THE ARDEN SHAKESPEARE

THE ARDEN EDITION OF THE
WORKS OF WILLIAM SHAKESPEARE

KING LEAR

Edited by
KENNETH MUIR

LONDON and NEW YORK

The general editors of the Arden Shakespeare have been
W. J. Craig (1899–1906), R. H. Case (1909–44),
Una Ellis-Fermor (1946–58), Harold F. Brooks (1952–82),
Harold Jenkins (1958–82) and Brian Morris (1975–82)

Present general editor: Richard Proudfoot

This edition of *King Lear*, by Kenneth Muir,
first published in 1972 by
Methuen & Co. Ltd
Reprinted 1975

First published as a University Paperback in 1964
Reprinted eight times
Reprinted with corrections 1972
Reprinted eight times
Reprinted with new appendix 1985
Reprinted 1986 and 1987

Reprinted 1989, 1991
by Routledge
11 New Fetter Lane, London EC4P 4EE
29 West 35th Street, New York, NY 10001

Editorial matter © 1972 Methuen & Co. Ltd

ISBN (hardbound) 0 416 76110 0
ISBN (paperback) 0 415 02692 X

Printed in England by
Clays Ltd, St Ives plc

CONTENTS

GENERAL EDITOR'S PREFACE

WHEN it was proposed, in 1946, to re-issue the Arden Shakespeare, little more was intended than a limited revision, bringing introductions and collations into line with the work of recent years and modifying appendices whenever additions were necessary or the material had been accepted into the common body of knowledge. In the main part of each volume the form of the original page was to be undisturbed, in order that the stereotype plates of those originals might still be used. This meant that practically no alterations could be made in the text, which was based on the Cambridge edition of 1863–6 (revised, 1891–3), and that any alterations in the commentary must be so arranged as to occupy the same space as the notes which they replaced.

It had been recognized from the first that in the case of a few plays it might be necessary to modify this restriction and it soon became clear that the first two volumes, *Macbeth* and *Love's Labour's Lost*, would prove more costly to produce if the stereotypes were retained than if they were abandoned. The two editors, therefore, who had gallantly endeavoured to preserve the original lay-out of the pages, found themselves freed from this necessity when their work was done or partly done, so that much of it had to be done again. As conditions became more stable, it became possible also to consider sparing their successors what they had experienced and at last to allow all editors to start afresh without tying them to the Cambridge text or to the lay-out of the original pages.

Thus a major change of policy came about by degrees, as the conditions of the years immediately after the war began to allow of it, and what had begun as a revision became a new edition.

This meant that publishers, editors, and general editor were faced with an entirely new responsibility: that of establishing the text of each play in place of a text which had hitherto been prescribed. Since we were unwilling to suspend activities until textual critics should be agreed that a text had been established as nearly authoritative for our day as that of the 1891–3 edition was held to be for its own, we decided to continue the work begun, in full awareness of the difficulties involved in publishing an edition such as this at a moment when there is not yet full agreement on a generally acceptable text. Each individual editor would thus be responsible for the text of his play, as well as for the introductions, collations, commentary, and appendices.

The policy of the original edition in respect of introductions, commentary, and appendices remains what it has always been; the lines laid down by those scholars who first designed its form have proved their worth throughout the past half-century. The introductions, though the emphasis must vary with the nature of the given play, include, together with the results of the editor's own thought and investigation, a survey of as many as possible of those studies which throw light upon the nature of the play or the problems surrounding it. The general commentary, which we have kept in its original position, at the foot of the page, provides such brief notes as may be required for the elucidation of specific passages or textual problems or for general comment and comparison; these often, therefore, serve to illustrate the general account given in the introduction.

The policy in respect of text is of necessity neither so simple nor so consistent as that of the editors of the original series, who were enjoined to use as their base the Cambridge text of 1891–3, and in most cases did so willingly, believing it to be as nearly authoritative as could be. Much has happened in the last fifty years, through the great extension of palæographical, bibliographical and textual scholarship; and our better understanding of (among other things) the nature and relations of Folio and Quarto texts has led us not always into more certainty, but sometimes rather into wholesome and chastened uncertainty. Each editor's text must now be his individual concern, since each play presents its own group of problems. Some of us may prove to have solved these in a way which posterity will repudiate. But an attempt will be made in every case to present the evidence for the editor's decisions fairly and to give at the same time representation to solutions other than that editor's own.

Una Ellis-Fermor

London, 1952

PREFACE

THIS revision of W. J. Craig's edition has been rendered simpler than it would otherwise have been by the publication of the Shakespeare Association Facsimile of the First Quarto, Dr J. Dover Wilson's facsimile of the Folio text, Sir Walter Greg's *The Variants of the First Quarto of 'King Lear'* (1939–40), and Professor G. I. Duthie's splendid edition (1949). I have used all these; and I have consulted the works listed in Tannenbaum's useful *Bibliography*, besides many more books and articles since published.

It has recently been suggested that a study of all the extant copies of the First Folio would reveal variants comparable in importance with those in the extant copies of the First Quarto. As no evidence has yet been produced that the text of *King Lear* contains any substantial variants, I am sceptical of this theory; but I have consulted facsimiles of two different copies of the Folio as well as the two originals accessible in Leeds, without discovering any variants. To have collated all extant copies of the Folio would have involved several years' work and the expenditure of several thousand pounds.

I prepared a text of the play some fifteen years ago for an amateur production; but that text has been extensively revised in the light of recent textual study. The Introduction and Appendices are entirely new; Craig's collations have been thoroughly revised; and though many of the notes have been adapted from his, few of them have been left unchanged.

I am indebted to Professor H. Kökeritz, Mr J. C. Maxwell, Mr J. M. Nosworthy, and Professor Harold Orton for some valuable suggestions; and to Mr A. C. Cawley, Mr H. H. Huxley, Mr Harold Fisch, Professor P. Alexander, and Mr J. M. Cameron for help of various kinds.

KENNETH MUIR

The University of Leeds
Christmas, 1950

I am further indebted to Mr Arthur Creedy, Mr R. T. Davies, Mr Arnold Davenport, Mr J. C. Maxwell, Mr G. K. Hunter, and Professors C. O. Brink and Simeon Potter for their assistance.

Liverpool, February 1952; December 1953

Some twenty years have elapsed since this edition went to press and the notes which have been added from time to time have now been inserted in their proper places. A few alterations have been made in the text and some misprints corrected. Charlton Hinman's great book, *The Printing and Proof-Reading of the First Folio of Shakespeare* (1963), has brought to light a number of variants in the text of *King Lear* but without necessitating any changes in the present text.

May 1971   **K. M.**

ABBREVIATIONS

Abbott	E. A. Abbott, *Shakespearian Grammar*, 1869.
Bradley	A. C. Bradley, *Shakespearean Tragedy*, ed. 1922.
E. K. Chambers	E. K. Chambers, *William Shakespeare*, 1930.
R. W. Chambers	R. W. Chambers, *King Lear*, 1940.
Coleridge	S. T. Coleridge, *Shakespearean Criticism*, ed. T. M. Raysor, 1930.
Danby	J. F. Danby, *Shakespeare's Doctrine of Nature*, 1949.
Duthie	G. I. Duthie, *King Lear*, 1949.
Furness	H. H. Furness, *King Lear* (Variorum), 1908.
Granville-Barker	H. Granville-Barker, *Prefaces to Shakespeare*, I, 1927.
Greg	W. W. Greg, *The Variants in the First Quarto of 'King Lear'*, 1940.
Heilman	R. B. Heilman, *This Great Stage*, 1948.
Kittredge	G. L. Kittredge, *Sixteen Plays of Shakespeare*, 1946.
Knight	G. Wilson Knight, *The Wheel of Fire*, 1949.
Florio	J. Florio's translation of Montaigne's *Essays* (Temple ed.).
Onions	C. T. Onions, *Shakespeare Glossary*, 1911.
Perrett	W. Perrett, *The Story of King Lear*, 1904.
Taylor	G. C. Taylor, *Shakespeare's Debt to Montaigne*, 1925.

E.L.H.	*English Literary History.*
E.S.	*English Studies.*
M.L.N.	*Modern Language Notes.*
M.L.Q.	*Modern Language Quarterly.*
M.L.R.	*Modern Language Review.*
N.Q.	*Notes and Queries.*
P.M.L.A.	*Publications of the Modern Language Association of America.*
P.Q.	*Philological Quarterly.*
R.E.S.	*Review of English Studies.*
S.A.B.	*Shakespeare Association Bulletin.*
S.P.	*Studies in Philology.*
T.L.S.	*Times Literary Supplement.*
Q1, Q2, Q3	Quartos published 1608, 1619, 1655.
F1, F2, F3, F4	Folios published 1623, 1632, 1663, 1685.

The usual abbreviations are used for the books of the Bible and Shakespeare's plays and poems are referred to by the abbreviations listed in C. T. Onions, *A Shakespeare Glossary* (1911, revised edition 1946).

INTRODUCTION

I. TEXT

King Lear was first printed in 1608, the imprint of the First Quarto (Q1) being—

> LONDON, / Printed for *Nathaniel Butter*, and are to be sold at his shop in *Pauls* / Church-yard at the signe of the Pide Bull neere / St. *Austins* Gate. 1608.

This is often known as the 'Pied Bull' Quarto. Twelve copies exist of it, but these are in ten different states because proof-reading was carried on simultaneously with the printing. Corrections were made in the formes after the printing had begun, and corrected sheets were subsequently bound up with uncorrected sheets. The total number of variants in the twelve extant copies is 167, though some of the emendations were incorrect.[1]

The Second Quarto (Q2), in spite of the evidence of the title-page ('Printed for Nathaniel Butter. / 1608'), was actually printed[2] in 1619 from a copy of Q1 in which

> sheets D, F, G, H were in the original, and sheets C (probably), E, K in the corrected state.

The third appearance of the play was in the First Folio of Shakespeare's plays (1623), where it occupies pages 283–309 of the section devoted to Tragedies. The F text was printed from a copy of Q1 in which sheet D was in the corrected state, sheets H and K in the uncorrected state, and sheets E and G probably in the uncorrected state. The state of the other sheets is not known.[3] This

---

1. W. W. Greg, *The Variants in the First Quarto of 'King Lear'*. Sir Walter Greg shows that sheets B, I, and L exist in only one state; the outer forme of C exists in one state, the inner forme in three; both the outer and inner formes of K exist in two states; the outer formes of D, E, and G, and the inner formes of F and H exits in two states.

2. W. W. Greg, *op. cit.*, p. 189. Cf. A. W. Pollard, *Shakespeare's Fight with the Pirates*, 1920, pp. viii ff., and E. K. Chambers, *William Shakespeare*, 1930, I. 133 ff.

3. Greg, *op. cit.*, pp. 144–9. But A. S. Cairncross has since argued, *R.E.S.* (1955), pp. 252–8, that the F compositor used a copy of Q2 as well as one of Q1. This would mean that on certain pages some errors of Q2 were probably carried over into the F text. The theory has been questioned.

copy of Q1 had been substantially altered, probably to bring it into line with the prompt-book used by Shakespeare's company. This involved the deletion of some 300 lines of the Q text, the addition of some 100 lines which had been omitted from Q, and a very large number of verbal alterations.

A modern editor will, of course, restore these omitted lines, whether his text is based mainly on the Quarto or on the Folio. There is now fairly general agreement that the F text is not only more accurately printed, but also much nearer to what Shakespeare wrote, than that of Q. Miss M. Doran, indeed, in her *Text of 'King Lear'* (1931), argued that Q was printed from Shakespeare's own autograph MS., and F from a transcript of the same MS. in a later state; but in a later article she seems to withdraw from this position.[1] Mr M. R. Ridley, in the Preface to his edition (1935), guessed that

> F was set from a better transcript of a common original than that which was available for Q.

His edition follows Q wherever it makes tolerable sense, and sometimes where it does not. He could not have given a more convincing demonstration of the relative badness of the Q text. A third critic, Mr Van Dam, goes even further.[2] He thinks that Q

> belongs to the class of printed plays nearest to Shakespeare's originals,

and that F was printed from

> the revised prompt-book, one remove farther from Shakespeare's original than the prompt-book text which served as copy for the Q.

Apart from these three critics, it is generally accepted that Q is substantially inferior to F, and that the latter must therefore serve as the basis of a modern text.

There is less agreement about the reasons for the peculiar nature of the Q text. Sir Edmund Chambers and Sir Walter Greg thought that the text was obtained by the use of shorthand during an actual performance. Dr J. Quincy Adams points to readings in Q which could be explained by the use of Timothy Bright's system of shorthand, *Characterie*;[3] but Miss Doran, Mr W. Matthews, and Profes-

---

1. *R.E.S.*, 1941, p. 474.
2. *Materials for the Study of the Old English Drama*, x (1935), 79.
3. E. K. Chambers, *op. cit.*, 1. 465–6; Greg, *op. cit.*, p. 187. Cf. *Neophilologus*, xviii (1933), 252–7; *The Library*, xvii (1936–7), 172–83; Greg, *The Editorial Problem in Shakespeare*, 1942, pp. 88–101; Adams, *Modern Philology*, xxxi, 135–63.

sor G. I. Duthie,[1] who has made a study of the three possible systems of shorthand,[2] believe that they were all too primitive and clumsy to have provided such a text as the Quarto of *King Lear*. Professor Leo Kirschbaum has propounded the theory[3]

> that a bad quarto was created by a reporter's memorizing from a theatrical MS. Mnemonic phenomena which adumbrate a single memory; stage-directions which are like those of the prompt-books; patches of correctly lined blank verse; small patches of perfect reproduction in the midst of wild confusion; isolated bibliographical links of spelling, punctuation, capital-ization between the good and bad texts . . . these shew us a reporter imperfectly remembering what he has seen on the written page.

This does not seem to me to be very credible. A man who perused the prompt-book for any length of time would have aroused sus-picions unless he were the 'book-keeper' himself, who is ruled out by other considerations. If, on the other hand, he took the prompt-book away from the theatre, he could have made a copy of it in a shorter time than he would have taken to learn it; and such a surreptitious borrowing would presuppose great carelessness on the part of the book-keeper. Yet *King Lear* does not have quite the same characteristics as known piratical texts, such as the First Quarto of *Hamlet*, where certain parts are more accurately reported than others—presumably because the actors who took those parts were guilty of reconstructing the text from memory. In the Quarto of *King Lear*, as Duthie points out,[4]

> there is no consistent variation in the standard of the reporting of the speeches of different characters.

It was left to Duthie to put forward a plausible theory about the Q text. He suggests that it is 'a memorial reconstruction made by the entire company', perhaps made

> during a provincial tour, the company having left the prompt-book (and the author's manuscript also, if the prompt-book was a transcript) in London.

There are various difficulties about this theory: some speeches are

1. Doran, *Modern Philology*, xxxiii (1935–6), 139 ff.; W. Matthews, *Modern Language Review*, xxvii (1932), 243 ff.; Duthie, *King Lear*, 1949, pp. 73–5; *Elizabethan Shorthand and the First Quarto of King Lear*, 1949.

2. Bright's *Characterie*, Bales's *Brachygraphie*, Willis's *Stenographie*.

3. *Modern Language Notes*, 1944, pp. 197–8. Cf. Kirschbaum's *True Text of 'King Lear'* (1945), where the theory is applied to this play; and *P.M.L.A.*, 1945, pp. 697–715.

4. *Op. cit.*, p. 75.

assigned to the wrong characters in Q, but for this the printer may be to blame; and the stage-directions are so bad that Duthie is constrained to admit that the copy for Q 'could not have served conveniently as a prompt-book', and that therefore a transcription was made of the rough copy scribbled at dictation speed.[1] Kirschbaum argues against the theory that bad quartos were stenographic reports by protesting that it is a libel on Elizabethan actors:[2]

> Did the Elizabethan actor customarily jumble his own lines, borrow phrases and lines from other actors, anticipate and recollect his own and other actors' lines, jump ten or more lines because of similar phraseology in two passages, sometimes with the consequent omission of other actors' speeches?

If, however, we assume that some of the bad quartos were based on memorial reconstructions by actors in the provinces, months or even years after they had last performed the play, it is easy to imagine that their version would be very inaccurate. The comparative accuracy of the Quarto of *King Lear*—compared, for example, with *Hamlet* Q1—suggests that the company was at full strength, and that there was no long interval between the last performance and the reconstruction of the prompt-book.

Duthie emphasizes that this is only a working hypothesis; and Kirschbaum has forcibly outlined his objections to it:[3]

> A supposed tour by the King's men in which they did not possess their prompt-book . . . sets up a second hypothesis to bulwark a first hypothesis, that of plural memorial transmission . . . this second hypothesis demands a third to account for the missing prompt-book. And a fourth . . . to explain why actors on a provincial tour should make not an abridged version but one considerably longer than the prompt-book used around 1620 in the city. Furthermore, that Burbadge and his co-actors 'habitually' delivered their lines as Q gives these lines is an extremely dubious hypothetical corollary to any complex of hypotheses. . . Time after time, for particular Q corruptions Professor Duthie has to give involved explanations in which actor, scribe, and compositor play an unbelievably complex game of simultaneous error.

We may recognize the force of these objections, without necessarily adopting Kirschbaum's own theory of a single reporter.

Dr Alice Walker in *Textual Problems of the First Folio* (1953) suggests that the copy for Q1 was provided by the actors who played the parts of Goneril and Regan, and that in those scenes in

1. Duthie, *op. cit.*, pp. 75–116 (esp. pp. 76–7, 115).
2. Kirschbaum, *True Text*, p. 6.   3. *R.E.S.*, April, 1951, p. 169.

which they do not appear, where they would have to rely on the manuscript alone, their text is better than recent editors have supposed. Although it may be doubted whether we need to assume that two actors were involved, Dr Walker's theory is attractive. She would not deny that on the whole the First Folio provides the better text.

The present text of the play, therefore, is based on F; but since the F texts of other plays contain numerous errors and 'sophistications' (i.e. unauthorized 'improvements'), we shall accept Q readings not only where the F readings are manifestly corrupt, but also where Q seems palpably superior. It is not impossible that true readings were preserved by the memories of actors, and so reproduced in Q, though by some accident they have not been preserved in F. Q appeared only three years after Shakespeare wrote the play; and in the fourteen years that elapsed before Q, corrected by the prompt-book, was sent to the printers, errors and deliberate changes would have been made. Moreover, as Greg points out,[1] since the F copy was an altered copy of Q, some mistakes in the latter are certain to have been left uncorrected—

> Thus it is only when the readings of the two differ that there is any strong ground for supposing that the Folio preserves that of the prompt-book; the negative inference, that where the two agree the prompt-book had the same reading, is much weaker. And so we reach the remarkable conclusion that the testimony of the Quarto and Folio together is of appreciably less authority than that of the Folio alone.

We ought therefore to be more prepared to introduce emendations in the text of F where it agrees with Q, than where it differs.

It should be added that Q is punctuated mostly with commas, and that it contains a large amount of mislineation.[2] Even F prints passages as prose which modern editors invariably print as verse.

2. DATE

On 16 March 1603 Samuel Harsnett's *Declaration of Egregious Popishe Impostures* was entered in the Stationers' Register; and as Shakespeare makes considerable use of this book throughout the play we can be certain that it was not written until after that date.

1. *Neophilologus*, 1933, pp. 261–2.
2. Duthie, *op. cit.*, p. 90, cites Edward Hubler who, in *The Parrott Presentation Volume*, ed. H. Craig, estimates that of the verse-lines which Q prints as verse, 650 are divided incorrectly, 1,580 correctly; that 500 lines of verse are printed as prose; and that 61 lines of prose are printed as verse. In an unpublished paper P. Alexander argues that the punctuation of Q resembles that of good quartos.

From the evidence of the title-page of Q1 and of the Stationers'
Register we know that the play was performed on 26 December
1606. The title-page runs as follows—

> M. William Shak-speare: / *HIS* / True Chronicle Historie of the
> life and / death of King LEAR and his three / Daughters. *With the
> vnfortunate life of* Edgar, *sonne* / and heire to the Earle of Gloster,
> and his / sullen and assumed humor of / TOM of Bedlam: / *As it
> was played before the Kings Maiestie at Whitehall vpon* / *S*. Stephans
> *night in Christmas Hollidayes*. / By his Maiesties seruants playing
> vsually at the Gloabe / on the Bancke-side.

Although this Quarto was dated 1608 we know that the Court
performance was in 1606, and not 1607, because the entry in the
Stationers' Register on 26 November 1607 reads as follows—

> Na. Butter. Io. Busby. Entred for their copie vnder thandes of
> Sir Geo. Buck knight & Thwardens A booke called. Mr William
> Shakespeare his historye of Kynge Lear as yt was played before
> the kings maiestie at Whitehall vppon St Stephans night at
> Christmas Last by his maiesties servantes playing usually at the
> globe on the Banksyde   vjd.

The play was therefore written between March 1603 and Christmas 1606.

It is usually assumed that 'these late eclipses in the sun and
moon' (I. ii. 100) must have been suggested by the eclipse of the
sun of October 1605, preceded by an eclipse of the moon in the
previous month. Professor G. B. Harrison, indeed, quotes from a
pamphlet entitled *Strange fearful & true newes which happened at
Carlstadt, in the Kingdome of Croatia*, which was published in February
1606, and argues that there is a similarity of phrase, sentiment and
rhythm between this passage and the remarks of Gloucester and
Edmund[1]—

> If these mundane & moueable bodies be mutually impressiue &
> impressible, nature constant in her Periodes, & reason experi-
> ence & Iugment in man, be of any power or credit. The great
> coniunction of the two superior bodies *Saturne* & *Iupiter*, consti-
> pated with so many seuerall coniunctions and radiations of other
> planets, and in the same place very neare, in parle together as it
> were for some strange decree of great consequence. The Earth's
> and Moone's late and horrible obscurations, the frequent Ecclip-
> sations of the fixed bodyes; by the wandring, the [vn-]fixed
> stars, I meane the planets, within these fewe yeares more then
> ordinary, shall without doubt (salued diuine inhibition) haue
> their effects no lesse admirable, then the positiues vnusuall.

1. *T.L.S.*, 30 Nov. 1933, p. 856.

Which PEVCER with many more too long to rehearse out of continuall obseruation and the consent of all Authors noted to be, new Leagues, Traytrous Designements, Catching at Kingdomes, translation of Empyre, downefall of menn in Authoritye, æmulations, Ambition, Innouations, Factious Sects, Schisms and much disturbance and trobles in religion and matters of the Church, with many other thinges infallible in sequent such orbicall positions and Phænomenes.

If we accepted Harrison's theory we should have to suppose that *King Lear* was written in the last ten months of 1606. But astrological jargon inevitably varies little; and there are closer parallels with Gloucester's remarks in Florio's *Montaigne*. There were several earlier eclipses that would still be remembered by the audience. In 1601, for example, there was an eclipse of the sun on 24 December, preceded by two eclipses of the moon on 15 June and 9 December. But Shakespeare may not have been referring to any particular pair of eclipses; and even supposing a reference was intended to the eclipses of 1605, he might have cunningly inserted the reference because he knew these eclipses were expected later in the year. It is therefore possible that the play was begun before September 1605; or, indeed, that the reference to the eclipses was a later addition. But the most usual hypothesis is that Shakespeare wrote *King Lear* in the winter of 1605–6, and that he used the 1605 edition of *The True Chronicle History of King Leir* which was published after 8 May 1605, when it was entered in the Stationers' Register.

There are three obstacles in the way of this dating. First, the entry for *King Leir* in S.R. referred to the play as a 'Tragecall historie'. Originally it was called a 'Tragedie', but the word has been altered in the Register. This suggests that the story of the play was already known as a tragedy. The title-page of *King Leir* calls it *The True Chronicle History*; and this might seem to show that the mistake in the Register was not due to the publisher.

Secondly, the title-page of the source play proclaims that the text is 'as it hath bene diuers and sundry times lately acted'. Greg pertinently remarks that he finds

it very difficult to believe that this respectable but old-fashioned play, dating back in all probability to about 1590 had been 'diuers and sundry times lately acted' in 1605, especially if the playhouse manuscript had been for years in the hands of stationers.

But if the play had not been recently acted it looks very much as though the publishers resurrected the play after a lapse of eleven years, in the hope that it would be mistaken for Shakespeare's new play, or at least derive some reflected glory from it.[1]

Thirdly, there is not much doubt that *Macbeth* was written by the summer of 1606; and if *King Lear* has to be dated early in 1606, Shakespeare must have been working overtime. Metrical tests, for what they are worth, tend to show that *King Lear* was written before *Macbeth*. It would be easier in some ways, therefore, if we could push back *King Lear* into the winter of 1604–5. The relationship of Shakespeare's play to *King Leir* is discussed on a later page; it need only be said here that this is not an insuperable objection to dating the play before the publication of *King Leir*.

It has recently been argued[2] that Shakespeare was influenced by William Strachey's sonnet 'On Sejanus', published with Jonson's play after 6 August 1605—

> How high a Poore man showes in low estate
> Whose Base is firme, and whole Frame competent,
> That sees this *Cedar*, made the Shrub of Fate,
> Th'on's little, lasting; Th'others confluence spent.
> And as the Lightning comes behind the Thunder
> From the torne Cloud, yet first inuades our Sense,
> So euery violent Fortune, that to wonder
> Hoists men aloft, is a cleere euidence
> Of a vaunt-curring blow the *Fates* have giuen
> To his forst state; swift Lightning blindes his eyes,
> While Thunder, from comparison-hating Heauen
> Dischargeth on his height, and there it lyes:
> If men will shun swolne *Fortunes* ruinous blastes,
> Let them vse Temperance. Nothing violent lastes.

The idea of the lightning as a vaunt-courier is used by Lear in his address to the storm; and he uses *invades* in the same metaphorical sense (III. iv. 7). It may be added that the phrases 'poor man . . . in low estate', 'fortune's ruinous blasts', and 'violent fortune' may be compared with Desdemona's 'downright violence and storm of fortunes' as well as with the opening lines of Act IV of *King Lear*. Here Edgar mentions 'the lowest and most dejected thing of

---

1. W. W. Greg, *The Library*, xx. 381–4. It has been suggested that Scene xxvi of *King Leir* was written not long after the Armada year, or perhaps when the Armada was expected. Another indication of the date is afforded by Daniel's sonnet (*Delia*, 1594) 'At the Author's going into Italie'. The opening line, 'O whither, poore forsaken, shall I goe', resembles *Leir*, 329, 'Now whither, poore forsaken, shall I goe'. Daniel is thought to have gone to Italy before 1590. There is a similar line in *Mucedorus*. There are close parallels with *Edward II* and *Richard III*; but it is impossible to tell in what order *King Leir* and these two plays were written.

2. See G. Ashe, *N.Q.*, 25 Nov. 1950.

Fortune', and he proceeds virtually to identify fortune and the wind—

> The wretch that thou hast blown unto the worst
> Owes nothing to thy blasts.

But it would appear that Strachey, not Shakespeare, was the debtor; and this means that the storm-scenes of *King Lear*, and possibly the opening lines of Act IV, must have been written by 2 November 1604, when *Sejanus* was first registered, unless we assume that the sonnet could have been added to the copy for the play after it had been licensed. Professor Leo Kirschbaum called my attention to another link between *King Lear* and *Sejanus*. Shakespeare, who acted in Jonson's play, remembered a description of two flatterers in the first scene:

> There be two,
> Know more, then honest councells: whose close brests
> Were they rip'd up to light, it would be found
> A poore, and idle sinne, to which their trunkes
> Had not been made fit organs. These can lye,
> Flatter, and sweare, forsweare, deprave, informe,
> Smile, and betray; make guilty men; then beg
> The forfeit lives, to get the livings; cut
> Mens throats with whisperings; sell to gaping sutors
> The emptie smoake, that flies about the Palace;
> Laugh, when their patron laughes; sweat, when he sweates;
> Be hot, and cold with him; change every moode,
> Habit, and garbe, as often as he varies;
> Observe him, as his watch observes his clock;
> And true as turkise in the dear lords ring,
> Looke well, or ill with him . . .

There can be little doubt that these lines contributed to Kent's attack on Oswald (II. ii. 69 ff.) and possibly to other lines in the same scene (95–101) and to Kent's account of himself (I. iv. 32 'honest counsel'). Lear later uses the word 'deprav'd' of Goneril's conduct (II. iv. 134). In any case, there is good reason to believe that *King Lear* was partly written by 6 August 1605; and, taken in conjunction with other evidence, the connection of the play with Strachey's sonnet establishes the winter of 1604–5 as the most probable date.[1]

---

1. Mr Ashe thinks that Strachey collaborated with Jonson in the first version of *Sejanus*, and with Shakespeare in the writing of *King Lear* and *Timon of Athens*. There is no direct evidence that Strachey was a dramatist, though he is known to have been a poet. He was a Cambridge graduate, and the word *sizes* is used in *King Lear* (II. iv. 173) in a specifically Cambridge sense; but even if this use was confined to Cambridge men, Shakespeare might have picked it up from Strachey

If *King Lear* was written in the winter of 1604–5 the date would fit in with the political situation, for between 1604 and 1607 King James was trying to get Parliament to approve of the union of England and Scotland and referring in speech after speech to the misfortunes that division brought to early Britain.[1] Professor Draper thinks that Shakespeare intended his play to illustrate the evils of disunion.[2]

This dating receives some support from the verbal affiliations of *King Lear* with *Othello*, *Measure for Measure*, and *Timon of Athens*, which appear to be more substantial than those with *Macbeth* and *Antony and Cleopatra*. *Othello* was probably written before the publication of the First Quarto of *Hamlet*;[3] and Bradley has pointed out a number of striking parallels between *Othello* and *King Lear*.[4] They inculde words which are not used by Shakespeare except in these two plays,[5] several words which are used in a sense peculiar to the two plays,[6] and two or three phrases.[7]

There are fewer verbal echoes of *Measure for Measure* in *King Lear*, but we may notice the phrase 'furred gown' which appears in both plays,[8] 'unaccommodated' which is linked with 'accommodations',[9] 'warped' used only in these plays and in *All's Well that Ends Well*,[10] and 'evasion' used only in these plays and in *Troilus and Cressida*.[11] More significant, perhaps, is the fact that themes dealt with in *Measure for Measure* recur in *King Lear*: the truancy of the Duke may be compared with Lear's abdication from respon-

---

or another. The references to fortune in Strachey's sonnet do not particularly resemble the allegory of fortune in *Timon*. The word *confluence*, used once in *Timon*, is also to be found in Florio's translation of Montaigne, from which Shakespeare may have taken it. As he uses the word *estate* nearly sixty times at all periods of his career, we can deduce nothing from the eight appearances of the word in *Timon*. Cf. *N.Q.*, 6 Jan. 1951.

1. J. W. Draper, *Studies in Philology*, 1937, pp. 178–85.

2. Shakespeare's company visited Dover on 4 Oct. 1605; but as there had been a previous visit in September 1597, we need not suppose that the description of Dover Cliff was inspired by the 1605 visit.

3. See A. Hart, *T.L.S.*, 10 Oct. 1935.

4. *Shakespearean Tragedy*, ed. 1922, pp. 441–3.

5. E.g. waterish, besort, potential, unbonetted, deficient.

6. E.g. decline (i. ii. 69–70; *Oth.*, iii. iii. 265), slack (ii. iv. 243; *Oth.*, iv. iii.88), commit (iii. iv. 79; *Oth.*, iv. ii. 72), secure (iv. i. 20; *Oth.*, i. iii. 10).

7. E.g. fortune's alms (i. i. 277; *Oth.*, iii. iv. 122), stand in hard cure (iii. vi. 98; stand in bold cure, *Oth.*, ii. i. 51), safer sense (iv. vi. 81; my safer guides, *Oth.*, ii. iii. 205), perforce must wither (iv. ii. 35; needs must wither, *Oth.*, v. ii. 15). Cf. note on v. iii. 275.

8. iv. vi. 163; *Meas.*, iii. ii. 8. Also used by Florio. Cf. Appendix 6.

9. iii. iv. 104–5; *Meas.*, iii. i. 14.

10. iii. vi. 52; *Meas.*, iii. i. 142; *All's W.*, v. iii. 49.

11. i. ii. 124; *Meas.*, i. i. 51; *Troil.*, ii. i. 75, ii. ii. 67, ii. iii. 123.

sibility; the debate on justice and authority which runs all through *Measure for Measure* reappears in the mad scenes of *King Lear*; the idea of 'the oddest frame of sense' in madness is repeated in the 'reason in madness' of the King;[1] the Duke's advice to Claudio in prison and his later comfort to Isabella[2]—

> That life is better life, past fearing death,
> Than that which lives to fear.—

look forward to several of Edgar's speeches; and his words—[3]

> O! our lives' sweetness,
> That we the pain of death would hourly die
> Rather than die at once!—

recall Claudio's fight for life. The turn of thought 'Keep me in patience' occurs in both plays;[4] and the next words in *Measure for Measure*—

> and with ripen'd time
> Unfold the evil which is here wrapt up
> In countenance!—

seem to be echoed in two passages in *King Lear*[5]—

> Time shall unfold what plighted cunning hides;

> in the mature time

and Isabella's lines about Angelo[6]—

> His filth within being cast, he would appear
> A pond as deep as hell.—

have been used by Dr Edith Sitwell as a commentary on Edgar's words: 'Nero is an angler in the Lake of Darkness.'

There are many resemblances between *King Lear* and *Timon of Athens*. The theme of ingratitude is prominent in both; both have many references to the lower animals; both stress the natural goodness of the poor in contrast to the viciousness of the rich; and their versification is similar. Bradley also draws attention to a number of verbal parallels,[7] and to a resemblance between the Fool's words and song in II. iv and the Poet's allegory of Fortune in the opening scene of *Timon of Athens*.[8] But if there is structural weakness in *Timon of Athens*, few critics would now agree with Bradley when he finds it in *King Lear* also.

1. *Meas.*, v. i. 61.   2. *Ibid.*, v. i. 402.   3. v. iii. 183–5.
4. *Meas.*, v. i. 116; cf. *Lr.*, I. v. 44.   5. I. i. 279; IV. vi. 272.
6. *Meas.*, III. i. 93–4. Cf. note to III. vi. 6–7 *post*.
7. I. iv. 148 (*Tim.*, II. ii. 122); IV. i. 20 (*Tim.*, IV. iii. 76); II. iv. 171 (*Tim.*, v. i. 134).
8. II. iv. 65 ff.

These links with other plays suggest that *King Lear* may well have been written soon after *Measure for Measure* and *Othello*, and not long before *Timon of Athens*.[1]

3. SOURCES

One of the sources of *King Lear* was an old chronicle play which had been published in 1605, *The True Chronicle History of King Leir*. From its nature this play would seem to belong to the sixteenth century; and it so happens that a *kinge leare* was performed at the Rose Theatre by the combined Queen's and Sussex's men during an unsuccessful season early in April 1594. It was not then a new play and it probably belonged to the Queen's men. On 14 May of the same year the play was entered in the Stationers' Register, though no edition is known to have appeared for eleven years.[2] No one knows who wrote the play, though H. Dugdale Sykes argued strongly for Peele's authorship.[3] It is by no means a good play, and few people will see any substance in the perverse view of Tolstoy:

> However strange this opinion may seem to worshippers of Shakespeare, yet the whole of this old drama is incomparably and in every respect superior to Shakespeare's adaptation. It is so, firstly, because it has not got the utterly superfluous characters of the villain Edmund and the unlifelike Gloucester and Edgar, who only distract one's attention; secondly, because it has not got the completely false effects of Lear running about the heath, his conversations with the fool and all these impossible disguises, failures to recognize, and accumulated deaths; and above all, because in this drama there is the simple, natural, and deeply touching character of Leir and the yet more touching and clearly defined character of Cordella, both absent in Shakespeare. Therefore there is in the older drama—instead of Shake-

1. This date would also fit in with the possibility that Shakespeare was influenced by the madness of Bryan Annesley. See note on p. xxxix *post*.

2. Cf. W. W. Greg, *The Library*, xx. 378–9; E. K. Chambers, *William Shakespeare*, I. 469; S. Lee, *Leir*, 1909, pp. x–xvi.

3. H. D. Sykes, *Sidelights on Shakespeare*, 1919, pp. 126–42. He mentions a number of words and phrases which appear in Peele's known works and also in *King Leir*. Some of these are too common to tell us anything about the authorship, e.g. 'To be enrolled in chronicles of fame'; 'The truest friend that ever'; 'good fellows'. Even 'heir indubitate' (*Leir*, 42) is to be found not in Peele's acknowledged works, but in two plays Sykes has elsewhere argued to be his, *The Troublesome Raigne* and *Alphonsus*: and it is to be found in Warner, *Albion's England*, VIII. 38. Lee, *op. cit.*, p. xxi, argues against Peele's authorship because his plays were not published anonymously. He suggests that it may have been written by the author of *Locrine* or by William Rankins.

speare's long drawn scene of Lear's interview with Cordelia and of Cordelia's unnecessary murder—the exquisite scene of the interview between Leir and Cordella, unequalled by any in all Shakespeare's dramas.[1]

A brief summary of the plot of *King Leir* will show the extent to which Shakespeare deviated from it. In the first scene, Leir plans a sudden strategem to trick Cordella into marriage:

> fayre *Cordella* vowes
> No liking to a Monarch, vnlesse loue allowes . . .
> Yet, if my policy may her beguyle,
> Ile match her to some King within this Ile . . .
> I am resolu'd, and euen now my mind
> Doth meditate a sudden stratagem,
> To try which of my daughters loues me best:
> Which till I know, I cannot be in rest.
> This graunted, when they ioyntly shall contend,
> Each to exceed the other in their loue:
> Then at the vantage will I take *Cordella*,
> Euen as she doth protest she loues me best,
> Ile say, then, daughter, graunt me one request,
> To shew thou louest me as thy sisters doe,
> Accept a husband, whom my selfe will woo.
> This sayd, she cannot well deny my sute . . .
> Then will I tryumph in my policy,
> And match her with a King of Brittany.

The honest Perillus (Kent) comments on this scheme:

> Thus fathers think their children to beguile,
> And oftentimes themselues do first repent,
> When heauenly powers do frustrate their intent.

Leir's plan is betrayed to Gonorill and Ragan by the time-serving Skalliger (Sc. 2). The wicked sisters, who are jealous of Cordella, flatter their father and promise to marry anyone he may appoint. Cordella refuses to flatter and Leir, though not banishing her, determines to divide the kingdom between her sisters (Sc. 3). The Gallian King decides to visit Brittayne in disguise to see whether Leir's three daughters are as beautiful as they are reputed to be (Sc. 4). Accompanied by the bluff Lord Mumford he woos and weds Cordella, whom he meets bewailing her lot (Sc. 7). Meanwhile Cornwall and Cambria draw lots for their shares of the kingdom, and Perillus makes an ineffectual attempt to prevent Cordella from losing her share (Sc. 6). These seven scenes of the old play Shakespeare condenses into one; and some critics have

1. *Tolstoy on Shakespeare*, 1907, pp. 43–4.

argued that his first scene is a failure. Professor Allardyce Nicoll, for example, declares that the author of the old play[1]

> At least provided his main characters with normal and appreciable motives, whereas Shakespeare has left us with something which simply cannot be tolerated on the stage, for to find an explanation of Lear's decisions and demeanour in this first scene we need to know the subsequent development of the plot; by themselves they are perfectly unintelligible.

Yet it is perfectly possible to perform the first scene of *King Lear* in such a way as to make the motives of the three sisters intelligible; and the irrationality of Lear is ultimately more credible, and certainly more tragic, than the futile cunning of his prototype. The scene is a kind of prologue; and by making it as short as possible Shakespeare was able to concentrate on the tragic results of the King's foolishness.

The old play continues with a scene in which Perillus laments Leir's stupidity, though he decides not to desert him (Sc. 8). Leir is ill-treated by his favoured daughters, and the Gallian King decides to send ambassadors to invite him to visit Gallia (Sc. 9–16). The man bribed by Ragan to murder Leir is stricken with remorse just as he is about to do the deed (Sc. 17–19). Cordella and her husband decide to go in disguise to Brittayne, accompanied by Mumford (Sc. 20–1). But Leir and Perillus escape to Gallia and there encounter the Gallian King, Cordella, and Mumford, disguised as countryfolk. Leir is reconciled to his daughter (Sc. 22–4). The Gallian King invades Brittayne on Leir's behalf, defeats the army of Cornwall and Cambria, and reinstates Leir who, we assume, lives happily for the rest of his life (Sc. 25–32). There is nothing about Cordella's death, whether by murder or suicide. It will be noticed that there is no equivalent here for the story of Gloucester. Leir is not so old as Shakespeare's hero—nor is he in any of Shakespeare's sources—and he is lachrymose and pathetic, without the rage, the energy, or the tragic grandeur of Lear. He is driven out, but not into a storm; and he never loses his sanity. Shakespeare omits Ragan's direct attempt on her father's life; he adds the Fool; and he substitutes the banished Kent for the unbanished Perillus.

There are some resemblances between the two plays in thought and expression, though the extent of Shakespeare's echoes has been variously estimated. Sir Walter Greg details some forty parallels, but some of these might easily be accidental.[2] The 'single-line asides in which Cordella comments on the protestations of her

1. *Studies in Shakespeare*, 1927, pp. 154–5.   2. *The Library*, xx. 386–97.

hypocritical sisters' and the scene in which Leir and Cordella kneel to each other were clearly remembered by Shakespeare, the latter both in the reconciliation scene and in the scene where Lear and Cordelia are led away to prison[1]—

> O! look upon me, Sir,
> And hold your hand in benediction o'er me.
> No, Sir, you must not kneel.

> When thou dost ask me blessing, I'll kneel down
> And ask of thee forgiveness.

In the old play Leir and Cordella keep on kneeling and rising until the scene topples over into absurdity; and before they have finished the Gallian King and Mumford also join in. But Shakespeare realized the inherent pathos of the scene, and transmuted it for his own purposes.

The following verbal parallels are mostly taken from Greg's list, though a few have been added. Ragan's words to Leir (269–70)—

> I haue right noble Suters to my loue,
> No worse than Kings, and happely I loue one . . .

may be echoed in Cordelia's lines (I. i. 99–101)—

> Happily, when I shall wed,
> That lord whose hand must take my plight shall carry
> Half my love with him.

Leir's words (512)—

> I am as kind as is the Pellican—

may have suggested (III. iv. 73–4)—

> Judicious punishment! 'twas this flesh begot
> Those pelican daughters.

Perillus's description of Leir (755)—

> But he, the myrrour of mild patience,
> Puts vp all wrongs, and neuer giues reply.—

certainly resembles Lear's words (III. ii. 37–8)—

> No, I will be the pattern of all patience;
> I will say nothing.

Leir's remark to Gonorill (844)—

> poore soule, she breeds yong bones.—

---

1. Cf. *Leir* (Malone Society), 254, 274, 2295 ff. Three scenes are given in Appendix 1, pp. 207–20 *post.*

and her reply, in which she uses the same phrase, may have suggested Lear's curse (II. iv. 160–1)—

> Strike her young bones,
> You taking airs, with lameness!

Leir remarks to Perillus (1111)—

> think me but the shadow of my selfe.—

and the phrase may have suggested the Fool's retort (I. iv. 228), 'Lear's shadow'. Cambria declares (1909) that

> The heauens are iust, and hate impiety;

Edgar tells his brother (v. iii. 169–70) that

> The Gods are just,[1] and of our pleasant vices
> Make instruments to plague us.

Leir's words, not spoken in Ragan's presence (2144)—

> Ah, cruell *Ragan*, did I giue thee all.—

are echoed in Lear's words to Regan (II. iv. 248)—

> I gave you all.

But perhaps the most significant parallel is the last. Perillus upbraids Gonorill with the words (2581)—

> Nay, peace thou monster, shame vnto thy sexe,
> Thou fiend in likenesse of a human creature.

Four lines later, Leir asks Ragan 'Knowest thou these letters?'— letters which she snatches and tears. In *King Lear*, Albany urges Goneril (IV. ii. 59–61)—

> See thyself, devil!
> Proper deformity shows not in the fiend
> So horrid as in woman;

and in the last scene he says to her (v. iii. 153–9)—

> Shut your mouth, dame,
> Or with this paper shall I stople it . . .
> Thou worse than any name, read thine own evil:
> No tearing, lady; I perceive you know it.
> *Gon.* Say, if I do, the laws are mine, not thine:
> Who can arraign me for't?
> *Alb.*   Most monstrous! O!
> Know'st thou this paper?

'Shame', 'fiend', and 'know'st thou' are common to both passages; 'monster', 'sex', and 'these letters' are echoed in 'monstrous',

1. Cf. III. iv. 36, 'show the Heavens more just'.

'woman', and 'this paper'; and the stage direction in the old play was remembered in Shakespeare's 'no tearing'. This last parallel can hardly be put down to coincidence; and Greg thinks[1] that cumulatively the parallels show that as Shakespeare wrote—

> ideas, phrases, cadences from the old play still floated in his memory below the level of conscious thought, and that now and again one or another helped to fashion the words that flowed from his pen.

He believes, in fact, that there is clear evidence that Shakespeare had read *King Leir* carefully not long before he wrote his own play. Elsewhere, Greg pointed out two apparent echoes of *King Leir* in *Hamlet*; and from this he deduces that Shakespeare must have read the old play in manuscript.[2] But is it really necessary to suppose that Shakespeare had read *King Leir*? If echoes of Coleridge's reading could coalesce years later in *The Ancient Mariner*, echoes which are in some instances closer than anything of *Leir* in *Lear*, why could not Shakespeare have got all he needed from memories of the old play which he might have seen performed in 1594, or before? From such a performance, ten or fifteen years before, he might well have recalled the main outlines of the piece, as well as a few vivid scenes and chance phrases. It might even be suggested that there is a possibility that Shakespeare acted in *King Leir*; and as Perillus is on the stage when all save one of the above parallel passages are spoken, that may have been Shakespeare's role.

Shakespeare had doubtless read Holinshed's account, and seen the cut illustrating Cordeilla's suicide with a dagger; but he borrowed little from it. Goneril's line—

> Sir, I love you more than word can wield the matter—

is fairly close to Holinshed's version—

> she loued him more than toong could expresse;

but Cordelia's answer—

> I love your Majesty
> According to my bond; no more nor less—

is not, except in the last few words, very close to Holinshed—

> I protest vnto you, that I haue loued you euer, and will continuallie (while I liue) loue you as my naturall father . . . asser-

---

1. *Op. cit.*, p. 397.
2. *T.L.S.*, 9 March 1940. The passages are *Leir*, 1467 ff., and *Ham.*, III. iii. 73 ff.; *Leir*, 2453–62, and *Ham.*, v. i. 16 ff. The second of these seems to be a valid parallel; but it is possible that Shakespeare and the author of *Leir* both echoed the Ur-*Hamlet*.

taine your selfe, that so much as you haue, so much you are
worth, and so much I loue you, and no more.

From Holinshed, too, Shakespeare may have derived the ducal
titles of Cornwall and Albania, though he gives Goneril and Regan
to the alternative husbands. Perrett has suggested that Cordelia's
avowal of disinterestedness (IV. iv. 23 ff.)—

> O dear father!
> It is thy business that I go about; ...
> No blown ambition doth our arms incite,
> But love, dear love, and our ag'd father's right.—

was inserted in the play because in Holinshed's account Cordeilla
is not entirely disinterested—

> Aganippus caused a mightie armie to be put in a readinesse, and
> likewise a great nauie of ships to be rigged, to passe ouer into
> Britaine with Leir his father in law, to see him againe restored to
> his kingdome. It was accorded, that Cordeilla should also go
> with him to take possession of the land, the which he promised to
> leaue vnto hir, as the rightfull inheritour after his decesse, not-
> withstanding any former grant made to hir sisters or to their
> husbands in anie maner of wise.

Greg shows[1] that the treatment of a foreign invasion of England
was a ticklish business for a dramatist of Shakespeare's day, and
he argues that Cordelia persuaded her husband

> to abandon his purpose of wresting a portion of the kingdom for
> himself and retire to his own land, thus leaving her free to use his
> army in defence of her father.

Two pages before the Leir story there is an account of how
Corineus wrestles with Gogmagog. He

> did so double his force that he got the vpper hand of the giant,
> and cast him downe headlong from one of the rocks there, not
> farre from Douer, and so dispatched him: by reason whereof the
> place was named long after, *the fall or leape of Gogmagog*, but after-
> ward it was called *The fall of Douer*.

---

1. *M.L.R.*, 1940, pp. 431–46. Greg seeks to show that when France and
Cordelia 'planned their invasion, they cannot possibly have known of Lear's
rejection by his elder daughters, for the simple reason that it had not yet happened'; and he suggests that France 'incensed at some fresh insult to Cordelia,
departed in a rage, determined to wrest by force her portion from ... Albany and
Cornwall. Such is the situation when France and Cordelia land at Dover.' This
is to scrutinize the chronology of the play too curiously, for an invasion could
not in any case be planned and executed in the two or three days that have elapsed
since the first scene of the play—as Greg himself points out.

This passage probably accounts for Shakespeare's choice of Dover for Gloucester's attempted suicide; and it is possible that Edgar's description of the imaginary fiend with eyes like two full moons was influenced by Holinshed's account of Gogmagog.

From Spenser's account in *The Faerie Queene*, Shakespeare probably derived the form of Cordelia's name and also her death by hanging, a method of suicide dictated to Spenser by his need of a rhyme:

> And ouercommen kept in prison long,
> Til wearie of that wretched life, her selfe she hong.

Many critics have echoed Johnson's complaint that

> Shakespeare has suffered the virtue of Cordelia to perish in a just cause, contrary to the natural ideas of justice, to the hope of the reader, and, what is yet more strange, to the faith of the chronicles.

But in all the sources known to have been used by Shakespeare, with the one exception of the old play, Cordelia commits suicide. By telescoping the battle fought by Cordelia to restore Lear to the throne with the one in which she is captured by her foes, Shakespeare humanizes the plot. He gives Cordelia a comforter in prison, 'the father she herself has saved from despair'.[1] He removes 'the cruel feature which Geoffrey's story shares with the Greek tale of Antigone': Cordelia is slain—but not by herself. It has been suggested that Gloucester's words (IV. vi. 39–40)—

> My snuff and loathed part of nature should
> Burn itself out—

may have been derived from Spenser's lines—

> But true it is, that when the oyle is spent,
> The light goes out, and weeke is throwne away;

but the comparison of human life to a lamp was a commonplace.

There is some evidence that Shakespeare had read John Higgins's account of Cordila in the 1574 edition of *The Mirror for Magistrates*. The agreement that Lear

> threescore knightes and squires
> Should alwayes haue, attending on him still at cal

may be compared with Goneril's reference to 'a hundred knights and squires'; and the subsequent reductions of the train were followed by Shakespeare. Higgins makes Cordila tell how, on hearing of the ill-treatment of her father, she

---

1. R. W. Chambers, *King Lear*, 1940, p. 21.

> besought my king with teares vpon my knee,
> That he would aide my father;

and Cordelia says (IV. iv. 26) that France

> My mourning and importun'd tears hath pitied.

The lines contrasting Cordila's former life with that in prison—

> From sight of princely wights, to place where theues do dwell:
> From deinty beddes of downe, to be of strawe full fayne—

may be compared with Cordelia's lines (IV. vii. 38–40)—

> And wast thou *fain*, poor father,
> To hovel thee with swine and rogues forlorn,
> In short and musty *straw*?—

and the vision of Despair, inciting Cordila to suicide, may be compared with Edmund's lines—

> To lay the blame upon her own despair,
> That she fordid herself.

Higgins, alone of the authors Shakespeare is likely to have read, speaks of the 'king of *Fraunce*'; he, unlike the author of *Leir*, Spenser, and Holinshed, uses the form 'Albany'; he alone gives the evil sisters their Shakespearian husbands; and his spelling of Gonerell is nearer to Shakespeare's than Holinshed's Gonorilla. His King of France 'deemde that vertue was of dowries all the best'; and Shakespeare's declares that 'She is herself a dowry'[1] (I. i. 240). Higgins, finally, provided a hint for 'What need one?'[2] (II. iv. 261) in the lines—

1. Greg compares Holinshed's words, 'onlie moued thereto . . . for respect of hir person and amiable vertues'.

2. Greg compares Holinshed again: 'scarslie they would allow him one seruant to wait vpon him'.

The above discussion of Shakespeare's treatment of his sources owes a good deal to the exhaustive work by W. Perrett, *The Story of King Lear*, 1904, cf. pp. 189, 214–15, 274. He points out that '& squires' is omitted in the 1587 edition of *The Mirror for Magistrates* in the first of the above quotations, and that Cordila's tears are omitted from the second passage. This would seem to prove that Shakespeare used the 1574 or 1575 editions of *The Mirror*: but there is one passage in the 1587 edition, and not in the earlier ones, which is close to Cordelia's speech (I. i. 94–103):

> For nature so doth binde and duty mee compell,
> To loue you, as I ought my father, well.
> Yet shortely I may chaunce, if Fortune will,
> To finde in heart to beare another more good will.
> Thus much I sayd of nuptiall loues that ment.

Shakespeare, as Mr Perrett suggests, might have derived Cordelia's lines from Camden's *Remaines* (1605): 'Yet she did think that one day it would come to pass that she should affect another more fervently, meaning her Husband, when she

Bereaude him of his seruantes all saue one,
Bad him content him selfe with that or none.

was married, who, being made one flesh with her, she was to cleave fast to, forsaking Father and Mother, kiffe and kin.' The only other evidence that Shakespeare had read Camden's *Remaines* is the Fool's remark (I. iv. 197), 'That's a sheal'd peascod', which may be compared with Camden's reference to Richard II's device of 'a Pescod branch with the cods open, but the Pease out, as it is vpon his Robe in his Monument at Westminster'. Shakespeare, perhaps, might have picked this up from some other source; and he could easily have invented, or borrowed from the marriage service, Cordelia's reference to conjugal duties. The possibility that Shakespeare consulted two editions of *The Mirror for Magistrates* is supported by another faint parallel with the 1587 edition which substitutes 'Their former loue and friendship waxed cold' for the line in the 1574 edition, 'Thought well they might, be by his leaue, or sans so bolde'. Cf. I. ii. 103, 'Love cools, friendship falls off.' (Cf. note on III. vi. 6–7.)

Perrett also argues (*op. cit.*, pp. 280 ff.) that Shakespeare, led by a marginal note in Holinshed, had also consulted Geoffrey who describes the distribution of two-thirds of the kingdom immediately after Goneril and Regan have given their answers. Only two accessible sources (Geoffrey and Perceforest) suggest that there was to be an unequal division, the best share going to Cordelia. The pretexts for reducing Lear's train are also to be found in Geoffrey, and in no other known version accessible to Shakespeare. Perrett thinks that Geoffrey's Lear is closer to Shakespeare's in character than any other; and he points out some possible verbal echoes (cf. I. i. 251, 254; I. ii. 176). Shakespeare might have invented these details independently, or used another source no longer extant. Perrett's analysis of the various versions of the Lear story is nevertheless very informative. These versions include those of Henry of Huntingdon (1139), Wace (1155), Layamon (*c.* 1205), Robert of Gloucester (1300), Robert Mannyng (1338), Caxton (1480), Fabyan (1516), Polydore Vergil (1534), Stow (1565), and some forty others. D. F. Atkinson (*E.L.H.*, 1936, pp. 63–6) has suggested the possibility that Shakespeare was influenced by Gerard Legh's *The Accedens of Armory*, 1562, fol. 165. Legh emphasizes Leir's rage at Cordeilla's answer: 'his irefull hart straight braided out wrothful wordes of wreke and reuenge: enforcyng her to shun the rage, thus thundered out against her.' In none of the versions certainly used by Shakespeare does Lear tell Cordelia to avoid his presence; but such a detail requires no source.

S. Musgrove, *R.E.S.* (1956), pp. 294–8, suggests that Shakespeare took the names of some of his characters from Camden's *Remaines*. Camden mentions that Oswald means 'House-ruler or Steward'; that Eadgar is derived from '*Eadig-ar, Happy,* or *blessed honor,* or *power*'; and that Edmund is derived from '*Eadmund,* Happy, or blessed, peace'. Musgrove suggests that Shakespeare's eye may have been caught by the next sentence and that this would explain why Edmund does not live up to his name: 'Our Lawyers yet doe acknowledge *Mund* for *Peace* in their word *Mundbrech,* for breach of *Peace*.' Musgrove shows too that Hakluyt in his early pages refers to Edgar as 'Pacificus', and as one who conceived the idea ' "of the whole and onely one mysticall citie universall" under the protection of British peace and justice' (p. 6). There are references to two Edmunds, another Edgar, and an Oswald on neighbouring pages (pp. 8–9). The names of various earls of Kent and Gloucester are to be found in the early pages of Hakluyt and in Camden. Camden mentions Caius with the words on his monument, FVI CAIVS (cf. v. iii. 280–9). In the section on Impresas Camden quotes 'Ex nihilo nihil' (cf. I. i. 89, I. iv. 130).

It is likely that the old play gave Shakespeare the idea of writing on King Lear; but he had long been familiar with the versions of Holinshed and Spenser, and also with *The Mirror for Magistrates*. As we have seen, he was cheerfully eclectic in his use of sources, combining details and phrases from each. On the one hand he rejected the happy ending of *King Leir*, and gave form to its formlessness; on the other hand he rejected the undramatic elements of the versions of Spenser, Holinshed, and Higgins, in which the defeat and suicide of the heroine come as an epilogue irrelevant to the story of Lear himself. The suicide of Cordelia would have been intolerable to a sensitive audience, and her murder necessitated the punishment of the guilty: Goneril and Regan could not be suffered to escape, if Cordelia were to die; and Lear could not, without anticlimax, be restored to the throne. Out of a moral story with a happy ending and an irrelevant, despairing epilogue, Shakespeare created a homogeneous tragedy. Some of the means of bringing about this transformation were to be found in the source of the underplot.

It is well known that the story of the Paphlagonian King in Sidney's *Arcadia* provided Shakespeare with the Gloucester underplot. Sidney drew special attention to the episode,[1] with the remark that it was

> worthy to be remembered for the unused examples therein, as well of true natural goodnes, as of wretched ungratefulness.

Gloucester's words (I. i. 31–2)—

> He hath been out nine years, and away he shall again—

may have been suggested by the remark that Plexirtus was 'called home by his father'.[2] Edgar's disguise as a beggar may have been prompted by the plight of the Paphlagonian King, with alms his 'onelie sustenaunce'.[3] The storm may be derived from the 'haile', 'the pride of the winde', and 'the tempests furie' of 'so extreame and foule a storme'.[4] Gloucester's reference to 'unnatural dealing' (III. iii. 1–2) may be taken from Sidney's phrase describing the 'vnnaturall dealings' of the wicked son. Regan's complaint that the blinded Gloucester moves all hearts against them (IV. v. 10–11) and her promise that

> Preferment falls on him that cuts him off   (IV. v. 38)

may be derived from the words of Leonatus—

> In deede our state is such, as though nothing is so needfull vnto

1. F. Pyle, *M.L.R.*, Oct. 1948, pp. 449–55.   2. *Ibid.*   3. *Ibid.*
4. Cf. Appendix, p. 229.

vs as pittie, yet nothing is more daungerous vnto vs, then to make our selues so knowne as may stirre pittie.

The duel between Edgar and Edmund may be traced to Shakespeare's preoccupation with the chivalric *Arcadia*.[1] Both Gloucester and Lear die partly of joy. Gloucester's 'flawed heart', on his becoming reconciled to Edgar,

> Alack, too weak the conflict to support!
> 'Twixt two extremes of passion, joy and grief,
> Burst smilingly;   (v. iii. 196–8)

and Lear dies believing that Cordelia, after all, lives. The hint for both scenes is to be found in Sidney's words[2]—

> after he had kist him, and forst his sonne to accept honour of him (as of his newe-become subiect) euen in a moment died, as it should seeme: his hart broken with vnkindnes & affliction, stretched so farre beyond his limits with this excesse of comfort, as it was able no longer to keep safe his roial spirits.

Shakespeare, then, took rather more than the bare bones of the underplot from *Arcadia*. The characters, too, of the blind King, and of the good son, Leonatus, are not unlike those of Gloucester and Edgar. Edmund, in his relations with Goneril and Regan, exhibits characteristics which are not to be found in Plexirtus; and, while he is flamboyantly hypocritical in the early part of the play, there is no reason to suspect the genuineness of his repentance in the last scene, in contrast to Plexirtus who in defeat merely

> thought better by humblenes to creepe, where by pride he could not march.

Mr Fitzroy Pyle has argued further[3] that the main plot of the play may also be influenced by *Arcadia*, not merely in the parallelism of the good and evil children in both plots—a father receiving kindness from the child he has wronged and evil from the child he has favoured—but also because Sidney's story is more tragic than that of *King Leir*. It presents

> evil at the height of its power, ruthless, tyrannical, utterly destructive and sadistic, drying up through fear the springs of human feeling in ordinary men. Goodness, in the persons of the two principal characters, is intellectually far inferior, suffers in consequence grievous affliction of mind and body, and shows

1. F. Pyle, *op. cit.*
2. R. W. Chambers, *King Lear*, 1940, p. 44, and Perrett, *op. cit.*, p. 212. Shakespeare uses the word *long-engraffed* (i. i. 296); both Sidney and Florio use *engraffed*. Cf. also note on iv. i. 10.
3. *Op. cit.*

strength only in resignation, kindness of heart, and service gladly given. In the handling of the story there is a hint of that largeness of scope and suggestiveness that belongs to high tragedy. . . . Surely it would seem that in transforming the *King Leir* play Shakespeare's imagination was fired less by it than by the 'source' of his Gloucester plot.

Sidney's king does not live happily ever after; and it is pointed out in different parts of *Arcadia*[1] that

To be fit to govern country or dependants we must learn to govern ourselves, that whoever breaks the marriage bond 'dissolues al humanitie', and that the laws fold us within assured bounds, 'which once broken mans nature infinitely rangeth'.

Shakespeare, Mr Pyle concludes, made this familiar doctrine

the basis of his whole play and explored it in all its ramifications —even to the length asserted by Sidney, that when the bounds of law are broken we should be glad 'we may finde any hope that mankind is not growen monstrous'.

Another critic has suggested that the Gloucester plot may have been influenced by another chapter in *Arcadia*.[2] The story of Plangus, son of the King of Iberia, introduces a stratagem similar to Edmund's when he wishes to persuade his father of Edgar's guilt—

He would bring him into a place where he should heare all that passed. . . The poore *Plangus* (being subiect to that only disadvantage of honest harts, credulitie) was perswaded by him.

Later on, Plangus is discovered, as Edmund describes Edgar, 'in the dark, his sharp sword out'—

The King affrighted called his guard, . . . who found indeed *Plangus* with his sword in his hand.

Plangus's stepmother defends him to his father in such a way as to make the latter more suspicious. She would tell him—

I dare take it upon my death, that he is no such sonne, as many of like might have bene, who loved greatnes so well, as to build their greatnes upon their fathers ruine.

Soon, we are told,

all *Plangus* actions began to be translated into the language of suspition.

1. Pyle, *op. cit.*, and Sidney, *Works*, ed. Feuillerat, II. 175, 94, 195–6.
2. D. M. McKeithan, *University of Texas Bulletin*, 8 July 1934, pp. 45–9. Cf. Sidney, *op. cit.*, II. xv. 242–9, and *Lear*, I. ii. 36–90.

Shakespeare would have found this story only a few pages after that of the Paphlagonian King.

Between the stories of the Paphlagonian King and of Plangus there is a dialogue in *terza rima* between Plangus and Basilius, which is supposed to be versified by Basilius himself from an actual conversation. The general tenor of the debate between the two men about the rights and wrongs of suicide, on the justice of the gods, and on the slaughter of the innocent may have caught Shakespeare's eye before he wrote of the attempted suicide of Gloucester and of the death of Cordelia. Plangus, like Gloucester, contemplates suicide because he thinks that men are merely

> Balles to the starres, and thralles to Fortunes raigne;
>   Turnd from themselves, infected with their cage,
>   Where death is feard, and life is held with paine.
> Like players pla'st to fill a filthy stage.
>   Where chaunge of thoughts one foole to other shewes,
>   And all but jests, save onely sorrowes rage.
> The child feeles that; the man that feeling knowes,
>   With cries first borne, the presage of his life,
>   Where wit but serves, to have true tast of woes . . .
> Griefe onely makes his wretched state to see
>   (Even like a toppe which nought but whipping moves)
>   This man, this talking beast, this walking tree.
> Griefe is the stone which finest judgement proves:
>   For who grieves not hath but a blockish braine,
>   Since cause of griefe no cause from life removes.

With these lines may be compared several passages in *King Lear*—

> As flies to wanton boys, are we to th'Gods;
> They kill us for their sport.   (IV. i. 36–7)

> O! our lives' sweetness,
> That we the pain of death would hourly die
> Rather than die at once!   (v. iii. 183–5)

> I am even
> The natural fool of Fortune.   (IV. vi. 188–9)

> we came crying hither:
> Thou know'st the first time that we smell the air
> We wawl and cry. . .
> When we are born, we cry that we are come
> To this great stage of fools. This' a good block!
>   (IV. vi. 176–81)

> Howl, howl, howl! O! you are men of stones:
>   (v. iii. 256)

It will be noticed that Sidney's 'blockish' follows soon after 'stage' and 'fools', just as Lear's obscure word 'block' follows immediately after 'stage of fools'. The cause of Plangus's grief is that Erona, whom he loves, has been unjustly condemned to death. Basilius, however, warns Plangus not to blaspheme and argues, much as Edgar does, that if we could see clearly we should know that the gods were just. Plangus's repeated question, 'Must *Erona* dye?', and his complaint that the gods fail to answer prayers—

> Let doltes in haste some altars faire erect
> To those high powers, which idly sit above,
> And vertue do in greatest need neglect—

may be compared with the juxtaposition of Albany's prayer for the safety of Lear and of Cordelia, and Lear's entrance with her dead body. There is also a resemblance between Basilius's words—

> But such we are with inward tempest blowne
> Of mindes quite contrarie—

and Lear's remark (III. iv. 12) about the tempest in his mind.[1]

Yet another critic has argued that Shakespeare derived 'one of his best-known images' and perhaps 'some of the interpretations of God and nature found in King Lear' from an episode in the third book of *Arcadia*; but the two conceptions of nature to be found in both *King Lear* and *Arcadia* are also to be found elsewhere.[2]

Lamb thought that 'the situation of Andrugio and Lucio' in Marston's *Antonio and Mellida* (III. i) resembled that of Lear and Kent.[3] There is a closer parallel with the same dramatist's *The Malcontent* (IV. iii), in which Pietro, in disguise, describes his own feigned suicide by leaping from a cliff into the sea. This scene may have given a hint to Shakespeare when he wrote of Gloucester's attempted suicide.[4] Some details of the mad scenes in *Titus Andronicus* are repeated in *King Lear*. Marcus kills a fly with 'slender gilded wings' (III. ii. 61. Cf. *Lear*, IV. i. 36, IV. vi. 112); Titus gets Lucius to try his skill at archery (IV. iii. Cf. *Lear*, IV. vi. 87); like Lear, he solicits the gods for justice (IV. iii. 15, 39, 49–51, 79); he produces an imaginary petition (IV. iii. 105. Cf. *Lear*, IV. vi. 137) and he uses the words[5]—

---

1. Cf. Muir and Danby, *N.Q.*, 4 Feb. 1950, pp. 49–51. See also notes on IV. vi. 136 and IV. iii. 17–24.

2. William A. Armstrong, *T.L.S.*, 14 Oct. 1949. Cf. Sidney, *op. cit.*, III. x. 406–10, and *Lr.*, IV. i. 36–7, IV. ii. 32–3, IV. iii. 33–5.

3. C. Lamb, *Specimens*, 1890, p. 66.

4. Seneca's *Thebais* opens with a long scene in which Oedipus asks Antigone to let him stumble over a precipice.

5. v. ii. 21; cf. *Lr.*, IV. vi. 175.

I am not mad; I know thee well enough.

The Aaron–Tamora–Saturninus triangle resembles the later triangle of Edmund–Goneril–Albany; and Aaron has something in common with Edmund.

Shakespeare's use of two other books, Harsnett's *Declaration* and Florio's translation of Montaigne, is discussed in the Appendices.[1]

This account of the sources of the play may serve to throw some light on Shakespeare's method of creating a unity from heterogeneous materials. When he amplified and complicated his original fable, his *donnée*, he pressed into his service incidents, ideas, phrases, and even words from books and plays; and the remarkable richness of texture apparent in *King Lear* may be explained, at least in part, by Shakespeare's use of such a method. It is difficult to agree with Mr Richard H. Perkinson who, while admitting Shakespeare's purposeful rearrangement of his material, asserts[2] that he was

> content to utilize the loose episodic structure associated with the chronicle play,

and that he deliberately sacrificed the probability of his sources. The play, far from exhibiting any signs of loose, episodic structure, is more closely knit than any of the tragedies, except *Othello*.

1. Shakespeare took Edgar's dialect in IV. vi from *The London Prodigal*, a play performed by his company. Roland M. Smith (*M.L.Q.*, 1946, pp. 153 ff.) argued that Shakespeare derived some details of the play from R. Johnson's *Tom a Lincolne* (1607); but the resemblances appear to be fortuitous.

2. *Philological Quarterly*, XXII (1943), 315–29. It will have been noticed that in none of the fifty or sixty versions of the Lear story in existence before Shakespeare's play does the old king go mad. This may well have been Shakespeare's own invention; but he may have been acquainted with the story of Brian Annesley, a gentleman pensioner of Queen Elizabeth, who in October 1603 was 'altogether unfit to govern himself or his estate'. Two of his daughters, Lady Wildgoose and Lady Sandys, tried to get him certified as insane, so that they could get his estate; but the youngest daughter, Cordell, wrote to Cecil, claiming that her father's services to the late queen 'deserved a better agnomination, than at his last gasp to be recorded and registered a Lunatic', and urging that he and his estate be put under the care of Sir James Croft. When Annesley died, the Wildgooses contested the will, but it was upheld by the court of Chancery. A few years later, early in 1608, Cordell Annesley married Sir William Harvey, the widower of the Dowager Countess of Southampton, and thus the step-father of Shakespeare's patron. It is possible, therefore, that Lear's madness was suggested to the poet by the madness of Annesley and the loyalty of his Cordelia. (Cf. G. M. Young, *Today and Yesterday*, 1948, pp. 300–1; Salisbury MSS. ix (1930), 262, 266; C. C. Stopes, *The Third Earl of Southampton*, 1922, p. 274.)

4. *KING LEAR*, 1605–1950

King Lear, as we have seen, was probably performed early in 1605, with Burbage in the title-role and Armin as the Fool. A few years later we hear of the play being performed by Sir Richard Cholmeley's players at Gowthwaite Hall in Yorkshire on Candlemas 1609–10. The actors, who were apparently recusants, used the published Quarto. Lear was probably played by Christopher Simpson, the Fool by William Harrison, and Cordelia by Thomas Pant.[1]

To judge from the records of performances, the play seems to have been less popular than *Hamlet* or *Othello*. After the Restoration, it was acted by Betterton who first used the text more or less as Shakespeare wrote it and then, after 1681, Tate's notorious adaptation which held the stage for a century and a half. Garrick, though he omitted many of Tate's additions, retained the interpolated love-scenes between Edgar and Cordelia, and also the happy ending. Addison complained that the play in Tate's version had lost half its beauty;[2] but the actors cannot be severely blamed since several critics approved of the happy ending. Samuel Johnson himself confessed—

> I was many years ago so shocked by Cordelia's death, that I know not whether I ever endured to read again the last scenes of the play till I undertook to revise them as editor.

At the beginning of the nineteenth century, critical opinion turned against the happy ending, and Lamb attacked it in a famous essay[3]—

> It is not enough that Cordelia is a daughter, she must shine as a lover too. Tate has put his hook into the nostrils of this Leviathan, for Garrick and his followers, the showmen of the scene, to draw the mighty beast about more easily. A happy ending!—as if the living martyrdom that Lear had gone through—the flaying of his feelings alive, did not make a fair dismissal from the stage of life the only decorous thing for him. If he is to live and be happy after, if he could sustain this world's burden after, why all this pudder and preparation—why torment us with all this unnecessary sympathy? As if the childish pleasure of getting his gilt robes and sceptre again could tempt him to act over again his misused station—as if at his years, and with his experience, anything was left but to die.

---

1. Cf. Sisson, *R.E.S.*, 1942, pp. 134–43.

2. See *The Spectator*, 16 April 1711. D. Nichol Smith, *Shakespeare in the Eighteenth Century*, 1928, pp. 20–5, has an account of the versions of *King Lear* between 1681 and 1823.

3. *Works* (ed. W. Macdonald), III, p. 33.

In 1823, Kean, influenced mainly by Lamb and Hazlitt, restored the tragic ending, though he still kept the love-scenes, and still excluded the Fool. It was not until 1838 that Macready, with some misgivings, reintroduced the Fool. Later in the century, there was a famous production in which the stars were Henry Irving and Ellen Terry; and during the last twenty years there have been several notable Lears, including Gielgud, Devlin, Wolfit, and Olivier. In the 1950 season at Stratford-on-Avon, Gielgud gave a magnificent performance, which was prevented from achieving its full effect only by the unsatisfactory staging of the storm-scenes.

There is comparatively little criticism of the play before the nineteenth century. Joseph Warton's papers in *The Adventurer* (1753–4) and Richardson's *Essays* (1784) are not without interest; and if Warton complains that the plot of Edmund against his brother 'destroys the unity of the fable', that the blinding of Gloucester ought not to be exhibited on the stage, and that the cruelty of the daughters is too savage and unnatural, he calls attention to many good qualities in the play, including the judicious contrast between the assumed madness of Edgar and the real distraction of Lear.

With Lamb's essay, mentioned above, Coleridge's lectures, Hazlitt's *Characters of Shakespeare's Plays* (1817), and occasional comments by Keats and Shelley, we arrive at a conception of the play not essentially different from that generally held today. Schlegel was the first to realize the dramatic function of the under-plot (1808). There have been scores of interpretations of the play since the Romantic period, including those of Dowden (1875), Bradley (1904), Swinburne (1909), Wilson Knight (1930), R. W. Chambers (1940), Bickersteth (1947), Heilman (1948), and Danby (1949), to all of which we shall have occasion to return.

5. THE PLAY

Exasperated by the difference between his experience as a reader of *King Lear* and his experience of Tate's version in the theatre, Lamb proclaimed that the play could not be represented on the stage. Bradley, likewise, argued that it was too huge for the stage. Other critics have followed suit; and it has recently been stated[1] that

> by the verdict of criticism and theatrical experience alike, *King Lear* is a poor stage play.

A few critics have realized that a poor stage play is, when all

1. Tucker Brooke, *Essays on Shakespeare*, 1948, p. 57.

qualifications have been made, a poor play. This, in fact, was Thackeray's opinion[1]—

> We all found the play a bore.... It is almost blasphemy to say that a play of Shakespeare's is bad; but I can't help it, if I think so.

Professor Allardyce Nicoll argued some years ago[2] that

> Shakespeare, through exhaustion or haste, had failed to think out the scheme and possibilities of *King Lear* as he had thought out and considered the scheme and possibilities of *Othello*:

and Mr J. Middleton Murry complains that the play is lacking in poetic spontaneity.[3] Shakespeare, he believes, was 'working against his natural bent'. He was 'spurring his imagination, which in consequence was something less than imagination'. In spite of the pains lavished by Shakespeare on the play, Mr Murry thinks that *Coriolanus* is much finer, and that it represents

> the return from effort to spontaneity, from artefact to creation, from inhumanity to humanity.

Perhaps the explanation of this singular judgment is to be found in Murry's belief that Shakespeare had experienced his plays before writing them. He found it intolerable to believe, we may suppose, that Shakespeare had experienced the suffering that lies at the heart of *King Lear*, just as once, as he confesses, he averted his eyes from the Crucifixion. That this is a plausible explanation can be seen from remarks he lets slip in his chapter on the play. He speaks of Shakespeare's 'uncontrollable despair', of his 'horrible primitive revulsion against sex'. The play is an 'exploitation of partial despair', 'an enforced utterance' made at a time when silence would have been 'more wholesome and more natural'. It was Shakespeare's 'deliberate prophylactic against his own incoherence'. Murry's verdict remains astonishing if only because he so seldom disagrees with Keats; and Keats has described for us in unforgettable lines his own sensations about the play[4]—

> Once again the fierce dispute
> Betwixt damnation and impassion'd clay
> Must I burn through;—

and in one of his letters he declared[5] that

> The excellence of every art is in its intensity, capable of making all disagreeables evaporate, from their being in close relation-

1. *Letters*, ed. Ray, 1945, II. 292.   2. *Studies in Shakespeare*, 1927, p. 157.
3. J. M. Murry, *Shakespeare*, 1936, pp. 337–51.
4. *Poems*, ed. H. W. Garrod, p. 482.
5. *Letters*, ed. M. B. Forman, 1948, p. 71.

ship with Beauty and Truth. Examine *King Lear*, and you will find this exemplified throughout.

This intensity has been recognized by most competent critics, and it was this that led Coleridge to call the play[1] 'the most tremendous effort of Shakespeare as a poet', and made Shelley describe[2] it as 'the most perfect specimen of dramatic poetry existing in the world'. It might, nevertheless, be a great poem and a bad stage play, either because it makes impossible demands on the actor, or because of alleged faults of construction more apparent to the spectator than to the reader. Yet in our own time the play has been strikingly successful on the stage, the role of Lear having been filled creditably, and even brilliantly, by actors who have failed in the supposedly easier parts of Macbeth and Othello; and few readers of Harley Granville-Barker's *Preface* would be prepared to deny the adequacy of Shakespeare's dramatic technique or the actability of the play. Lamb thought that the storm scenes were the most difficult to perform; but if Lear is permitted to act the storm (as his speeches suggest he should) and if the stage effects are neither too realistic nor too clever, the scenes can be overwhelming.[3]

The mad scenes are perhaps more difficult because some members of every audience are inclined to laugh. The omission of the trial of Goneril and Regan from the Folio has been taken to indicate that this scene was unsuccessful in Shakespeare's lifetime. This would not be at all surprising since the Elizabethans were prepared to find madness entertaining. Even Granville-Barker had doubts about the actability of this scene:[4] but though few members of an audience would spot the Horatian allusions and the Latin puns, the symbolic significance of the trial of the two daughters by a mad beggar, a dying Fool, and a serving-man is perfectly clear. *He hath put down the mighty from their seat, and hath exalted the humble and meek.*

No performance of a great play, or of a great piece of music, can be ideal; but a performance, if not too defective, can give us an experience we should not get from a reading of the text or a perusal of the score at home. Drama, especially, is a communal art, re-

1. Coleridge, *Table Talk*, 29 Dec. 1822.

2. Shelley, *A Defence of Poetry*, 1909, p. 134.

3. The invention of electric light and the banishment of realistic scenery has simplified the producer's task since the days of Garrick; but in Komisarjevsky's Stratford production a film of storm clouds projected on the cyclorama effectually distracted our attention from what was being said by the actors. On the other hand, those who try to suggest the storm solely by means of canned music have seldom or never obtained satisfactory results. Thunder and lightning are necessary, and if they are used to punctuate, rather than to accompany Lear's words, they need not prevent us from hearing a single one of them.

4. *Prefaces to Shakespeare*, 1927, I. 227.

quiring an audience to participate in the performance; and Bradley, with all his critical insight, missed something in his ideal theatre of the mind, that his valet might have got in the gallery of the Lyceum theatre.

It is worth noting that the alleged theatrical weaknesses of the play have been analysed most effectively by Bradley himself who yet seems to have had little experience of the play in the theatre. He complains of the structural weakness of the fourth act and of the first part of the fifth, of the disadvantages of the double action, which in his opinion outweighed the advantages, and of a number of gross improbabilities.[1] He points out, for example, that Edgar would be unlikely to write to Edmund when he could speak with him, and that Gloucester would have noticed the improbability; that Gloucester had no need to go to Dover for the purpose of committing suicide; and that it is strange that he should show no surprise when Edgar drops into dialect during his encounter with Oswald; that there is no good reason why Edgar should not reveal himself to his father, or why Kent should preserve his disguise until the last scene; that Edmund, after he has received his fatal wound, delays unnecessarily in telling of the danger to Lear and Cordelia; and that it is absurd for Edgar to return from his hiding-place to soliloquize in his father's castle. Now it is perfectly true that the scene between the mad king and the blinded Gloucester is strictly supererogatory to the plot, but it is never felt to be superfluous, even from the theatrical point of view. Parts of the underplot, especially that which concerns Edmund's intrigues with Goneril and Regan, are not presented in detail, and we are left to piece it together from hints and guesses: this is not a dramatic fault since it has the effect of concentrating our attention on Lear himself. Most of the improbabilities mentioned by Bradley would not be noticed in the theatre, and they cannot therefore detract from the effectiveness of *King Lear* as a stage play. Apart from this, there is something to be said in defence of every one of the improbabilities. Edmund's forged letter, which he pretended was thrown through the window, might be regarded as a more plausible method of broaching conspiracy than by word of mouth because the writer could deny his handwriting, or pretend he was making an assay of his brother's virtue; and Gloucester, having swallowed a camel, was not likely to strain at a gnat. Gloucester decides to jump off Dover cliff primarily because Shakespeare wants all his characters to congregate at Dover for the last act of the play. But it may be argued that the reiterated question, 'Wherefore to Dover?', recalls the cliff to

1. *Op. cit.*, 1922, pp. 254–8, 445.

Gloucester's mind, and in his half-crazed state he has an irrational urge to end his life there. The case-histories of suicides contain stranger obsessive characteristics than this. Nor does it seem necessary that Gloucester should express surprise when Edgar begins to speak in dialect. Either he could appear surprised without words, or he could assume that his other senses had become imperfect with the loss of his sight. Shakespeare had prepared the way by making Gloucester comment, earlier in the scene, on the improvement in Poor Tom's speech. Edgar, in real life, would perhaps have revealed himself to his father; but the conventions of romance and of poetic drama do not always coincide with those of real life. Shakespeare reconciles the two by making Edgar refer to his conduct as a 'fault', or miscalculation. He had wished, we may suppose, not only to overcome his father's desire for suicide, but also to convince him that the gods were not spiteful. He may also have delayed the revelation of his identity in order to impose a penance on his father, and to guarantee the genuineness and permanence of his repentance. R. W. Chambers, not altogether fancifully, thinks that Gloucester, guided by Edgar, is climbing the mountain of Purgatory[1]—

> We begin to see the world as Keats saw it—not so much as a Vale of Tears as a Vale of Soul-making.

There is, too, a suggestion that Edgar wished to rehabilitate himself in the eyes of the world, and punish Edmund, before revealing himself. There is nothing improbable in any of these motives, and the dramatist is bound to explain only those things that would otherwise seem incredible. Indeed, a certain mystery in the characters prevents them from seeming mechanical, just as in real life we can classify our acquaintances, not our friends. A similar defence may be offered of Kent's wish to conceal his identity. Edmund's delay in revealing the danger to Lear and Cordelia may be explained by his loyalty to Goneril, or by the gradual workings of repentance;[2] and Edgar appears to return to his father's courtyard only on a stage with representational scenery—on Shakespeare's own stage the presence of Kent in the stocks would be forgotten, and the audience would certainly not assume that Edgar was in the neighbourhood of the castle.[3]

1. *Op. cit.*, p. 48. Cf. Keats, *Letters*, 1948, pp. 355 ff.
2. Cf. Masefield, *Shakespeare*, p. 193, and G. W. Knight, *The Wheel of Fire*, 1949, p. 206.
3. Bradley has other perplexities, to which I append short answers. (1) Why should Edgar meekly avoid his father? (Because Edmund had made him believe that his life is in danger.) (2) Lear speaks of having to dismiss fifty followers,

The improbabilities, then, are unlikely to be noticed during a performance; and those detected in the study can be explained away in the study. On the question of time, indeed, as we have seen,[1] Shakespeare preserves a calculated vagueness. We are allowed to think that the King of France invades Britain because of the ill-usage Lear has received from Goneril and Regan, though he could not have heard of Lear's sufferings before the invasion had been set in motion. If we notice the impossibility we are driven to believe that the motive of the invasion is to recover by force Cordelia's share of the kingdom; but this is later contradicted by Cordelia's own claim that the invasion is entirely in her father's interest. This confusion, which could be avoided only by slowing up the action, was the result of cunning rather than carelessness. The same thing may be said of Shakespeare's treatment of place. The vagueness is apparently designed[2]

---

though Goneril has not mentioned a number. (Perhaps Lear hears during his brief absence from the stage that Goneril had dismissed half his train before consulting him on the matter; or maybe he is a telepathist.) (3) Lear and Goneril both send off messengers and tell them to bring back an answer, though both are following them with the greatest speed. (Presumably both Goneril and Lear expected to meet their returning messengers on the road. Kent and Oswald, however, are both commanded by Regan to follow her to Gloucester's house.) (4) Why does Burgundy rather than France have the first refusal? (Because Lear does not wish to insult France by offering Cordelia's hand without a dowry.) (5) Why does Shakespeare neglect to tell us about the fate of the Fool? (There is no particular reason, except novel-readers' insatiable curiosity, why we should be told. It is appropriate that the professional jester should fade out when he is no longer needed.) (6) When Lear arrives at Gloucester's house the Fool implies that most of his train have deserted him; but Regan says that he is attended with a desperate train, and we hear in Act iii that he has thirty-six knights in quest of him. (Shakespeare wished to give the impression in ii. iv that Lear was deserted by his followers. The thirty-six 'hot questrists' seem to have just arrived at Gloucester's house in iii. vii, following Lear from Goneril's; but even if they had arrived earlier, and they are the desperate train mentioned by Regan, who is hardly a reliable witness, they might be regarded by Kent as a small train compared with Lear's accustomed escort.) (7) In iv. iii, Kent refers to a letter sent to Cordelia, though it had been a verbal message (iii. i). (He may have sent a letter as well as a verbal message, or Shakespeare may have forgotten, or hoped that his audience had.) (8) Kent, on finding the King in the storm, does not halloo as he had arranged to do. (Either the actor could insert an halloo, or else the King's plight made Kent forget the arrangement.) (9) Cordelia does not reveal Kent's identity to the gentleman, in spite of the promise in iii. i. (Perhaps Shakespeare changed his mind.)

It may be admitted that in Nos. 7, 8, and 9, Shakespeare was guilty of trivial inconsistencies; but they would certainly not be noticed during a performance. And it may be worth while to mention that all three relate to two scenes that are textually unreliable. There are cuts in iii. i in both Q and F; and iv. iii is omitted by F altogether.

1. Cf. p. xxx *ante.*   2. Greg, *M.L.R.*, 1940, p. 432.

to prevent topographical difficulties impeding the rapidity of the action.

So much for the alleged faults of *King Lear* as an acting play. We may turn now to broader questions of interpretation.

R. G. Collingwood has remarked[1] that

apart from the idea of the family, intellectually conceived as a principle of social morality, the tragedy of Lear would not exist.

One theme of the play, expressed in plot and underplot, is the parent–child relationship. To a child, the father may be 'both loved protector and unjustly obstructing tyrant'; and to a parent the child may be 'both loving supporter of age and ruthless usurper and rival'.[2] This ambivalent attitude is distributed between the good and evil children of Lear and Gloucester.[3] Lear has reached the age when he should 'renounce love, choose death, and make friends with the necessity of dying'.[4] The play opens with his decision to abdicate, so that he may crawl unburthened towards death; but the love-test he imposes shows that he still retains the desire for love, and his actions in the first scene reveal only too plainly that he wishes to retain the authority he is ostensibly renouncing. This is a universal theme; for though, since a king has more to renounce than a subject, Lear's royalty is important, yet, as Goethe pointed out[5]—

Ein alter Mann ist stets ein König Lear,

because he is reluctant to admit that the young have lives of their own to lead, and because there is always a conflict between youth and age. Children often seem to their parents to be ungrateful; and the old must in some degree be deserted by the young. But in *King Lear* such common human feelings are magnified. The selfishness and ingratitude of children, no longer trammelled by the restraints of morality or modified by filial affection, are projected into the monstrous figures of Goneril and Regan; and family bickering is enlarged into an internecine struggle, destroying the peace of Britain, and accompanied by a storm in the cosmos itself.

The play is not only a tragedy of parents and children, of pride and ingratitude: it is also a tragedy of kingship. Power corrupts not

1. *The Principles of Art*, 1938, p. 295.

2. M. Bodkin, *Archetypal Patterns in Poetry*, 1934, pp. 15–16.

3. In *The Master Builder* the ambivalence is expressed in the single figure of Hilda who is loved and feared by Solness, and who loves and destroys him.

4. S. Freud, *Collected Papers*, IV (1934), 236. Cf. G. Orwell, *Polemic*, March 1947; W. Empson, *The Structure of Complex Words*, 1951, p. 125.

5. Goethe, *Gedichte*, 1925, II. 103 ('An aged man is always a King Lear.'). The poem is quoted by G. Landauer, *Shakespeare*, 1920, II. 127.

only the possessor's capacity for loving, but the spontaneity of others' love. He can never be sure that the professed love of friends and relations is disinterested, since it may easily be purposeful flattery. What is more, the appetite for flattery grows by what it feeds on; those who refuse to flatter are hated and banished, while the flatterers are rewarded. In the first scene of the play, Lear is a foolish old man who has been described[1] with pardonable exaggeration as an

> arrogant old idiot, destitute of any decent human quality and incapable of any reasonable act,

who is led in the vanity of dotage to stage a scene to gratify his craving for affection. When Cordelia refuses to barter her love for material profit, Lear banishes both her and the one man who dares to take her part. This violation of the duties of kingship is the initial deed from which the tragedy springs. As the play progresses, Lear's subconscious realization that he has committed a sinful mistake gradually rises into his consciousness. The cruelty of Goneril and Regan makes him admit that he has banished the one daughter who loved him disinterestedly; but it is not until near the end of the second act that he experiences an emotion not purely egotistical—when he argues the difference between the bare animal necessities and human needs. In the storm, more sinned against than sinning, Lear learns 'the art of our necessities', and so becomes aware of the common humanity he shares with the poor naked wretches. He exhorts pomp to 'shake the superflux to them', as Gloucester was later to pray that distribution should

> undo excess,
> And each man have enough.

The repetition is significant, and it completely disproves Schücking's argument that as Shakespeare elsewhere displays little social sense we should not assume that Lear in acquiring this compassion was being purified.[2] Shakespeare, after all, was not cut off from the Christian tradition, with its insistence on the duty of charity;[3] and though he doubtless believed in an hierarchical rather than in an equalitarian society, there is no reason to think that he would have looked on the wish of Lear and Gloucester to shake the superflux to the less fortunate as a symptom of madness.

Yet Lear, on the appearance of Poor Tom, does go mad. Obsessed as he is with the thought of filial ingratitude, it needs

---

1. By Bridie.
2. Schücking, *Character Problems in Shakespeare's Plays*, 1922, p. 186.
3. Cf. J. F. Danby, *Shakespeare's Doctrine of Nature*, 1949, pp. 185–9.

only a little shock to drive him over the frontiers of sanity. The Bedlam beggar provides him with a living example of the poverty he has been pitying; and by tearing off his clothes he identifies himself with unaccommodated man, the 'poor, bare, forked animal'. In one sense this is the central moment of the play—a dramatic answer to the Psalmist's question: 'What is man that Thou art mindful of him?' Stripped of his proud array, stripped of everything except the basic necessities, man's life is cheap as beast's. But this is only an interim report on the human condition: it is not the answer provided by the play as a whole.

In the trial scene, Lear is concerned with justice—'a kind of wild justice'—and with the cause of hardness of heart. When he next appears, in the fourth act, we see him in a new stage of self-knowledge. He realizes that he has been flattered like a dog, and that a king is merely a man. He inveighs against sex, partly because, as the Elizabethans knew, certain kinds of madness are accompanied by such an obsession, and partly because sexual desire has led to the birth of unnatural children, if indeed their unnaturalness does not prove that their mother's tomb sepulchres an adulteress. Lear returns to the subject of justice and authority in his next long speech. 'A dog's obeyed in office.' All men are sinners, and successful men cloak their crimes and vices by the power of gold. Justice is merely an instrument of the rich and powerful to oppress the poor and weak. But since all are equally guilty, none does offend. Since all are miserable sinners, all have an equal right to be forgiven. This speech continues the analysis of authority begun in *Measure for Measure*; and, as I have suggested elsewhere, the praise of Order and the analysis of Authority may be regarded as the thesis and antithesis of the Shakespearian dialectic.[1] It has often been observed that Lear's diatribes on sex and gold resemble the invective of the disillusioned Timon.

The old Lear died in the storm. The new Lear is born in the scene in which he is reunited with Cordelia. His madness marked the end of the wilful, egotistical monarch. He is resurrected as a fully human being. We can tell from his protest—

You do me wrong to take me out o'th'grave—   (iv. vii. 45)

that the awakening into life is a painful process. After the reconciliation, Lear makes only two more appearances. In the scene in which he is being led off to prison he has apparently overcome the desire for vengeance: he has left behind him all those attributes of kingship which had prevented him from attaining his full stature

1. Cf. K. Muir, *Modern Quarterly Miscellany*, 1947, pp. 64–6. I have borrowed several phrases from this article, '*Timon of Athens* and the Cash-Nexus'.

as a man; he has even passed beyond his own pride. At the beginning of the play, he is incapable of disinterested love, for he uses the love of others to minister to his own egotism. His prolonged agony and his utter loss of everything free his heart from the bondage of the selfhood. He unlearns hatred, and learns love and humility.[1] He loses the world and gains his soul—

> We two alone will sing like birds i'th'cage:
> When thou dost ask me blessing, I'll kneel down,
> And ask of thee forgiveness.   (v. iii. 9–11)

The play is not, as some of our grandfathers believed, pessimistic and pagan: it is rather an attempt to provide an answer to the undermining of traditional ideas by the new philosophy that called all in doubt.[2] Shakespeare goes back to a pre-Christian world and builds up from the nature of man himself, and not from revealed religion, those same moral and religious ideas that were being undermined. In a world of lust, cruelty, and greed, with extremes of wealth and poverty, man reduced to his essentials needs not wealth, nor power, nor even physical freedom, but rather patience, stoical fortitude, and love; needs, perhaps, above all, mutual forgiveness, the exchange of charity, and those sacrifices on which the gods, if there are any gods, throw incense—

> A life of sins forgiven, of reciprocated charity, of clear vision, and of joyous song—what is this but the traditional heaven transferred to earth?—

asks Bickersteth.[3] J. C. Maxwell was right when he said[4] that

> King Lear is a Christian play about a pagan world. . . . The fact that Shakespeare can assume in his audience a different religious standpoint from that of any of his characters gives him a peculiar freedom, and makes possible an unusual complexity and richness.

Some have thought that Shakespeare, as well as Gloucester, believed that

> As flies to wanton boys, are we to th'Gods:
> They kill us for their sport.   (iv. i. 36–7)

---

1. Cf. W. H. Auden's description of parabolic art; but in a later essay, *Horizon*, Aug. 1949, p. 87, Auden argues strangely that since Lear repents he is not a tragic hero.

2. T. Spencer, *Shakespeare and the Nature of Man*, 1943, pp. 135 ff.

3. *The Golden World of 'King Lear'*, 1947, p. 10.

4. *M.L.R.* xlv (April 1950), 142 ff. E. Welsford, *The Fool*, 1935, p. 268, points out 'that the metaphysical comfort of the Scriptures is deliberately omitted, though not therefore necessarily denied'. See also Oscar J. Campbell, *E.L.H.*, June 1948.

Others have supposed that he would have subscribed to Kent's exclamation that the stars governed our condition; or, more plausibly, that he would have agreed with Edgar's stern summing-up—

> The Gods are just, and of our pleasant vices
> Make instruments to plague us.   (v. iii. 169–70)

But all these, and other, statements about the gods are appropriate to the characters who speak them, and to the immediate situation in which they are spoken. Shakespeare remains in the background; but he shows us his pagan characters groping their way towards a recognition of the values traditional in his society.

In spite of Swinburne's eloquent pages on *King Lear*,[1] Shakespeare's vision of the world was not essentially pessimistic. The tragic writer is necessarily selective; and it would be as foolish to regard the author of the Romances as optimistic, as to suppose that the author of the Tragedies was necessarily a pessimist. Heroes of Romances survive; heroes of Tragedies usually die. Nor is the world of the tragedies, the world of *King Lear* in particular, exclusively evil. In the other scale we have to put the loyalty of Kent and the Fool, the fortitude and forgiveness of Edgar and Cordelia, the humanity of Cornwall's servant. Nor does evil finally triumph, for the will to power is self-destructive.[2] Heilman shows that the 'reason in madness' theme is balanced by that of 'madness in reason'. The three wicked children are all destroyed by their superficially sane pursuit of self-interest. They all believe in looking after themselves; they all implicitly deny that we are members one of another; they all assume that man is a competitive rather than a co-operative animal[3]—

> But the paradox is that these free minds, unburdened by any conventional or traditional allegiances, become slaves to the uncontrolled animal desire, mechanisms for the attainment of irrational objectives.

Goneril and Regan become centaurs, their rational minds instruments of the animal body. Their moral code, apparently so efficient and utilitarian,

> ruins the basis of human order . . . destroys the soul of its practitioner;

---

1. *A Study of Shakespeare*, 1879 (ed. 1918), pp. 171–2; *Three Plays of Shakespeare*, ed. 1909, p. 16.
2. J. Macmurray, *The Clue to History*, 1938, p. 237.
3. *This Great Stage*, 1948, pp. 225–53.

and yet, in spite of the dreadful cost, it cannot even ensure success in this world. Edmund, who believes only in his own will, and seems at first to be as ruthless as Iago, is moved by the story of his father's death to do some good 'in spite of his own nature'; and he is constrained to admit that there is a moral order in the universe.

Yet Shakespeare was certainly in a ruthless mood when he wrote *King Lear*, and his religious attitude provides no easy comfort, and makes no concessions to sentimentality. But we see Cordelia and Kent uncontaminated by the evil around them; we see Lear and Gloucester painfully learning wisdom; we see Albany increase in moral stature as he frees himself from his infatuation; and we see Edgar change from a credulous fool to a brave and saintly champion. 'Pessimism does not consist in seeing evil injure good,' said Heilman justly; it is rather the inability to see good, 'or to discover total depravity, but no grace'. It is not pessimism but realism to recognize that without Edmunds there could be no Cordelias.

But Cordelia dies. To some critics—and even Bradley seems to be undecided on the question—it would have been better if Shakespeare had allowed the miseries of Lear to be concluded in the reconciliation scene. Such critics, if mistaken, are at least not so far astray as others who have pretended that Cordelia's death is a punishment for her original obstinacy. Her death is even less a fitting punishment for her 'fault' than Lear's own agony is an appropriate punishment for his foolishness. It is right that the final scenes of the play should make us shrink, but wrong that we should wish them altered. When Lear banished Cordelia and when Gloucester committed adultery they unleashed horrors—treachery, blindness, madness, murder, suicide, and war—and the innocent are at least as vulnerable as the guilty. Indeed, it may be said, it is because of her very virtues that Cordelia is chosen to be a victim of the ruthless destiny that broods over the tragic scene, just as in the old legends it was always the pure and innocent who were chosen to propitiate the dragon, and just as in ancient Mexico it was always the most beautiful of the captives who were slain on the bloody altar of Tezcatlipoca. Cordelia's honesty is not the best policy; and her virtue is literally its own reward. Of those critics who complain that she died guiltless we can only enquire if they would rather she had died guilty. There is, of course, something gratuitous and supererogatory about her death, since it could have been averted if Edmund had spoken a few minutes earlier; and Shakespeare seems to underline the futility of Albany's prayer for the safety of Lear and of Cordelia. This does not mean that the gods kill us for their sport: it means simply that they do not intervene to prevent us from killing each other.

But we are mainly concerned with the effect of Cordelia's death on Lear himself. It destroys his dream of a happy life in prison, and it hastens his final dissolution; though his actual death-blow is not his bereavement but his joy when he imagines that Cordelia is not dead after all. That joy was based on an illusion. The earlier joy of reconciliation, however short-lived, was not an illusion: and its significance is not wholly eradicated by Cordelia's death. Lear's own death is a dramatic necessity, for a happy ending (in the conventional sense) was unthinkable for one who 'had learnt too much too late'.[1]

It was Bradley who suggested that the play might be called 'The Redemption of King Lear'; and the account given above of the development of his character is partly based on his analysis. Schücking, however, argues[2] that it is not

> really consistent with Shakespeare's philosophy to see in this sequence of events an ascent of the character to a higher plane, a process of purification and perfection.

Lear in his madness

> does little more than follow the beaten track of the melancholy type.

His attacks on society, however profound they may seem, are the result of his mental derangement; and at the end of the play he is not purified by suffering, but rather

> a nature completely transformed, whose extraordinary vital forces are extinguished, or about to be extinguished.

Schücking concludes, therefore, that it shows a complete misunderstanding of the play 'to regard Lear as greater at the close than at the beginning'. It is true, of course, that some of Lear's most impressive criticisms of society are spoken in his madness; that he becomes progressively more feeble; and that in the last scene there are signs of his approaching dissolution: yet the three moments in the play crucial to Bradley's theory of Lear's development—his recognition of error, his compassion for the poor, and his kneeling to Cordelia—occur either before or after his madness.[3]

1. Mark Van Doren, *Shakespeare*, 1939, p. 250.   2. *Op. cit.*, pp. 186–9.
3. Cf. I. v. 24; III. iv. 28; IV. vii. 45 ff.

His resemblance to the melancholic type[1] is superficial, though other dramatists had criticized society through the mouth of a malcontent as Shakespeare did through the mouth of a madman. Schücking seems to be only partially aware of the paradox that Lear when ostensibly sane cannot distinguish between Cordelia and her wicked sisters: he acquires wisdom by going mad, and his wildest speeches are a mixture of matter and impertinency— 'reason in madness'. In the same way, Gloucester before he lost his eyes was spiritually blind, and could not tell the difference between a good son and a bad.[2] He confesses this in the lines:

> I stumbled when I saw. Full oft 'tis seen,
> Our means secure us, and our mere defects
> Prove our commodities.

The whole play is built on this double paradox, which could be overlooked only by a critic who was determined to regard Shakespeare's technique as 'primitive'.[3]

A good deal of attention has been paid in recent years to the imagery of *King Lear*. As early as 1879, one industrious critic pointed out the prevalence of animal imagery—133 separate mentions of sixty-four different animals—and several later critics have commented on the significance of these figures.[4] This imagery is designed partly to show man's place in the Chain of Being, and to bring out the sub-human nature of the evil characters, partly to show man's weakness compared with the animals, and partly to compare human existence to the life of the jungle. It has been said that a scene by Racine is 'the explanation which closes for the time a series of negotiations between wild beasts'. There are scenes in *King Lear* to which the description might more aptly be applied. Yet Shakespeare knew, as well as a later poet,[5] that humanity is bound to assert itself:

1. A psychiatrist who took part in a recent amateur production of the play commented on the clinical accuracy with which Shakespeare depicted Lear's manic state in iv. vi.

2. This is why Gloucester's blinding is not an irrelevant horror, and not even something that should have been described by a messenger. Because of its importance as a visual symbol it had to be carried out in full view of the audience. By this means, as J. I. M. Stewart puts it (*Character and Motive in Shakespeare*, p. 23), Shakespeare achieved 'the powerful effect of a suddenly realized imagery; the oppressive atmosphere of the play here condensing in a ghastly dew'.

3. Cf. R. B. Heilman, *op. cit.*, pp. 41 ff., 173 ff.

4. *New Sh. Soc. Trans.*, 1877–9, pp. 385–405; G. W. Knight, *The Wheel of Fire*, 1949, pp. 185 ff.; Spurgeon, *Shakespeare's Imagery*, 1935, p. 342; Bradley, *op. cit.*, p. 266; Heilman, *op. cit.*, pp. 92 ff., 105 ff.; W. H. Clemen, *The Development of Shakespeare's Imagery*, 1951, pp. 133–53.

5. W. H. Auden, *Another Time*, 1940, p. 52.

> the striped and vigorous tiger can move
> With style through the borough of murder; the ape
> Is really at home in the parish
> Of grimacing and licking; but we have
> Failed as their pupils.

According to Miss Spurgeon,[1] the iterative image of the play is that

> of a human body in anguished movement, tugged, wrenched, beaten, pierced, stung, scourged, dislocated, flayed, gashed, scalded, tortured, and finally broken on the rack.

The image expresses the suffering not only of Lear, but of man; and the suffering itself is perhaps more important than its causes. At times Lear's voice seems to blend with that of Job[2] in demanding of the gods why the righteous man is smitten. Lear is suffering man, *homo patiens*; and throughout the play we hear words that express that suffering by recalling the derivation of *Patience*, and the fortitude needed to bear it.

> You Heavens, give me that patience, patience I need!
> I will be the pattern of all patience.
> I will endure.
> Thou must be patient.
> Men must endure . . .
> The wonder is he hath endur'd so long.

We have already referred to the significance of the images relating to the blinding of Gloucester, and to the double paradox of reason in madness and madness in reason. Another recurrent theme is that of clothes,[3] civilized man being contrasted with essential man. This cluster of ideas shows how wealth can pervert justice, and it reminds us that the lady clad in proud array ought to consider the plight of the poor naked wretches. The rights of the poor, the weak, and the aged are contrasted in the play with the doctrine of the survival of the fittest; and if we are to believe Danby,[4] Shakespeare presents two contrasting views of nature—

1. *Op. cit.*, p. 339.
2. Cf. Knight, *op. cit.*, p. 191. W. H. Gardner, *Gerard Manley Hopkins*, 1. 175, points out that 'Job's story is one of trial through suffering, while Lear's is one of purgation; but the stature and bearing of the sufferers give them a universal significance. The storm in *Lear* may be considered as much a symbol of divine intervention and judgement as the lightning and whirlwind which preceded the voice of God in *Job*.' That Shakespeare was recalling, perhaps unconsciously, the story of Job can be guessed from Lear's references to boils.
3. Cf. p. xlix *ante*, and Heilman, *op. cit.*, pp. 67 ff.
4. *Op. cit.*, pp. 20 ff. Danby goes on to suggest that Shakespeare was thus dramatizing the conflict between medieval society and nascent capitalism.

the traditional view of Hooker and Bacon, which assumes that nature is benignant, rational, and divinely ordered; and the view of the rationalists that man is governed by appetite and self-interest. There is nothing impossible in the assumption that Shakespeare was conscious, in a wider sense, of the two conceptions of nature; for he would have found them in Montaigne, in Sidney, and in Holland's preface to his translation of Pliny. H. F. there contrasts the pagan and the Christian views of nature—

> And though Pliny and the rest were not able by Nature's light to search so far as to find out the God of Nature, who sitteth in the glorie of light which none attaineth, but contrariwise in the vanitie of their imagination bewrayed the ignorance of foolish hearts, some doting upon Nature herselfe, and others upon speciall creatures as their God.

Something has been said of the underplot in the section of the introduction dealing with sources. Schlegel explained that its function was to universalize the tragedy[1]—

> Were Lear alone to suffer from his daughters, the impression would be limited to the powerful compassion felt by us for his private misfortune. But two such unheard-of examples taking place at the same time have the appearance of a great commotion in the moral world; the picture becomes gigantic, and fills us with such alarm as we should entertain at the idea that the heavenly bodies might one day fall from their appointed orbits.

Coleridge complained of the gross improbability of the opening situation of the play;[2] but the improbability is acceptable during a performance because of the artistic law that two improbabilities are easier to accept than one. Furthermore, as Dowden pointed out,[3]

> one story of horror serves as a means of approach to the other, and helps us to conceive its magnitude.

Wilson Knight has written eloquently on the grotesque element in the play;[4] and he points out that the Fool 'sees the potentialities of comedy in Lear's behaviour'. Most critics have tended to sentimentalize the Fool; and Granville-Barker remarks justly that the producer today is faced with the difficulty that the Fool 'is all etherealized by the Higher Criticism'.[5] We are usually told that by his jests the Fool tries to take Lear's mind off his obsession with

1. *Lectures on Dramatic Art*, 1808.
2. *Shakespearian Criticism*, ed. Raysor, i. 59.
3. *Shakespeare His Mind and Art*, 1879, p. 265.   4. *Op. cit.*, pp. 160 ff.
5. *Op. cit.*, p. 200.

his daughters' ingratitude. Nothing could be further from the truth. Nearly every one of his jests reminds Lear of the sorrow that is gnawing at his heart. He may 'labour to outjest' his master's 'heart-struck injuries'; but it might almost be said that these jests, coming on top of Lear's afflictions, and concerned as they are with the afflictions, help to drive him mad. He stands, perhaps, for worldly common sense;[1] he is not without malice,[2] and he can never forgive Lear's treatment of Cordelia. He began to pine away on Cordelia's banishment, and his bitter jokes continually remind the King of his injustice. He is 'not merely a touching figure who might easily have been drawn from life'; he is also 'the sage-fool who sees the truth'.[3] His dramatic function is of great importance. He provides not so much comic relief as a safety-valve for the emotions of the audience. Lear's conduct is absurd, if judged critically; and the representation of madness is apt to arouse more laughter than sympathy. The Fool was therefore inserted to draw the laughs of the audience, and so preserve Lear's sublimity. This is near to Hazlitt's view.[4] He declared that

> the contrast would be too painful, the shock too great, but for the intervention of the fool, whose well-timed levity comes in to break the continuity of feeling when it no longer can be borne, and to bring into play again the fibres of the heart just as they are growing rigid from over-strained excitement.

But Keats was also right when he commented in the margin of his copy of Hazlitt's book—

> And is it really thus? Or as it has appeared to me? Does not the Fool by his very levity give a finishing-touch to the pathos; making what without him would be within our heart-reach nearly unfathomable. The Fool's words are merely the simplest translation of Poetry as high as Lear's.

The Fool's character and function are both ambiguous, and all through the play Shakespeare is continually inverting the orthodox view of wisdom and foolishness. In the storm-scenes there is a wild quartet of madness—Lear, Poor Tom, the Fool, and the elements themselves—in which the Fool seems almost to stand for sanity. He fades from the picture when he is no longer needed, since Lear can act as his own Fool. As Miss Welsford says,[5]

> Lear's tragedy is the investing of the King with motley: it is also the crowning and apotheosis of the Fool.

1. Orwell's description cited by Empson.   2. Empson, *op. cit.*, p. 133.
3. E. Welsford, *The Fool*, 1935, p. 253.
4. *Characters of Shakespeare's Plays*, 1926, p. 121.   5. *Op. cit.*, p. 269.

Hazlitt began his essay on the play with the wish that he could pass it over, and say nothing about it. His words must be echoed by every editor—

> All that we can say must fall far short of the subject, or even what we ourselves conceive of it.

6. RECENT CRITICISM

Besides a large number of articles and chapters on *King Lear*, several books have been published in the last two decades. Russell A. Fraser in *Shakespeare's Poetics in Relation to King Lear* (1962) discusses the iconology of the play and Shakespeare's treatment of Elizabethan commonplaces on providence, order, fortune, anarchy, will, etc. Maynard Mack in *King Lear in our Time* (1965) eloquently restates the significance of the play, with some mordant comments on some recent productions. William R. Elton in *King Lear and the Gods* (1966) provides a learned and subtle discussion of the religious ideas of the play, concluding that Shakespeare's attitude was in this play more sceptical than Christian. Nicholas Brooke in *Shakespeare: King Lear* (1963) gives a valuable scene-by-scene commentary on the action of the play. Helen Gardner's *King Lear* (1967) is also illuminating. There are nine articles on the play in *Shakespeare Survey 13* (1960); and Barbara Everett in an article in *Critical Quarterly*, II (1960), pp. 325–39, complained that modern critics, including the present editor, had tried to turn the play into a partial, or total, Christian allegory. There were a number of replies in the same journal, III (1961), pp. 67–72. The most valuable recent edition is that of G. I. Duthie and J. Dover Wilson (1960): from this some improvements have been made in the present text.

POSTSCRIPT (1978)

A new impression enables me to mention two admirable books on the play: *Some Facets of King Lear* (1974), edited by Rosalie L. Colie and F. T. Flahiff and *An Essay on King Lear* (1974), by S. L. Goldberg.

KING LEAR

DRAMATIS PERSONÆ

LEAR, *King of Britain.*
KING OF FRANCE.
DUKE OF BURGUNDY.
DUKE OF CORNWALL, *Husband to Regan.*
DUKE OF ALBANY, *Husband to Goneril.*
EARL OF KENT.
EARL OF GLOUCESTER.
EDGAR, *Son to Gloucester.*
EDMUND, *Bastard son to Gloucester.*
CURAN, *a Courtier.*
OSWALD, *Steward to Goneril.*
Old Man, Tenant to Gloucester.
Doctor.
Fool.
An Officer, employed by Edmund.
Gentleman, Attendant on Cordelia.
A Herald.
Servants to Cornwall.
GONERIL,
REGAN, } *Daughters to Lear.*
CORDELIA,

*Knights of Lear's train, Officers, Messengers,
Soldiers, and Attendants.*

SCENE: *Britain.*

KING LEAR

ACT I

SCENE I.—[*A State Room in King Lear's Palace.*]

Enter KENT, GLOUCESTER, *and* EDMUND.

Kent. I thought the King had more affected the Duke of
Albany than Cornwall.

Glou. It did always seem so to us; but now, in the division
of the kingdom, it appears not which of the Dukes he
values most; for equalities are so weigh'd that curi-   5
osity in neither can make choice of either's moiety.

Kent. Is not this your son, my Lord?

ACT I

Scene i

S.D. *A . . . Palace*] Capell; *not in Q, F.*   *Edmund*] *F;* Bastard *Q.*   3. so] *not
in F2–4.*   4. kingdom] *F;* kingdomes *Q.*   5. equalities] *Q;* qualities *F.*
6. neither] nature *Q3.*

Scene I] The opening dialogue introduces the underplot, and gives us a
glimpse of Kent before his intervention
at l. 119.

1. *had . . . affected*] had more regard
for. See *1H6,* v. v. 57.

2. *Albany*] Holinshed tells us that
Albany extended 'from the river
Humber to the point of Caithness'.
Albanacte, who owned it, gave his
name to it.

5. *values*] esteems. Cf. II. ii. 142 and
H5, I. ii. 269.

equalities . . . weigh'd] equalities,
shares are so balanced, one against the
other, or perhaps are so carefully considered and adjusted. 'Elizabethan
usage often pluralizes abstract nouns
when two or more persons or things
are in question' (Kittredge). F 'quali-

ties' has been accepted by a few editors: it may be a slip by the compositor,
or a scribal correction (Duthie). But it
may be the correct reading, and refer
to the mental and moral qualities of
the dukes.

5–6. *that . . . moiety*] that the most
careful scrutiny of either share could
not induce either of the dukes to prefer
his fellow's portion to his own.

curiosity] the most minute and scrupulous attention or examination. Cf.
I. ii. 4, I. iv. 67 *post,* and *Tim.,* IV. iii.
303. See also Baret, *Alvearie,* 1580:
'Curiositie, piked [i.e. picked] diligence'.

6. *moiety*] share, not necessarily half.
Cf. *1H4,* III. i. 96: 'Methinks my
moiety, north from Burton here, / In
quantity equals not one of yours.'

3

Glou. His breeding, Sir, hath been at my charge: I have
so often blush'd to acknowledge him, that now I am
braz'd to't.   10

Kent. I cannot conceive you.

Glou. Sir, this young fellow's mother could; whereupon
she grew round-womb'd, and had, indeed, Sir, a son
for her cradle ere she had a husband for her bed. Do
you smell a fault?   15

Kent. I cannot wish the fault undone, the issue of it being
so proper.

Glou. But I have a son, Sir, by order of law, some year
elder than this, who yet is no dearer in my account:
though this knave came something saucily to the   20
world before he was sent for, yet was his mother
fair; there was good sport at his making, and the
whoreson must be acknowledged. Do you know this
noble gentleman, Edmund?

Edm. No, my Lord.   25

Glou. My Lord of Kent: remember him hereafter as my
honourable friend.

Edm. My services to your Lordship.

10. to't] *F;* to it *Q.*   13. round-womb'd] *unhyphened Q, F.*   18. a son, Sir] *F;*
Sir a son *Q.*   year] yeares *Q3.*   20. something] somewhat *F3–4.*   to] *F;*
into *Q;* in *Q3.*   22. the] he *Q3.*   24. noble gentleman] Nobleman *F2–4.*
25. *Edm.*] *F; Bast. Q (and throughout).*   26–8. *Glou.* . . . Lordship] *Glo.* My
services to your Lordship. unrable friend. *Q3.*

10. *braz'd*] made insensible, hardened, literally 'plated with brass'. Cf.
Ham., III. iv. 37.

11. *conceive*] Kent uses the word in
the sense of 'understand'; Gloucester
puns on it in his next speech. Van Dam
thinks the quibble is only possible if the
word is used intransitively, and urges
the omission of *you.* This improvement
is not absolutely necessary.

12. *mother*] Coleridge, *Shakespearean
Criticism*, ed. Raysor, i. 56, says that
Edmund 'hears his mother and the
circumstances of his birth spoken of
with a most degrading and licentious
levity'. But Kittredge argues that
Edmund, though on the stage, does
not hear this conversation.

15. *fault*] perhaps a quibble on the
two meanings of the word: (*a*) mis-
deed, (*b*) loss of scent by hounds.
Shakespeare often compares sin to a
bad smell. Cf. *Ham.*, III. iii. 36.

17. *proper*] handsome. Cf. *Oth.*, IV.
iii. 35.

18. *some year*] about a year. Cf. *Shr.*,
IV. iii. 189.

19. *account*] estimation. Cf. *Mer. V.*,
III. ii. 157.

20. *knave*] fellow—not implying
moral disapproval.

24. *Edmund*] The name was perhaps
suggested to Shakespeare by the
Edmund Peckham and the Edmunds
mentioned many times by Harsnett.

28. *services*] i.e. duty.

Kent. I must love you, and sue to know you better.
Edm. Sir, I shall study deserving.   30
Glou. He hath been out nine years, and away he shall
    again. The King is coming.

    Sennet. Enter one bearing a coronet, KING LEAR, CORNWALL,
    ALBANY, GONERIL, REGAN, CORDELIA, *and Attendants.*

Lear. Attend the Lords of France and Burgundy,
    Gloucester.
Glou. I shall, my Liege.   [*Exeunt Gloucester and Edmund.*
Lear. Meantime, we shall express our darker purpose.   35
    Give me the map there. Know that we have divided
    In three our kingdom; and 'tis our fast intent
    To shake all cares and business from our age,
    Conferring them on younger strengths, while we   39
    Unburthen'd crawl toward death. Our son of Cornwall,
    And you, our no less loving son of Albany,
    We have this hour a constant will to publish
    Our daughters' several dowers, that future strife

32. *Sennet*] F; *Sound a Sennet* Q.   *one . . . coronet*] Q; *not in* F.   33. the] my
Q.   34. Liege] Q; Lord F.   *Exeunt . . . Edmund*] Capell; *Exit* F; *not in* Q.
35. we shall] F; we will Q.   darker] dark Q3.   purpose] F; purposes Q.
36. Give . . . there] F; The map there Q; Give me the map here F3-4.   Know
that] F; Know Q.   37. fast] F; first Q.   38. from our age] F; of our state Q.
39. Conferring] F; Confirming Q.   strengths] F; years Q.   39-44. while . . .
now] F; *not in* Q.

31. *out*] in foreign parts, pushing his
fortunes. Cf. *Gent.*, i. iii. 7.

31-2. *away . . . again*] Perhaps these
words seal Gloucester's doom.

32. S.D. Sennet] a particular set of
notes on the trumpet or cornet, sounded at the entrance or exit of a company
or procession. It is distinct from a
flourish. Cf. Marston, *Antonio and
Mellida*, I. 1: 'The Cornets sound a
sennet . . . they embrace, at which the
cornets sound a flourish.'

    coronet] intended for Cordelia.

33. *Attend*] wait on them, usher into
our presence.

35. *our darker purpose*] our more
secret intention, i.e. the plan to give
the best share to the daughter who

loves him most. The councillors only
know of Lear's intention to divide
the kingdom, and of the shares designed for Goneril and Regan. Empson, *The Structure of Complex Words*,
p. 127, comments: 'We are directed
to the idea of renunciation by his
calling it a *darker* purpose; in the eyes
of the world it would be a gloomy
one.'

37. *fast*] fixed, unalterable. Cf. *Cor.*,
II. iii. 192.

38-40. *To . . . death*] Cf. *Leir*, 26-7:
'The world of me, I of the world am
weary, / And I would fayne resigne
these earthly cares.'

42. *constant will*] fixed purpose, *certa
voluntas*. Cf. 'fast intent', 37 *ante*.

May be prevented now. The Princes, France and
   Burgundy,
Great rivals in our youngest daughter's love,   45
Long in our court have made their amorous sojourn,
And here are to be answer'd. Tell me, my daughters,
(Since now we will divest us both of rule,
Interest of territory, cares of state)
Which of you shall we say doth love us most?   50
That we our largest bounty may extend
Where nature doth with merit challenge. Goneril,
Our eldest-born, speak first.

Gon. Sir, I love you more than word can wield the matter;
Dearer than eye-sight, space and liberty;   55
Beyond what can be valued rich or rare;
No less than life, with grace, health, beauty, honour;
As much as child e'er lov'd, or father found;
A love that makes breath poor and speech unable;
Beyond all manner of so much I love you.   60

---

44. Princes] *F;* two great Princes *Q;* Prince *F3–4.* 45. youngest] younger
F2–4. 47. me] *not in F3–4.* 48–9. Since . . . state] *F; not in Q.* 52. Where
. . . challenge] *F;* where merit doth most challenge it *Q.* 54. love] *F;* do
loue *Q.* word] *F;* words *Q.* wield] yield *conj. Capell;* weld *conj. Gould.*
55. and] *F;* or *Q.* 58. as] *F;* a *Q.* found] *F;* friend *Q.*

44. *prevented*] forestalled.

49. *Interest*] possession, the present
legal sense. Cf. 'interess'd', 84 *post,*
and *2H6,* III. i. 84.

52. *Where . . . challenge*] Steevens
explains, 'Where the claims of merit
are superadded to that of nature, i.e.
birth. Challenge, to make title to, to
claim as one's right.' Cf. *3H6,* III. ii.
86. Alternatively Steevens suggests
that nature = natural filial affection;
but it means rather 'paternal affection', and *merit,* in the context, means
'filial affection'. Cuningham, *N.Q.,*
16 May 1914, suggested that the line
should end 'challenge it', the word
'Goneril' being transferred to the
following line.

54. *Sir . . . matter*] more than I
can express in words. Cf. *Tit.,* III.
ii. 29: 'handle the theme'; and *R3,*
III. vii. 19. See *Leir,* 239: 'Which

cannot be in windy words rehearst.'

55. *space and liberty*] 'Space expresses
the idea of "freedom from confinement"; *liberty* adds the idea of "personal freedom in action"' (Kittredge).
Craig suggests the phrase means absolute freedom, 'ample room and verge
enough'. It may mean merely 'spacious liberty'.

56. *valued*] estimated. Cf. *Err.,* I. i.
24.

57. *No . . . life*] Cf. *Leir,* 241 : 'I thinke
my life inferiour to my loue.'

59. *unable*] weak, inadequate. Cf.
H5, Epilogue, 1.

60. *Beyond . . . much*] Johnson explains
'beyond all assignable quantity'.
Kittredge suggests that *manner* is the
emphatic word. Wright thinks *so much*
refers to the comparisons by which
Goneril had tried to measure her
love.

Cor. [*Aside.*] What shall Cordelia speak? Love, and be
    silent.

Lear. Of all these bounds, even from this line to this,
    With shadowy forests and with champains rich'd,
    With plenteous rivers and wide-skirted meads,
    We make thee lady: to thine and Albany's issues   65
    Be this perpetual. What says our second daughter
    Our dearest Regan, wife of Cornwall?

Reg. I am made of that self metal as my sister,
    And prize me at her worth. In my true heart
    I find she names my very deed of love;   70
    Only she comes too short: that I profess
    Myself an enemy to all other joys
    Which the most precious square of sense possesses,

---

61. *Aside*] *Pope; not in Q, F.*   speak] *F;* doe *Q.*   63. shadowy] *F;* shady
Q.   rich'd] rich *Collier MS.*   63–4. and with . . . rivers] *F; not in Q.*
65. thee] the *F3.*   issues] *F;* issue *Q.*   67. of Cornwall] *F;* to Cornwall,
speake *Q.*   68. I] *F;* Sir I *Q.*   that self metal] *F (hyphened);* the selfe
same metall *Q.*   as my sister] *F;* that my sister is *Q.*   69. me] you *conj.*
Mason.   worth. In . . . heart] *F;* worth in . . . heart, *Q;* worth in . . . heart.
Theobald (conj. Bishop).   71. comes too] *F;* came *Q.*   73. precious]
spacious *Keightley.*   square] spirit *Hanmer;* sphere *Collier MS.*   possesses]
Q; professes *F.*

---

61. *speak*] The Q 'doe' is a possible
reading, but it may be an actor's substitution, influenced by 225 *post*, 'I'll
do't before I speak' and 235–6. 'This
first speech of Cordelia's seems to me
more attractive and less commonplace
if we have her asking herself what *she*
shall say, and then gently but firmly
stilling the question with two commands to herself' (Duthie).

63. *shadowy*] shady. Cf. *Gent.*, v. iv. 2.
Henderson compares Florio's Montaigne, Temple ed., III. 379, 'shady
forrests'.

champains] unwooded plains. Cf.
Tw. N., II. v. 174. The word is often
spelt *champian* and *champion*.

rich'd] enriched.

64. *wide-skirted*] extensive.

67. *Our . . . Cornwall?*] The Q addition 'Speak' was probably suggested
by 53 *ante* and 85 *post*, but it completes
the line.

68. *self*] same. Cf. IV. iii. 34 and *Err.*,
v. i. 10.

69. *And . . . worth*] Three explanations have been given: (i) I estimate
myself her equal in the amount of my
affection for you. Cf. *Troil.*, IV. iv. 136;
(ii) I estimate my love as equal to hers;
(iii) Value me (imperative) the same
as her. Cf. *Leir*, 240, 'I prize my loue to
you at such a rate.'

70. *my . . . love*] my love as it actually
is. Delius explains 'the formal legal
definition of love'.

71. *that*] in that.

73. *most . . . sense*] variously explained: (i) sense absolute, sense in its
perfection. Cf. Bodenham, *Belvedere*,
ed. 1875, p. 73: 'Councell and good
advise is wisdom's square / And most
availing to the life of man'; (ii) the
most delicately sensitive part of my
nature (Wright); (iii) the choicest
estimate of sense. Cf. *Troil.*, v. ii. 133

And find I am alone felicitate
In your dear highness' love.
Cor. [*Aside.*]   Then poor Cordelia!   75
And yet not so; since I am sure my love's
More ponderous than my tongue.
Lear.   To thee and thine, hereditary ever,
Remain this ample third of our fair kingdom,
No less in space, validity, and pleasure,   80
Than that conferr'd on Goneril. Now, our joy,
Although our last, and least; to whose young love
The vines of France and milk of Burgundy
Strive to be interess'd; what can you say to draw
A third more opulent than your sisters? Speak.   85

---

74. alone] all one *Q3*.   75. *Aside*] *Pope; not in Q, F.*   77. ponderous] *F;*
richer *Q*.   my] their *conj. Warburton.*   81. conferr'd] *F;* confirm'd *Q*.
Now] *F; but now Q*.   82. our last, and] *F;* the last, not *Q;* our last, not
Pope.   least . . . love] *F;* least in our deare loue, *Q*.   83–4. The . . .
interess'd] *F; not in Q*.   84. interess'd] *Jennens;* interest *F*.   draw]
F; win *Q*.   85. Speak] *F; not in Q*.

(Moberley); (iv) the most advan-
tageous position on the board. Cf. 154
post (*N.Q.*, 7 Oct. 1905); (v) most delicate test of one's sensibility can claim
as joys; *square* means 'criterion' from
the carpenter's square (Kittredge);
(vi) Kinnear, *Cruces Shakespearianae*,
1883, p. 413, proposes *spirit* for *square*.
Cf. *Troil.*, I. i. 58 and III. iii. 106.
Perhaps the soundest explanation
would be a combination of (iii) and
(v), for the quotation 'To square the
general sex By Cressid's rule' suggests
a connection with the carpenter's
square.

possesses] A few editors keep F reading, which is likely to be a compositor's
error from the proximity of 'profess'
(71). Verity says that *professes* strikes a
wrong note, since Regan does not
mean to doubt the reality of sensuous
joys but to emphasize that she is hostile
to them because she knows the higher
joy of loving and being loved by Lear
—the greater the joys, the greater her
devotion in rejecting them for love of
her father.

74. *felicitate*] made happy. Cf. suffo-
cate (for suffocated), *Troil.*, I. iii. 125.

77. *ponderous*] perhaps suggested by
'metal' (68). Cordelia cannot produce
golden words, cannot 'coin her heart
in words', but her heart has love of a
better and weightier metal.

80. *validity*] value. Cf. *All's W.*, v.
iii. 192.

82. *our last, and least*] Most editors
follow the Q reading but the very
commonness of the expression would
tend to make an actor substitute it for
the F reading. Cf. *Leir*, 2657–8: 'To
thee last of all, / Not greeted last,
'cause thy desert was small'. Cordelia
was young, and small in stature.

83. *milk*] pastures, the effect for the
cause (Eccles).

84. *interess'd*] closely connected,
interested, concerned. Cf. Florio, *op.
cit.*, III. 111: 'And favour our childrens
causes against us, as men interested in
the same.'

85. *opulent*] McElwaine (*N.Q.*, 25
Nov. 1911) points out that Lear must
assign Cordelia her share during his

Cor. Nothing, my lord.

Lear. Nothing?

Cor. Nothing.

Lear. Nothing will come of nothing: speak again.

Cor. Unhappy that I am, I cannot heave   90
    My heart into my mouth: I love your Majesty
    According to my bond; no more nor less.

Lear. How, how, Cordelia! Mend your speech a little,
    Lest you may mar your fortunes.

Cor.   Good my Lord,
    You have begot me, bred me, lov'd me: I   95
    Return those duties back as are right fit,
    Obey you, love you, and most honour you.
    Why have my sisters husbands, if they say
    They love you all? Happily, when I shall wed,   99
    That lord whose hand must take my plight shall carry
    Half my love with him, half my care and duty:
    Sure I shall never marry like my sisters,

87–8.] *F; not in Q.*   89. Nothing will] *F;* How, nothing can *Q;* Nothing
can *Theobald.*   90. heave] have *Q3, F3–4.*   92. no] *F;* nor *Q.*   93.
How . . . Cordelia] *F;* Goe to, goe to *Q.*   94. you] *F;* it *Q.*   95. I]
Pope's lineation; I begins 96 Q, F.   96. fit] sit *Q3.*   99. Happily] *F;*
Happely *Q1;* Haply *Q2.*

life, for on his death she will only
inherit equally with/her sisters.

86. *Nothing*] This word is echoed
throughout the play. Henderson (cf.
Appendix, p. 235) refers to Florio, *op.
cit.*, III. 341 and *passim.*

89. *Nothing . . . nothing*] Cf. the proverbial '*ex nihilo nihil fit.*' Baldwin,
Shakespeare's Small Latine, II. 543, cites
Germbergius, *Carminum Proverbialium,*
1583, p. 154, and Persius, III. 84: 'de
nihilo nihilum, in nihilum nil posse
reverti.'

90–1. *heave . . . mouth*] Noble compares Ecclesiasticus, xxi. 26: 'The
heart of fooles is in their mouth: but
the mouth of the wise is in their heart.'

92. *bond*] filial obligation, bounden
duty. Cf. I. ii. 105 and II. iv. 176. See
Appendix pp. 221, 223, and 209 for
parallels in Holinshed, Spenser, and
Leir.

96. *Return . . . fit*] 'As they, the duties,
are right and fit to be returned'
(Craig). 'Those duties that are most
fitting', i.e. those mentioned in the
following line (Kittredge).

97–103. *Obey . . . my father all*]
Perrett, *op. cit.*, argues that Shakespeare may have derived the idea of
these lines from Camden's *Remaines.*
But he may have got it from the 1587
edition of *The Mirror for Magistrates,*
or borrowed it himself direct from the
marriage service. See Introduction,
p. xxxii. Baldwin, *Shakespeare's Petty
School,* p. 174, points out that Nowell in
his commentary on the Little Catechism puts 'obey' in the forefront as
does Cordelia: 'sacra scriptura liberos
iubet parentibus obtemperare, atque
inseruire: parentes timere charissimos
eos habere, eos colere et reuereri.'

100. *plight*] troth-plight.

To love my father all.
Lear. But goes thy heart with this?
Cor.   Ay, my good Lord.
Lear. So young, and so untender?   105
Cor. So young, my Lord, and true.
Lear. Let it be so; thy truth then be thy dower:
For, by the sacred radiance of the sun,
The mysteries of Hecate and the night,
By all the operation of the orbs   110
From whom we do exist and cease to be,
Here I disclaim all my paternal care,
Propinquity and property of blood,
And as a stranger to my heart and me
Hold thee from this for ever. The barbarous Scythian,
Or he that makes his generation messes   116
To gorge his appetite, shall to my bosom
Be as well neighbour'd, pitied, and reliev'd,

---

103. To . . . all] *Q; not in F.*   104. thy . . . this] *F;* this with thy heart
Q.   my good] *F;* good my *Q.*   107. Let] *F;* Well let *Q.*   thy
truth] *Q, F1–2;* the truth *F3–4.*   109. mysteries] *F2;* mistresse *Q;*
miseries *F.*   night] *F;* might *Q.*   110. operation] *Q, F;* operations
F2–4.   117. to my bosom] *F; not in Q.*

---

103. *all*] exclusively. Cf. *Tim.*, I. i.
139.

107. *thy . . . dower*] Cf. *Gent.*, III. i. 78:
'Then let her beauty be her wedding-
dower.'

109. *mysteries*] secret rites. Daniel
suggested that the man who prepared
Q for the F edition, wishing to correct
mistresse to *misteries*, wrote *eries* in the
margin but accidentally drew his pen
through the last six, instead of only the
last five, letters of *mistresse.*

Hecate] the goddess of the lower
world, and patroness of magic and
witchcraft, as in *Macbeth.* The word, as
usual in Shakespeare, is a dissyllable.
The exception, *1H6*, III. ii. 64, may not
be his.

110. *operation*] astrological influence.
Cf. *Ant.*, II. vii. 30.

113. *Propinquity*] close relationship.
property] closest blood relationship,
rising, as it were, to identity of blood
(Wright). Cf. *R2*, I. ii. 1, spoken by

Woodstock's brother: 'The part I had
in Woodstock's blood'.

115–17. *The . . . appetite*] The usual
explanation of *generation* is 'offspring'.
Cf. Matt., iii. 7. But Craig suggests it
means 'parents'. He points out that
progeny is used in the sense of 'ancestors'
(*Cor.*, I. viii. 12) and cites Chapman,
Byron's Tragedy, IV. ii. 126–32: 'to
teach . . . The Scythians to inter, not
eat, their parents'. Perrett cites Harrison, *Description of Britain*, IV, 'These
Scots were reputed for the most
Scithian-like and barbarous nation.
. . . For both Diodorus . . . & Strabo . . .
do seem to speake of a parceil of the
Irish nation that should inhabit Britain
in their time, which were giuen to the
eating of man's flesh, and therefore
called *Anthropophagi* . . . those Scots . . .
who vsed to feed on the buttocks of
boies and women's paps, as delicate
dishes.'

116. *messes*] portions of food.

As thou my sometime daughter.

Kent.   Good my Liege,—

Lear. Peace, Kent!   120
Come not between the Dragon and his wrath.
I lov'd her most, and thought to set my rest
On her kind nursery. Hence, and avoid my sight!
So be my grave my peace, as here I give
Her father's heart from her! Call France. Who stirs? 125
Call Burgundy. Cornwall and Albany,
With my two daughters' dowers digest the third;
Let pride, which she calls plainness, marry her.
I do invest you jointly with my power,
Pre-eminence, and all the large effects   130
That troop with majesty. Ourself, by monthly course,
With reservation of an hundred knights

---

119. Liege,—] *Rowe;* Liege. *Q, F.*   127. dowers] Dowres *F;* dower *Q.*
the] *F;* this *Q.*   129. with] *F;* in *Q.*

---

121. *Dragon*] Lear may refer to the dragon of Britain, which he would wear emblazoned on his helmet (Moberley). Cf. *The Birth of Merlin*, v. ii. 39–40: 'We have firm hope that tho' our dragon sleep / Merlin will us and our fair Kingdom keep.' But Shakespeare often refers to the dragon as a symbol of savage ferocity, e.g. *Cor.*, IV. vii. 23.

wrath] the object of his wrath. But J. C. Maxwell suggests to me that 'the notion conveyed appears to be that of Lear's wrath as an extension of his personality—a sort of anthropologist's "mana"—his union with which must remain intact if he himself is to hold together. A dragon cannot *be* a dragon without his wrath. The kind of disintegration which Lear is afraid of is what actually takes place.' Maxwell goes on to compare I. i. 168–9. Cf. *Anglia*, XXXIX, p. 45, where Dubislaw quotes Koppel to the same effect and cites *Ham.*, III. iv. 112.

122. *set my rest*] stake my all. Cf. *Rom.*, v. iii. 110. The idiom is taken from the game of primero. See Gascoigne, *Supposes*, III. 2: 'This amorous cause . . . may be compared to them

that play at primero: of whom one, peradventure, shall leese a great sum of money before he win one stake, and, at last, half in anger shall set up his rest, win it, and after that another, and another; till, at last, he draw the most part of the money to his heap, the other by little and little diminishing his rest, till he come as near the brink as erst the other was.' But here, as in the *Romeo and Juliet* passage, there is a quibble on the phrase.

123. *nursery*] nursing, tender care.

125. *Who stirs?*] i.e. Be quick! The courtiers are shocked into immobility.

127. *digest*] incorporate.

128. *Let . . . her*] let her pride be her dowry and win her a husband.

129. *with*] Cf. *2H4*, IV. v. 73. Elsewhere after *invest*, Shakespeare uses 'in'. Cf. *Meas.*, III. i. 96.

130. *large effects*] splendid accompaniments.

131. *troop with*] are associated with. Cf. *Rom.*, I. v. 50.

132. *reservation*] Cf. II. iv. 250. The word is a legal term, and means the action or fact of reserving (for oneself or another) some right, power or privilege.

By you to be sustain'd, shall our abode
Make with you by due turn. Only we shall retain
The name and all th'addition to a king; the sway,   135
Revenue, execution of the rest,
Beloved sons, be yours: which to confirm,
This coronet part between you.

Kent.   Royal Lear,
Whom I have ever honour'd as my King,
Lov'd as my father, as my master follow'd,   140
As my great patron thought on in my prayers,—
Lear. The bow is bent and drawn; make from the shaft.
Kent. Let it fall rather, though the fork invade
The region of my heart: be Kent unmannerly,   144
When Lear is mad. What would'st thou do, old man?
Think'st thou that duty shall have dread to speak
When power to flattery bows? To plainness
    honour's bound
When majesty falls to folly. Reserve thy state;
And, in thy best consideration, check   149
This hideous rashness: answer my life my judgment,

134. turn] *F;* turnes *Q.*   shall] *F;* still *Q.*   135. th'addition] *F;* the
additions *Q.*   138. between] *F;* betwixt *Q.*   139. my] a *F4.*   141.
prayers,—] *Rowe;* praiers. *Q, F.*   145. mad] *Q2, F;* man *Q1.*   would'st]
F4; wilt *Q;* wouldest *F1–3.*   148. falls] *F;* stoops *Q.*   Reserve thy
state] *F;* Reuerse thy doome *Q.*

135. *addition*] honours, titles, cere-
monial observances. Cf. *Mac.*, I. iii.
106. The plural form, as in Q, is more
usual; but see *N.E.D.*
   136. *Revenue*] accented on the second
syllable.
   142. *make from*] avoid.
   143. *fork*] a forked head on an arrow.
Ascham, *Toxophilus*, ed. Arber, p. 135,
describes it as 'hauing two points
stretching forward, and this English-
men do call a forke-head'.
   144. *The . . . heart*] The same
expression is used by Ford in *The
Lady's Trial*, III. iii. 27.
   145. *old man*] Kent's bluntness
increases Lear's rage.
   147. *plainness*] Cf. II. ii. 98.
   148. *Reserve thy state*] Duthie suggests

that the actor who played Kent was
influenced by the lines in *Leir*, 505–6,
567: 'Cease, good my Lords, and sue
not to reuerse / Our censure, which is
now irreuocable.' / 'Whose deeds haue
not deseru'd this ruthlesse doome'.
A conflation of these passages would
account for the Q reading. But cf. *Tit.*,
III. i. 24. Kent in the F reading is here
thinking more of Lear's safety than of
the injustice to Cordelia, though it is
this injustice which makes Kent
intervene.
   149. *best consideration*] as opposed to
the rashness of his first thoughts.
   150. *answer . . . judgment*] 'Let my
life be answerable for my judgment, or
I will stake my life on my opinion'
(Johnson).

Thy youngest daughter does not love thee least;
Nor are those empty-hearted whose low sounds
Reverb no hollowness. *Lear offers a fair*

Lear.   Kent, on thy life, no more. *warning*
                                                 to fools
Kent. My life I never held but as a pawn *Harshness*
To wage against thine enemies; nor fear to lose it, 155
Thy safety being motive.

Lear.   Out of my sight!

Kent. See better, Lear; and let me still remain
The true blank of thine eye.

Lear. Now, by Apollo,—

Kent.   Now, by Apollo, King, 159
Thou swear'st thy Gods in vain.

Lear.   O, vassal! miscreant!
[*Laying his hand upon his sword.*

Alb., *Corn.* Dear Sir, forbear.

---

152. empty-hearted] *hyphen not in Q, F.*   low sounds] *F;* low, sound *Q1;*
low sound *Q2.*   153. Reverb] *F;* Reuerbs *Q.*   thy] my *F3–4.*   154.
as a] *Q;* as *F.*   155. thine] *F;* thy *Q.*   nor] *Q;* nere *F.*   fear] fear'd
conj. Furness.   156. motive] *F;* the motiue *Q.*   159. Lear] *Q; Kear F.*
Kent] *Q; Lent F.*   160. O . . . miscreant] *F;* Vassall, recreant *Q.*   S.D.]
Rowe; not in Q, F.   161.] *F; not in Q.*

---

153. *Reverb*] Shakespeare probably
coined the word from reverberate.

hollowness] a quibble on the two
meanings of the word: concavity, and
insincerity. Cf. I. ii. 110 and *Ham.*, III.
ii. 218. Kittredge cites the proverb:
'Emptie vessels haue the loudest
sounds' (Greene, *George a Greene*, IV. 4;
ed. Collins, II. 210).

154. *held*] considered.

pawn] a stake hazarded in a wager;
the only instance in Shakespeare of its
use in this sense. He usually employs
the word in the sense of pledge, something given in security. Cf. *Gent.*, I. iii.
47. But see I. ii. 83 and *Cym.*, I. vi. 194,
where pawn (vb) is used in the sense
of stake. Capell thought there was an
allusion to the game of chess, and
there may have been a concealed pun.
Cf. note on *wage* (155).

155. *wage*] to stake, as in a wager; to
risk, to venture. Cf. *Cym.*, I. iv. 144.

But the preposition 'against' suggests
that Shakespeare was also thinking of
waging war.

156. *motive*] moving cause.

157. *still*] always.

158. *blank*] the white spot in the
centre of the target, the white. Cotgrave defines *Blanc* as 'the white or
mark of a pair of buts'. Kent implies
that he is the wise counsellor to whom
Lear should look for advice. There
may be a quibble on the white of
the eye in the ordinary sense of the
phrase.

159. *Apollo*] Leir in Layamon's
Brut also invokes Apollo. The pagan
setting is necessary to Shakespeare's
conception of the story.

160. *miscreant*] Perhaps, as Wright
suggests, the word is used in its original sense of misbeliever. Kent had
apparently referred contemptuously
to the gods.

Kent. Kill thy physician, and the fee bestow
 Upon the foul disease. Revoke thy gift;
 Or, whilst I can vent clamour from my throat,
 I'll tell thee thou dost evil.
Lear.   Hear me, recreant!   165
 On thine allegiance, hear me!
 That thou hast sought to make us break our vow,
 Which we durst never yet, and with strain'd pride
 To come betwixt our sentence and our power,
 Which nor our nature nor our place can bear,   170
 Our potency made good, take thy reward.
 Five days we do allot thee for provision
 To shield thee from disasters of the world;
 And on the sixth to turn thy hated back
 Upon our kingdom: if on the tenth day following   175

---

162. Kill] *F;* Doe, kill *Q.*   the fee] *Q;* thy fee *F.*   163. thy] the *F3–4.*
gift] *F;* doome *Q.*   166. thine] *F;* thy *Q.*   167. That] *F;* Since *Q.*
vow] *Q;* vowes *F.*   168. strain'd] *F;* straied *Q.*   169. betwixt] *F;*
betweene *Q.*   sentence] *Q;* Sentences *F.*   171. made] *Q1, F;* make
Q2–3.   172. Five] *F;* Foure *Q.*   173. disasters] *F;* diseases *Q;* defeascs
Q3; distresses *conj. Kinnear.*   174. sixth] *F4;* sixt *F;* fift *Q.*   175. on]
not in F2–4; one *Q3.*   tenth] seventh *Collier MS.*

---

162. *Kill*] Before this word Q inserts
'Doe'; this may be a F omission, or an
actor's addition.
 165. *recreant*] one who proves false to
his allegiance.
 167. *That*] seeing that.
 168. *strain'd*] forced, unnatural,
used beyond its province. Cf. *Rom.*, II.
iii. 19; *2H4*, I. i. 161; *Ado*, IV. i. 254.
 171. *Our . . . reward*] Malone
explains: 'As a proof that I am not a
mere threatener, that I have power as
well as will to punish, take the due
reward of thy demerits.' Craig suggests: 'You want me to take back my
power. Well I do, and you must take
the consequences.' Nichol Smith,
more simply, paraphrases: 'our royal
authority being maintained'. So
Coleridge, *op. cit.*, I, p. 61, says that
Kent's opposition displays 'Lear's
moral incapability of resigning the
sovereign power in the very moment
of disposing of it'. But I think the

phrase means 'our power backed up by
those to whom it has been delegated,
Cornwall and Albany'. This is substantially Steevens's explanation. Pope
and Boswell, accepting the reading of
Q2, assume that the line means: 'Take
thy reward in another sentence which
shall make good, shall establish, that
power.' The rhyme take–make is,
however, ugly.
 173. *disasters*] misfortunes. Many
editors prefer Q 'diseases', and
Malone thought the F printer altered
it because he did not know that diseases 'meant the slighter incon-
veniences, troubles, or distresses of the
world'. Duthie, however, points out
that the word *disease* occurs ten lines
earlier, and that the Q reading may be
a recollection.
 175. *tenth*] Collier MS. proposes
'seventh' and P. A. Daniel suggests
'se'nth', believing that the sense of the
passage requires this alteration. It

Thy banish'd trunk be found in our dominions,
The moment is thy death. Away! By Jupiter,
This shall not be revok'd.

Kent. Fare thee well, King; sith thus thou wilt appear,
Freedom lives hence, and banishment is here.   180
[*To Cordelia.*] The Gods to their dear shelter take thee,
    maid,
That justly think'st and hast most rightly said!
[*To Goneril and Regan.*] And your large speeches may
    your deeds approve,
That good effects may spring from words of love.
Thus Kent, O Princes! bids you all adieu;   185
He'll shape his old course in a country new.   [*Exit.*

Flourish. Re-enter GLOUCESTER, *with* FRANCE,
BURGUNDY, *and Attendants.*

Glou. Here's France and Burgundy, my noble Lord.
Lear. My Lord of Burgundy,
We first address toward you, who with this king
Hath rivall'd for our daughter. What, in the least,   190

179. Fare] *F; Why fare Q.*   sith] *F; since Q.*   thus] *Q1, F; not in
Q2–3.*   180. Freedom] *F; Friendship Q.*   181. S.D.] *Hanmer.*   dear
shelter] *F; protection Q.*   thee, maid] thee Maid *F; the maid Q.*   182.
justly think'st] *F; rightly thinks Q; justly thinks F4.*   hast] *Q1, F; hath
Q2.*   rightly] *F; iustly Q.*   183. S.D.] *Hanmer; not in Q, F.*   And
. . . speeches] *Q, F; And you, large speechers, Capell.*   186. Exit] *F; not
in Q.*   187. Glou.] *Q; Cor. F.*   188. of] *Q1, F; or Q2.*   189. toward]
F; towards Q.   this] *F; a Q.*

would certainly be more logical.

177. *Jupiter*] Perrett cites Harrison,
Description of Britain, IX, on the religion
of the ancient inhabitants. They
'honoured the said *Samothes* himselfe
vnder the name of *Dis* and *Saturne*;
also *Jupiter, Mars . . . Apollo, Diana* and
. . . *Hercules*'.

179–86. *Fare . . . country new*] Craig
comments: 'After the storm comes the
equanimity of Kent's rhymed lines.'
The lines sum up the situation, and
point the moral.

183. *approve*] prove true. Cf. II. ii.
156.

184. *effects*] deeds.

186. *shape . . . new*] Kent means that

he will, in a foreign land, pursue his
old ways of speaking plainly. For
'shape his course' see Marlowe,
Edward II, IV. v. 3: 'Shape we our
course to Ireland.'

S.D. Flourish] See note on 32 *ante.*

187. *Here's*] A singular verb is often
used, especially where it precedes the
subjects.

189. *address*] address myself.

this] Duthie argues for the Q reading. 'Burgundy will want a large
dowry since he, a Duke, has had the
temerity to set up as rival to a King.'
But the same point would be made by
stressing *king.*

190. *rivall'd*] competed.

Will you require in present dower with her,
Or cease your quest of love?

Bur.   Most royal Majesty,
I crave no more than hath your Highness offer'd,
Nor will you tender less.

Lear.   Right noble Burgundy,
When she was dear to us we did hold her so,   195
But now her price is fallen. Sir, there she stands:
If aught within that little-seeming substance,
Or all of it, with our displeasure piec'd,
And nothing more, may fitly like your Grace,
She's there, and she is yours.

Bur.   I know no answer.   200

Lear. Will you, with those infirmities she owes,
Unfriended, new-adopted to our hate,
Dower'd with our curse and stranger'd with our oath,
Take her, or leave her?

Bur.   Pardon me, royal Sir;
Election makes not up in such conditions.   205

---

192. Most] *F; not in Q.*   193. hath] *F;* what *Q, F3–4.*   195. did hold] held
F2–4.   196. fallen] fall'n *F3–4.*   197. little-seeming] *Collier (conj. S.
Walker); unhyphened Q, F.*   198. with our] without *Q3.*   piec'd] pierc'd
Pope.   199. more] *F;* else *Q.*   201. Will] *F;* Sir will *Q.*   203. Dower'd]
F; Couered *Q.*   204. Take her] Take leave *F3–4.*   205. in] *F;* on *Q.*

---

195. *so*] i.e. 'dear' at a high price.
'While we loved her, we were ready to
give her a large dowry.'

197. *that . . . substance*] Johnson
thinks *little seeming* is equivalent to
'ugly'; Steevens thinks that *seeming*
means 'specious'; Wright takes the
phrase to refer to Cordelia's small size;
Kittredge paraphrases: 'That little
creature, who seems to be something
real, but is in fact a mere vain *semblance*
of reality'. He suggests that *seeming-
substance* might be hyphened. Craig, I
think correctly, suggests that Lear is
referring ironically to Cordelia's blunt
professions of sincerity which she
had just contrasted with her sister's
alleged insincerity. As Schmidt points
out, *substance* commonly means *reality*
in opposition to *shadow*. I take the
phrase to mean, therefore, 'this

genuine creature, who refuses to
flatter'. Cf. II. ii. 96 ff. where Cornwall
is similarly ironical at Kent's expense.

198. *piec'd*] attached to it, in addition to it. Cf. III. vi. 2 and *Cor.*, II. iii.
220.

199. *may . . . Grace*] may please by
its fitness. Cf. II. ii. 87.

201. *owes*] owns. Cf. I. iv. 118.

203. *stranger'd*] made a stranger,
disowned.

205. *Election . . . up*] 'Election comes
to no decision', as in the phrase 'make
up one's mind' (Wright). 'No one can
choose.'

in such conditions] on such terms.
Schmidt, *Zur Textkritik*, p. 14, defended the F reading 'in' because
'conditions' referred to the 'qualities'
of Cordelia described by Lear, 202–4.
Cf. *H5*, IV. i. 108, *AYL.*, I. i. 48.

Lear. Then leave her, sir; for, by the power that made me,
　　I tell you all her wealth. [*To France.*] For you, great
　　　King,
　　I would not from your love make such a stray
　　To match you where I hate; therefore beseech you
　　T'avert your liking a more worthier way   210
　　Than on a wretch whom Nature is asham'd
　　Almost t'acknowledge hers.
France.　　　　　　　　　　This is most strange,
　　That she, whom even but now was your best object,
　　The argument of your praise, balm of your age,
　　The best, the dearest, should in this trice of time   215
　　Commit a thing so monstrous, to dismantle
　　So many folds of favour. Sure, her offence
　　Must be of such unnatural degree
　　That monsters it, or your fore-vouch'd affection

---

207. S.D.] *Pope; not in Q, F.*   210. T'avert] *F;* to auert *Q.*   212. t'acknow-
ledge] *F;* to acknowledge *Q.*   213. whom] *F;* that *Q;* who *F2.*   best]
Q; not in F.   215. The best, the] *F;* Most best, most *Q.*   217. folds]
fouls *Q3.*   219. your fore-vouch'd affection] *F;* you for voucht affections *Q.*

---

207. *For*] as for.
208. *make . . . stray*] stray so far.
209. *To*] as to. Cf. *R3*, III. ii. 27.
beseech] I beseech.
210. *T'avert . . . way*] to turn your
affections from the unworthy person
on whom they are now placed, and
place them on a better person.
more worthier] Shakespeare frequently uses the double comparative.
213. *whom*] The F reading is un-
grammatical, but not without parallels in Shakespeare. Presumably
France began to say 'whom you loved
most' and changed the construction in
the middle of the sentence.
best object] main object of love.
214. *argument*] subject, theme. Cf.
Ado, II. iii. 11.
215. *The best, the dearest*] This, the F
reading, may be a sophistication, but
as the Q reading is not demonstrably
better there is no good reason for
adopting it. For the double superlative
cf. *Ham.*, II. ii. 122.

216. *dismantle*] strip off.
217–20. *Sure . . . taint*] Malone, who
accepted Q reading, explains: 'Either
her offence must be monstrous, or if
she has not committed any such
offence, the affection you always professed to have for her must be tainted
and decayed.' Craig, following Johnson in assuming that *or* signifies *ere*,
explains: 'She must surely have committed some unspeakably horrid act,
ere the warm affection you always professed to hold her in, should thus
suddenly have changed to hate.' But F
fall makes perfectly good sense. Maxwell, following Delius, interprets:
'Either she has committed a monstrous offence, or your fore-vouch'd
affection must *now* be discredited as
having been all along unjustified.' As
the second *must* can be understood
there is no need to emend *affection* to
affections, or *fall* to *falls*, as Duthie and
Johnson suggest.
219. *monsters it*] makes it a monster.

Fall into taint; which to believe of her,   220
Must be a faith that reason without miracle
Should never plant in me.

Cor.   I yet beseech your Majesty,
(If for I want that glib and oily art
To speak and purpose not, since what I well intend,
I'll do't before I speak), that you make known   225
It is no vicious blot, murther or foulness,
No unchaste action, or dishonour'd step,
That hath depriv'd me of your grace and favour,
But even for want of that for which I am richer,
A still-soliciting eye, and such a tongue   230
That I am glad I have not, though not to have it
Hath lost me in your liking.

Lear.   Better thou
Hadst not been born than not t'have pleased me better.

France. Is it but this? a tardiness in nature
Which often leaves the history unspoke   235
That it intends to do? My Lord of Burgundy,
What say you to the lady? Love's not love

220. Fall] *F*; Falne *Q*.   222. Should] *F*; Could *Q*.   224. well] *Q*; will *F*.
225. make known] *F*; may know *Q*.   226. murther or] *Q, F*; nor other *Singer*
(*Collier MS.*).   227. unchaste] *F*; vncleane *Q*.   229. richer] *F*; rich *Q*.
230. still-soliciting] *hyphened Theobald*.   231. That] *F*; As *Q*.   232. Better] *F*;
Goe to, goe to, better *Q*.   232–3. Better . . . better] *divided as by Pope; F ends
line at* had'st, *Q at* borne.   233. t'have] *F*; to haue *Q*.   234. but] *F*; no more
but *Q*.   235. Which] *F*; That *Q*.   leaves] loves *Q3*.   236. intends to do]
intends *conj. A. Walker*.   237. Love's] *F*; Loue is *Q*.

220. *her*] emphatic (Kittredge).
221. *reason without miracle*] perhaps
a reference to the controversy about
natural religion, as in Montaigne,
op. cit., III, *passim*.
223. *If for*] even if you are enraged
with me because.
224. *purpose not*] i.e. to do what I
have promised.
226. *murther or*] Cordelia, with scorn,
mentions the worst vices she can think
of—vices which might have justified
Lear's treatment of her. The Collier
emendation is unnecessary, and absurd: for, as Kittredge points out,
'vicious blot' is not a definite kind of
'foulness'. Cordelia mentions murder

and unchastity as two examples of a
vicious blot.
227. *dishonour'd*] dishonourable.
229. *for which*] for want of which.
230. *still-soliciting*] always cadging.
232. *lost*] ruined. Cf. *Ant.*, IV. xii. 29.
liking] Cordelia deliberately uses a
colder word than love.
234. *tardiness in nature*] natural
reticence (Kittredge).
235. *history*] account. Schmidt explains as 'communication of what is in
the heart or inner life of man', comparing *Meas.*, I. i. 29.
237. *What . . . to*] i.e. Will you have.
Cf. *Shr.*, IV. iii. 17. 'What say you to a
neat's foot.'

When it is mingled with regards that stand
Aloof from th'entire point. Will you have her?
She is herself a dowry.

Bur.   Royal King,   240
Give but that portion which yourself propos'd,
And here I take Cordelia by the hand,
Duchess of Burgundy.

Lear. Nothing: I have sworn; I am firm.

Bur. I am sorry, then, you have so lost a father   245
That you must lose a husband.

Cor.   Peace be with Burgundy!
Since that respect and fortunes are his love,
I shall not be his wife.

France. Fairest Cordelia, that art most rich, being poor;
Most choice, forsaken; and most lov'd, despis'd!   250
Thee and thy virtues here I seize upon:
Be it lawful I take up what's cast away.
Gods, gods! 'tis strange that from their cold'st neglect
My love should kindle to inflam'd respect.   254
Thy dowerless daughter, King, thrown to my chance,
Is Queen of us, of ours, and our fair France:

238. regards] *F;* respects *Q.*   stand] *Pope;* stands *Q, F.*   240. a dowry] *F;*
and dowre *Q.*   King] *F;* Leir *Q.*   244. I am firm] *F; not in Q.*   247.
respect and fortunes] *F;* respects of fortune *Q.*   255. my] *F;* thy *Q.*

237–9. *Love's . . . point*] Cf. *Sonn.,*
cxvi. 2–6.

238. *regards*] considerations. Cf. *Oth.,*
I. i. 154. The Q reading was doubtless
suggested by 247 *post.*

stand] Though Q and F agree on the
reading *stands,* and though a plural
subject often has a singular verb, the
line sounds better without the s.

239. *entire*] essential, single.

247. *respect and fortunes*] mercenary
considerations—an example of hendiadys. Duthie denies that the phrase
means the same as the Q reading, but
he does not give his own interpretation. Perhaps the F version means
'what people think of me, and what
my dowry is'. Cf. *Ham.,* III. ii. 192–3:
'The instances that second marriage
move / Are base respects of thrift, but

none of love.' Heilman, *op. cit.,* p. 308,
points out that *regards, respect,* and
despis'd are all derived from words of
seeing, and that Shakespeare may
have 'embedded a number of bi-
lingual puns' in these lines.

249–50. *most rich . . . despis'd*] Noble,
Shakespeare's Biblical Knowledge, compares 2 Corinthians, vi. 10: 'As poore,
and yet making many rich: as hauing nothing, and yet possessing all
things'.

251. *I seize upon*] Perrett, *op. cit.,*
p. 280, compares Geoffrey of Monmouth's phrase 'se vero tantummodo
puellam captare'.

254. *My . . . respect*] Perrett cites
Geoffrey again: 'amore virginis in-
flammatus'.

255. *chance*] lot.

Not all the dukes of wat'rish Burgundy
Can buy this unpriz'd precious maid of me.
Bid them farewell, Cordelia, though unkind:
Thou losest here, a better where to find.   260

Lear. Thou hast her, France; let her be thine, for we
Have no such daughter, nor shall ever see
That face of hers again; therefore be gone
Without our grace, our love, our benison.
Come, noble Burgundy.   265

> [*Flourish. Exeunt Lear, Burgundy, Cornwall,*
> *Albany, Gloucester, and Attendants.*

France. Bid farewell to your sisters.

Cor. The jewels of our father, with wash'd eyes
Cordelia leaves you: I know you what you are;
And like a sister am most loth to call   269
Your faults as they are named. Love well our father:
To your professed bosoms I commit him:
But yet, alas! stood I within his grace,
I would prefer him to a better place.
So farewell to you both.

Reg. Prescribe not us our duty.

Gon.   Let your study   275

---

257. of] *F;* in *Q.*   258. Can] *F;* Shall *Q.*   265. *Flourish*] *F; not in Q.*
Exeunt ... Attendants] *Capell; Exit Lear and Burgundy Q; Exeunt F.*   267. The]
Q, F; Ye *Rowe.*   270. Love] *F;* vse *Q.*   273. prefer] perfer *F2.*   275.
Reg.] *F;* Gonorill *Q.*   duty] *F;* duties *Q.*   *Gon.*] *F;* Regan *Q.*

257. *wat'rish*] a quibble: abounding
in streams, and weak, diluted. Cf. *Oth.*,
III. iii. 15. R. A. Law, *Studies in
Philology*, 1936, p. 222, suggests that
Shakespeare may have had historical
characters in mind. Sargeaunt, *N.Q.*,
27 March 1909, suggests unnecessarily
that we should read *Duke's.*

258. *unpriz'd precious*] unappreciated
by others, but precious in my sight.

259. *though unkind*] though they have
treated you with unnatural cruelty.
Staunton thinks Shakespeare may
have intended *unkinn'd*, i.e. forsaken
by thy kindred. He compares *Ven.*,
703.

260. *here ... where*] 'These have the
power of nouns' (Johnson).

264. *benison*] blessing.

267. *The*] i.e. You, the. Several
editors follow Rowe's emendation, but
though 'the' and 'ye' are often difficult
to distinguish in MSS. cf. *Cæs.*, v. iii.
99, where the article is used in a voca-
tive phrase (Kittredge).

wash'd] i.e. with tears. Cf. *MND.*,
II. ii. 93.

270. *as ... named*] by their true ugly
names. Cf. 'To call a spade a spade'.

271. *professed*] 'Cordelia commits
her father to the love which her sisters
had professed, not to that which they
really feel' (Delius).

273. *prefer*] advance (cf. *R3*, IV. ii.
182), or recommend (cf. *Cym.*, II. iii.
49–51).

Be to content your lord, who hath receiv'd you
At Fortune's alms; you have obedience scanted,
And well are worth the want that you have wanted.

Cor. Time shall unfold what plighted cunning hides;
Who covers faults, at last with shame derides.   280
Well may you prosper!

France.   Come, my fair Cordelia.
                              [*Exeunt France and Cordelia.*

Gon. Sister, it is not little I have to say of what most
nearly appertains to us both. I think our father will
hence to-night.

Reg. That's most certain, and with you; next month   285
with us.

Gon. You see how full of changes his age is; the observation we have made of it hath not been little: he
always lov'd our sister most; and with what poor
judgment he hath now cast her off appears too   290
grossly.

Reg. 'Tis the infirmity of his age; yet he hath ever but
slenderly known himself.

Gon. The best and soundest of his time hath been but
rash; then must we look from his age, to receive not   295

---

278. want] *F;* worth *Q.*   279. plighted] pleated *Q.*   280. covers] *Q, F;*
cover *Jennens.*   with shame] *F;* shame them *Q.*   281. my] *F;* not in *Q.*
282–4.] *verse Q, F; prose Capell.*   282. little] *F;* a little *Q.*   288. not] *Q;*
not in F.   290. too] *Q, F;* too too *F2–4.*   291. grossly] *F;* grosse *Q.*
295. from . . . receive] *F;* to receiue from his age *Q.*

---

277. *At . . . alms*] 'When fortune was
doling out petty charities, not bestow-
ing bounteous awards' (Kittredge).
Cf. *Oth.,* III. iv. 122.

scanted] stinted, come short of.

278. *And . . . wanted*] and well
deserve (*a*) to be treated unkindly by
your husband, because of your own
lack of affection for your father; or
(*b*) to lose your share of the kingdom.
(*a*) is more probable.

are worth] Cf. II. iv. 43.

wanted] gone, or been, without.

279. *plighted*] folded, complicated,
and so, figuratively, dissembling. Q
and F words have the same sense. Cf.

Milton, *Comus,* 301, 'plighted', and
Lucrece, 93: 'Hiding base sin in pleats
of majesty.'

280–1. *Who . . . prosper*] Noble, *op.
cit.,* compares Proverbs, xxviii. 13: 'He
that hideth his sinnes, shall not prosper.' The implication is that Goneril
and Regan will not prosper.

280. *Who*] i.e. Time. Most editors
prefer the Q reading of this line; in
which case *Who* means 'Those who'.

291. *grossly*] obviously.

292–8. *'Tis . . . them*] Cf. *Leir,* 195:
'For he, you know, is alwayes in
extremes.'

295. *rash*] hasty, hot-headed.

alone the imperfections of long-engraffed condition, but therewithal the unruly waywardness that
infirm and choleric years bring with them.

Reg. Such unconstant starts are we like to have from him
as this of Kent's banishment.   300

Gon. There is further compliment of leave-taking between France and him. Pray you, let us hit together:
if our father carry authority with such disposition
as he bears, this last surrender of his will but offend
us.   305

Reg. We shall further think of it.

Gon. We must do something, and i'th'heat.   [*Exeunt.*

SCENE II.—[*The Earl of Gloucester's Castle.*]

Enter EDMUND, *with a letter.*

Edm. Thou, Nature, art my goddess; to thy law
My services are bound. Wherefore should I

---

296. imperfections] *F;* imperfection *Q.*
ingraffed *F;* long ingrafted *Q.*   297. the] *F; not in Q.*
stars *Q2.*   302. Pray you] Pray *Q.*
303. disposition] *F;* dispositions *Q.*

long-engraffed] *hyphened Pope;* long
299. starts] *Q1, F;*
let us] *F;* let's *Q.*   hit] *Q; sit F.*
306. of it] *F;* on't *Q.*

Scene II

S.D.] *Pope subst.*

296. *long-engraffed*] 'firmly imbed-
ded' (Kittredge). Q and F give
variants of the same word from Fr.
greffer.

296–7. *condition*] disposition. Cf.
Oth., IV. i. 204. Goneril's diagnosis is
near to the truth.

299. *unconstant starts*] sudden whims;
a metaphor from horsemanship. Cf.
Mac., III. iv. 63, and *Ven.*, 302.

301. *compliment*] formality. Cf. *Rom.*,
II. ii. 89.

302. *hit*] agree, act vigorously. Cf.
Leir, 1155–6, where Ragan says: 'Yet
will I make fayre weather, to procure /
Conuenient meanes, and then ile
strike it sure.' Schmidt adopts F 'sit',
explaining 'take counsel together'. Cf.
Per., II. iii. 92.

303–4. *carry . . . bears*] continues to
wield his authority, in spite of his
abdication, in the way we have just
seen.

304. *last surrender*] Empson, *op. cit.*,
p. 128, comments: 'a curious remark
that seems to imply previous renuncia-
tions'. But *last* means 'recent'. Cf. *Tp.*,
v. i. 153.

304–5. *offend us*] be a nuisance to us.

307. *do*] as opposed to *think.*

i'th'heat] i.e. strike while the iron is
hot (Steevens).

Scene II

1. *Nature*] William A. Armstrong,
T.L.S., 14 Oct. 1949, argues that
Shakespeare was influenced by the
epicurean atheism of Cecropia in

Stand in the plague of custom, and permit
The curiosity of nations to deprive me,
For that I am some twelve or fourteen moonshines   5
Lag of a brother? Why bastard? Wherefore base?
When my dimensions are as well compact,
My mind as generous, and my shape as true,
As honest madam's issue? Why brand they us
With base? with baseness? bastardy? base, base?   10
Who in the lusty stealth of nature take
More composition and fierce quality
Than doth, within a dull, stale, tired bed,

---

4. deprive] deprave *conj. A. Walker.*   10. With . . . base] *F;* with base, base
bastardie *Q.*   13. dull, stale] *F;* stale, dull *Q.*   tired] *F;* lyed *Q1;* lied *Q2.*

Sidney's *Arcadia* (ed. Feuillerat, pp. 406–7). But the ideas expressed there were not uncommon: they are discussed, for example, by Montaigne. John F. Danby, *op. cit.*, pp. 31–2, points out that 'Edmund worships a Goddess of whom neither Hooker nor Bacon would approve. . . No medieval devil ever bounced on the stage with a more scandalous self-announcement.' Draper, *Shakes. Jahr.*, 1938, p. 133, remarks that Edmund in taking Nature for his goddess 'so renounces both religion and the laws of human society'. See also Heilman, *op. cit.*, pp. 123–8. Kittredge cites Webster, *The Devil's Law Case*, IV. ii. 275–80.

3. *Stand . . . custom*] stand on, be dependent on pestilential custom. Wright aptly quotes from the Prayer-Book version of Ps., xxxviii. 17: 'And I truly am set in the plague.' See the Montaigne passage quoted in the Appendix, p. 237.

4. *curiosity*] squeamishness, false delicacy, over-particularity or fastidiousness. Cf. I. i. 5–6 *ante.* 'The nice distinctions which the laws of nations make in defiance of nature and common sense' (Kittredge).

deprive me] debar me, keep me out of my rights. Cf. *Hystorie of Hamblet*, IV: 'rather than he would deprive himself'. As Edmund is a younger son, he would not inherit even if

he were legitimate. Cf. *AYL.*, I. i. 49.

5. *For that*] because.

6. *Lag of*] behind in years. Cf. I. i. 18–19 and *R3*, II. i. 90.

base] *Bastard* has apparently no etymological connection with the adj. *base*, though 'base son' was used for 'bastard'. Edmund is protesting against the assumption that he is low and vile because he is illegitimate.

7. *dimensions*] proportions. Cf. *Mer. V.*, III. i. 62, and Tourneur, *The Atheist's Tragedy*, v. ii. 165–6: 'Me thinks, my parts, and my dimentions, are / As many, as large, as well compos'd as his.'

compact] put together, made. Cf. *Tit.*, v. iii. 88.

8. *generous*] gallant, high-spirited, courageous, befitting a person of noble birth. Cf. *Troil.*, II. ii. 154.

as true] as truly stamped, hit off, as true a likeness of my father. Cf. *Wint.*, v. i. 127. Kittredge thinks it means symmetrical.

9. *honest*] chaste.

11. *lusty . . . nature*] Cf. *Oth.*, III. iii. 338: 'stolen hours of lust'.

12. *More composition*] a fuller mixture. The Bastard in *John* (I. i. 88) has a 'large composition'.

fierce quality] more energetic quality.

13. *dull . . . tired*] referring to the occupants of the marriage bed, and their relations.

Go to th'creating a whole tribe of fops,
Got 'tween asleep and wake? Well then,   15
Legitimate Edgar, I must have your land:
Our father's love is to the bastard Edmund
As to th'legitimate. Fine word, 'legitimate'!
Well, my legitimate, if this letter speed,
And my invention thrive, Edmund the base   20
Shall top th'legitimate—: I grow, I prosper;
Now, gods, stand up for bastards!

Enter GLOUCESTER.

Glou. Kent banish'd thus! And France in choler parted!
And the King gone to-night! prescrib'd his power!

14. to] *not in F3–4.*   th'creating] *F;* the creating of *Q;* creating *Pope.*
15. asleep] *Capell;* a sleepe *Q1, F;* sleepe *Q2;* a-sleep *Pope.*   then] *F;* the *Q.*
18. Fine . . . 'legitimate'] *F; not in Q.*   21. top] *Capell (conj. Edwards);* tooth'
Q; to'th' *F;* toe *Hanmer;* be *Pope.*   24. prescrib'd] *F;* subscribd *Q.*

14. *th'creating*] Abbott points out that 'although this is a noun, and therefore preceded by "the", yet it is so far confused with the gerund as to be allowed the privilege of governing a direct object.'
fops] fools; not, as after the Restoration, dandies.
19. *speed*] prosper.
21. *Shall top th'legitimate*] This emendation was first suggested by Edwards in his *Canons of Criticism,* and first adopted by Capell. Greg argues that 'if the tail of the "p" were for any reason obscured, "top" would naturally be misread as "too".' Capell aptly points out that 'top' is opposed to 'base' (by a quibble), and connected with 'grow', which has no natural introduction unless preceded by 'top'. Duthie shows that although the F reading might be taken to mean 'shall attack my legitimate brother', Edmund is acting against him anyway by means of the letter. The context requires a word meaning 'overthrow' or 'surpass'. Johnson, following Hanmer, explained 'toe the legitimate' as 'kick him out . . . or to supplant him'.

Tannenbaum, *S.A.B.*, Jan. 1941, supports this reading, and cites *Mer.V.*, I. iii. 119: 'And foot me as you spurn a stranger cur.' On the whole, 'top' would seem to be preferable; and certainly an actor would find it easier to say with the right note of triumph.
22. *stand up*] Heilman, *op. cit.*, p. 314, suggests that there is a punning reference to tumescence.
23. *And . . . parted*] In the recorded parting between Lear and France, there is no appearance of any choler in France; but another interview is spoken of (I. i. 301), and France is described as 'hot-blooded'. Greg suggests, *M.L.R.*, 1940, p. 444, that France, 'incensed at some fresh insult to Cordelia, departed in a rage, determined to wrest by force her portion from . . . Albany and Cornwall'. Cf. note to IV. iii. 3.
24. *to-night*] last night (Greg).
prescrib'd] limited, restricted, confined within bounds (*N.E.D.*). This meaning is rare. The Q reading *subscribed* is explicable as an anticipation of III. vii. 63, also spoken by Gloucester.

Confin'd to exhibition! All this done   25
Upon the gad!—Edmund, how now! What news?
Edm. So please your Lordship, none.   [*Putting up the letter.*
Glou. Why so earnestly seek you to put up that letter?
Edm. I know no news, my Lord.
Glou. What paper were you reading?   30
Edm. Nothing, my Lord.
Glou. No? What needed then that terrible dispatch of it
into your pocket? The quality of nothing hath not
such need to hide itself. Let's see: come; if it be no-
thing, I shall not need spectacles.   35
Edm. I beseech you, Sir, pardon me; it is a letter from my
brother that I have not all o'erread, and for so much
as I have perus'd, I find it not fit for your o'erlooking.
Glou. Give me the letter, sir.
Edm. I shall offend, either to detain or give it. The con-   40
tents, as in part I understand them, are to blame.
Glou. Let's see, let's see.
Edm. I hope, for my brother's justification, he wrote this
but as an essay or taste of my virtue.
Glou. [Reads.] *This policy and reverence of age makes the*   45
world bitter to the best of our times; keeps our fortunes from
us till our oldness cannot relish them. I begin to find an idle

25. done] gone *F2–4*.   27. S.D.] *Rowe; not in Q, F*.   28. Why] Whe *F2*.   32.
needed] *F*; needes *Q*.   terrible] *F, Q2*; terribe *Q1*.   34. hide] hid *Q3*.   37. and]
F; not in Q.   38. o'erlooking] *F*; liking *Q*.   44. virtue] *F*; virtue. *A letter Q*.
45. S.D.] *F; not in Q*.   *and reverence*] *F; not in Q*.   46. *the best*] best *F2–4*.

25. *Confin'd to exhibition*] restricted to
an allowance. Cf. the use of the term
'exhibition' as a minor scholarship ten-
able at a university, and *Gent.*, I. iii. 69.

26. *Upon the gad*] suddenly, as if
pricked by a gad or goad. Cf. *Tit.*,
IV. i. 103, and *Tim.*, III. vi. 73, 'with
that spur' = with the same alacrity.

28. *earnestly*] eagerly. Cf. *Troil.*, IV.
ii. 41.

put up] i.e. in his pocket.

31. *Nothing*] Cf. note on I. i. 86.

32. *terrible dispatch*] fearful haste.

36. *pardon me*] excuse me from showing it to you.

38. *o'erlooking*] inspection. Cf. v. i. 50.

44. *essay . . . taste*] The words are

synonymous, meaning 'test'. To take
the 'assay' of a dish was to taste it. Cf.
2H4, II. iii. 52, and *John*, v. vi. 28. See
Appendix, p. 237.

45. *This . . . age*] the policy of rever-
encing age—hendiadys (Schmidt).
'Policy' suggests that it is a clever trick
on the part of the aged (Kittredge).

46. *bitter*] Whiter, in an unpublished note, points out that the word
was suggested by *taste* (44), and that it
suggests *relish*.

best . . . times] best years of our
lives. Cf. I. i. 294.

47. *relish*] appreciate. Cf. *Meas.*, III.
i. 34–8.

47–8. *to find . . . tyranny*] I begin to

*and fond bondage in the oppression of aged tyranny, who
sways, not as it hath power, but as it is suffer'd. Come to me,
that of this I may speak more. If our father would sleep till* 50
*I wak'd him, you should enjoy half his revenue for ever,
and live the beloved of your brother,* EDGAR.—Hum!
Conspiracy! 'Sleep till I wak'd him,—you should
enjoy half his revenue.' My son Edgar! Had he a
hand to write this? a heart and brain to breed it 55
in? When came you to this? Who brought it?

Edm. It was not brought me, my Lord; there's the cunning of it; I found it thrown in at the casement of my
closet.

Glou. You know the character to be your brother's? 60

Edm. If the matter were good, my Lord, I durst swear it
were his; but, in respect of that, I would fain think it
were not.

Glou. It is his.

Edm. It is his hand, my Lord; but I hope his heart is not 65
in the contents.

Glou. Has he never before sounded you in this business?

Edm. Never, my Lord. But I have heard him oft maintain
it to be fit that, sons at perfect age, and fathers declin'd, the father should be as ward to the son, and 70
the son manage his revenue.

---

53. Sleep] *F;* Slept *Q.*   wak'd] wakt *Q;* wake *F.*   55. brain] a brain
Rowe.   56. you to this] *F;* this to you *Q, F3–4.*   62. respect] *Q2, F;*
respect, *Q1.*   64. It is] *Q1, F;* Is it *Q2.*   his.] *F;* his? *Q.*   65. but] *not
in F2–4.*   67. Has] *F;* Hath *Q.*   before] *F;* hertofore *Q.*   68. heard
him oft] *F;* often heard him *Q.*   69–70. declin'd] *F;* declining *Q.*   70. the
father] *F;* his father *Q.*   ward] a ward *Q3.*   71. his] *F;* the *Q.*

---

feel that to be thus oppressed by an
aged and tyrannical father is nothing
but a state of vain and foolish servi-
tude.

47. find] feel.

48–9. who . . . suffer'd] who is able
to rule not by its strength but by our
tameness in putting up with it. Cf.
Troil., I. iii. 137: 'Troy in our weakness
stands, not in her strength.' See also
Cæs., I. iii. 104–5.

49. sways] rules. Cf. I. i. 135.

60. *character*] handwriting. Cf. *Ham.,*
IV. vii. 52.

67. *sounded*] a nautical metaphor.

69–70. *declin'd*] past their prime. Cf.
Oth., III. iii. 265.

70–1. *the father . . . revenue*] Sullivan
points out in his introduction to Pettie,
The Civile Conversation of . . . Guazzo,
1581 (ed. 1925), that there is a long
passage in the third conversation (*op.
cit.,* II. 65–73) on the foolishness of
fathers who cling to their power and

Glou. O villain, villain! His very opinion in the letter!
Abhorred villain! Unnatural, detested, brutish villain! worse than brutish! Go, sirrah, seek him; I'll
apprehend him. Abominable villain! Where is he?   75
Edm. I do not well know, my Lord. If it shall please you
to suspend your indignation against my brother till
you can derive from him better testimony of his
intent, you should run a certain course; where, if
you violently proceed against him, mistaking his   80
purpose, it would make a great gap in your own
honour, and shake in pieces the heart of his obedience. I dare pawn down my life for him, that he hath
writ this to feel my affection to your honour, and to
no other pretence of danger.   85

74. sirrah] *F;* sir *Q.*   I'll] Ile *F;* I *Q1;* I, *Q2;* Ay *Camb.*   78. his] *F;* this
Q.   79. should] *Q, F;* shall *Q2.*   81. own] *not in F2–4.*   83. that] *F;*
not in Q.   84. writ] *F;* wrote *Q.*   85. other] *F;* further *Q.*

possessions: 'The father is so desirous
of keping his paternall jurisdiction,
that though his children bee arived to
mans estate, and be perfectly accom-
plished every way, yet he will alowe
them neither more living, nor more
liberty then they had when they were
children. . . I thinke they have just
cause to bee mal contents, who knowing themselves to be sufficient men,
and to be so taken of every man, are
neverthelesse used by their father like
children: and therefore I cannot
blame them greatly, if in stead of
loving him, they complaine of death
for delaying the execution of that
judgement, which so long before was
pronounced agaynst him . . . adding,
that his living, will do him no good
when it falleth into his handes, for that,
by course of nature, he shall be constrained to forgoe it againe. . . If that
come by the fault of age, I will not say
that such men were wel worthy to
dwel amongest the Caspians, who
when the father is arrived to the age of
threescore and ten, kill him presently,
and give him to beastes to eat.' Similar
sentiments are expressed by Mon-

taigne. Cf. Appendix, p. 237, and
Florio, *op. cit.,* III. 96–107: 'It is meere
injustice to see an old, crazed, sinnow-
shronken, and nigh dead father . . . to
enjoy so many goods as would suffice
for the preferment and entertainment
of many children, and in the meane
while, for want of meanes, to suffer
them to lose their best dayes and
yeares . . .; whereby they are often cast
into dispaire, to seeke, by some way
how unlawfull soever to provide for
their necessaries. . . But a father over-
burthened with yeares . . . ought
willingly to distribute and bestow
them amongst those, to whom by
naturall decree they belong.'

70. *as . . . to*] under the guardian-
ship of.

73. *Abhorred*] detestable.

detested] detestable.

79. *you . . . course*] you would be
adopting a safe plan.

where] whereas.

81. *gap*] breach. Cf. *Wint.,* IV. iv. 198.

83. *pawn*] stake. Cf. I. i. 154.

84. *feel*] test. Cf. *H5,* IV. i. 131.

85. *pretence of danger*] dangerous
intention. Cf. *Gent.,* III. i. 47.

Glou. Think you so?

Edm. If your honour judge it meet, I will place you where
you shall hear us confer of this, and by an auricular
assurance have your satisfaction; and that without
any further delay than this very evening.   90

Glou. He cannot be such a monster—

Edm. Nor is not, sure.

Glou. —to his father, that so tenderly and entirely loves
him. Heaven and earth! Edmund, seek him out;
wind me into him, I pray you: frame the business   95
after your own wisdom. I would unstate myself to
be in a due resolution.

Edm. I will seek him, Sir, presently; convey the business
as I shall find means, and acquaint you withal.

Glou. These late eclipses in the sun and moon portend no   100
good to us: though the wisdom of Nature can reason
it thus and thus, yet Nature finds itself scourg'd by
the sequent effects. Love cools, friendship falls off,
brothers divide: in cities, mutinies; in countries,
discord; in palaces, treason; and the bond crack'd   105
'twixt son and father. This villain of mine comes

88. of] *not in F3–4.*   91. monster—] *Dyce;* Monster. *Q, F.*   92–4. Nor . . .
earth!] *Q; not in F.*   95. the] *F;* your *Q.*   96. to] *Q1, F;* ro *Q2.*   98.
will] *F;* shall *Q.*   99. find] *F;* see *Q.*   102. it] *F; not in Q.*   105.
discord] *F;* discords *Q.*   in palaces] *F;* palaces *Q.*   treason] treasons *Q3.*
and] *F; not in Q.*   106. 'twixt] *F;* betweene *Q.*

88. *auricular*] Shakespeare would
know the expression 'auricular confession'. It is used, for example, in the
preface of Brooke's *Romeus and Juliet.*
Florio, too, uses the word 'auricular'.
Cf. Appendix, p. 236.

95. *wind me into him*] worm your way
into his confidence for me (Kittredge).
'Wind' is to make cautious, indirect
advances. Cf. *Cor.,* III. iii. 64. There is
a good description of the process in
Polonius' instructions to Reynaldo,
Ham., II. i. 1–68.

frame] fashion, manage. Cf. *Wint.,*
v. i. 91; *2H4,* IV. i. 180.

96. *unstate myself*] forfeit my rank and
fortune. Cf. *Ant.,* III. xiii. 30.

96–7. *to . . . resolution*] to be convinced of his innocence, or even of his

guilt, and so freed from uncertainty.
Cf. *Oth.,* III. iii. 180.

98. *presently*] at once.

convey] manage.

100–11. *These . . . graves*] See Introduction, p. xviii, and Appendix, p.
237.

101. *the wisdom . . . Nature*] natural
philosophy, man's reason, scientific
knowledge.

101–2. *can . . . thus*] can offer explanations of eclipses.

102–3. *yet . . . effects*] yet the natural
world of man is afflicted by the disasters that follow.

103. *falls off*] revolts. Cf. *1H4,* I. iii.
94.

104. *mutinies*] riots, insurrections.

105. *bond*] Cf. I. i. 92.

under the prediction; there's son against father: the
King falls from bias of nature; there's father against
child. We have seen the best of our time: machina-
tions, hollowness, treachery, and all ruinous dis-		110
orders follow us disquietly to our graves. Find out
this villain, Edmund; it shall lose thee nothing: do
it carefully. And the noble and true-hearted Kent
banish'd! his offence, honesty! 'Tis strange.		[*Exit.*

Edm. This is the excellent foppery of the world, that,	115
when we are sick in fortune, often the surfeits of our
own behaviour, we make guilty of our disasters the
sun, the moon, and stars; as if we were villains on
necessity, fools by heavenly compulsion, knaves,
thieves, and treachers by spherical predominance,	120
drunkards, liars, and adulterers by an enforc'd
obedience of planetary influence; and all that we
are evil in, by a divine thrusting on. An admirable
evasion of whoremaster man, to lay his goatish
disposition to the charge of a star! My father com-	125
pounded with my mother under the dragon's tail,
and my nativity was under *Ursa major*; so that it
follows I am rough and lecherous. Fut! I should

106–11. This . . . graves] *F; not in Q.*	112. villain] villanie *Q3.*	114.
honesty] *F;* honest *Q.*	'Tis] *F;* strange *Q.*	S.D.] *F; not in Q.*	116.
surfeits] *F;* surfeit *Q.*	118. stars] *F;* the stars *Q.*	on] *F;* by *Q.*	120.
treachers] *F;* trecherers *Q.*	spherical] *F;* spiritual *Q.*	125. to] *Q; not in F.*
a star] *F;* stars *Q.*	128. Fut] *Q; not in F;* Tut *Jennens.*

107–9. *there's son . . . child*] Noble
compares Mark, xiii. 12. Hart, *Shakespeare and the Homilies*, quotes *Homilies*,
1640, pp. 295–6: 'The brother to seek,
and often to work the death of his
brother, the son of his father, the father
to seek or procure the death of his sons
being at man's age, and by their faults
to disinherit their innocent children,
and kinsmen their heirs for ever.'

108. *falls . . . nature*] goes against
natural instincts. The metaphor is
from bowls. Cf. *John*, II. i. 574–80.

109. *best . . . time*] Cf. 46 *ante.*

110. *hollowness*] falseness, insincerity.
Cf. I. i. 153.

111. *disquietly*] Cf. Appendix, p. 236.
'unquietly'.

115. *foppery*] stupidity.

116. *surfeits*] natural evil results, as
indigestion follows over-eating. Cf.
Cor., IV. i. 46.

118. *on*] by. Cf. *LLL.*, I. i. 149.

120. *treachers*] traitors. Cf. Spenser,
F.Q., II. i. 12.

spherical predominance] because a particular planet was most powerful at
the hour of our birth. Cf. *All's W.*,
I. i. 211.

123. *divine . . . on*] supernatural
impelling or incitement. Cf. *Mac.*,
I. iii. 130: 'supernatural soliciting'.

124. *goatish*] lascivious. Cf. *Oth.*, III.
iii. 180.

128. *Fut!*] 'Foot or 'Sfoot; Pooh!

have been that I am had the maidenliest star in the firmament twinkled on my bastardizing. Edgar—   130

Enter EDGAR.

and pat he comes, like the catastrophe of the old comedy: my cue is villanous melancholy, with a sigh like Tom o' Bedlam. O! these eclipses do portend these divisions. *Fa, sol, la, mi.*

Edg. How now, brother Edmund! What serious contemplation are you in?   135

Edm. I am thinking, brother, of a prediction I read this other day, what should follow these eclipses.

Edg. Do you busy yourself with that?

Edm. I promise you the effects he writes of succeed un-   140
happily; as of unnaturalness between the child and the parent; death, dearth, dissolutions of ancient amities; divisions in state; menaces and maledictions against King and nobles; needless diffidences,

129. maidenliest] *F3;* maidenlest *Q, F1–2.*   in] *F;* of *Q.*   130. bastardizing] *F;* bastardy *Q.*   Edgar] *Q; not in F.*   131. and pat] *Steevens;* and out *Q;* Pat *F.*   132. my cue] *F;* mine *Q.*   133. sigh] *Q2, F;* sith *Q1.*   Tom o'] *F;* them of *Q.*   133–4. do portend] portent *Q3.*   134. *Fa . . . mi] F; not in Q.*   139. with] *F;* about *Q.*   140. you] *not in F2–4.* writes] *F;* writ *Q.*   141–7. as . . . astronomical] *Q; not in F.*   143. amities] *Q1;* armies *Q2.*

130. *bastardizing*] extra-marital conception. The word is used by Florio. Cf. Appendix, p. 236.

133. *Tom o' Bedlam*] Tom was the name generally assumed by the bedlam beggar, or Abraham man. Cf. Audeley, *Fraternitye of Vagabondes,* 1565 (ed. 1880, p. 1): 'An Abraham man is he that walketh bare armed, and bare legged, and fayneth himself mad, and caryeth a packe of wool, or a stycke with baken on it, or such lyke toy, and nameth himselfe poore Tom.' See also Jonson, *The Devil is an Ass,* v. ii. 35, 'Your best song's Tom o' Bethlem.' Harsnett also mentions Bedlamites.

134. *Fa . . . mi*] Some have supposed that these musical notes may have been suggested to Edmund by the word 'division', which had the sense of

musical modulation. Cf. *1H4,* III. i. 211. A similar play on the two meanings of the word will be found in Beaumont and Fletcher, *The Coronation,* III. i (ed. Waller, viii. 269): 'Is it not pitty any division / Should be heard out of Musick?' It has also been suggested (*Notes and Queries,* 23 June 1928) that 'Edmund is evidently about to say "Father", but when he hears the sound of the first part of the word, his mischievous nature prompts him to supply, instead, the remaining syllables of the diabolical progression.' In any case, Edmund sings to himself so as to pretend that he is unaware of Edgar's approach.

137–8. *this other day*] the other day.

140. *succeed*] turn out.

144. *diffidences*] suspicions, cases of

banishment of friends, dissipation of cohorts, nup-   145
tial breaches, and I know not what.

Edg. How long have you been a sectary astronomical?

Edm. When saw you my father last?

Edg. The night gone by.

Edm. Spake you with him?   150

Edg. Ay, two hours together.

Edm. Parted you in good terms? Found you no displeasure in him by word nor countenance?

Edg. None at all.

Edm. Bethink yourself wherein you may have offended   155
him; and at my entreaty forbear his presence until
some little time hath qualified the heat of his displeasure, which at this instant so rageth in him that
with the mischief of your person it would scarcely
allay.   160

Edg. Some villain hath done me wrong.

Edm. That's my fear. I pray you have a continent forbearance till the speed of his rage goes slower, and
as I say, retire with me to my lodging, from whence
I will fitly bring you to hear my Lord speak. Pray   165

---

145. dissipation of cohorts] denegation of contracts *conj. Kinnear.*   cohorts]
courts *Steevens;* comforts *Jennens.*   148. When] *F;* Come, come, when *Q.*
149. The] *F;* Why, the *Q.*   151. Ay] I *F; not in Q.*   153. nor] *F;* or *Q.*
155. may] *not in F3–4.*   156. until] *F;* till *Q.*   159. scarcely] *F;* scarce *Q.*
162. fear] *F;* feare brother *Q.*   162–9. I . . . Brother] *F; not in Q.*

---

mutual distrust. Cf. *1H6*, III. iii. 10.

145. *dissipation of cohorts*] Craig
remarks that 'this does not read like
Shakespeare', and suggests that he
may have written 'disputation of con-
sorts', i.e. wrangling among comrades.
But, as Kittredge points out, 'The
word *cohorts* fits the era of the play as
Shakespeare seems to have imagined
that era . . . though the fabulous Lear's
reign was long before' the Roman
occupation. Schmidt thinks that these
lines 141–7, peculiar to Q, are spurious, since they contain six words to be
found nowhere else in Shakespeare.
But of these *menace* (as a noun) and
dissipation are to be found in Florio's
Montaigne, *malediction, astronomical,*

and *cohort* were not uncommon, and
Shakespeare uses elsewhere in the play
words cognate to *unnaturalness.* It may
be added that Florio also uses *sectary.*
The cohorts were melting away, presumably by the desertion of the soldiers.

147. *sectary astronomical*] believer in,
or student of, astrology.

156. *forbear . . . presence*] avoid meeting him.

157. *qualified*] mitigated. Cf. *Oth.,* II.
iii. 31.

162–3. *have . . . forbearance*] restrain
your feelings, and keep away. Cf. 156
ante.

165. *fitly*] opportunely. Cf. *Tim.,* III.
iv. 111.

ye, go; there's my key. If you do stir abroad, go
arm'd.

Edg. Arm'd, brother!

Edm. Brother, I advise you to the best. I am no honest
man if there be any good meaning toward you; I   170
have told you what I have seen and heard; but
faintly, nothing like the image and horror of it;
pray you, away.

Edg. Shall I hear from you anon?

Edm. I do serve you in this business.   [*Exit Edgar.*   175
A credulous father, and a brother noble,
Whose nature is so far from doing harms
That he suspects none; on whose foolish honesty
My practices ride easy! I see the business.
Let me, if not by birth, have lands by wit: 180
All with me's meet that I can fashion fit.   [*Exit.*

SCENE III.—[*A Room in the Duke of Albany's Palace.*]

Enter GONERIL, *and* OSWALD, *her Steward.*

Gon. Did my father strike my gentleman for chiding of
his Fool?

Osw. Ay, Madam.

166. ye] *F;* you *Rowe.*   169. best] *F;* best, goe arm'd *Q.*   170. toward] *F;*
towards *Q.*   175. S.D.] *Q1; after 174 Q2; Exit (after 174) F.*

Scene III

S.D. *A Room . . . Palace*] *Capell; The Palace Rowe; not in Q, F.*   *Oswald, her
Steward*] *Collier; Gentleman Q1; A Gentleman Q2; Steward F.*   3. *Osw.*]
Collier; Gent. Q; Stew. F.   Ay] I *F;* Yes *Q.*

170. *meaning*] intention.
172. *faintly*] euphemistically.
image and horror] horrible reality—
the horror which an exact description
would fill you with.
176. *credulous father*] Geoffrey of
Monmouth uses the expression *credulus
ergo pater* about Lear (Perrett, *op. cit.,*
p. 280).
179. *practices*] intrigues.
ride] Cf. *Tw.N.,* III. iv. 318, *Wint.,*
I. ii. 94.

181. *All . . . fit*] To me everything is
fitting and justifiable that I can utilize
for my purposes; the end justifies the
means.
fashion fit] make fitting.

Scene III

1–2. *chiding . . . Fool*] Empson, *op. cit.,*
p. 129, comments: 'So it is the Fool
who causes the beginning of the storm
against Lear, rather than his shadowy
train of deboshed knights.'

Gon. By day and night, he wrongs me; every hour
　　　　He flashes into one gross crime or other,　　　　　5
　　　　That sets us all at odds: I'll not endure it:
　　　　His knights grow riotous, and himself upbraids us
　　　　On every trifle. When he returns from hunting
　　　　I will not speak with him; say I am sick:
　　　　If you come slack of former services,　　　　　　10
　　　　You shall do well; the fault of it I'll answer.
Osw. He's coming, Madam; I hear him.　　　　[*Horns within.*
Gon. Put on what weary negligence you please,
　　　　You and your fellows; I'd have it come to question:
　　　　If he distaste it, let him to my sister,　　　　　15
　　　　Whose mind and mine, I know, in that are one,
　　　　Not to be over-rul'd. Idle old man,
　　　　That still would manage those authorities
　　　　That he hath given away! Now, by my life,
　　　　Old fools are babes again, and must be us'd　　　20
　　　　With checks as flatteries, when they are seen abus'd.
　　　　Remember what I have said.
Osw.　　　　　　　　　Well, Madam.
Gon. And let his knights have colder looks among you;

4. night, he] *F;* night he *Q.*　　　7. upbraids] *Q2, F;* obrayds *Q1.*　　　12. S.D.]
Capell; not in Q, F.　　　14. fellows] *F;* fellow seruants *Q1;* fellow-seruants
Q2.　　　to] *F;* in *Q.*　　　15. di taste] *F;* dislike *Q.*　　　my] *F;* our *Q.*
17–21. Not . . . abus'd] *Q; not in F.*　　　21. checks . . . abus'd] like flatt'rers
when they're seen t'abuse us *Theobald.*　　　22. have said] *F;* tell you *Q.*
Well] *F;* Very well *Q.*

4. *By . . . night*] probably an oath.
Cf. *H8,* I. ii. 213. But Craig explains
the phrase as 'at all times'. Kittredge
points out that Lear swears by day and
night, I. i. 108–9.

5. *flashes*] Cf. *Ham.,* II. i. 33.
crime] offence.

8. *hunting*] In the story of Lear as
told in Layamon's *Brut* the two dukes
covenanted with Lear 'that they would
provide for the king Hawks and
hounds that he might ride over all the
country and live in bliss while he
lived'. Lear's hunting is mentioned
elsewhere in the poem.

10. *come . . . services*] are less serviceable, less duteous to him, than formerly. Cf. II. iv. 243 and *Oth.,* IV. iii. 88.

11. *answer*] be answerable for.

14. *to question*] to be discussed.

15. *distaste*] dislike. Cf. *Troil.,* II. ii.
66. See note to I. iv. 2 *post.*

17. *Idle*] foolish.

21. *With . . . abus'd*] with rebukes as
well as soothing words, when they (the
old fools) are seen to be deluded. Tyrwhitt thought the antecedent of they
was *flatteries,* but Kittredge argued
that this 'interpretation forces one
to emphasize *they,* and that spoils
the metre'. Johnson points out a
play on the words *used* and *abused,*
and he explains: 'Old men must
be treated with checks, when as
they are seen to be deceived with
flatteries.'

What grows of it, no matter; advise your fellows so:
I would breed from hence occasions, and I shall,   25
That I may speak: I'll write straight to my sister
To hold my very course. Prepare for dinner.   [*Exeunt.*

SCENE IV.—[*A Hall in the same.*]

Enter KENT, *disguised.*

Kent. If but as well I other accents borrow,
That can my speech defuse, my good intent
May carry through itself to that full issue
For which I raz'd my likeness. Now, banish'd Kent,
If thou canst serve where thou dost stand condemn'd,   5
So may it come, thy master, whom thou lov'st,
Shall find thee full of labours.

Horns within. Enter LEAR, *Knights, and
Attendants.*

25–6. I would . . . speak] *Q; not in F.*   27. very] *Q; not in F.*   S.D.]
F; Exit Q.

Scene IV
S.D. *A Hall . . . same*] *Capell; not in Q, F.   disguised*] *Rowe; not in Q, F.*
1. well] *Q1;* will *F.*   2. That] *Q, F;* And *Rowe, Pope, Johnson, Theobald.*
defuse] *Q, F;* disuse *Rowe, Pope, Johnson;* diffuse *Theobald;* deface *Capell;*
disguise *conj. Jennens.*   6. So . . . come] *F; not in Q.*   7. labours] *F;*
labour *Q.   Horns within*] *F; not in Q.   Knights*] *Rowe; not in Q, F.   At-*
tendants] *F; not in Q.*

25. *breed*] Cf. *grows* in the previous
line and I. ii. 55, III. vi. 74.
occasions] opportunities. Cf. *Oth.,*
II. i. 246.
26. *straight*] immediately.

Scene IV
2. *defuse*] disorder, confuse, render
indistinct, speak broad, disguise.
Cf. *H5,* v. ii. 61, 'defused attire';
Wiv., IV. iv. 54, 'diffused (i.e. un-
couth) song'. Dyce cites Palsgrave,
Lesclarcissement': '*Dyffuse* harde to be
vnderstande, *diffuse.*' Wright cites
Lyly, *Euphues,* ed. Arber, p. 64:
'defused determination'; and Armin,

Nest of Ninnies, 1880, p. 48: 'it is hard
that the taste of one Apple should
distaste the whole lumpe of this
defused Chaios.'
2–4. *my good . . . likeness*] I may be
able to carry out the good purpose
which made me so disguise myself, i.e.
to attend on the King.
4. *raz'd . . . likeness*] obliterated my
former appearance. As Kent had probably shaved his beard, there may be a
quibble on *raz'd* and *razor.*
6. *So . . . come*] either a parenthetical
wish, referring to Kent's hope of serving his master, or else it may mean 'so
it may happen that'.

Lear. Let me not stay a jot for dinner: go, get it ready.

[*Exit an Attendant.*

How now! what art thou?

Kent. A man, Sir.   10

Lear. What dost thou profess? What would'st thou with
     us?

Kent. I do profess to be no less than I seem; to serve him
     truly that will put me in trust; to love him that is
     honest; to converse with him that is wise, and says   15
     little; to fear judgment; to fight when I cannot
     choose; and to eat no fish.

Lear. What art thou?

Kent. A very honest-hearted fellow, and as poor as the
     King.   20

Lear. If thou be'st as poor for a subject as he is for a King,
     thou art poor enough. What would'st thou?

Kent. Service.

Lear. Who would'st thou serve?

Kent. You.   25

Lear. Dost thou know me, fellow?

Kent. No, Sir; but you have that in your countenance
     which I would fain call master.

Lear. What's that?

Kent. Authority.   30

Lear. What services canst thou do?

8. S.D.] *Malone; not in Q, F.*   15. says] say *Steevens.*   18. art] are *F2.*
21. be'st] *F;* be *Q.*   he is] *Q;* hee's *F.*   22. thou art] *Q2, F;* thar't *Q1.*
24. Who] Whom *F2-4.*   29. What's] What's is *Q3.*   31. services]
service *Q3.*   thou] *Q2, F; not in Q1.*

8. *stay*] wait. Cf. *Gent.,* I. ii. 131.
  jot] moment.
  11. *What . . . profess*] What is your
job? Lear uses *profess* 'in the sense of
trade or *calling*'. Kent replies in the
sense of *assertion* (Delius).
  15. *converse*] consort. Accented on
the first syllable.
  16. *fear judgment*] by an earthly, or a
heavenly, judge. Cf. Ps., i. 6 (cited
Noble, *op. cit.*).
  16–17. *when . . . choose*] when I must.
Cf. *All's W.,* I. i. 158.
  17. *eat no fish*] two explanations:

(*a*) I am a loyal protestant (Warburton). Cf. Marston *The Dutch Courtezan,*
I. ii (ed. Wood, p. 76) : 'Yet I trust I am
none of the wicked that eate fish a
Fridaies.' (*b*) I am no weakling
(Capell). Cf. *2H4,* IV. iii. 99: 'these
demure boys who never come to any
proof; for thin drink doth so over-cool
their bloods, and making many fish
meals'. From *Rom.,* I. i. 36, it seems
possible that Kent's meaning is
indecent.
  27. *countenance*] bearing—not merely
'face' (Kittredge).

Kent. I can keep honest counsel, ride, run, mar a curious
tale in telling it, and deliver a plain message bluntly;
that which ordinary men are fit for, I am qualified in,
and the best of me is diligence.   35

Lear. How old art thou?

Kent. Not so young, Sir, to love a woman for singing, nor
so old to dote on her for anything; I have years on
my back forty-eight.

Lear. Follow me; thou shalt serve me; if I like thee no   40
worse after dinner I will not part from thee yet.
Dinner, ho! dinner! Where's my knave? my Fool?
Go you and call my Fool hither.   [*Exit an Attendant.*

Enter OSWALD.

You, you, sirrah, where's my daughter?

Osw. So please you—   [*Exit.*   45

Lear. What says the fellow there? Call the clotpoll back.
                                        [*Exit a Knight.*
Where's my Fool, ho? I think the world's asleep.

Re-enter Knight.

How now! where's that mongrel?

Knight. He says, my Lord, your daughter is not well.

Lear. Why came not the slave back to me when I call'd   50
him?

Knight. Sir, he answered me in the roundest manner, he
would not.

Lear. He would not!

Knight. My Lord, I know not what the matter is; but, to   55
my judgment, your Highness is not entertain'd with

32. counsel] counsailes *F2–4.*   37. Sir] *F; not in Q.*   40. thou] that
F2.   me; . . . me;] *Rowe;* me, . . . me, *Q, F.*   43. S.D.] *Capell; Enter
Steward (44) Q, F.*   44. You, you] *F;* you *Q.*   45. S.D.] *Dyce; not in Q, F.*
46. S.D.] *Dyce; not in Q, F.*   49. daughter] *Q;* Daughters *F1–2.*   52. me]
not in F3–4.   54. He] *Q2, F;* A *Q.*

32. *keep . . . counsel*] keep an honourable secret.

curious] elaborate, complicated, elegant, nice.

37. *to love*] as to love.

42. *knave*] boy. Cf. I. i. 20.

45. *So please you*] Oswald is carry-

ing out instructions. Cf. I. iii. 13.

46. *clotpoll*] clod-pate, blockhead.
Cf. *Troil.,* II. i. 128, and *Tw.N.,* III. iv.
208.

52. *roundest*] plainest, rudest. Cf.
Ham., III. i. 191.

56. *entertain'd*] treated.

that ceremonious affection as you were wont; there's
a great abatement of kindness appears as well in the
general dependants as in the Duke himself also and
your daughter.   60

Lear. Ha! say'st thou so?

Knight. I beseech you, pardon me, my Lord, if I be mistaken; for my duty cannot be silent when I think
your Highness wrong'd.

Lear. Thou but rememb'rest me of mine own conception: 65
I have perceived a most faint neglect of late; which I
have rather blamed as mine own jealous curiosity
than as a very pretence and purpose of unkindness:
I will look further into't. But where's my Fool? I
have not seen him this two days.   70

Knight. Since my young Lady's going into France, Sir,
the Fool hath much pined away.

Lear. No more of that; I have noted it well. Go you, and
tell my daughter I would speak with her.

                                    [*Exit an Attendant.*

Go you, call hither my Fool.   [*Exit an Attendant.* 75

Re-enter OSWALD.

O! you sir, you, come you hither, sir.
Who am I, sir?

Osw. My Lady's father.

Lear. 'My Lady's father!' my Lord's knave: you whoreson dog! you slave! you cur!   80

58. of kindness] *F; not in Q.*   64. wrong'd] *Q, F;* is wronged *Q2.*   65.
mine] my *F3–4.*   67. mine] my *F4.*   68. purpose] *F;* purport *Q.*
69. my] *F;* this *Q.*   74, 75. S.D.s] *Dyce; not in Q, F.*   75. *Re-enter Oswald*]
Collier; Enter Steward *F; not in Q.*   76. you sir, you] *F1–2;* you sir, you sir *Q;*
you sir *F3–4.*   hither, sir] *F;* hither *Q.*

65. *rememb'rest*] remindest. Cf. *Wint.,*
III. ii. 231.

   conception] idea.

66. *most faint*] hardly perceptible, or,
more probably, dull, languid, cold,
'weary negligence'. Cf. I. iii. 13. In
Leir, 2262, the King speaks of Gonorill's treatment: 'But euery day her
kindnesse did grow cold.'

67. *curiosity*] 'a punctilious jealousy,

resulting from a scrupulous watchful-
ness of his own dignity' (Steevens). Cf.
I. i. 5–6 and I. ii. 4.

68. *very pretence*] an actual intention.
Cf. I. ii. 85.

70. *this*] these.

71–2. *Since . . . away*] By this delicate
stroke Shakespeare gives us an insight
into the characters of Cordelia, Lear,
and the Fool.

Osw. I am none of these, my Lord; I beseech your pardon.
Lear. Do you bandy looks with me, you rascal? [*Striking him.*
Osw. I'll not be strucken, my Lord.
Kent. Nor tripp'd neither, you base foot-ball player.

[*Tripping up his heels.*

Lear. I thank thee, fellow; thou serv'st me, and I'll love   85
thee.
Kent. Come, sir, arise, away! I'll teach you differences:
away, away! If you will measure your lubber's
length again, tarry; but away! Go to; have you
wisdom? [*Exit Oswald.*] So.   90
Lear. Now, my friendly knave, I thank thee: there's
earnest of thy service.   [*Gives Kent money.*

Enter Fool.

Fool. Let me hire him too: here's my coxcomb.

[*Offers Kent his cap.*

Lear. How now, my pretty knave! how dost thou?
Fool. Sirrah, you were best take my coxcomb.   95

81. these] *F;* this *Q.*   your pardon] *F;* you pardon me *Q.*   82. S.D.]
Rowe; not in Q, F.   83. strucken] *F;* struck *Q.*   84. S.D.] *Rowe; not
in Q, F.*   87. arise, away] *F; not in Q.*   89. Go to] *F; not in Q.*   89–
90. have . . . So] *F;* you haue wisedome *Q.*   90. S.D.] *Theobald, subst.*
91. my] *F; not in Q.*   92. *Gives Kent money*] *Capell, subst.*   93. S.D.] *Rowe,
subst.*

82. *bandy*] exchange, hit to and fro, as in the game of tennis. Cf. II. iv. 173 and *Shr.*, v. ii. 172. Cotgrave has: 'To bandy against, at Tennis; and (by metaphor) to pursue with all insolencie.'

83. *strucken*] struck. Cf. *Cor.*, IV. v. 156.

84. *foot-ball*] Football, perhaps suggested by 'bandy' (82), was regarded as a low game in Shakespeare's day. It was played by idle boys in the streets to the great annoyance of the citizens.

87. *I'll . . . differences*] I'll teach you your position, the difference between yourself and the king.

88–9. *measure . . . length*] Cf. *Cym.*, I. ii. 25; *MND.*, III. ii. 429; *Rom.*, III. iii. 70.

89–90. *have . . . wisdom?*] 'Are you in your senses?' Cf. *2H4*, v. v. 49. Or it may simply mean, 'Have you the sense to make yourself scarce?' Schmidt argues that this is not a question, but an imperative. Neither F nor Q has a question mark.

90. *So*] That's right!

92. *earnest*] earnest-money, a small sum paid to secure a bargain, hansel. Cf. *Mac.*, I. iii. 104.

93. *coxcomb*] the cap of the professional fool. Cf. Minshew, *Ductor in Linguas*, 1617: 'Natural idiots and fools have, and still accustom themselves to wear, cock's feathers, or a hat with the neck and head of a cock on the top, with a bell thereon.'

95. *you were best*] you had better. Cf. Speed, *Chronicle*, p. 1136: 'My counsel is that you were best to yield.'

Kent. Why, Fool?

Fool. Why? for taking one's part that's out of favour.
　　Nay, and thou canst not smile as the wind sits,
　　thou'lt catch cold shortly: there, take my coxcomb.
　　Why, this fellow has banish'd two on's daughters, 　　100
　　and did the third a blessing against his will: if thou
　　follow him thou must needs wear my coxcomb.
　　How now, Nuncle! Would I had two coxcombs and
　　two daughters!

Lear. Why, my boy? 　　　　　　　　　　　　　　105

Fool. If I gave them all my living, I'd keep my coxcombs
　　myself. There's mine; beg another of thy daughters.

Lear. Take heed, sirrah; the whip.

Fool. Truth's a dog must to kennel; he must be whipp'd
　　out when the Lady's Brach may stand by th'fire 　　110
　　and stink.

96. *Kent.* Why, Fool?] *Q; Lear.* Why my Boy *F.* 　　97. one's] *F, Q2;*
on's *Q.* 　　that's] that is *F4.* 　　99. thou'lt] *F;* thou't *Q.* 　　100. has]
F; hath *Q.* 　　on's] *Q1, F;* of his *Q2–3.* 　　101. did] *F;* done *Q.* 　　106.
gave] give *F3–4.* 　　all my] *F;* any *Q.* 　　I'd] I'll *Rowe.* 　　coxcombs]
Q1, F; coxcombe *Q2–3, F2–4.* 　　109. Truth's] *F;* Truth is *Q.* 　　dog]
F; dog that *Q.* 　　110. the Lady's] *New Camb. (conj. Letherland);* the Lady
F; Ladie oth'e *Q.*

96. Kent.] wrongly given to Lear
by F.

98. *and*] a common variant of *an*,
meaning if.

smile . . . sits] back the stronger side.
Cf. II. ii. 72–8 *post.*

99. *catch cold*] be turned out of doors;
or, perhaps, it merely means 'it will be
the worse for you.'

100. *banish'd . . . daughters*] This may
mean that Lear had made Goneril and
Regan independent, and so lost their
love and obedience (Capell); but the
Fool deliberately uses the word
banish'd, to glance at Lear's treatment
of Cordelia.

on's] of his.

101. *a blessing . . . will*] By cursing
and banishing Cordelia, Lear had
made her Queen of France, and saved
her from marrying Burgundy.

103. *Nuncle*] contracted from *mine
uncle.* 'It seems to have been the customary appellation of the licensed fool
to his superiors' (Nares).

106. *living*] property. Cf. *Mer.V.*,
v. i. 286.

107. *There's . . . daughters*] 'Thus he
calls Lear a double-dyed fool' (Kittredge).

108. *whip*] Fools were commonly
whipped. Cf. *AYL.*, I. ii. 90 ff.

110. *the Lady's Brach*] Most editors
follow Steevens in reading *Lady, the
brach,*—Lady being a common name
for hound. Cf. *1H4*, III. i. 240. Brach,
in Shakespeare's day, was generally
used as 'a mannerly name for all
hound bitches'. Sir Thomas More,
Comfort against Tribulation, 1573, p.
199: 'I am so cunning that I cannot
tell whether among them a bitch be a
bitch, but as I remember she is no
bitch, but a brach.' Duthie conjectures 'Liar the Brach', though retaining the F reading in his text. He re-

Lear. A pestilent gall to me!

Fool. Sirrah, I'll teach thee a speech.

Lear. Do.

Fool. Mark it, Nuncle: 115
    Have more than thou showest,
    Speak less than thou knowest,
    Lend less than thou owest,
    Ride more than thou goest,
    Learn more than thou trowest,   120
    Set less than thou throwest;
    Leave thy drink and thy whore,
    And keep in-a-door,
    And thou shalt have more
    Than two tens to a score.   125

Kent. This is nothing, Fool.

Fool. Then 'tis like the breath of an unfee'd lawyer; you

---

112. gall] *F;* gull *Q.*   115. Nuncle] *F;* vncle *Q.*   117. less] more
Jennens.   123. in-a-door] *Capell;* in a doore *Q, F;* in dore *F3–4.*   126.
Kent] *F; Lear Q.*   127. 'tis] *F; not in Q; it is F4.*

---

marks: 'It has been implied that Truth is a dog of low social status—the Lady Brach is pictured as of high social status.' Perhaps the antithesis is not between Truth and Falsehood, but between Truth and Flattery. Shakespeare often associates dogs with flatterers.

112. *A . . . me!*] a passionate remembrance of Oswald's insolence (Moberly); 'a plague take me for my folly' in banishing Cordelia (Craig); or a reference to the Fool's satirical gibes (Kittredge). Cf. 'bitter Fool' (135).

gall] irritation, sore, produced by rubbing and chafing. But the word also means 'the secretion of the liver, bile', something intensely bitter. Cf. previous note.

116–23. *Have . . . door*] Florio, *Second Fruites,* pp. 101–5, has some similar rhymed proverbs: 'The bottom of your purse or heart, / To anie man do not empart. / Do not giue your selfe to plaie, / Vnles you purpose to de-

caie . . . / Shun wine, dice, and letchery, / Else will you come to beggery.'

116. *Have . . . showest*] Don't parade your wealth.

117. *Speak . . . knowest*] Be reticent, don't tell all you know.

118. *owest*] ownest. Cf. *R2,* IV. i. 185.

119. *goest*] walkest. Cf. *Sonn.,* cxxx. 11.

120. *Learn . . . trowest*] Don't believe all you hear; or 'Ascertain much, and don't indulge in guessing' (Tovey).

121. *Set . . . throwest*] Don't stake all your winnings at a single throw.

123. *in-a-door*] indoors.

124–5. *And . . . score*] meaning, I suppose, that for each pound one would have more than twenty shillings.

126. *nothing*] Cf. notes to I. i. 86 and I. iv. 127–8.

127. *Then . . . lawyer*] See Appendix, p. 237.

127–8. *you . . . for't*] Cf. *Leir,* 654: 'He lou'd me not, and therfore gaue me nothing.'

gave me nothing for't. Can you make no use of nothing, Nuncle?

Lear. Why no, boy; nothing can be made out of nothing.   130

Fool. [*To Kent.*] Prithee, tell him, so much the rent of his
land comes to: he will not believe a Fool.

Lear. A bitter Fool!

Fool. Dost thou know the difference, my boy, between a
bitter Fool and a sweet one?   135

Lear. No, lad; teach me.

Fool.   That lord that counsell'd thee
                    To give away thy land,
                Come place him here by me,
                    Do thou for him stand: 140
                The sweet and bitter fool
                    Will presently appear;
                The one in motley here,
                    The other found out there.

Lear. Dost thou call me fool, boy?   145

Fool. All thy other titles thou hast given away; that thou
wast born with.

Kent. This is not altogether Fool, my Lord.

Fool. No, faith, lords and great men will not let me; if I
had a monopoly out, they would have part on't: 150

---

128. gave] *F;* give *F3–4.*   for't] for it *Q2–3.*   129. Nuncle] *F;* vncle *Q.*
131. S.D.] *Rowe; not in Q, F.*   134. thou] *F; not in Q.*   135. one] *F;*
foole *Q.*   137–52. That . . . snatching] *Q; not in F.*   150. out] *Q;* on't
Pope.   150–1. on't: and ladies] *Capell;* an't, and Ladies *Q1 corr.;* an't, and
lodes *Q1 uncorr.;* on't, and lodes *Q2–3.*

---

133. *bitter*] sarcastic. Cf. 112 *ante.*

137. *That lord*] Skalliger, a lord in
the old play, who gives advice to Leir
about the division of the kingdom, may
have been in Shakespear's mind here;
but Kittredge thinks the Fool implies
that nobody gave Lear such idiotic
advice.

140. *Do . . . stand*] impersonate
him. Hanmer read 'Or do'; White
argued for 'And do'; the Cambridge editors suggested the line
should read: 'Do thou there for him
stand.'

142. *presently*] at once.

144. *there*] He points at Lear, who is
the bitter fool.

146–7. *thou . . . with*] i.e. Lear was a
born fool.

149. *No . . . me;*] The Fool takes
'altogether fool' to mean not 'entirely
a fool', but 'one who has all the folly
that there is' (Kittredge).

150. *monopoly out*] i.e. one granted.
In spite of the Declaratory Act against
monopolies, passed at the end of Elizabeth's reign, James I constantly
granted them to his needy courtiers,
and there was a great popular outcry
in consequence.

and ladies too, they will not let me have all the fool
to myself; they'll be snatching. Nuncle, give me an
egg, and I'll give thee two crowns.

Lear. What two crowns shall they be?

Fool. Why, after I have cut the egg i'th'middle and eat   155
up the meat, the two crowns of the egg. When thou
clovest thy crown i'th'middle, and gav'st away
both parts, thou bor'st thine ass on thy back o'er
the dirt: thou hadst little wit in thy bald crown
when thou gav'st thy golden one away. If I speak   160
like myself in this let him be whipp'd that first finds
it so.

> *Fools had ne'er less grace in a year;*
> *For wise men are grown foppish,*
> *And know not how their wits to wear,*   165
> *Their manners are so apish.*

Lear. When were you wont to be so full of songs, sirrah?

Fool. I have used it, Nuncle, e'er since thou mad'st thy
daughters thy mothers; for when thou gav'st them
the rod and putt'st down thine own breeches,   170

> *Then they for sudden joy did weep,*
> *And I for sorrow sung,*

151. the] *Q1; not in Q2–3.*   152–3. Nuncle . . . egg] *F;* giue me an egge
Nuncle *Q.*   157. crown] *Q;* Crownes *F.*   158. thine] *F;* thy *Q.*   on
thy] at'h *Q1.*   162. so] sooth *Warburton.*   163. grace] *F;* wit *Q.*
165. *And*] *F;* They *Q.*   to] *F;* doe *Q.*   168. e'er] ere *F;* euer *Q.*
169. mothers] *F;* mother *Q.*   171. *Then they*] *verse Theobald; prose Q, F.*
171–4. *for . . . among*] *verse F; prose Q.*

154. *What . . . be?*] The answer to the
Fool's riddle is obvious, but Lear is
deliberately acting as a stooge.

158–9. *thou . . . dirt*] The Fool refers
to Æsop's fable of the man, his two
sons, and the ass. Warner had retold it
in *Albion's England* (1586), 1602.

161. *like myself*] like a fool, foolishly
outspoken.

162. *so*] i.e. true. The implication is
that Lear himself should be whipped
already.

163–6. Fools . . . apish] Johnson
explains: 'There was never a time
when fools were less in favour than
now, and the reason is they were never

so little wanted, for wise men now
supply their place.' Malone cites Lyly,
Mother Bombie, II. iii (ed. Bond, III,
p. 191): 'I thinke Gentlemen had
neuer lesse wit in a yeere.'

164. foppish] foolish.

166. apish] See Appendix, p. 242.
The word is also used by Armin, *op.
cit.,* p. 49.

168. *used it*] made a practice of it.
Cf. *Ham.,* III. ii. 50.

171–4. Then . . . among] Rollins,
M.L.R., 1920, p. 87, points out that
the Fool is adapting an old ballad:
'Some men for sodayne ioye do wepe, /
And some in sorrow syng: / When that

> *That such a king should play bo-peep,*
> *And go the fools among.*

Prithee, Nuncle, keep a schoolmaster that can   175
teach thy Fool to lie: I would fain learn to lie.

Lear. And you lie, sirrah, we'll have you whipp'd.

Fool. I marvel what kin thou and thy daughters are:
they'll have me whipp'd for speaking true, thou'lt
have me whipp'd for lying; and sometimes I am   180
whipp'd for holding my peace. I had rather be any
kind o'thing than a fool; and yet I would not be
thee, Nuncle; thou hast pared thy wit o'both sides,
and left nothing i'th'middle: here comes one o'the
parings.   185

Enter GONERIL.

Lear. How now, daughter! what makes that frontlet
on? You are too much of late i'th'frown.

Fool. Thou wast a pretty fellow when thou hadst no need
to care for her frowning; now thou art an O without
a figure. I am better than thou art now; I am a   190

174. *fools*] Q; Foole *F1–2*.   176. learn to] *F*; learnto Q *corr.*; learne Q
uncorr.   177. And] *Q1, F*; If *Q2–3*.   sirrah] *F*; *not in* Q.   179.
thou'lt] *F*; thou wilt Q.   180. sometimes] *F*; sometime Q.   182. o']
F; of Q.   183. o'] *F*; a Q.   184. i'th] *F*; in the Q.   o'] *F*; of Q.
187. You] *F*; me thinks you Q.   of late] *F*; alate Q.   189. frowning] *F*;
frowne Q.   now thou] Q *corr., F*; thou thou *Q1 uncorr., Q2–3*.

they lie in daunger depe, / To put
away mournyng.' Steevens compares
a song in Heywood's *Rape of Lucrece*,
1608 (*Works*, ed. Pearson, v. 179):
'Some men for sudden joy gan weep, /
But I for sorrow sing.'

173. play bo-peep] Cotgrave thus
translates *Faire les doux yeux*. Harsnett
uses the phrase metaphorically. See
Appendix, p. 240. The implication is
that Lear has blinded himself, hidden
himself (i.e. abdicated), or played silly
pranks. From Dekker, *Satiromastix* (ed.
Pearson, I. 257), the game seems to
have been more like hide-and-seek
than the modern bo-peep: 'Our
vnhandsome-fac'd Poet does play at
bo-peepes with your Grace, and cryes

"all-hidde" as boyes doe' (cited
Kittredge).

186. *makes*] is doing.

frontlet] Perrett takes this to be a
'generic name for a coronet or small
crown'. Cf. *N.E.D.* But a frontlet was
a band worn either for ornament, or,
at night, to remove wrinkles. Lear is
clearly referring to Goneril's frowning
forehead. Steevens cites *Zepheria*, 1594,
xxvii: 'But now my sunne it fits thou
take thy set, / And vayle thy face with
frownes as with a frontlet.' Wright
compares 'frontier' (*1H4*, I. iii. 19).

189–90. *an . . . figure*] a mere cipher.
Florio, *Second Fruites*, p. 149, uses the
same conceit: 'Doo not you knowe
that nobilitie is now a daies like vnto

Fool, thou art nothing. [*To Goneril.*] Yes, forsooth,
I will hold my tongue; so your face bids me, though
you say nothing.
    Mum, Mum:
    He that keeps nor crust nor crumb,   195
    Weary of all, shall want some.
That's a sheal'd peascod.   [*Pointing to Lear.*

Gon. Not only, Sir, this your all-licens'd Fool,
    But other of your insolent retinue
    Do hourly carp and quarrel, breaking forth   200
    In rank and not-to-be-endured riots. Sir,
    I had thought, by making this well known unto you,
    To have found a safe redress; but now grow fearful,
    By what yourself too late have spoke and done,
    That you protect this course, and put it on   205
    By your allowance; which if you should, the fault
    Would not 'scape censure, nor the redresses sleep,
    Which, in the tender of a wholesome weal,

---

191. S.D.] *Pope; not in Q, F.*   195. nor crust] *F;* neither crust *Q.*   nor
crumb] not crum *F1–2.*   197. S.D.] *Johnson; not in Q, F.*   199. other]
Q, F; others *Johnson.*   201. and . . . Sir] *Craig; without hyphens, Capell;* and
(not . . . riots,) Sir *Q;* and (not . . . endur'd) riots *Sir. F1;* (and . . . endured)
riots *Sir. F2;* (and . . . endured) riots, *Sir F3–4.*   202. known] know *F4.*
205. it] *F; not in Q.*   207. redresses] *F;* redresse *Q.*

---

a cipher of nothing in arithmetick, which if it haue no number added vnto it, it sommes nothing, euen so if there be no valor, ritches, or knowledge ioyned vnto nobilitie, it makes nothing, and is neither regarded nor honoured.'

197. *sheal'd peascod*] shelled peapod. Camden, *Remaines* (ed. 1629, p. 181, cited Perrett) mentions Richard II's device of 'a Pescod branch with the cods open, but the Pease out, as it is vpon his Robe in his Monument at Westminster'.

200. *carp*] find fault, prate.

201. *rank*] gross, excessive. Cf. *Ham.*, I. ii. 136.

203. *safe*] sure. Cf. *3H6*, IV. vii. 52.

204. *too late*] Lear has been tardy in reproving his retinue.

205. *put it on*] instigate it. Cf. *Cor.*, II. iii. 264.

206. *allowance*] approbation (Malone). Cf. *Oth.*, I. i. 128. Huloet, *Dictionary*, 1572, has: 'Allowance, acceptation or estimation.'

206–11 *which . . . proceeding*] If you should do this, I will censure you for it, and take steps to check the riotous behaviour of your knights. My disciplinary measures, due to my desire to have a healthy state, may well offend you; and I should be accused of lacking in filial duty, were it not that everyone would recognize the necessity of my actions. Goneril's speech is deliberately tortuous, but the meaning is clear.

208. *Which*] i.e. the redresses.

tender] strong desire for. Cf. *Gent.*, IV. iv. 145, and *1H4*, V. iv. 49.

Might in their working do you that offence,
Which else were shame, that then necessity   210
Will call discreet proceeding.

Fool. For you know, Nuncle,
    The hedge-sparrow fed the cuckoo so long,
    That it's had it head bit off by it young.
So out went the candle, and we were left darkling.   215

Lear. Are you our daughter?

Gon. I would you would make use of your good wisdom,
Whereof I know you are fraught; and put away
These dispositions which of late transport you
From what you rightly are.   220

Fool. May not an ass know when a cart draws the horse?
Whoop, Jug! I love thee.

Lear. Does any here know me? This is not Lear:
    Does Lear walk thus? speak thus? Where are his
      eyes?
    Either his notion weakens, his discernings   225
    Are lethargied—Ha! waking? 'tis not so.
    Who is it that can tell me who I am?

Fool. Lear's shadow.

210. Which] *F;* that *Q.*   211. Will] *F;* must *Q.*   proceeding] *F;*
proceedings *Q.*   212. know] *F;* trow *Q.*   213–14.] *verse Pope; prose Q, F.*
214. it's had] *F;* it had *Q, F2.*   it head] *Q, F1;* its head *F2–4.*   by it]
F1–2; beit *Q1–2;* be it *Q3;* by it's *F3–4.*   217. I] *F;* Come sir, I *Q.*   your]
F; that *Q.*   219. which] *F;* that *Q.*   transport] *F;* transforme *Q.*
223. Does] *F;* Doth *Q.*   This] *F;* Why this *Q.*   224. Does] *F;* doth *Q.*
225. weakens] *F;* weakness *Q.*   his²] *F;* or his *Q;* or's *Craig (conj. S. Walker).*
226. lethargied—] *Rowe;* Lethergied. *F;* lethergie *Q.*   Ha! waking] *F;*
sleeping or wakeing, ha! sure *Q.*   228.] *assigned to Lear Q.*

213–14. *The ... young*] This couplet
may have been proverbial.

214. *it ... it*] its ... its.

215. *So ... darkling*] Cf. Spenser,
Faerie Queene, II. x. 30: 'But true it is,
that when the oyle is spent, / The light
goes out, and weeke is throwne away; /
So when he had resigned his regiment, / His daughter gan despise his
drouping day.'

218. *fraught*] stored.

219. *dispositions*] states of mind,
temperamental fits.

transport] Cf. *Cor.,* I. i. 77.

221. *May ... horse?*] May not a

Fool see that there is something
obviously wrong, when a daughter
gives instructions to her royal
father?

222. *Whoop ... thee*] possibly, as
Steevens was informed, a quotation
from an old song. Jug is a nickname
for Joan. Presumably there is no connection between this and the more
modern refrain 'Little brown jug,
don't I love thee?'

225. *notion*] intellectual power. Cf.
Mac., III. i. 83.

226. *waking?*] Am I awake?

228. *Lear's shadow*] Cf. *Leir,* IIII:

Lear. I would learn that; for by the marks of sovereignty,
knowledge, and reason, I should be false persuaded   230
I had daughters.
Fool. Which they will make an obedient father.
Lear. Your name, fair gentlewoman?
Gon. This admiration, Sir, is much o'th'savour
Of other your new pranks. I do beseech you   235
To understand my purposes aright:
As you are old and reverend, should be wise.
Here do you keep a hundred knights and squires;
Men so disorder'd, so debosh'd, and bold,
That this our court, infected with their manners,   240
Shows like a riotous inn: epicurism and lust
Makes it more like a tavern or a brothel
Than a grac'd palace. The shame itself doth speak
For instant remedy; be then desir'd

229–32. I ... father] *Q; not in F.*   230. false] halfe *conj. Anon.*   232. they] *Q3;* they, *Q1–2.*   234. This admiration, Sir] *F;* Come, sir, this admiration *Q.*   savour] *Q, F;* fauour *Q3, Capell.*   236. To] *F; not in Q.*   237. should] *Q1, F;* you should *Q2–3; not in Steevens conj.*   238. a] *Q, F;* one *Q2–3.*   239. debosh'd] *F;* deboyst *Q;* debauch'd *Pope.*   242. Makes it] *F;* make *Q.*   or a] *F;* or *Q.*   243. grac'd] *F;* great *Q.*   244. then] *F;* thou *Q.*

'And think me but the shaddow of myselfe.'

229–32. *I . . . father*] These two speeches are omitted by F. Q ascribes *Lear's shadow* to Lear himself; and editors assume that his two speeches have been erroneously run together, with the incorporation of the Fool's intervening words. Nosworthy, however, thinks that Lear repeats the Fool's words as a question. The omission could arise from the repetition of the words, and the propinquity of the three *Lears.* But it is safer to assume that Lear ignores the Fool's remark, and follows his own train of thought.

230. *false*] i.e. falsely. Perhaps we should hyphen *false-persuaded.* Shakespeare has 'false-derived' (*2H4,* iv. i. 190), 'false-played' (*Ant.,* iv. xiv. 19).

232. *Which*] i.e. *whom,* relating to the 'I' of Lear's speech.

234. *admiration*] affected astonishment.

235. *other your*] other of your.

237. *should*] Q2 inserts *you* before this word, but it can be understood from the preceding clause.

239. *disorder'd*] disorderly.

debosh'd] a variant of *debauched.* Cf. *All's W.,* ii. iii. 145, and Cotgrave, who thus translates *desbauché.* See Appendix, p. 236.

241. *Shows*] appears. Cf. *Cor.,* iv. v. 68.

epicurism] gluttony, riotous living. Cf. Appendix, p. 236.

242. *tavern . . . brothel*] *tavern* refers to *epicurism* and *brothel* to *lust.*

243. *grac'd*] honourable, the abode of stately decorum, 'graced with the presence of a sovereign' (Warburton).

244. *desir'd*] requested.

By her, that else will take the thing she begs,   245
A little to disquantity your train;
And the remainders, that shall still depend,
To be such men as may besort your age,
Which know themselves and you.

Lear.   Darkness and devils!
Saddle my horses; call my train together.   250
Degenerate bastard! I'll not trouble thee:
Yet have I left a daughter.

Gon. You strike my people, and your disorder'd rabble
Make servants of their betters.

Enter ALBANY.

Lear. Woe, that too late repents; O! Sir, are you come?   255
Is it your will? Speak, Sir. Prepare my horses.
Ingratitude, thou marble-hearted fiend,
More hideous, when thou show'st thee in a child,
Than the sea-monster.

Alb.   Pray, Sir, be patient.

Lear. [*To Goneril.*] Detested kite! thou liest.   260

247. remainders] *F;* remainder *Q.*   249. Which] *F;* that *Q1;* And *Q2–3.*
254. S.D.] *F; Enter Duke Q.*   255. Woe] *F;* We *Q.*   repents] *F;*
repent's *Q1;* repent's vs *Q2–3.*   O . . . come?] *Q; not in F.*   256. Speak,
Sir] *F;* that wee *Q.*   my] *F;* any *Q.*   259. *Alb.* Pray . . . patient] *F;*
not in *Q.*   260. *Lear*] *F; not in Q.*   S.D.] *Rowe; not in Q, F.*   liest] *F;*
list *Q1;* lessen *Q2–3.*

246. *disquantity*] reduce the size of.
247. *remainders*] those who remain.
Cf. *Cym.*, I. i. 129.
    depend] attend you as dependants.
248. *besort*] suit. Cf. *Oth.*, I. iii. 239.
255. *Woe, that*] woe to him that.
Florio, *Second Fruites,* p. 165, gives the
proverb: 'Yet, but too late repents the
ratt, / If once her taile be caught by
the cat.'
257. *marble-hearted*] Cf. 'marble-
breasted' (*Tw.N.*, v. i. 127).
259. *the sea-monster*] 'the' is the
generic article (Kittredge). Lear is not
referring to any specific monster. Cf.
Mer.V., III. ii. 57. Upton suggests that
the reference is to the hippopotamus,
a symbol of impiety and ingratitude.
Plutarch, *Morals* (tr. P. Holland),

p. 1300, mentions a picture in the
temple of Minerva at Sais, in which is
the figure of a river-horse, denoting
'murder, impudence, violence, and
injustice'. But the hippo is a river-
monster, not a sea-monster. Other
editors suggest that Lear was referring
to the whale. Craig argues that Shakespeare was thinking of those monsters
of classical antiquity slain by Hercules
and Perseus.
260. *kite*] Armstrong, *Shakespeare's
Imagination,* 1946, pp. 12, 17, points
out that to Shakespeare the kite 'is a
despicable creature symbolic of cow-
ardice, meanness, cruelty and death',
and he shows that a reference to the
bird is normally accompanied by
allusions to bed, death, spirits, birds,

My train are men of choice and rarest parts,
That all particulars of duty know,
And in the most exact regard support
The worships of their name. O most small fault,
How ugly didst thou in Cordelia show!   265
Which, like an engine, wrench'd my frame of
    nature
From the fix'd place, drew from my heart all love,
And added to the gall. O Lear, Lear, Lear!
Beat at this gate, that let thy folly in,   [*Striking his head.*
And thy dear judgment out! Go, go, my people.   270
                        [*Exeunt Kent and Knights.*

Alb. My Lord, I am guiltless, as I am ignorant
Of what hath moved you.

Lear.   It may be so, my Lord.
Hear, Nature, hear! dear Goddess, hear!
Suspend thy purpose, if thou didst intend
To make this creature fruitful!   275
Into her womb convey sterility!
Dry up in her the organs of increase,
And from her derogate body never spring
A babe to honour her! If she must teem,

261. train are] *F;* traine, and *Q.*   266. Which] *F;* That *Q.*   268. Lear,
Lear, Lear!] *F;* Lear, Lear! *Q.*   269. S.D.] *Pope; not in Q, F.*   270.
S.D.] *New Camb.*   272. Of . . . you] *F; not in Q.*   273. Hear, Nature]
F; Hark, Nature *Q.*   Goddess, hear!] *F;* Goddesse *Q.*

and food. In the present context we
have 'marble-hearted' (257), 'devils'
(249), and 'epicurism' (241).

261. *choice*] choicest, the superlative
being understood from 'rarest'.

263–4. *And . . . name*] and are most
particular in living up to the honourable reputation they have earned.

263. *in . . . regard*] the smallest
details. Cf. *Ham.*, II. ii. 79.

264. *worships*] honour. 'Abstract
nouns are often pluralized when they
refer to more than one person'
(Kittredge).

266. *engine*] Edwards and later
critics assume that this is the rack; but
Kittredge points out that the rack does

not wrench the human frame *from its
fixed place,* and suggests that the 'figure
is that of a building that is thrown off
its foundation ("the fix'd place") by a
powerful mechanical contrivance.'
Maxwell suggests (privately) that 'the
picture called up by the passage, as a
whole, is rather of Lear's frame being
prised apart, once a lever has been
introduced far enough to get purchase.' He compares I. i. 168–9.

278. *derogate*] debased, degraded.
Cf. *Cym.*, II. i. 48. The word, like
'sterility' (276) and 'disnatur'd' (281),
is used by Florio. Cf. Appendix, p.
236.

279. *teem*] have offspring.

Create her child of spleen, that it may live   280
And be a thwart disnatur'd torment to her!
Let it stamp wrinkles in her brow of youth,
With cadent tears fret channels in her cheeks,
Turn all her mother's pains and benefits
To laughter and contempt, that she may feel   285
How sharper than a serpent's tooth it is
To have a thankless child! Away, away!   [*Exit.*

Alb. Now, Gods that we adore, whereof comes this?
Gon. Never afflict yourself to know more of it:
But let his disposition have that scope   290
As dotage gives it.

Re-enter LEAR.

Lear. What! fifty of my followers at a clap;
Within a fortnight!
Alb.   What's the matter, Sir?
Lear. I'll tell thee. [*To Goneril.*] Life and death! I am
 masham'd
That thou hast power to shake my manhood thus,   295
That these hot tears, which break from me perforce,

---

281. thwart] *F;* thourt *Q.*   disnatur'd] *F;* disuetur'd *Q1–2;* disventur'd *Q3.*
283. cadent] *F;* accent *Q;* candent *Warburton.*   285. that . . . feel] *F, Q2;*
that shee may feele, that she may feele *Q1.*   287. Away, away!] *F;* goe,
goe, my people? *Q.*   S.D.] *F; not in Q.*   289. more of it] *F;* the cause *Q;*
of it *F2–4.*   291. As] *F;* That *Q.*   S.D.] *F; not in Q.*   293. What's] *F;*
What is *Q.*   296. which] *F;* that *Q.*

---

280. *child of spleen*] a child consisting
only of spleen.

281. *thwart*] cross-grained, perverse.
disnatur'd] without natural affection.
Steevens quotes Daniel, *Hymen's
Triumph,* II. iv. 89: 'I am not so disnatured a man, / Nor so ill borne, to
disesteeme her loue.'

283. *cadent*] falling. Perhaps Shakespeare's coinage.
fret] wear away.

284. *her . . . pains*] Goneril's maternal
cares.

286. *How . . . tooth*] Malone compares Ps., cxl. 3. 'They have sharpened
their tongues like a Serpent.'

288. *Gods . . . adore*] Empson, *The
Structure of Complex Words,* p. 130, comments: 'Perhaps implying that Nature
was not one of the regular gods and
should not be prayed to'.

290. *disposition*] humour.

291. *As*] The relative construction
'that . . . as' is found elsewhere in
Shakespeare (cf. Abbott, 280), and
there is no need to adopt the Q reading.

292. *fifty*] See Introduction, p.
xxxi.
at a clap] Shakespeare could have
found the phrase in Harsnett. See
Appendix, p. 240.

Should make thee worth them. Blasts and fogs upon
  thee!
Th'untented woundings of a father's curse
Pierce every sense about thee! Old fond eyes,
Beweep this cause again, I'll pluck ye out,   300
And cast you, with the waters that you loose,
To temper clay. Yea, is't come to this?
Ha! Let it be so: I have another daughter,
Who, I am sure, is kind and comfortable:
When she shall hear this of thee, with her nails   305
She'll flay thy wolvish visage. Thou shalt find
That I'll resume the shape which thou dost think
I have cast off for ever.   [*Exit.*

Gon. Do you mark that?

Alb. I cannot be so partial, Goneril,   310
To the great love I bear you,—

Gon. Pray you, content. What, Oswald, ho!
[*To the Fool.*] You, sir, more knave than fool, after
  your master.

Fool. Nuncle Lear, Nuncle Lear! tarry, take the Fool
  with thee.   315

---

297. thee . . . Blasts] *F;* the worst blasts *Q.*   297–8. upon thee! / Th'untented]
F; vpon the vntender *Q uncorr.*, *Q2–3;* vpon the vntented *Q corr.*   299. Pierce]
Q corr., F; Peruse *Q uncorr., Q2–3.*   thee! Old] *F;* the old *Q.*   300. this
cause] *Q, F1;* thee once *F2–4.*   ye] *F;* you *Q.*   301. cast you] *F;* you cast *Q.*
loose] *F1–2, Staunton;* make *Q;* lose *F3–4.*   302. Yea . . . this?] *Q1;* Yea, is it
. . . this? *Q2–3; not in F.*   303. Ha! Let it be so] *F; not in Q.*   I have another]
F; Yet haue I left a *Q;* yet I have left a *Steevens.*   304. Who] *F;* Whom *Q.*
308. ever] *F;* euer, thou shalt I warrant thee *Q.*   S.D.] *Q2, F; not in Q1.*
309. that?] *F;* that my Lord *Q.*   311. you,—] *Theobald;* you. *F;* you, *Q.*
312. Pray you, content.] *F;* come sir no more *Q.*   What, Oswald, ho!] *F; not
in Q.*   313. You, sir] *F;* you *Q.*   314. take] *F;* and take *Q.*   315–16. with
thee. A] *F;* with a *Q.*

---

298. *Th'untented woundings*] wounds
too deep to be cleaned with a *tent*, a
roll of lint.

299. *fond*] foolish.

300. *Beweep*] Cf. *Sonn.*, xxix. 2. The
meaning is 'If you weep for'.

301. *loose*] There is no good reason
for altering the F reading; for though
loose is a frequent spelling of *lose*, the
word does not certainly mean that
here. Kittredge interprets: 'waste—

since these tears are of no avail'.
Staunton, retaining *loose*, explains it as
'discharge', as in the phrase 'to loose
an arrow'. But the word can also mean
'emit', and this would seem to be the
sense here. There may, however, be a
quibble on *loose* and *lose*.

304. *comfortable*] comforting, ready
to give comfort. Cf. *All's W.*, I. i.
86.

314–15. *take . . . thee*] There is a

             A fox, when one has caught her,
             And such a daughter,
             Should sure to the slaughter,
             If my cap would buy a halter;
             So the Fool follows after.   [*Exit.*   320
Gon. This man hath had good counsel. A hundred knights!
       'Tis politic and safe to let him keep
       At point a hundred knights; yes, that on every dream,
       Each buzz, each fancy, each complaint, dislike,
       He may enguard his dotage with their powers,   325
       And hold our lives in mercy. Oswald, I say!
Alb. Well, you may fear too far.
Gon.   Safer than trust too far.
       Let me still take away the harms I fear,
       Not fear still to be taken: I know his heart.
       What he hath utter'd I have writ my sister;   330
       If she sustain him and his hundred knights,
       When I have show'd th'unfitness,—

                 Re-enter OSWALD.

                           How now, Oswald!
       What, have you writ that letter to my sister?
Osw. Ay, madam.
Gon. Take you some company, and away to horse: 335
       Inform her full of my particular fear;

320. S.D.] *F; not in Q.*   321–32. This . . . unfitness] *F; not in Q.*   331. she]
F; she'll *F3–4.*   332. unfitness,—] *Rowe;* vnfitnesse. *F.*   S.D.] *F; not in Q.*
How now, Oswald] *F;* What Oswald, ho. *Oswald.* Here Madam *Q.*   333.
that] *F;* this *Q.*   334. Ay] I *F;* Yes *Q.*   336. fear] *F;* feares *Q.*

double meaning in this: (i) take me
with you, (ii) take the epithet 'fool'
with you. Kittredge remarks that this
was a regular farewell gibe.

318. *Should sure*] should certainly be
sent.

319, 320. *halter . . . after*] pronounced
hauter and auter. Cf. Ellis, *English
Pronunciation,* II. 193–201.

323. *At point*] in armed readiness.
Cf. *Ham.,* I. ii. 200.

324. *buzz*] rumour. Cf. Chapman
The Widow's Tears, II. i (ed. Pearson,
II. 24): 'Thinke 'twas but a Buzz

deuis'd by him to set your braines a
work.' See also *Ham.,* IV. v. 90:
'buzzers'.

325. *enguard*] protect. Cf. 'ensteep'
(*Oth.,* II. i. 70), 'englut' (*Oth.,* I. iii. 57),
and 'engirt' (*2H4,* v. i. 99).

326. *in mercy*] in jeopardy. Cf. the
legal term *In misericordia.*

328. *still*] always.

329. *Not . . . taken*] rather than continue in the fear of being overtaken by
harm.

336. *particular*] own, personal, individual.

And thereto add such reasons of your own
As may compact it more. Get you gone,
And hasten your return.   [*Exit Oswald.*

                    No, no, my Lord,
This milky gentleness and course of yours   340
Though I condemn not, yet, under pardon,
You are much more attax'd for want of wisdom
Than prais'd for harmful mildness.

Alb. How far your eyes may pierce I cannot tell:
Striving to better, oft we mar what's well.   345

Gon. Nay, then—

Alb. Well, well; th'event.   [*Exeunt.*

---

339. hasten] *Q corr., F; after Q uncorr., Q2–3.*   S.D.] *Rowe; not in Q, F.*   No
no] *F; now Q.*   340. milky] *Q corr., F; mildie Q uncorr., Q2–3.*   341.
condemn] *F; dislike Q; condemn it Pope.*   342. You are] *F2–4; Y'are Q;
Your are F1.*   attax'd for] *Duthie (conj. Greg); alapt Q uncorr., Q2–3; attaskt
for Q corr.; at task for F.*   343. prais'd] *F; praise Q.*   345. better, oft] *F;
better ought Q.*   347. th'event] *the 'uent F; the euent Q.*

338. *compact*] confirm, make substantial, fortify. Cotgrave has: '*Affermir*; to strengthen, fortifie, confirm, assure, compact.'

340. *This . . . yours*] this mild and gentle course of action of yours—hendiadys. Tovey compares *John*, v. ii. 133.

milky] Cf. *Mac.*, i. v. 18.

341. *condemn not*] Pope and most editors insert 'it' between these words. This regularizes the metre; but as Abbott (*483) points out, the voice can linger hesitatingly on 'yet' if the F reading is retained.

342. *attax'd*] Greg's emendation (*Variants*, pp. 141–2, 153–5). He suggests that the copy for Q had *atatxt*: this was misread as *alapt* by the compositor; the corrector emended to

attaskt: and this was emended in the F to *at task*. H. W. Crundell, *N.Q.*, 26 Jan. 1935, suggests *attach'd*, meaning *accused*, and cites from *N.E.D.* a quotation from Nashe: 'They shall not easily be attached of any notable absurditie.' The main objection to the F reading is that a past participle is needed, or expected, to balance *praised*. None of the three readings ('attaskt', 'at task for' and 'ataxt') are to be found elsewhere, but *attax'd* is a plausible Shakespearian coinage.

343. *harmful mildness*] dangerous lenity.

345. *Striving . . . well*] Cf. 'let well alone' and *Sonn.*, ciii. 9–10.

347. *th'event*] Let us see what happens.

SCENE V.—[*Court before the Same.*]

Enter LEAR, KENT, *and Fool.*

Lear. Go you before to Gloucester with these letters.
Acquaint my daughter no further with any thing you
know than comes from her demand out of the letter.
If your diligence be not speedy I shall be there afore
you.   5

Kent. I will not sleep, my Lord, till I have delivered your
letter.   [*Exit.*

Fool. If a man's brains were in's heels, were't not in
danger of kibes?

Lear. Ay, boy.   10

Fool. Then, I prithee, be merry; thy wit shall not go slip-
shod.

Lear. Ha, ha, ha!

Fool. Shalt see thy other daughter will use thee kindly;

Scene v

S.D. *Court . . . Same*] Capell.   *Enter . . . Fool*] Q*2–3*; *Enter Lear* Q*1*; *Enter Lear,*
Kent, Gentleman, and Fool F.   4. afore] F; before Q.   8. brains] Q, F;
brain *Pope.*   were] where Q*1*.   in's] F; in his Q, F*3–4*.   were't] *Rowe;*
wert Q, F.   11. not] F; ne'er Q.

1. *Gloucester*] i.e. the town of that name, near which the residence of the Duke was.

these letters] this letter. Cf. 3 *post.*

3. *than . . . letter*] than the perusal of the letter suggests to her to ask you.

demand] question.

out of] suggested by.

8. *If . . . heels*] Armin, *op. cit.*, p. 56, speaking of 'the cleane fooles of this world', says 'that the braine is now lodged in the foote, and therevpon comes it that many make their head their foote'. Cf. III. ii. 31–4.

brains] Furness takes the word to be used as a singular, *brains* and *brain* being used more or less interchangeably.

were't] it = his brain.

9. *kibes*] chilblains, chapped heels, cf. *Ham.*, v. i. 153; and Beaumont and Fletcher, *Love's Cure*, II. i. 120: 'scabs,

chilblains, and kib'd heels'. Kibby is used in Devonshire and Cornwall for *sore, chapped* (cf. Halliwell, *Dictionary of Archaic and Provincial Words*, 1878). The Fool is referring to Kent's promise to be speedy. Kittredge compares Hoccleve, *Male Regle*, 232, 'No more than hir wit were in hire heele'.

11–12. *thy . . . slip-shod*] You will never have to wear slippers because of chilblains, for you show you have no wit, even in your heels, in undertaking your journey to Regan.

slip-shod] slippered, in slip-shoes or slippers. Cf. Jonson, *Alchemist*, I. i. 46: 'Your feete in mouldy slippers, for your kibes'.

14. *kindly*] a play on the two senses of the word: (i) affectionately, (ii) after her kind, according to her nature. Cf. *Ant.*, v. ii. 264.

     for though she's as like this as a crab's like an apple, 15
     yet I can tell what I can tell.

Lear. What canst tell, boy?

Fool. She will taste as like this as a crab does to a crab.
     Thou canst tell why one's nose stands i'th'middle
     on's face? 20

Lear. No.

Fool. Why, to keep one's eyes of either side's nose, that
     what a man cannot smell out, he may spy into.

Lear. I did her wrong,—

Fool. Canst tell how an oyster makes his shell? 25

Lear. No.

Fool. Nor I neither; but I can tell why a snail has a house.

Lear. Why?

Fool. Why, to put's head in; not to give it away to his
     daughters, and leave his horns without a case. 30

Lear. I will forget my nature. So kind a father! Be my
     horses ready?

Fool. Thy asses are gone about 'em. The reason why the
     seven stars are no mo than seven is a pretty reason.

Lear. Because they are not eight? 35

Fool. Yes, indeed: thou would'st make a good Fool.

---

15. she's] she is *Q2–3*.   crab's] *F;* crab is *Q.*   16. can tell what] *F;*
con what *Q.*   17. What . . . boy?] *F;* Why, what canst tell, my boy? *Q.*
18. She will] *F;* sheel *Q.*   does] *F;* doth *Q.*   19. Thou canst] *F;* canst
thou *F3–4;* canst not *Q.*   stands] stande *Q1.*   20. on's] *F;* of his *Q.*
22. one's] *F;* his *Q.*   of] *F;* on *Q.*   side's] *Q1, F;* side his *Q2–3.*   23.
he] a *Q1.*   29. put's] *F;* put his *Q.*   away to] away unto *Q2–3.*
30. daughters] *F;* daughter *Q.*   33. 'em] *F;* them *Q.*   34. mo] *F;* more
Q, F4.   36. indeed] *F; not in Q.*

---

15. *she*] Regan.

this] Goneril.

as like . . . apple] i.e. she is like her
in appearance. Wright compares
Lyly, *Euphues*, ed. Arber, p. 120: 'The
sower Crabbe hath the shew of an
Apple as well as the sweet Pippin.'

20. *on's*] of his.

22. *of*] on. Cf. *Shr.*, IV. i. 71: 'Both of
one horse'.

side's] side of his.

27. *snail*] See note to III. iv. 152.

29. *put's*] put his.

30. *horns*] 'The Fool does not mean
to call Lear a cuckold: he simply
accepts horns as the inevitable adorn-
ment of married men' (Kittredge).

31. *forget . . . nature*] i.e. cease to be
a kind father.

33–4. *the seven stars*] the Pleiades. Cf.
1H4, I. ii. 16. See Amos, v. 8 and Job,
xxxviii. 31, marginal note in A.V. to
Pleiades: 'Cimah or the seven stars'.
Cf. note to III. iv. 152.

34. *mo*] more.

pretty] apt, neat.

Lear. To take't again perforce! Monster Ingratitude!

Fool. If thou wert my Fool, Nuncle, I'd have thee beaten
　　for being old before thy time.

Lear. How's that?　　　　　　　　　　　　　　　　40

Fool. Thou should'st not have been old till thou hadst
　　been wise.

Lear. O! let me not be mad, not mad, sweet heaven;
　　Keep me in temper; I would not be mad!

Enter Gentleman.

How now! Are the horses ready?　　　　　　　45

Gent. Ready, my Lord.

Lear. Come, boy.

Fool. She that's a maid now, and laughs at my departure,
　　Shall not be a maid long, unless things be cut shorter.

　　　　　　　　　　　　　　　　　　　　[Exeunt.

38. thou wert] you wert *F2;* you were *F3–4.*　　41. till] *F;* before *Q.*　　43.
not mad] *F; not in Q.*　　heaven;] *F;* heauen! I would not be mad *Q.*
44. S.D.] *Theobald; not in Q, F.*　　45. How now!] *F; not in Q.*　　48. that's a]
F; that is *Q;* that is a *Capell.*　　49. unless] *F;* except *Q.*

37. *To . . . perforce*] Either he is, as
Johnson suggests, 'meditating on his
resumption of royalty', perhaps with
the help of Cornwall and Regan (cf.
I. iv. 306–8); or he is thinking of
Goneril's monstrous ingratitude in
taking away the privileges she had
agreed to grant him (Steevens).

43. *mad*] the first premonition.

44. *in temper*] in my normal condition of mind.

48–9. *She . . . shorter*] addressed to the
audience. Several editors assume that
Shakespeare was not responsible for
the couplet. The maid who sees only
the funny side of the Fool's gibes, and
does not realize that Lear is going on a
tragic journey is such a simpleton that
she won't know how to preserve her
virginity. The rhyme *departure–shorter*
was accurate in Elizabethan pronunciation. The word *departure* is a
homonymic pun.

ACT II

SCENE I.—[*A Court within the Castle of the Earl of Gloucester.*]

Enter EDMUND *and* CURAN, *meeting.*

Edm. Save thee, Curan.

Cur. And you, sir. I have been with your father, and given him notice that the Duke of Cornwall and Regan his Duchess will be here with him this night.

Edm. How comes that? 5

Cur. Nay, I know not. You have heard of the news abroad? I mean the whisper'd ones, for they are yet but ear-bussing arguments.

Edm. Not I: pray you, what are they?

Cur. Have you heard of no likely wars toward, 'twixt the 10 Dukes of Cornwall and Albany?

Edm. Not a word.

Cur. You may do then, in time. Fare you well, sir. [*Exit.*

Edm. The Duke be here to-night! The better! best!
This weaves itself perforce into my business. 15
My father hath set guard to take my brother;

ACT II

Scene i

S.D. *A Court . . . Gloucester*] Malone; *not in* Q, F. *Enter . . . meeting*] Q1, *subst.;*
Enter Bastard and Curan, severally F. 2. you] Q; your F1. 3. Regan] F;
not in Q. 4. this] F; to Q. 7. they] F; there Q. 8. ear-bussing] Q;
eare-kissing F. 10–12. Have . . . word] Q1, F; *not in* Q2–3. 10. toward]
F; towards Q1. the] F; the two Q1. 13. do] F; *not in* Q. S.D.]
F; *not in* Q.

1. *Save thee*] God save thee—a common salutation.

8. *ear-bussing*] ear-kissing, the F reading, has the same meaning, but is probably a sophistication. Collier suggests that a quibble may have been intended on *bussing* (kissing), and *buzzing* (whispering). Cf. i. iv. 324.

arguments] subjects of conversation.

10. *toward*] impending. Cf. iii. iii. 19 and iv. vi. 206.

14. *The better!*] so much the better.

And I have one thing, of a queasy question,
Which I must act. Briefness and Fortune, work!
Brother, a word; descend: brother, I say!

Enter EDGAR.

My father watches: O Sir! fly this place;   20
Intelligence is given where you are hid;
You have now the good advantage of the night.
Have you not spoken 'gainst the Duke of Cornwall?
He's coming hither, now, i'th'night, i'th'haste,
And Regan with him; have you nothing said   25
Upon his party 'gainst the Duke of Albany?
Advise yourself.
Edg.   I am sure on't, not a word.
Edm. I hear my father coming; pardon me;
In cunning I must draw my sword upon you;
Draw; seem to defend yourself; now quit you well.   30
Yield; come before my father. Light, ho! here!
Fly, brother. Torches! torches! So, farewell. [*Exit Edgar.*
Some blood drawn on me would beget opinion
                              [*Wounds his arm.*

18. I must act] *F; must aske Q.*   work] *F; helpe Q.*   19. S.D.] *So
Theobald; at 15 Q1; at 18 Q2–3, F.*   20. Sir] *F; not in Q.*   23. 'gainst]
against *Q2–3.*   Cornwall?] *F; Cornwall ought Q.*   26. 'gainst] *F;*
against *Q.*   27. yourself] *F; your- Q.*   29. cunning] *F; crauing Q.*
30. Draw] *F; not in Q.*   31. ho] *F; not in Q.*   32. brother] *F; brother flie
Q.*   torches!] *not in F2–4.*   S.D.] *F; not in Q.*   33. S.D.] *Rowe; not in Q, F.*

17. *of . . . question*] of a kind that
requires careful handling, if he is not
to make a mess of it.

queasy] sickly, liable to vomit.

18. *Briefness*] promptitude, immediate action, speed. Cf. *Per.*, v. ii. 280.

24. *i'th'haste*] in great haste. For
instances of the use of the definite
article in adverbial phrases, see
Abbott, 91.

26. *Upon his party*] on his side; not
against him (as in 23 *ante*), but against
Albany. Schmidt gives several instances where the phrase means 'upon
the side of'. Cf. *John*, I. i. 34; *R2*, III. ii.
203; *Cor.*, I. i. 238. It is unlikely, therefore, that the passage means 'reflecting
upon his party, which is soon to be

opposed to Albany in the coming
struggle'. Craig, however, cites *Mac.*,
IV. iii. 131: 'My first false speaking /
Was this upon myself'—where *upon*
means *against*.

27. *Advise yourself*] consider. Cf.
Tw.N., IV. ii. 102.

on't] of it.

29. *In cunning*] to avoid the appearance of collusion.

30. *quit you well*] give a good account
of yourself, fight well. Cf. 1 Sam., iv. 9:
'Be strong, and quit yourselves like
men, and fight.'

31. *Yield*] spoken loudly, so as to be
overheard.

33–4. *beget…endeavour*] make people
think I have had a desperate fight.

Of my more fierce endeavour: I have seen drunkards
Do more than this in sport. Father! father!   35
Stop, stop! No help?

Enter GLOUCESTER, *and Servants with torches.*

Glou.   Now, Edmund, where's the villain?
Edm. Here stood he in the dark, his sharp sword out,
    Mumbling of wicked charms, conjuring the moon
    To stand auspicious mistress.
Glou.   But where is he?
Edm. Look, Sir, I bleed.
Glou.   Where is the villain, Edmund?   40
Edm. Fled this way, Sir, when by no means he could—
Glou. Pursue him, ho! Go after.   [*Exeunt some Servants.*
                    'By no means' what?
Edm. Persuade me to the murther of your lordship;
    But that I told him, the revenging Gods
    'Gainst parricides did all the thunder bend;   45
    Spoke with how manifold and strong a bond
    The child was bound to th'father; Sir, in fine,
    Seeing how loathly opposite I stood
    To his unnatural purpose, in fell motion,

36. *and . . . torches*] *F; not in Q.*   where's] *F; where is Q.*   38. Mumbling]
F; warbling *Q.*   39. stand] *F;* stand's *Q1;* stand his *Q2–3.*   41. Sir,
when] *Q, F;* sir. When *Capell.*   could—] *Q;* could. *F1.*   42. ho!] *F;
not in Q.*   S.D.] *Dyce; not in Q, F.*   43. to the] to *F3–4.*   44. revenging]
F; reuengiue *Q.*   45. the thunder] *F;* their thunders *Q.*   47. in] *F;*
in a *Q.*   49. in] *F;* with *Q.*

34–5. *I . . . sport*] Young gallants,
under the influence of drink, would
wound themselves in order to pledge
the health of their mistresses in blood
mingled with their drink. See, e.g.,
Jonson, *Cynthia's Revels,* IV. i. 200–9:
'I would see how *Loue* could worke . . .
by letting this gallant expresse himselfe . . . with stabbing himselfe and
drinking healths, and writing lan-
guishing letters in his bloud.' Kittredge
cites *The Man in the Moone,* 1609 (ed.
Halliwell, p. 43): 'He hath let his
owne blood . . . and quaffed an health
thereof in praise of his mistresse.'
38. *Mumbling . . . charms*] Edmund

plays on Gloucester's superstitions.
39. *auspicious mistress*] The same
phrase is used in *All's W.,* III. iii. 8.
40. *I bleed*] Edmund must gain time
to allow Edgar to escape; he does not
wish to be confronted with him until
Gloucester is convinced of his guilt.
44. *that*] when that, 'when' being
understood from 41 *ante.* Cf. I. i. 167,
where That = since that.
45. *bend*] aim.
48. *loathly opposite*] bitterly opposed
(Kittredge).
49. *fell*] deadly, fierce.
    motion] thrust—a fencing term. Cf.
Tw.N., III. iv. 303.

With his prepared sword he charges home   50
My unprovided body, lanch'd mine arm:
And when he saw my best alarum'd spirits
Bold in the quarrel's right, roused to th'encounter,
Or whether gasted by the noise I made,
Full suddenly he fled.
Glou.   Let him fly far: 55
Not in this land shall he remain uncaught;
And found—dispatch. The noble Duke my master,
My worthy arch and patron, comes to-night:
By his authority I will proclaim it,
That he which finds him shall deserve our thanks,   60

51. lanch'd] *Q;* latch'd *F;* lanced *Theobald.*   52. And when] *F;* But when
Q; But whe'r *Furness (conj. Staunton).*   53. quarrel's right] *Q2–3, F;* quarrels,
rights *Q1.*   54. gasted] 'ghasted *Jennens;* gaster'd *conj. Craig.*   55. Full] *F;*
but *Q.*   58. worthy] worth *F4.*

50. *prepared*] unsheathed and ready.
Cf. *Rom.,* I. i. 116.

charges home] makes a home thrust at.

51. *unprovided*] unprotected. Cf. *R3,*
III. ii. 75.

lanch'd] pierced, wounded, the old
form of *lanced.* Wright quotes *Holly-
band, French Dictionary,* 1593: 'Poindre,
to stick, to lanch.' Duthie defends
latch'd, the F reading, which could
mean 'catch', 'to pull or strike swiftly
off, out, up'. He cites Stewart,
Cronicles (1858), 383: 'Lymnis war
lachit hard of be the kne.' Here *lachit*
means 'struck'. But even if Shakespeare read Stewart when writing
Macbeth there is no evidence that he
had read it before he wrote *King Lear,*
and no evidence that the word was
used with this meaning in England
in Shakespeare's time. The meaning
'caught' would give tolerable sense,
but the Q reading gives a better sense
it implies that Edgar had drawn blood.
The corrector might easily misread
lāch'd.

52. *And*] The Q reading 'But' is
more logical, perhaps; but Edmund is
feigning agitation. See next note.

when] Staunton's suggestion, 'whe'r'
= whether, adopted by Furness, is

attractive, as it makes a logical construction; but Verity argues that we
do not here want symmetry, 'the
broken, disjointed style of the whole
speech being intended to indicate
Edmund's feigned agitation'.

alarum'd spirits] energies roused to
action, as by a trumpet.

53. *Bold . . . right*] emboldened by the
justice of his cause.

54. *gasted*] frightened. Cf. Palsgrave,
Lesclarcissement, 1530: 'I gast him as
sore as he was this twelve months.'
Shakespeare uses 'gastness' (*Oth.,* v. i.
106). Elizabethans erroneously supposed that 'gastfull' was etymolo-
gically connected with '*ghost*'. Harsnett, *op. cit.,* pp. 137, 73, uses the
phrases 'gastful opinions' and 'God-
gastring Giants'. (Shakespeare may
have intended a quibble on *gasted* and
ghosted; Edgar, frightened, vanished
like a ghost at cock-crow.)

55. *Let . . . far*] however far he flies.

57. *And . . . dispatch*] and when he is
found, kill him. Brae, *N.Q.,* 1852,
argues that *dispatch* means 'Get on with
your story.'

58. *worthy*] honourable.

arch and patron] chief patron (hendiadys).

Bringing the murderous coward to the stake;
He that conceals him, death.

Edm. When I dissuaded him from his intent,
And found him pight to do it, with curst speech
I threaten'd to discover him: he replied,   65
'Thou unpossessing bastard! dost thou think,
If I would stand against thee, would the reposal
Of any trust, virtue, or worth in thee
Make thy words faith'd? No: what I should deny,—
As this I would; ay, though thou didst produce   70
My very character—I'ld turn it all
To thy suggestion, plot, and damned practice:
And thou must make a dullard of the world,
If they not thought the profits of my death
Were very pregnant and potential spirits   75
To make thee seek it.'

---

61. coward] *F; caytife Q.*   67. would the] *F; could the Q.*   reposal] *F;*
reposure *Q.*   69. what I should] *Q; what should I F; what, should I*
Schmidt.   70. ay] I *Q; not in F.*   71. I'ld] I'll *F4.*   72. practice] *F;*
pretence *Q.*   75. spirits] *F, Rowe, Delius, Schmidt, Harrison; spurres Q, most edd.*

---

61. *Bringing . . . stake*] Craig suggests that it was customary to chain captives to a stake of wood, and he cites Chaucer, *The Knight's Tale*, 1693–4: 'And he that is at meschief, shal be take, / And noght slayn, but be broght un-to the stake.' But Gloucester probably means 'Bringing Edgar to the place of execution', not implying that he is to be burned at the stake.

62. *death*] the same elliptical form of expression as 57 *ante.*

64. *pight*] fully determined, from *pitched.*

curst] sharp, harsh, angry.

66. *unpossessing*] incapable of holding property, and so beggarly.

67. *would stand*] should stand.

reposal] placing.

68. *virtue . . . worth*] or your own virtue, or worth.

69. *faith'd*] credited.

71. *character*] handwriting. Cf. I. ii. 60.

72. *suggestion*] evil instigation. Cf. *Oth.*, II. iii. 358 and *Mac.*, I. iii. 134.

practice] treacherous device. Cf. v. iii. 150.

73. *make . . . world*] suppose everyone to be stupid. Cf. *Cym.*, v. v. 265.

74. *If . . . thought*] The auxiliary was not required, when the negative preceded the verb. Cf. Abbott, *305, and IV. ii. 2.

75. *pregnant*] obvious, readily conceivable (Craig); ready (Johnson); productive of something, teeming with incitements (Furness).

potential] powerful.

spirits] Schmidt, almost the only editor who retains F reading, interprets 'evil spirits'; it might mean 'incitements'. In several passages in other plays Shakespeare juxtaposes 'potent' and 'spirits'. Cf. *Tp.*, I. ii. 275 ('potent ministers'); *John*, II. i. 358 ('potents, fiery kindled spirits'); *Mac.*, IV. i. 76 ('more potent than the first' spirit); *Ham.*, II. ii. 631 ('very potent with such spirits'); *Ham.*, v. ii. 364 ('The potent poison quite o'ercrows my spirit'). In view of these parallels,

Glou.   O strange and fast'ned villain!
   Would he deny his letter, said he? I never got him.
                                         [*Tucket within.*
   Hark! the Duke's trumpets. I know not why he comes.
   All ports I'll bar; the villain shall not 'scape;
   The Duke must grant me that: besides his picture   80
   I will send far and near, that all the kingdom
   May have due note of him; and of my land,
   Loyal and natural boy, I'll work the means
   To make thee capable.

             Enter CORNWALL, REGAN, *and Attendants.*

Corn. How now, my noble friend! since I came hither   85
   Which I can call but now, I have heard strange news.
Reg. If it be true, all vengeance comes too short
   Which can pursue th'offender. How dost, my Lord?

76. O strange] *F;* Strong *Q.*   77. said he?] *F; not in Q.*   I . . . him] *Q;
not in F.*   S.D.] after *seek it* (76) *F; not in Q.*   78. why] *Q;* wher *F.*
82. due] *F; not in Q.*   84. S.D.] *F, subst.; Enter the Duke of Cornwall Q.*
86. strange news] *Q;* strangenesse *F.*   88. dost] does *F2–4.*

it is needless to adopt the Q reading, though Duthie suggests that the F compositor may have corrupted *spurres* into *spirits* by confusion with *profits* in the preceding line; or that a scribe misread the playhouse MS. and miscorrected Q.

76. *O strange*] Gloucester is concerned with Edgar's apparent unnaturalness, rather than his recklessness. Cf. Q reading.

fast'ned] inveterate, hardened. It is probably a metaphor from the hardening of cement.

77. *got*] begot.

Tucket] Gloucester recognizes the Duke's special trumpet-call.

78. *why*] Kirschbaum, defending the F reading 'where', argues that Gloucester 'is apprehensive . . . that Edgar may escape by the open door through which the duke will enter'. But there is no reason to think that Edgar is still in the castle precincts.

79. *ports*] seaports, or, less probably,

means of exit, gates. Cf. *Troil.,* IV. iv. 113. Craig compares Kyd, *Soliman and Perseda,* II. i. 332–6: 'But for Assurance that he may not scape, / Weele lay the ports and hauens round about; / And let a proclamation straight be made / That he that can bring foorth the murtherer / Shall haue three thousand Duckets for his paines.'

83. *Loyal and natural*] Cf. III. v. 2–3: 'nature thus gives way to loyalty.' Gloucester is quibbling on the two meanings of *natural,* 'bastard' and 'feeling natural affection' (opposed to the unnaturalness of his legitimate son). But since *natural* could mean legitimate as well as illegitimate, he may also imply that Edmund is now his rightful heir.

84. *capable*] able to inherit. *N.E.D.* quotes from Guillim, *Heraldry,* 1610, II. 5 (1660), 65: 'Bastards are not capable of their father's patrimony.'

87. *If . . . vengeance*] Cf. *Leir,* 1582: 'If it be so, that shee doth seeke reuenge'.

Glou. O! Madam, my old heart is crack'd, it's crack'd.

Reg. What! did my father's godson seek your life?   90
    He whom my father nam'd, your Edgar?

Glou. O! Lady, Lady, shame would have it hid.

Reg. Was he not companion with the riotous knights
    That tended upon my father?

Glou. I know not, Madam; 'tis too bad, too bad.   95

Edm. Yes, Madam, he was of that consort.

Reg. No marvel then though he were ill affected;
    'Tis they have put him on the old man's death,
    To have th'expense and waste of his revenues.
    I have this present evening from my sister   100
    Been well inform'd of them, and with such cautions
    That if they come to sojourn at my house,
    I'll not be there.

Corn.   Nor I, assure thee, Regan.
    Edmund, I hear that you have shown your father
    A child-like office.

Edm.   It was my duty, Sir.   105

Glou. He did bewray his practice; and receiv'd
    This hurt you see, striving to apprehend him.

Corn. Is he pursued?

---

89. O!] *F; not in Q.*   it's] *F; is Q.*   91. nam'd, your] *F;* named your *Q.*
92. O!] *F;* I *Q.*   94. tended upon] *F;* tends vpon *Q;* tend upon *Theobald;*
tended on *Hanmer.*   96. of that consort] *F; not in Q, Capell.*   99. th'expense
and waste] *F;* these—and wast *Q uncorr., Q2–3;* the wast and spoyle *Q corr.;*
the spence and waste *conj. Greg;* the fee and waste *conj. Maxwell.*   his] *F,*
Q corr.; this his *Q uncorr., Q2–3; not in F2–4.*   104. hear] *F;* heard *Q.*
105. It was] *F;* twas *Q;* It is *F3–4.*   106. bewray] *F;* betray *Q.*

96. *Yes*] Kittredge suggests the word
should be 'prolonged and dissyllabic',
presumably to fill out the metre and to
suggest Edmund's feigned hesitation
in speaking of Edgar's guilt.

consort] set. The accent is on the
second syllable. Cf. *Gent.*, IV. i. 64. The
word is often used contemptuously.
Cf. *Rom.*, III. i. 49.

97. *ill affected*] disloyal.

98. *put him on*] incited him to.

99. *th'expense and waste*] the privilege of spending and squandering.
Greg, *Variants*, pp. 155–6, discusses
the reading of Q1. He thinks there

is a remote possibility that Shakespeare wrote 'the spence and waste',
th'expence being a F sophistication.
The copy for Q must have been
illegible at this point, but the uncorrected version looks like a genuine
attempt to decipher the copy, the
corrected version being an emendation.

105. *child-like*] filial.

106. *bewray*] discover, disclose. Cf.
Matt., xxvi. 73. There is no suggestion
of treachery in this word, unlike
'betray'.

107. *apprehend*] arrest.

Glou.   Ay, my good Lord.
Corn. If he be taken he shall never more
    Be fear'd of doing harm; make your own purpose,   110
    How in my strength you please. For you, Edmund,
    Whose virtue and obedience doth this instant
    So much commend itself, you shall be ours:
    Natures of such deep trust we shall much need;
    You we first seize on.
Edm.   I shall serve you, Sir,   115
    Truly, however else.
Glou.   For him I thank your Grace.
Corn. You know not why we came to visit you,—
Reg. Thus out of season, threading dark-ey'd night:
    Occasions, noble Gloucester, of some prize,
    Wherein we must have use of your advice.   120
    Our father he hath writ, so hath our sister,
    Of differences, which I best thought it fit
    To answer from our home; the several messengers

---

111. For] *Q, F1;* as for *F2-4, Jennens.*   112. this instant] *Q, F;* in this instance *Jennens (conj. Heath);* at this instant *conj. Capell.*   115. Sir] *F; not in Q, Jennens.*   118. threading] *F;* threatning *Q.*   119. prize] *F, Q2-3;* prise *Q uncorr.;* poyse *Q corr.;* price *Capell (conj. Johnson).*   122. differences] *F, Q corr.;* defences *Q uncorr., Q2-3.*   best] *F, Q uncorr., Q2-3;* lest *Q corr.;* least *Wright, Camb.*   thought] *Q;* though *F.*   123. home] *F, Q corr.;* hand *Q uncorr., Q2-3.*

---

110. *Be . . . harm*] be feared, lest he should do mischief.

110–11. *make . . . please*] carry out your plans for his capture, and make what use you like of my authority and resources for that purpose.

112. *virtue . . . obedience*] virtuous obedience. Hence the singular vb.

118. *Thus*] Regan takes the words out of her husband's mouth, and thereby shows that he is subordinate.

threading . . . night] traversing the darkness, with a quibble on the eye of a needle, and the dark eyes of Night. Heywood, *Love's Mistress,* III. i. 4, speaks of 'negro night, the black-eyed Queene' (cited Kittredge).

119. *prize*] importance. Greg, *Variants,* shows that as the Q used as copy

for F was here in its corrected state, the F reading must have come from the playhouse MS. and not from the uncorrected Q. The Q compositor misread *o* as *r* in III. iv. 6 (contentious/ crulentious); the corrector presumably did the same in the present passage.

122. *differences*] quarrels.

which] referring, as Delius points out, not to *differences,* but to a letter Lear has *writ.*

122–3. *I . . . home*] She wishes to answer the letters away from home, so that the King cannot quarter himself there before she has consulted with Goneril; who, we learn, is also coming to Gloucester's castle (cf. II. iv. 182).

123. *from*] away from. Cf. *Ham.,* III. ii. 22.

From hence attend dispatch. Our good old friend,
Lay comforts to your bosom, and bestow   125
Your needful counsel to our businesses,
Which craves the instant use.

Glou.   I serve you, Madam.
Your Graces are right welcome.   [*Flourish. Exeunt.*

SCENE II.—[*Before Gloucester's Castle.*]

Enter KENT *and* OSWALD, *severally.*

Osw. Good dawning to thee, friend: art of this house?
Kent. Ay.
Osw. Where may we set our horses?
Kent. I'th'mire.
Osw. Prithee, if thou lov'st me, tell me.   5
Kent. I love thee not.
Osw. Why, then I care not for thee.
Kent. If I had thee in Lipsbury pinfold, I would make
      thee care for me.
Osw. Why dost thou use me thus? I know thee not.   10

---

126. businesses] *F;* business *Q.*   128. *Flourish*] *F; not in Q, F2–4.   Exeunt*] *not in Q.*

Scene II

S.D. *Before . . . Castle*] Capell; *not in Q, F.*   severally] *F; not in Q.*   1.
dawning] *F;* deuen *Q uncorr.;* euen *Q corr.,* Q2–3.   this] *F;* the *Q.*   4.
I'th'] *F;* It'h *Q1;* In the *Q2–3.*   5. lov'st] *F;* loue *Q.*

124. *attend dispatch*] are waiting to be
dispatched.

127. *craves . . . use*] requires to be
done at once.

Scene II

1. *dawning*] It is still dark (cf. 30),
and the sun has still not risen by the
end of the scene. As Greg suggests, the
copy for Q was probably 'dauen', and
the F reading was a substitution of a
more common form of the word.

of this house] a servant here. Cf.
North's *Plutarch (Coriolanus)*, Temple
ed., p. 35: 'They of the house spy-
ing him, wondred what he should
be.'

8. *Lipsbury pinfold*] A pinfold is a
pound, a pen in which stray cattle are
confined. Nares suggests the phrase
means 'between my teeth' (i.e. in my
clutches), *Lipsbury* meaning Liptown.
In Fletcher, *Wit at Several Weapons*, I.
i (ed. Glover, ix. 71), 'to purchase lip-
land' means 'to procure a kiss'; and
Kittredge cites *Luc.*, 679: 'Entombs
her outcry in her *lips'* sweet *fold*'. Hilda
M. Hulme suggests that there is a
quibble on two senses of *lip*: 'to kiss'
and 'to shear'. Nosworthy cites
Middleton, *The Changeling*, III. iii:
'Have you read Lipsius?' Here the
name is introduced for the sake of the
pun on the first syllable.

Kent. Fellow, I know thee.

Osw. What dost thou know me for?

Kent. A knave, a rascal, an eater of broken meats; a base, proud, shallow, beggarly, three-suited, hundred-pound, filthy worsted-stocking knave; a lily-livered,   15
action-taking, whoreson, glass-gazing, super-serviceable, finical rogue; one-trunk-inheriting slave; one that wouldst be a bawd in way of good service, and art nothing but the composition of a knave, beggar, coward, pandar, and the son and heir of a   20
mongrel bitch: one whom I will beat into clamorous whining if thou deni'st the least syllable of thy addition.

Osw. Why, what a monstrous fellow art thou, thus to rail on one that is neither known of thee nor knows thee!   25

Kent. What a brazen-fac'd varlet art thou, to deny thou

---

14. three-suited] *F;* three suyted *Q uncorr.;* three shewted *Q corr.,* *Q2–3.*
16. action-taking] *F;* action-taking knaue, a *Q.*   16–17. super-serviceable, finical] *F;* super finicall *Q.*   17. one-trunk-inheriting] *F3;* one trunk-inheriting *F1–2; no hyphens Q.*   21. one] *F; not in Q.*   clamorous] *Q,* *F3–4;* clamours *F1–2.*   22. deni'st] *F;* denie *Q.*   thy] *F;* the *Q.*   24. Why] *F; not in Q.*   25. that is] *F;* that's *Q.*

---

13. *A knave . . .*] In this speech Kent attacks Oswald as a cowardly menial who parades as a gentleman (Kittredge).

eater . . . meats] one who eats up remains of food. Cf. *Cor.,* IV. v. 35, and *Cym.,* II. iii. 119.

14. *three-suited*] Cf. Edgar's words, III. iv. 133. Servants were apparently given three suits of clothes a year. Wright quotes Jonson, *The Silent Woman,* III. i. 38–42: 'Who giues you your maintenance, I pray you? Who allowes you your horse-meat, and man's meat? your three sutes of apparell a yeere? your foure paire of stockings, one silke, three worsted?'

14–15. *hundred-pound*] probably a hit at James I's profuse creation of knights. Steevens quotes Middleton, *The Phoenix,* IV. iii. 55: 'How's this? am I us'd like a hundred-pound gentleman?'

15. *worsted-stocking*] Cf. Jonson's

words quoted in note on l. 14. Gentlemen wore silk stockings.

lily-livered] white-livered, without blood in it, and hence cowardly. Cf. *Mac.,* v. iii. 15; *2H4,* IV. iii. 113; *Mer.V.,* III. ii. 86; *Tw.N.,* III. ii. 65–7.

16. *action-taking*] one who goes to law, instead of fighting.

glass-gazing] vain, foppish. Cf. *R3,* I. i. 15.

16–17. *super-serviceable*] above his work (Wright); over-officious (Johnson); ready to serve his master in dishonourable ways, 'a bawd in the way of good service' (Kittredge).

17. *finical*] affectedly fastidious.

one-trunk-inheriting] possessing only one trunkful of effects.

19. *composition*] compound, mixture.

20. *heir*] inheriting the mongrel bitch's characteristics.

22–3. *thy addition*] the titles I've given you. Cf. I. i. 135.

knowest me! Is it two days since I tripp'd up thy
heels and beat thee before the King? Draw, you
rogue; for though it be night, yet the moon shines:
I'll make a sop o'th'moonshine of you.   30
                              [*Drawing his sword.*
You whoreson cullionly barber-monger, draw.

Osw. Away! I have nothing to do with thee.

Kent. Draw, you rascal; you come with letters against the
King, and take Vanity the puppet's part against the
royalty of her father. Draw, you rogue, or I'll so   35
carbonado your shanks: draw, you rascal; come
your ways.

Osw. Help, ho! murther! help!

Kent. Strike, you slave; stand, rogue, stand; you neat
slave, strike.   [*Beats him.*   40

Osw. Help, ho! murther! murther!

---

27. since] *F;* agoe since *Q.*   27–8. tripp'd . . . thee] *F;* beat thee, and tript vp
thy heeles *Q.*   29. yet] *F; not in Q.*   30. o'th'] *F;* of the *Q.*   of] *F;* a' *Q.*
S.D.] *Rowe; not in Q, F.*   31. You] *F;* draw you *Q.*   cullionly] cully only
Q3.   33. come with] *F;* bring *Q.*   40. strike] *F, Q uncorr.;* strike? *Q corr.*
S.D.] *Rowe; not in Q, F.*   41. murther! murther] *F;* murther, helpe *Q.*

---

30. *a sop . . . moonshine*] The ground is
drenched in moonlight, and Kent proposes to pierce him with his sword, to
allow the moonlight, or the reflection
of the moon in a pond, to soak into
him, as when a piece of toast or a wafer
is set floating in a prepared drink. Or
perhaps, as Entwistle suggests, Kent
means to steep Oswald in his own
blood, 'by the consenting light of the
moon'. The existence of a dish, called
'eggs in moonshine' (eggs fried in oil or
butter, covered with slices of onions
and seasoned with verjuice, nutmeg,
and salt), made Farmer and others
suppose that there was a quibbling
reference to a dish with a similar name.
Nosworthy compares Porter, *Two
Angry Women of Abington* (1599), 2333:
'Ile cut thee out in collops and
egges.'

31. *cullionly*] rascally, base, vile;
from cullion. Cf. *Shr.,* IV. ii. 20.

barber-monger] a constant patron of
the barber's shop.

34. *Vanity*] Kittredge says that
morality plays with allegorical
characters were performed in puppet-
shows. Marlowe, *The Jew of Malta,* II.
iii (881), mentions Lady Vanity. Cf.
Jonson, *Volpone,* II. iii. 21, and *The
Devil is an Ass,* I. i. 42. Kent is, of
course, referring to Goneril.

36. *carbonado*] to scotch, or cut cross-
wise, a piece of meat before broiling or
grilling it. Cf. *Cor.,* IV. v. 199. It was
frequently used in a metaphorical
sense. Cf. Nashe, *Have With You to
Saffron Walden,* ed. McKerrow, III. 17:
'I will deliuer him to thee, to be
scotcht and carbonadoed.'

36–7. *come your ways*] come along.
Cf. *Ham.,* I. iii. 135. The phrase is still
current in Northern England.

39. *neat*] elegant, foppish (cf. Chapman, *All Fools,* v. ii: 'that neate spruce
slaue'); or, perhaps, as Walker suggests, pure, unmixed, as in the phrase
'neat wine'; or Shakespeare may have
had both meanings in mind.

Enter EDMUND, *with his rapier drawn.*

Edm. How now! What's the matter? Part!

Kent. With you, goodman boy, if you please: come, I'll
flesh ye; come on, young master.

Enter CORNWALL, REGAN, GLOUCESTER, *and Servants.*

Glou. Weapons! arms! What's the matter here?   45

Corn. Keep peace, upon your lives:
He dies that strikes again. What is the matter?

Reg. The messengers from our sister and the King.

Corn. What is your difference? speak.

Osw. I am scarce in breath, my Lord.   50

Kent. No marvel, you have so bestirr'd your valour.
You cowardly rascal, nature disclaims in thee: a
tailor made thee.

---

41. S.D.] *Furness; Enter Bastard, Cornewall, Regan, Gloster, Servants* F*; Enter
Edmund with his rapier drawn, Gloster, the Duke and Dutchesse* Q.   42. Part] *F;
not in* Q*; Parts them Grant White.*   43. if] *F;* and Q*; an Staunton.*   44. ye]
F; you Q.   S.D.] *Staunton; see S.D. 41 ante.*   49. What is] *F;* whats Q.

42. *matter*] subject of the quarrel.

Part!] Grant White, following
Dyce's conjecture, took the unitali-
cized 'Part' of F to be a S.D., and
nearly all later editors have done the
same. Schmidt, one of the few editors
who retains *Part* in the text, has to
argue that Kent quibbles on the word
in his 'with you', i.e. 'I will depart
with you.' This is barely possible; but
the interpretation given below is more
probable, and to keep *Part* in the text
thus separates the retort from the
words that evoke it.

43. *With you*] i.e. the quarrel is with
you.

goodman boy] a title of mock respect
to an impudent youth. Cf. *Rom.,* I.
v. 79.

44. *flesh*] initiate. It was originally a
hunting term. See Palsgrave, *Lesclarcissement*: 'Flesche as we do an hounde,
when we give him any parte of a wyld
beast, to encourage him to run well'.
The word was often used in connection
with fighting. Cf. *1H4,* v. iv. 133, and

Beaumont and Fletcher, *Wit at
Several Weapons,* I. i (ed. Glover, ix. 78):
'The first that flesht me a Soldier, Sir, /
was that great battel of *Alcazar*.'

49. *difference*] quarrel. Cf. II. i. 122.

51. *your valour*] Craig suggests that
this may be a mock title, and he compares *Troil.,* I. iii. 176.

52. *disclaims in thee*] renounces any
claim to have produced you. Cf. Jonson, *The Case is Altered,* v. xii. 67–8:
'*Count F.* Is not *Rachel* then thy
daughter? / *Jaq.* No, I disclaime in
her.' Gifford points out that two instances of *disclaim in* in Jonson's *Every
Man in his Humour* were altered to *disclaim* in the Jonson Folio, and he suggests that the phrase was becoming
obsolete.

52–3. *a . . . thee*] proverbial. Cf. *Cym.,*
IV. ii. 81; Jonson, *The Staple of News,*
I. ii. 110–11: 'Thence comes your
prouerbe; The Taylor makes the
man.' Apperson, *English Proverbs,* pp.
616–17, gives some variants and see
Ham., III. ii. 37 ff.

Corn. Thou art a strange fellow; a tailor make a man?

Kent. A tailor, sir: a stone-cutter or a painter could not   55
have made him so ill, though they had been but two
years o'th'trade.

Corn. Speak yet, how grew your quarrel?

Osw. This ancient ruffian, Sir, whose life I have spar'd at
suit of his grey beard,—   60

Kent. Thou whoreson zed! thou unnecessary letter! My
Lord, if you will give me leave, I will tread this unbolted villain into mortar, and daub the wall of a
jakes with him. Spare my grey beard, you wagtail?

Corn. Peace, sirrah!   65
You beastly knave, know you no reverence?

Kent. Yes, sir; but anger hath a privilege.

55. A] *F; I, a Q.*   56. they] *F; hee Q.*   57. years] *F; houres Q.*   o'th]
F3; oth' F1–2; at the *Q.*   58. *Corn.] F; Glost. Q.*   59. This] The *F3–4.*
60. grey beard,—] *Rowe;* gray-beard. *Q,F1–2;* gray beard. *F3.*   62. you will]
F; you'l *Q.*   63. wall] *F;* walles *Q.*   63–4. a jakes] Iaques *Q3.*   65.
sirrah] *F;* sir *Q.*   66. know you] *F;* you haue *Q.*   67. hath] *F;* has *Q.*

57. *years*] Greg, *Editorial Problem,*
p. 91, points out that the Q reading is
a vulgarization. 'Shakespeare knows
that art is long.' Nosworthy compares
Porter, *Two Angry Women of Abington,*
1786–8: 'thou whorson refuge of a
Taylor, that wert prentise to a Taylor
halfe an age, and because if thou hadst
serued ten ages thou wouldst prooue
a botcher'.

o'th'trade] Duthie cites *Meas.,* II. i.
192.

61. *Thou . . . letter*] This title is given
to the letter Z because it was generally
ignored in the dictionaries of the time.
Baret omits it altogether in his
Alvearie, and Rider in his *Dictionary,*
ed. 1640, says it is not used in Latin.
Jonson, *English Grammar,* ed. Herford
and Simpson, VIII. 492, writes: 'Z is a
letter often heard amongst us, but
seldome seene.' Jonson was echoing
Mulcaster's *Elementarie,* 1582.

62–3. *unbolted*] Tollet says that unbolted mortar is made of unsifted lime,
the lumps of which have to be broken
up by treading on them with wooden
shoes. But 'coarse' is a curious epithet

to apply to Oswald, the glass-gazing,
finical, barber-monger; and Kittredge
explains 'this fellow who is a rascal
through-and-through'.   Perhaps   a
quibble is intended: an unbolted
villain might be a released or un-
restrained one; or, since *unbolt* is used
in the sense of *reveal* (*Tim.,* I. i. 51), unbolted might mean *apparent.* It has
been suggested to me that since Boult
(in *Pericles*) has a name suitable to his
trade, *unbolted* might be taken to mean
'effeminate' or 'impotent'.

63. *mortar*] Steevens compares Massinger, *A New Way to Pay Old Debts,*
I. i: 'I will . . . tread you into mortar.'

64. *jakes*] privy.

wagtail] Cf. silly-ducking, 100 *post.*
Kittredge comments that the wagtail
is so called 'from the spasmodic up-
and-down jerking of its tail. Oswald is
too scared to stand still. Kent may
merely mean that Oswald is obsequious.

66. *beastly*] beast-like, irrational, and
perhaps disgusting.

67. *anger . . . privilege*] Cf. *John,* IV.
iii. 32.

Corn. Why art thou angry?

Kent. That such a slave as this should wear a sword,
    Who wears no honesty. Such smiling rogues as these,   70
    Like rats, oft bite the holy cords a-twain
    Which are too intrince t'unloose; smooth every
        passion
    That in the natures of their lords rebel;
    Bring oil to fire, snow to their colder moods;
    Renege, affirm, and turn their halcyon beaks   75
    With every gale and vary of their masters,
    Knowing nought, like dogs, but following.
    A plague upon your epileptic visage!
    Smoile you my speeches, as I were a Fool?

70. Who] *F;* That *Q.*   71. the holy] *F;* those *Q.*   a-twain] *F3;* a twain *F1;*
in twain *Q.*   72. too intrince] *Capell;* t'intrince *F;* to intrench *Q.*   t'un-
loose] *F;* to inloose *Q.*   74. Bring] *Q;* Being *F.*   fire] *F;* stir *Q.*   their]
Q; the *F.*   75. Renege] *F2–4;* Reneag *Q;* Reuenge *F1.*   76. gale] *Q;*
gall *F1.*   77. dogs] *F;* dayes *Q.*   79. Smoile] *F1–3, Q;* smile *F4.*

71. *holy cords*] natural bonds of affection. Editors think that the reference is to the bonds between parent and child; but the context suggests that Kent is referring to the bonds of matrimony.

72. *intrince*] abbreviated from *intrinsicate* (cf. *Ant.*, v. ii. 307), from Ital. *intrinsecato*, but confused in sense with *intricato* (*N.E.D.*). Wright thinks it is a compound of *intrinsic* and *intricate*. It means intricate, involved, entangled, tightly drawn.

smooth] flatter. Cf. *R3*, i. iii. 48; *Rom.*, III. ii. 98; *Tit.*, v. ii. 140.

74. *Bring*] Both Q and F readings make excellent sense. Duthie explains: 'Kent means that the flatterers *are* oil to the flame of their masters' wrath, that they feed it and keep it burning . . . just as when their masters are in, say, a melancholy mood . . . the flatterers are snow to that mood.' He compares *2H6*, v. ii. 51 ff.

75. *Renege*] deny. Cf. *Ant.*, I. i. 8.

75–6. *turn . . . gale*] This refers to the belief that the halcyon, or kingfisher, if hung up by the tail or beak, would turn with the wind. T. Lupton, *Tenth*

Book of Notable Things, says that 'A little byrde called the King's Fisher, being hanged up in the ayre by the neck, his nebbe, or bill, will be always direct or straight gainst the wind.' Cf. Marlowe, *The Jew of Malta*, I. i. 38–9: 'But now how stands the wind? / Into what corner peeres my *Halcions* bill?' Sir Thomas Browne exposed the belief as a vulgar error; but, according to Green, *Shakespeare and the Emblem Writers*, p. 393, it was still prevalent in some parts of England in the middle of the nineteenth century.

76. *gale and vary*] varying gale (hendiadys).

78. *epileptic*] Oswald pale, and trembling with fright, was yet smiling and trying hard to put on a look of lofty unconcern.

79. *Smoile*] Q and F agree here substantially. Presumably Kent remembers to speak in dialect, and unless the passage is corrupt he means 'smile at'.

as . . . Fool] as if I were a professional jester, trying to make you laugh; or, less likely, as if I were foolish, and your butt.

Goose, if I had you upon Sarum plain,   80
 I'd drive ye cackling home to Camelot.
Corn. What! art thou mad, old fellow?
Glou. How fell you out? say that.
Kent. No contraries hold more antipathy
 Than I and such a knave.   85
Corn. Why dost thou call him knave? What is his fault?
Kent. His countenance likes me not.
Corn. No more, perchance, does mine, nor his, nor hers.
Kent. Sir, 'tis my occupation to be plain:
 I have seen better faces in my time   90
 Than stands on any shoulder that I see
 Before me at this instant.
Corn.   This is some fellow,
 Who, having been prais'd for bluntness, doth affect
 A saucy roughness, and constrains the garb
 Quite from his nature: he cannot flatter, he,   95
 An honest mind and plain, he must speak truth:

80. if] *Q2–3, F;* and *Q1.* 81. drive ye] *F;* send you *Q.* 86. What is his fault?] *F;* What's his offence? *Q.* 88. does] doth *Q2–3.* nor . . . nor] *F;* or . . . or *Q.* 91. Than] *Q2;* Then *Q3, F;* That *Q.* 92. some] *F;* a *Q.* 96. An . . . and] *F;* He must be *Q.*

80–1. *Goose . . . Camelot*] Camelot, the residence of King Arthur, has been identified with Winchester (cf. Malory, *Morte Darthur*, ii. 19). Others suppose Camelot to have been in Somerset or Wales; and there are said to have been flocks of geese on the moors near the former site. Capell thought that there was an allusion to a 'Winchester goose', a syphilitic swelling (so called because the Southwark brothels were on land 'within the jurisdiction of the Bishop of Winchester') or a person suffering therefrom. E. A. Armstrong, *Shakespeare's Imagination*, pp. 57–65, shows that the goose often appears as part of a chain of ideas, including disease, bitterness, seasoning, and restraint. In this context we have 'plague' (78), 'lily-livered' (15, rather remote), 'saucy' (94), and 'cords' (71). Cf. ii. iv. 45–63, where some of the same associations recur. But the allusion to the Winchester goose was probably unconscious, and is not likely to have been noticed by an audience.

80. *Sarum plain*] Hulme cites Udall's translation of Erasmus' *Apopthegemes*, where 'his malaparte tongue' is linked with 'Thom Trouthe, or plain Sarisburie'.

87. *likes*] pleases. Cf. i. i. 199.

91. *shoulder*] Shoulder is often, if not always, employed by Shakespeare for the part between the shoulders.

94–5. *constrains . . . nature*] forces on himself a demeanour, a character, quite opposed to what is really his (Craig). But it is more likely that his = its, and that Cornwall means that Kent 'distorts the style of straightforward speaking quite from its nature, which is sincerity; whereas he makes it a cloak for craft' (Clarke).

94. *garb*] style, manner, fashion, especially of speech; it does not mean 'fashion of dress'.

And they will take it, so; if not, he's plain.
These kind of knaves I know, which in this plainness
Harbour more craft and more corrupter ends
Than twenty silly-ducking observants,   100
That stretch their duties nicely.

Kent.   Sir, in good faith, in sincere verity,
Under th'allowance of your great aspect,
Whose influence, like the wreath of radiant fire
On flick'ring Phœbus' front,—

Corn.   What mean'st by this?

Kent.   To go out of my dialect, which you discommend   106
so much. I know, sir, I am no flatterer: he that
beguil'd you in a plain accent was a plain knave;
which for my part I will not be, though I should win
your displeasure to entreat me to't.   110

97. And] An *Pope.*   take it] *F;* tak't *Q.*   100. silly-ducking] *F;* silly
ducking *Q.*   102. faith] *F;* sooth *Q, Steevens.*   in sincere] *F;* or in sincere *Q.*
103. great] *F;* graund *Q.*   105. On] *F;* In *Q.*   flick'ring] *Duthie;* flicking
F; flitkering *Q;* flickering *Pope.*   front,—] *Rowe;* front. *Q, F.*   by] *F;*
thou by *Q.*   106. dialect] *F;* dialogue *Q.*   110. to't] to it *Q2–3.*

99. *Harbour*] Abbott *412 points out
that the two nouns connected by 'of'
(*kind of knaves*) seem regarded as a
compound noun with plural termi-
nation.

more . . . ends] Shakespeare often uses
the double comparative. Ridley points
out that Cornwall has given an admirable character sketch of Iago.

100. *silly-ducking*] ludicrously obsequious. Cf. 'silly-stately', *1H6,* IV.
vii. 72.

observants] obsequious attendants.

101. *stretch . . . nicely*] are particular
to carry out their courtly duties
punctiliously.

103–5. *Under . . . front*] Florio, *A
Worlde of Wordes,* 1598, uses the same
affected language in his Epistle Dedi-
catory: 'But as to me, and manie more
the glorious and gracious sunne-shine
of your Honor hath infused light and
life: so may my lesser borrowed light,
after a principal respect to your
benigne aspect, and influence, affoorde
some lustre to some others.'

103. *allowance*] approval. Cf. I. iv.
206.

aspect] the accent is on the second
syllable. Kent is quibbling on the two
meanings of the word, (i) appearance,
(ii) the relative positions of the
heavenly bodies as they appear to an
observer . . . and the influence attri-
buted thereto (Onions).

104. *influence*] astrological power
exercised by the heavenly bodies:
Kent implies ironically that Cornwall
is a heavenly body.

105. *front*] forehead.

106. *dialect*] manner of speaking,
language.

107–8. *he . . . accent*] the type of man
Cornwall has been describing, 96–105.

109–10. *though . . . to't*] This has not
been explained satisfactorily. 'Though
I should win you, displeased as you
now are, to like me so well as to entreat
me to be a knave' (Johnson). 'Though
I should so far win over, appease, your
wrath, that you should entreat me to
answer it again' (Craig). 'I will not be

Corn. What was th'offence you gave him?

Osw. I never gave him any:
    It pleas'd the King his master very late
    To strike at me, upon his misconstruction;
    When he, compact, and flattering his displeasure,   115
    Tripp'd me behind; being down, insulted, rail'd,
    And put upon him such a deal of man,
    That worthied him, got praises of the King
    For him attempting who was self-subdu'd;
    And, in the fleshment of this dread exploit,   120
    Drew on me here again.

Kent.   None of these rogues and cowards
    But Ajax is their fool.

Corn.   Fetch forth the stocks!
    You stubborn ancient knave, you reverend braggart,
    We'll teach you.

Kent.   Sir, I am too old to learn.

---

111. What was th'] *F;* what's the *Q.*   115. compact] *F;* coniunct *Q.*   117.
man] *F;* man, that *Q.*   120. fleshment] *F;* flechuent *Q.*   dread] *Q;*
dead *F.*   122. Fetch . . . stocks] *F;* Bring forth the stocks, ho? *Q.*   123.
ancient] *F;* ausrent *Q uncorr.;* miscreant *Q corr.,* *Q2–3.*   reverend] vnreuerent
Q2–3.   124. Sir] *F; not in Q.*

a plain knave, though as a great in-
ducement to be such, though to
entreat me, induce me, to it, I should
win your displeasure, a thing far more
desirable in my eyes than your favour'
(Craig, alternatively). 'Even if I could
induce you to lay aside your displeasure so far as to beg me to be one'
(Kittredge). Schmidt suggests, I think
rightly, that 'your displeasure' is the
opposite to the usual style of address,
'your grace'. The passage might then
mean: 'Though I should convert your
grace, who is not gracious to me, to
a more amiable frame of mind, so that
instead of being annoyed with me you
actually *entreat* me to be a plain knave,
i.e. a flatterer.'

115. *compact*] in league with the
King. The Q reading means the same.

116. *being . . . insulted*] exulted over
me when I was down. Cotgrave defines *insulter*, 'to insult, crow, vaunt,

or triumph over'. Cf. *AYL.,* iii. v. 36.

117. *put . . . man*] made himself out
such a hero.

118. *worthied him*] won honour for
himself (Kittredge); gave him the
appearance of worth (Craig). Abbott
derives *worthied* from the adj.; Schmidt
from *worthy* = hero; Perrett from
M.E. *wurthien* = dignify.

119. *For . . . who*] for assailing one
who.

120. *fleshment*] the action of 'flesh-
ing'; hence, the excitement resulting
from a first success. Cf. ii. ii. 44.

122. *But . . . fool*] Ajax is (by their
own account) a fool in comparison
with *them* (Kittredge). 'Ajax in brag-
ging is a fool to them' (Capell). In
Troilus and Cressida Ajax is treated
as a fool by the rogue and coward,
Thersites.

123. *stubborn*] rough, fierce.
reverend] aged.

Call not your stocks for me; I serve the King,   125
On whose employment I was sent to you;
You shall do small respect, show too bold malice
Against the grace and person of my master,
Stocking his messenger.
Corn.   Fetch forth the stocks!
As I have life and honour, there shall he sit till noon.
Reg. Till noon! till night, my Lord; and all night too.   131
Kent. Why, Madam, if I were your father's dog,
You should not use me so.
Reg.   Sir, being his knave, I will.
Corn. This is a fellow of the self-same colour
Our sister speaks of. Come, bring away the stocks.   135
                                    [*Stocks brought out.*

Glou. Let me beseech your Grace not to do so.
His fault is much, and the good King his master
Will check him for't: your purpos'd low correction
Is such as basest and contemned'st wretches
For pilf'rings and most common trespasses   140
Are punish'd with: the King must take it ill,
That he, so slightly valued in his messenger,

126. employment] *F;* imployments *Q.*   127. shall] *F;* should *Q.*   respect]
Q; respects *F.*   129. Stocking] *F;* Stobing *Q uncorr.;* Stopping *Q corr.*
133. should] *F;* could *Q.*   134. self-same colour] *F;* selfe same nature *Q1;*
same nature *Q2–3.*   135. speaks] speake *Q1.*   S.D.] *Dyce; after 133 F;*
not in Q.   137–41. His . . . with] *Q; not in F.*   139. contemned'st] *Capell;*
contaned *Q uncorr.;* temnest *Q corr.,* *Q2–3.*   141. must] *Q;* his master,
needs must *F.*   142. he] *F;* he's *Q, F3–4.*

128. *grace and person*] i.e. an insult to
the Crown, and a personal insult
too.

129. *stocks*] G. M. Young points out,
T.L.S., 30 Sept. 1949, p. 633, that in
the Rawdon Hastings MSS. iv there
are 'some briefe notes of orders to be
observed' in the household of the fifth
Earl of Huntingdon (who succeeded
in 1604). Kent's punishment was
'strictly in accordance with the dis-
cipline observed in a great house of the
time'. Young quotes, p. 327: 'Whoso-
ever shall be unseemly stout or urge
any quarrell in mealetyme and will not

be silenced . . . that he be presently
taken from the table and carryed to the
porter's lodge, and there to be sett in
the stockes. . . That if any doe un-
seamly behave themselves towards
there betters, the offence to be
punnyshed first by the stockes.'

133. *should*] would.

134. *colour*] kind, complexion. Cf.
AYL., I. ii. 107.

135. *bring away*] bring here, bring
along. Cf. *Meas.,* II. i. 41.

138. *check*] rebuke.

140. *pilf'rings*] Cf. Appendix, p.
236.

Should have him thus restrained.

Corn.   I'll answer that.

Reg. My sister may receive it much more worse
To have her gentleman abus'd, assaulted,   145
For following her affairs. Put in his legs.

                      [Kent is put in the stocks.

Corn. Come, my Lord, away.

            [Exeunt all but Gloucester and Kent.

Glou. I am sorry for thee, friend; 'tis the Duke's pleasure,
Whose disposition, all the world well knows,
Will not be rubb'd nor stopp'd: I'll entreat for thee.   150

Kent. Pray, do not, Sir. I have watch'd and travell'd
    hard;
Some time I shall sleep out, the rest I'll whistle.
A good man's fortune may grow out at heels:
Give you good morrow!

Glou. The Duke's to blame in this; 'twill be ill taken.   *[Exit.*

Kent. Good King, that must approve the common saw,   156
Thou out of heaven's benediction com'st
To the warm sun!

---

145. gentleman] Gentlemen *Q1*.   146. For . . . legs] *Q; not in F.*   S.D.]
Pope; after 143 Rowe; not in Q, F.   147. Come . . . away] *F, Q2–3;* Come, my
good lord, away *Q1 (assigned to Regan).*   S.D.] *Dyce; Exit Q2, F; not in Q1.*
148. Duke's] *Q;* Duke *F1.*   151. Pray] *F;* Pray you *Q.*   152. out] ont *Q1.*
155. taken] *F;* tooke *Q.*   S.D.] *not in Q1.*

143. *answer*] be answerable for.

145. *assaulted*] Cf. Appendix, p. 236.

147. *Come . . . away*] Q gives these
words to Regan. But, as Kirchbaum
points out, Cornwall sees that Gloucester is reluctant to leave Kent, and
orders him to follow. 'Nevertheless,
Gloucester remains, though obviously
nervous.'

150. *rubb'd*] impeded. A *rub* in bowls
is an obstacle by which a bowl is
diverted from its proper course.

151. *watch'd*] gone without sleep.

154. *Give*] i.e. God give.

155. *taken*] received.

156. *approve*] confirm.

157–8. *heaven's . . . sun!*] This proverb, derived presumably from those
who leave the shade to go into the hot
sun, and so go from better to worse, is

to be found in Heywood, *Proverbs*
1546 (ed. 1874, p. 115): 'In your
running from him to me, yee runne /
Out of God's blessing into the warme
sunne.' It is to be found in Lyly,
Euphues (ed. Arber, pp. 196, 320), in
Holinshed, *Chronicles* (ed. 1577, I. 33),
and in Pettie, *Petite Pallace* (ed. 1908,
II. 146). Kittredge cites Howell, *Den-
drologia*, 1640, p. 13: 'And now I am
come from God's blessing to the warme
Sun, who is a little too prodigall of his
beames here.' P. L. Carver, *M.L.R.*,
1930, p. 478, shows that in translating
Ab equis ad asinos, Palsgrave, *Acolastus*,
has 'from the hall into the kitchen, or
out of Christe's blessing into a warme
sonne (now I am well promoted)', i.e.
humiliated or degraded. Carver therefore interprets Kent's words: 'You are

Approach, thou beacon to this under globe,
That by thy comfortable beams I may   160
Peruse this letter. Nothing almost sees miracles,
But misery: I know 'tis from Cordelia,
Who hath most fortunately been inform'd
Of my obscured course; and shall find time
From this enormous state, seeking to give   165
Losses their remedies. All weary and o'erwatch'd,
Take vantage, heavy eyes, not to behold
This shameful lodging.
Fortune, good night; smile once more; turn thy wheel!
                              [*He sleeps.*

weel of
fortune

161. miracles] *F; my rackles Q uncorr.; my wracke Q corr., Q2–3.*   163. most]
not *Q uncorr.*   164–5. shall . . . From] shee'll . . . For *conj. Daniel;* she'll . . .
From *Staunton.*   166. their] and *Q uncorr.*   o'erwatch'd] *F;* ouerwatch *Q1;*
ouer-watch *Q2–3.*   167. Take] Late *Q uncorr.*   168–9.] *two lines, the first
ending* night *Q, F.*   smile . . . turn] *F;* Smile, once more turne *Q1–2.*

destined to learn in all its bitterness the
meaning of the proverb which speaks
of exchanging power and dignity for
impotence and humiliation.' This is
doubtless correct, though the proverb
does not always have the implication
of humiliation. Cf. *Leir,* 1154: 'he
came from bad to worse.'

159. *under globe*] Cf. 'lower world',
R2, III. ii. 38.

160. *comfortable*] comforting, help-
ful.

161–2. *Nothing . . . misery*] for, when
we are in despair, any relief seems
miraculous (Kittredge). Cf. IV. i. 2–6.

164. *obscured*] in disguise.

course] course of action.

164–6. *and . . . remedies*] The passage
is probably corrupt. Jennens started
the idea that Kent was reading to himself divided portions of Cordelia's
letter. It would not be light enough to
make out the words clearly. Perhaps,
too, as White suggests, Kent is too
sleepy to concentrate. Staunton's
reading of *she'll* for *shall* is unnecessary,

since *who* is understood; unless, indeed,
Kent is saying that he will himself find
time. E. Sullivan, *T.L.S.,* 20 Dec.
1923, suggests that *From* = away from
(cf. II. i. 123) and that the passage
means that Cordelia 'removed as she
is from the lawless state of things pre-
vailing here, will be sure to find time
when seeking to provide remedies'.
This is not very satisfactory, as from
III. i. 30 it looks as though this letter
informs Kent that France is planning
an invasion. Cuningham, *N.Q.,* 28
March 1914, wanted to emend *From* to
Form = restore. In any case, the meaning of the passage is that Cordelia will
somehow intervene.

165. *enormous*] out of the norm,
irregular, lawless. Not used elsewhere
in Shakespeare. Cf. Appendix, p. 236.

state] state of things.

166. *o'er-watched*] Cf. 151 *ante,* and
Cæs., IV. iii. 241.

167–8. *Take . . . lodging*] take the
opportunity afforded by sleep of not
seeing the stocks.

SCENE III.—[*A Wood.*]

Enter EDGAR.

Edg. I heard myself proclaim'd;
And by the happy hollow of a tree
Escap'd the hunt. No port is free; no place,
That guard, and most unusual vigilance,
Does not attend my taking. Whiles I may 'scape,   5
I will preserve myself; and am bethought
To take the basest and most poorest shape
That ever penury, in contempt of man,
Brought near to beast; my face I'll grime with filth,
Blanket my loins, elf all my hairs in knots,   10
And with presented nakedness outface
The winds and persecutions of the sky.
The country gives me proof and precedent
Of Bedlam beggars, who, with roaring voices,
Strike in their numb'd and mortified bare arms   15

Scene III

1. heard] *F;* hear *Q.*   4. unusual] vnusall *Q2–3, F1–2.*   5. Does] *F;* dost *Q.*   taking. Whiles] *F;* taking while *Q.*   10. elf] *F;* else *Q, F2;* put *F3–4.*   hairs] *F;* hair *Q, F4.*   in] *F;* with *Q.*   12. winds] *F;* wind *Q.* persecutions] *F;* persecution *Q.*   15. Strike] *Q, F;* Stick *Furness (conj. S. Walker).*   and] *not in Q uncorr.*   bare] *Q; not in F.*

S.D.] F has no scene division, and presumably Kent remained on the stage during Edgar's speech, though he must not be supposed to be in the immediate neighbourhood of the castle. It is possible that F text represents a version of the play performed on a platform, without an inner stage or gallery. See *R.E.S.*, 1940, pp. 300–3; 1946, p. 229.

2. *happy*] opportune.

3. *port*] Cf. II. i. 79.

5. *attend my taking*] await to capture me.

6. *am bethought*] have got the idea.

8. *in . . . man*] to show how contemptible a creature man is.

10. *elf*] tangle into elf-locks; matted **hair**, caused by neglect, was called

'elf-locks', and elves were blamed for them. Cf. *Rom.*, I. iv. 89–91. In an anonymous pamphlet, *O per se O,* possibly by Dekker, reprinted in Judges, *The Elizabethan Underworld,* p. 371, the Abram cove is described as 'a lusty strong rogue . . . his hair long and filthily knotted, for he keeps no barber'.

11. *presented*] exposed to view, as on a stage.

outface] brave. Cf. *Mer.V.,* IV. ii. 17.

13. *proof*] example.

15. *numb'd*] Cf. Appendix, p. 236.

mortified] made insensible to pain. Dekker, *Bellman of London,* 1608 (ed. 1904, p. 99), describes an Abraham man: 'You see pinnes stuck in sundry

Pins, wooden pricks, nails, sprigs of rosemary;
And with this horrible object, from low farms,
Poor pelting villages, sheep-cotes, and mills,
Sometime with lunatic bans, sometime with prayers,
Enforce their charity. Poor Turlygod! poor Tom!   20
That's something yet: Edgar I nothing am.   [*Exit.*

---

16. Pins] *Q, F;* Pies *Q uncorr.*   17. from] *Q, F;* frame *Q uncorr.*   farms] *F;*
seruice *Q.*   18. sheep-cotes] *Q;* sheeps-coates *F.*   19. Sometime] *Q;*
Sometimes *F.*   sometime] sometimes *F2–4.*   20. Turlygod] *Q, F;*
Tuelygod *Q uncorr.*

places of his naked flesh, especially in
his armes, which paine hee gladly puts
himselfe to . . . onely to make you
beleeve he is out of his wits. He calls
himselfe by the name of *Poore Tom.*'
See also Appendix, pp. 240–1.

bare] Kirschbaum regards this word
as an interpolation, a recollection of
'presented nakedness' (l. 11).

16. *pricks*] skewers.
sprigs] Cf. Appendix, p. 236.
17. *object*] spectacle. Cf. v. iii. 237.
low] lowly. Cf. *AYL.,* II. iii. 68.
18. *pelting*] petty, paltry. Cf. *R2,* II.
i. 60; and Golding, tr. Ovid's *Metamorphoses,* VIII. 804–5: 'one cotage
afterward / Receyved them, and that
was but a pelting one in deede.'
19. *bans*] curses.
20. *Poor . . . Tom!*] Edgar practises
the Bedlam beggar's whine (Kittredge).
Turlygod] Nothing is known of this
name, though some have supposed it
to be a corruption of Turlupin, the
name given to a sect of half-mad
beggars in Paris 1600, who used to

perform their religious services naked.
C. Mackay, *Glossary of Obscure Words
and Phrases,* 1887, pp. 429–30, suggests
that the word is an anglicized form of
Tuir-le-guid, 'one who beseeches or
importunes for alms with a doleful
pertinacity'. *Guid* in Gaelic signifies
importunity, and *Tuir* means 'to relate
with a mournful cadence, to whine, to
chant dolefully'. Roland M. Smith,
M.L.Q., 1946, p. 168, rejects this
interpretation and suggests the word
is derived from the Ir. *Toirdhealbhach
God,* which means 'stammering Turley' or possibly 'mad Turley' (reading
gealt for *god*). None of these suggestions
is satisfactory.
poor Tom] Cf. I. ii. 133 and note to
l. 15 above.
21. *That's . . . am*] There is some
hope for me as Poor Tom; I am nothing, I am doomed, as Edgar. Or
possibly the words mean merely 'I am
no longer Edgar'.
am] The rhyme, owing to the pronunciation of Tom, was probably a
good one.

SCENE IV.—[*Before Gloucester's Castle. Kent in
the Stocks.*]

Enter LEAR, *Fool, and Gentleman.*

Lear. 'Tis strange that they should so depart from home,
    And not send back my messenger.
Gent.   As I learn'd,
    The night before there was no purpose in them
    Of this remove.
Kent.   Hail to thee, noble master!
Lear. Ha!   5
    Mak'st thou this shame thy pastime?
Kent.   No, my Lord.
Fool. Ha, ha! he wears cruel garters. Horses are tied by
    the heads, dogs and bears by th'neck, monkeys by
    th'loins, and men by th'legs: when a man's over-
    lusty at legs then he wears wooden nether-stocks.   10
Lear. What's he that hath so much thy place mistook
    To set thee here?

Scene IV

S.D. *Before . . . Castle*] Pope, subst.; not in Q, F.   *Kent . . . Stocks*] Dyce; not in
Q, F.   *Enter . . . Gentleman*] F; Enter King Q1; Enter King and a Knight Q2–3.
1. home] F; hence Q.   2. messenger] Q; Messengers F1–2.   Gent.] F;
Knight. Q.   3. in them] F; not in Q.   4. this] F; his Q.   5. Ha!] F;
How, Q.   6. thy] Q; ahy F1.   No, my Lord.] F; not in Q.   7. he] F;
looke he Q.   tied] tide tide F2.   8. heads] F; heeles Q.   9. man's] Q;
man F; man is F2–4.   10. then] hen Q2; when Q3.

1–2. '*Tis . . . messenger*] Cf. *Leir*,
1355–6: 'I wonder that the Messenger
doth stay, / Whom we dispatcht for
Cambria so long since.'

4. *remove*] change of residence. Cf.
All's W., v. iii. 131.

7. *cruel*] a pun on *cruel* and *crewel*, i.e.
thin, worsted yarn. Cf. *Two Angry
Women of Abington*, 1599 (Malone Soc.
489–90): 'heele haue / His Cruel
garters crosse about the knee.' Greene,
Menaphon, ed. Arber, p. 36, has the
same pun: 'with his sheep-hook
fringed with cruel to signifie he was
chief of the savages'.

7–9. *Horses . . . legs*] Cf. Harsnett,
Appendix, p. 241.

9–10. *over-lusty at legs*] too much of a
vagabond (Kittredge). Cf. Dekker,
The Seven Deadly Sins of London, ed.
Arber, p. 31: 'tradesmen as if they
were dancing galliards are lusty at
legs and never stand still'. See also
Massinger, *Virgin Martyr*, IV. ii. 13;
Middleton, *Blurt Master Constable*,
I. i. 91.

10. *nether-stocks*] stockings. What we
now call knee-breeches were then
called upper-stocks. Kittredge cites
Harington, *Apology*, ed. 1814, p. 26:
'Wooden stocks were fitter for them
than silk stockings.' The same jest is
made by Lyly, *Mother Bombie*, v. iii.

12. *To*] as to.

Kent.   It is both he and she,
　　Your son and daughter.
Lear. No.
Kent. Yes.   15
Lear. No, I say.
Kent. I say, yea.
Lear. No, no; they would not.
Kent. Yes, yes, they have.
Lear. By Jupiter, I swear, no.   20
Kent. By Juno, I swear, ay.
Lear.   They durst not do't,
　　They could not, would not do't; 'tis worse than
　　　　murther,
　　To do upon respect such violent outrage.
　　Resolve me, with all modest haste, which way
　　Thou might'st deserve, or they impose, this usage,   25
　　Coming from us.
Kent.   My Lord, when at their home
　　I did commend your Highness' letters to them,
　　Ere I was risen from the place that show'd
　　My duty kneeling, came there a reeking post,
　　Stew'd in his haste, half breathless, panting forth   30
　　From Goneril his mistress salutations;
　　Deliver'd letters, spite of intermission,

18–19. *Lear.* No ... have] *Q ; not in F.*   19. Yes, yes] *New Camb. (conj. Maxwell) ;*
Yes *Q.*   21–2. *Kent.* By ... ay. *Lear*] *F ; not in Q.*   21, 22. do't] do it *Q 2–3.*
22. could ... would] *F ;* would ... could *Q.*   25. might'st] may'st *Q.*   impose]
F ; purpose *Q.*   30. panting] *Q ;* painting *F.*   31. salutations] salutation *F 2–4.*

14–21. *No ... ay*] These lines are a
conflation of Q and F. Kirschbaum
argues that the reporter restates 20–1
in 18–19, then recollects 20 and
attaches it to Lear's next speech. But
the two speeches omitted by F are so
effective in their context that it is difficult to believe they were added by the
actors. Duthie remarks that the effect
of climax in the passage seems to bear
the stamp of Shakespearian calcu-
lation.

23. *upon respect*] There are two explanations: (i) upon the respect due to
the king's messenger (Johnson) or

upon Respect, personified (Malone);
(ii) deliberately. Cf. *John*, IV. ii. 214:
'when, perchance, it frowns / More
upon humour than advised respect'.
Cf. also *Ham.*, III. i. 68.

24. *Resolve*] satisfy, answer. Cf. *R3*,
IV. ii. 26.

modest] becoming, sober, reasonable.
Cf. IV. vii. 5.

25. *might'st*] could'st.

27. *commend*] commit, deliver. Cf.
All's W., v. i. 31.

32. *spite of intermission*] though my
business was interrupted and the answer delayed which I was to receive.

Which presently they read: on whose contents
They summon'd up their meiny, straight took horse;
Commanded me to follow, and attend   35
The leisure of their answer; gave me cold looks:
And meeting here the other messenger,
Whose welcome, I perceiv'd, had poison'd mine,
Being the very fellow which of late
Display'd so saucily against your Highness,   40
Having more man than wit about me, drew:
He rais'd the house with loud and coward cries.
Your son and daughter found this trespass worth
The shame which here it suffers.

Fool. Winter's not gone yet, if the wild-geese fly that way. 45
        Fathers that wear rags
           Do make their children blind,
        But fathers that bear bags
           Shall see their children kind.
        Fortune, that arrant whore,   50
        Ne'er turns the key to th'poor.
But for all this thou shalt have as many dolours for
thy daughters as thou canst tell in a year.

Lear. O! how this mother swells up toward my heart;
    Hysterica passio! down, thou climbing sorrow!   55

---

33. whose] *Q; those F.*   34. meiny] *F;* men *Q.*   39. which] *F;* that *Q.*   44.
The] *F;* This *Q.*   45–53. Winter's . . . year] *F; not in Q.*   45. wild] *F2;* wil'd
F1.   52–3. for thy] *F;* for thy deare *F2–4;* from thy deare *Theobald;* from thy
Singer.   55. Hysterica] *F4; Historica Q, F1–2; Hystorica F3.*

33. *presently*] immediately.
34. *meiny*] household, servants. See
Appendix, p. 240.
40. *Display'd*] acted ostentatiously.
41. *more . . . wit*] more courage than
sense.
   drew] drew his sword.
42. *rais'd . . . house*] awakened the
servants.
45. *wild-geese*] Cf. note on II. ii. 80–1
and *saucily* (40), *blind* (47), *dolours* (52),
and *stocks* (62). Possibly an allusion to
Lady Wild-goose (see Introduction,
p. xxxix).
48. *bear bags*] hang on to the money-
bags.

51. *turns the key*] opens the door. Cf.
III. vii. 62.
52. *dolours*] a pun on dollars, the
English name for the Spanish peso and
the German thaler. Cf. *Tp.*, II. i. 19,
and *Meas.*, I. ii. 50.
   for] on account of, owing to.
53. *tell*] a quibble, the word meaning both *relate* and *count*.
54–5. *mother . . . Hysterica passio*] The
symptoms of this malady are described
by Drayton, *Polyolbion*, VII. 19–28.
Richard Mainy, one of the people
mentioned in Harsnett's pamphlet,
suffered from the mother, and it is
alluded to more than once. See

Thy element's below. Where is this daughter?

Kent. With the Earl, Sir; here within.

Lear. Follow me not; stay here.   [*Exit.*

Gent. Made you no more offence but what you speak of?

Kent. None.   60

How chance the King comes with so small a number?

Fool. And thou hadst been set i'th'stocks for that question, thou'dst well deserv'd it.

Kent. Why, Fool?

Fool. We'll set thee to school to an ant, to teach thee   65
there's no labouring i'th'winter. All that follow
their noses are led by their eyes but blind men; and
there's not a nose among twenty but can smell him
that's stinking. Let go thy hold when a great wheel
runs down a hill, lest it break thy neck with follow-   70

---

57. here] *F; not in Q.*   58. here.] *F; there? Q1;* there. *Q2–3.*   S.D.]
F; not in Q.   59. but] *F;* then *Q.*   60. None] *F;* no, *Q.*   61. the] *Q;*
the the *F.*   number] *F;* traine *Q.*   62. And] *Q1, F;* If *Q2–3;* An *Pope.*
68. twenty] *F;* a 100 *Q.*   69. stinking] sinking *conj. Mason.*   70–1.
following;] *F;* following it, *Q.*

Appendix, p. 239. Edward Jordan,
*A Brief Discourse of a Disease called the
Suffocation of the Mother,* 1605, p. 5,
writes: 'This disease is called by
diverse names amongst our authors,
Passio Hysterica, Suffocatio, Priefocatio,
and *Strangulatus uteri, Caducus Matricis,*
i.e. in English, the Mother or the
Suffocation of the Mother, because,
most commonly, it takes them with
choking in the throat; and it is an
affect of the mother or wombe, wherein the principal parts of the bodie
by consent do suffer diversely according to the diversitie of the causes
and diseases wherewith the ma-
trix is offended.' Craig thinks the
word may be only a contraction of
smother.

56. *element*] proper place.

59. *Made . . . offence*] For examples of
this form, see *Meas.,* IV. ii. 198–9;
AYL., III. v. 117.

61. *How chance*] how does it happen
that.

65. *ant*] The ant lays up a store of

food during the summer, and the Fool
implies that in the winter of Lear's
fortunes his followers have deserted
him, because they can no longer make
anything out of him. Cf. the verses 79–
82 below. Alternatively, or addition-
ally, he may be telling Kent that he is
foolish to remain with the King. Baldwin, *Shakespere's Small Latine and Lesse
Greeke,* I. 620–1, points out that Shakespeare may have been influenced by
the fable of the Fly and the Ant as told
by Camerarius: '*At ego aestate mediocri
labore exerceor, vt hyeme quietam &
securam vitam possim degere.*'

69. *stinking*] Mason wished to emend
to *sinking,* with which Steevens compared *Ant.,* III. x. 26. Malone defended
stinking, and compared *All's W.,* v. ii.
4–6: 'I am now, sir, muddied in fortune's mood, and smell somewhat
strong of her strong displeasure.'
Those who can see that the king is
ruined have deserted him, and even
the blind should be able to smell the
stench of fortune's displeasure.

ing; but the great one that goes upward, let him
draw thee after. When a wise man gives thee better
counsel, give me mine again: I would have none but
knaves follow it, since a Fool gives it.

<blockquote>

That sir which serves and seeks for gain,   75
  And follows but for form,
Will pack when it begins to rain,
  And leave thee in the storm.
But I will tarry; the Fool will stay,
  And let the wise man fly: 80
The knave turns Fool that runs away;
  The Fool no knave, perdy.
</blockquote>

Kent. Where learn'd you this, Fool?
Fool. Not i'th'stocks, Fool.

Re-enter LEAR, *with* GLOUCESTER.

Lear. Deny to speak with me! They are sick! They are
  weary!   85
They have travell'd all the night! Mere fetches, ay,

---

71. upward] *F;* vp the hill *Q.* 73. have] *Q;* hause *F1.* 75. That sir] That,
sir, *F4.* which] *F;* that *Q.* and seeks] *F; not in Q.* 77. begins] begin *Q1.*
78. the] a *F4.* 79. But] And *F3–4.* 81–2. The knave ... knave] The fool
turns knave that runs away, The knave no fool *Collier (conj. Johnson).* 84. Fool]
F; not in Q. S.D.] *Capell, based on Q; after 82 F.* 86. have] *F; not in Q.*
all the night] *F;* hard to night *Q.* fetches, ay] *conj. Capell;* fetches *F;* Iustice I *Q.*

---

73. *have*] J. Sledd, *M.L.N.*, 1940,
p. 595, suggests that the F reading,
hause, may be a variant of *halse*, meaning *beseech* or *abjure*, and derived from
O.E. *halsian.*

75. *sir*] man.

76. *form*] Cf. *Meas.*, II. iv. 12, and
Oth., I. i. 50. The man is 'trimmed in
forms and visages of duty', but has no
inner feelings of loyalty. He serves
because of his master's rank.

77. *pack*] be off.

79–82. *But ... perdy*] Enid Welsford,
The Fool, 1935, pp. 255–6, 267, com-
menting on these lines, and rejecting
Johnson's emendation, shows that the
Fool, like Erasmus in *The Praise of
Folly*, is playing upon the various
meanings and relations of the words
'fool' and 'knave'. His decision to stay

with Lear is 'the unambiguous wisdom
of the madman who sees the truth'. He
does not wish Kent to follow his advice
to desert the King, for it is only the
advice of a fool. 'The knave who runs
away comes out into the open, and is
at once seen as the abject contemptible
ludicrous creature that he has always
been. The fool is at least true to himself.' Kittredge similarly interprets:
'The fellow that forsakes his master is
(from the point of view of the higher
wisdom) a fool, since true wisdom
implies fidelity; and the fool who, like
me, remains faithful is, at all events, no
knave.'

84. *Not ... Fool*] Kent, too, is a loyal
fool, and not a politic knave.

85. *Deny*] refuse. Cf. *R3*, v. iii. 343.

86. *fetches*] tricks, subterfuges, ruses,

The images of revolt and flying off.
Fetch me a better answer.

Glou.   My dear Lord,
You know the fiery quality of the Duke;
How unremovable and fix'd he is   90
In his own course.

Lear. Vengeance! plague! death! confusion!
Fiery! what quality? Why, Gloucester, Gloucester,
I'd speak with the Duke of Cornwall and his wife.

Glou. Well, my good Lord, I have inform'd them so.   95

Lear. Inform'd them! Dost thou understand me, man?

Glou. Ay, my good Lord.

Lear. The King would speak with Cornwall; the dear
    father
Would with his daughter speak, commands, tends
    service:
Are they inform'd of this? My breath and blood!   100
Fiery! the fiery Duke! Tell the hot Duke that—
No, but not yet; may be he is not well:
Infirmity doth still neglect all office
Whereto our health is bound; we are not ourselves

92. plague! death!] *F;* death, plague *Q.*   93. Fiery! what quality?] *F;*
what fierie quality, *Q.*   95–6. Well . . . man?] *F; not in Q.*   98. father]
fate *Q uncorr.*   99. with his] with the *Q uncorr.*   commands, tends] *F;*
come and tends *Q uncorr.;* commands her *Q corr., Q2–3.*   100. Are . . . blood!]
F; not in Q.   101. Fiery . . . Duke!] *F;* The fierie Duke *Q uncorr.;* Fierie Duke
Q corr.   that—] *F;* that Lear *Q.*   102. No] mo *Q uncorr.*

contrivances, acts of tacking (nautical).

ay] This may be an interpolation by
the actor, or an accidental omission by
F. On the whole, although there is no
reason why the line should be made
regular, it is improved by the retention of this word.

87. *images*] signs, symbols. The word,
Craig suggests, may here be disyllabic,
though this is surely improbable.

flying off] revolt, desertion. Cf. *Ant.*,
II. ii. 155.

89. *quality*] nature, disposition. Cf.
Tw.N., III. i. 70.

90. *unremovable*] stubbornly firm.
Cf. *Tim.*, v. i. 227.

99. *commands, tends*] The corrected

reading of Q, *commands her seruice*,
could not have been in the copy, for
the original compositor could not have
misread *her* as *tends*. Although F here
may have been printed from an uncorrected sheet, and *tends* may therefore be a reproduction of a Q error, the
word makes sense. Schmidt suggests
that it is an apheitc form of *attends*:
Greg, that it means *offers*. Lear commands her service, tenders his own;
and this may be taken as a conciliatory
afterthought, or as an ironical re-
inforcement of his words. Cf. Greg,
Variants, pp. 161–2, and Duthie, *op.
cit.*, pp. 143–4.

101. *hot*] hot-tempered, passionate.
103. *office*] duty.

When Nature, being oppress'd, commands the mind 105
To suffer with the body. I'll forbear;
And am fall'n out with my more headier will,
To take the indispos'd and sickly fit
For the sound man. Death on my state! wherefore
                                                        [Looking on Kent.
Should he sit here? This act persuades me 110
That this remotion of the Duke and her
Is practice only. Give me my servant forth.
Go tell the Duke and's wife I'd speak with them,
Now, presently: bid them come forth and hear me,
Or at their chamber-door I'll beat the drum 115
Till it cry sleep to death.
Glou. I would have all well betwixt you.   *[Exit.*
Lear. O me! my heart, my rising heart! but, down!
Fool. Cry to it, Nuncle, as the cockney did to the eels

---

105. commands] command *Q1.*   109. S.D.] *Johnson; not in Q, F.*   113. Go]
F; not in Q.   I'd] Ile *Q.*   117. S.D.] *F; not in Q.*   118. O me ... down]
F; O my heart, my heart *Q.*

107. *am ... will*] am angry with my more headlong impulse.

headier] impetuous or headlong, rather than headstrong. Cf. Ascham, *Toxophilus*, ed. Arber, p. 85: 'Wales being headye, and rebelling many yeares against us'.

108. *To take*] for taking.

109. *my state*] my royal power.

111. *remotion*] keeping aloof, as in *Tim.*, IV. ii. 346. But Lear may be referring to their removal. Cf. II. iv. 4.

112. *practice*] craft, trickery.

forth] out of the stocks.

114. *presently*] at once.

116. *Till ... death*] till the noise of the drum has been the death of sleep, so that they give up all idea of sleeping. Cf. *Mac.*, II. ii. 42.

117. *I ... well*] Cf. *Leir*, 831, 'I feare that all things go not well.'

119. *cockney*] Halliwell and Dyce suspect that there is an allusion to some lost story. A cockney could be a spoilt child, a cook, a Londoner, or an affected woman. Cotgrave defines *Coquine* as a beggar woman, also a cockney, *simper-de-cockit*, nice thing. Meres, *Wit's Treasury*, 1598, cited *N.E.D.*, has: 'Many cockney and wanton women are often sick.' The present use of the word is difficult to determine, as affected woman, cook, and Londoner would all fit the context. Perhaps the heroine of the story was all three. She was so unfamiliar with eels that she did not know that they should be killed before cooking. Cf. Lyly, *Euphues*, ed. Arber, p. 103: 'But why cast I the effects of this vnnaturalnesse in thy teeth, seeing I my selfe was the cause? I made thee a *wanton*, and thou hast made me a foole: I brought thee vp like a *cockney*, and thou hast handled me like a *cockescombe*.' J. C. Maxwell points out to me that the italicized words reappear in the present context, and that the situation recalls that of *Euphues*, where Ferardo complains of his daughter's ingratitude: 'I had thought that my hoary haires should haue found comforte by thy golden lockes, and my

when she put 'em i'th'paste alive; she knapp'd   120
'em o'th'coxcombs with a stick, and cried 'Down,
wantons, down!' 'Twas her brother that, in pure
kindness to his horse, buttered his hay.

Re-enter GLOUCESTER, *with* CORNWALL, REGAN,
and Servants.

Lear. Good morrow to you both.
Corn.   Hail to your Grace!
                                    [*Kent is set at liberty.*
Reg. I am glad to see your Highness.   125
Lear. Regan, I think you are; I know what reason
I have to think so: if thou shouldst not be glad,
I would divorce me from thy mother's tomb,
Sepulchring an adult'ress. [*To Kent.*] O! are you free?
Some other time for that. [*Exit Kent.*] Beloved Regan,
Thy sister's naught: O Regan! she hath tied   131
Sharp-tooth'd unkindness, like a vulture, here.
                                    [*Points to his heart.*

---

120. when she] when hee *F2–4.*   put 'em] *F;* put vm *Q1;* put them *Q2–3, F4.*
i'th'] *F;* it'h *Q1;* vp i' th *Q2–3.*   120–1. knapp'd 'em o'th'] *F;* rapt um ath *Q.*
122. her] his *F3–4.*   123. S.D.] *F, subst.; Enter Duke and Regan Q.*   124. *&c.*
Corn.] *F; Duke Q.*   S.D.] *F; not in Q.*   126. you] *Q;* your *F.*   128. divorce]
deuose *Q uncorr.*   mother's] *Q;* Mother *F.*   tomb] fruit *Q uncorr.*   129.
S.D.] *Rowe; not in Q, F.*   O] *F;* Yea *Q.*   130. S.D.] *Ringler.*   131. sister's]
sister is *Q.*   tied] tired *Sympson.*   132. S.D.] *Pope; not in Q, F.*

---

rotten age great ease by thy rype
years. . . Would I had neuer lyued to
be so olde, or thou to be so obstinate.
. . . Is this the comfort that the parent
reapeth for all his care? Is obstinacy
payed for obedyence, slubbernenesse,
rendred for duetie, malycious desper-
atenesse, for filiall feare?'

120. *knapp'd*] rapped. Jamieson,
Scottish Dictionary, defines knap as 'to
strike smartly, as "knap the nail on the
head"'. Cf. Ps., xlvi. 9.

121–2. *Down . . . down!*] Down, you
playful creatures, down (Kittredge).
But even without Robert Graves's
poem of this title one might suspect
that the phrase was equivocal.

123. *buttered his hay*] A common trick

of cheating ostlers was to grease the
hay of horses committed to their care;
the horses, disliking grease, were kept
from feeding, and the ostler could
steal their provender. The cockney's
brother, however, did it in all innocence.

124. *Good morrow*] It is now evening,
so that Lear's greeting is ironical.

128. *mother's tomb*] At the opening of
King Leir, there is a reference to the
funeral of the Queen.

129. *Sepulchring*] as being the
sepulchre of. The accent is on the
second syllable.

132. *like a vulture*] an allusion to the
torture of Prometheus. See Appendix,
p. 241.

I can scarce speak to thee; thou'lt not believe
With how deprav'd a quality—O Regan!
Reg. I pray you, Sir, take patience. I have hope   135
You less know how to value her desert
Than she to scant her duty.
Lear.   Say? how is that?
Reg. I cannot think my sister in the least
Would fail her obligation. If, Sir, perchance
She have restrain'd the riots of your followers,   140
'Tis on such ground, and to such wholesome end,
As clears her from all blame.
Lear.   My curses on her!
Reg. O, Sir! you are old;
Nature in you stands on the very verge
Of her confine: you should be rul'd and led   145
By some discretion that discerns your state
Better than you yourself. Therefore I pray you
That to our sister you do make return;
Say you have wrong'd her.
Lear.   Ask her forgiveness?
Do you but mark how this becomes the house: 150
'Dear daughter, I confess that I am old;

133. thou'lt] *F;* thout *Q.*   134. With how deprav'd] *F;* Of how depriued
Q corr., Q2; Of how deptoued *Q uncorr.*   quality—] *Rowe;* quality. *F;*
qualitie, *Q.*   135. you] *F; not in Q.*   137. scant] *F;* slacke *Q.*   137–42.
Lear. Say . . . blame.] *F; not in Q.*   144. in] *F;* on *Q.*   145. her] *Q;* his *F.*
147. pray you] *F;* pray *Q.*   149. her.] *F;* her Sir? *Q.*   150. but] *F; not
in Q.*

134. *quality*] manner, disposition.

135–7. *I have . . . duty*] Johnson and
other critics (inc. Greg, *T.L.S.*, 9 Nov.
1933) have pointed out that Shakespeare says the opposite of what he
intends. But the double negative does
not, here and frequently in Shakespeare, make an affirmative. Regan
means: 'I hope you undervalue her
dutifulness, rather than that she has
come short in it.' Perhaps Shakespeare
meant Regan to say the opposite of
this, and so tell the truth against her
will.

137. *scant*] Cf. I. i. 277; II. iv. 173;
III. ii. 67.

145. *confine*] assigned limit; or Regan
may mean that Lear is imprisoned in
the flesh and about to be released by
death.

146. *discretion*] the abstract for the
concrete, i.e. discreet person. Cf.
'houseless poverty', III. iv. 26.

state] condition of mind; or, your
dependent position.

150. *house*] the royal house (Perrett);
family relations (Kittredge).

151–3. *Dear . . . food*] Heilman, *op.
cit.*, pp. 142–3, says that Lear is here
'the ironic critic of a violation of
Nature which is symbolized by the
father's being a suppliant to his child.

    Age is unnecessary: on my knees I beg   [*Kneeling*.
    That you'll vouchsafe me raiment, bed, and food.'
Reg. Good sir, no more; these are unsightly tricks.
    Return you to my sister.
Lear. [*Rising*.]   Never, Regan.   155
    ╱She hath abated me of half my train;
    Look'd black upon me; struck me with her tongue,
    Most serpent-like, upon the very heart.
    All the stor'd vengeances of Heaven fall
    On her ingrateful top! Strike her young bones,   160
    You taking airs, with lameness!
Corn.   Fie, Sir, fie!
Lear. You nimble lightnings, dart your blinding flames
    Into her scornful eyes! Infect her beauty,
    You fen-suck'd fogs, drawn by the pow'rful sun,

---

152. S.D.] *Dyce; not in Q,F.*   155. Never] *F;* No *Q.*   157. black] back *Q 2–3.*
161. Fie, Sir, fie!] *F;* Fie he sir *Q.*   162. *Lear.*] *Q 2; Le. F; not in Q.*

. . . Lear's ironic prayer is a ruthlessly logical display of the doctrine of the survival of the fittest . . . age is a crime in a world where the chief value is physical force.'

152. *Age . . . unnecessary*] Old people are useless. Johnson explained: 'Old age has few wants.'

156. *abated*] deprived, curtailed. Hilda M. Hulme, *M.L.R.*, 1951, p. 322, shows that the word was used in Warwickshire in this sense.

157. *struck . . . tongue*] Cf. *Leir*, 1048: 'I will so toung-whip him.'

159. *stor'd vengeances*] Cf. Beaumont and Fletcher, *The Coxcomb*, I. i. 22: 'Let all the stored vengeance of heaven's justice'.

160. *top*] head.

young bones] Cf. *Leir*, 844–7: '*Leir.* Alas, not I: poore soule, she breeds yong bones, / And that is it makes her so tutchy sure. / *Gon.* What, breeds young bones already! you will make / An honest woman of me then, belike.' The same expression, 'young bones', for unborn progeny, is to be found in Tourneur, *The Atheist's Tragedy*, IV.

iii. 172, and in Ford, *The Broken Heart*. II. i. Kellett, *Suggestions*, p. 40, remarks that 'the curse gains greatly in meaning if we assume that Shakespeare's Lear, like the old playwright's Leir, knew or suspected that Goneril had already an unborn child.' Kittredge declares that the context makes it certain that the yong bones are Goneril's own; and Perrett urges that since the embryo is well protected, it could not be hurt by taking airs. But this is not a decisive objection. Cf. *Ham.*, I. i. 163. Perrett's other objection, that Lear would not curse an innocent unborn child, is invalid. Cf. I. iv. 279 ff.

161. *taking*] infecting, blasting. Cf. *Wiv.*, IV. iv. 32, and Palsgrave, *op. cit.*, 'taken, as children's limbs are by the fairies'.

164. *fen-suck'd*] sucked up from the fens by the heat of the sun. Cf. *MND.*, II. i. 90. In another passage, *Tp.*, II. ii. 1–2, Shakespeare uses five words that appear together in the present context: 'All the infections that the sun sucks up / From bogs, fens, flats on Prosper fall.'

To fall and blister her!   165
Reg. O the blest Gods! so will you wish on me,
When the rash mood is on.
Lear. No, Regan, thou shalt never have my curse:
Thy tender-hefted nature shall not give
Thee o'er to harshness: her eyes are fierce, but thine 170
Do comfort and not burn. 'Tis not in thee
To grudge my pleasures, to cut off my train,
To bandy hasty words, to scant my sizes,

---

165. blister her] *Muir;* blister *F;* blast her pride *Q;* blister pride *Schmidt;* blister her pride *Duthie.*   167. is on] *F; not in Q.*   169. Thy] *F;* The *Q.*   tender-hefted] *F;* tender hested *Q1-2;* tender hasted *Q3;* tender-hearted *Rowe.* 170. Thee] the *Q1.*   o'er] are *Q3.*

---

165. *blister her*] The Q reading is unlikely to be right, because it was deliberately corrected by F; but the F reading is not convincing as it stands. Schmidt's *blister pride* is easier to speak, and the compositor may have thought that *pride* as well as *blast her* was marked for deletion. Duthie's reading, *blister her pride,* if the -er of *blister* is elided as he suggests, would be indistinguishable in the theatre from *blister pride.* The reading in the text can be spoken with plenty of venom. For a similar use of *blister* cf. *Tp.,* I. ii. 323: 'blister you all o'er'; and *Ham.,* III. iv. 42–4. Duthie argues that the Q reading is a memorial corruption (cf. I. iv. 297). But it must be admitted that *blast* and *infection* were also closely associated in Shakespeare's mind, and *blast* and *blister* were probably thought to have a common derivation, so that the substitution of one for the other would be simple enough. It is not impossible that Shakespeare suggested or allowed an emendation which by some accident never got into the prompt-book. Nosworthy conjectures *blister o'er.*

169. *tender-hefted*] set in a delicate 'haft' or bodily frame; hence womanly, gentle (*N.E.D.*). Florio uses the word *hafted,* 'handled' (cf. Appendix, p. 236). Shakespeare elsewhere (*Wint.,* II. i. 45) uses *heft* to mean 'heaving', as

in retching; and Steevens, followed by Kittredge, explains: 'heaved (i.e. moved, swayed) by tender emotions only'. Schmidt (*Lexicon*) suggests the word means 'tender-handled', gentle to touch or approach, affable. If the Q reading *tender hested* were accepted, it might mean, since *hest* = command, commanded by tenderness, 'a nature which is governed by gentle dispositions'. I am not satisfied with any of these explanations. Wright cites Cotgrave, *op. cit.*: '*Emmanché:* . . . Helued, set into a haft. *Lasche emmanché:* Lazie, idle, slothfull, weake, feeble, loose ioynted, faint-hearted'. But he does not draw the conclusion that if *lasche emmanché* can mean 'faint-hearted', then *tender-hefted* may reasonably be taken to mean 'tender-hearted'.

171. *Do . . . burn*] Malone compares *Tim.,* v. i. 134.

173. *bandy*] Cf. I. iv. 82 and note.

sizes] allowances. Cotgrave, *op. cit.,* defines *Mesure:* 'scantling, rule, square, proportion, size'. A sizar is a poor scholar who used to obtain allowances from the college buttery-hatch. In *Leir,* Perillus complains (763): 'His pension she hath halfe restrain'd from him.' Skalliger urges Gonorill (801): 'The large allowance which he hath from you . . . / Therefore abbridge it halfe.'

And, in conclusion to oppose the bolt
Against my coming in: thou better know'st   175
The offices of nature, bond of childhood,
Effects of courtesy, dues of gratitude;
Thy half o'th'kingdom hast thou not forgot,
Wherein I thee endow'd.

Reg.   Good sir, to th'purpose.
Lear. Who put my man i'th'stocks?   [*Tucket within.*
Corn.   What trumpet's that?
Reg. I know't, my sister's: this approves her letter,   181
   That she would soon be here.

Enter OSWALD.

                    Is your Lady come?
Lear. This is a slave, whose easy-borrow'd pride
   Dwells in the fickle grace of her he follows.
   Out, varlet, from my sight!
Corn.   What means your Grace?
Lear. Who stock'd my servant? Regan, I have good
      hope   186
   Thou didst not know on't. Who comes here?

Enter GONERIL.

                    O Heavens
   If you do love old men, if your sweet sway
   Allow obedience, if you yourselves are old,

178. o'th'] *F*; of the *Q.*   180. S.D.] *F, after 179; not in Q.*   181. sister's] sister *Q3.*   letter] *F*; letters *Q.*   182. S.D.] *Dyce; Enter Steward (after that, 180) Q, after* stocks *F.*   183. easy-borrow'd] *hyphened Theobald.*   184. fickle] *Q*; fickly *F1–2*; sickly *F3–4.*   he] a *Q1.*   186. *Lear*] *F*; *Gon. Q.*   stock'd] *F*; struck *Q.*   187. on't] *F*; ant *Q1–2.*   S.D.] *Johnson; at 185 Q,F.*   188. your] *F*; you *Q.*   189. you] *F*; not in *Q.*

176. *offices*] duties.
   bond of childhood] a child's duty to her parents.
   177. *Effects*] workings, manifestations. Cf. *H8*, II. iv. 86.
   181. *I know't*] Regan probably recognized some distinguishing note or tune (Steevens). Cf. *Oth.*, II. i. 180.
   approves] confirms, is in accordance with. Cf. II. ii. 156.
   183. *easy-borrow'd*] 'borrowed with-

out the trouble of doing anything to justify it' (Moberly), as one who borrows money without offering any security. Perhaps Theobald was wrong to hyphen the words; *easy* may mean 'coolly impudent'.
   184. *fickle*] The F reading was probably due to a remembrance of l. 108 *ante.*
   189. *Allow*] approve of. Cf. *allowance,* I. iv. 206.

Make it your cause; send down and take my part!   190
[*To Goneril.*] Art not asham'd to look upon this beard?
O Regan! will you take her by the hand?
Gon. Why not by th'hand, sir? How have I offended?
All's not offence that indiscretion finds
And dotage terms so.
Lear.   O sides! you are too tough;   195
Will you yet hold? How came my man i'th'stocks?
Corn. I set him there, Sir; but his own disorders
Deserv'd much less advancement.
Lear.   You! did you?
Reg. I pray you, father, being weak, seem so.
If, till the expiration of your month,   200
You will return and sojourn with my sister,
Dismissing half your train, come then to me:
I am now from home, and out of that provision
Which shall be needful for your entertainment.
Lear. Return to her? and fifty men dismiss'd?   205
No, rather I abjure all roofs, and choose
To wage against the enmity o'th'air;
To be a comrade with the wolf and owl,
Necessity's sharp pinch! Return with her!
Why, the hot-blooded France, that dowerless took   210
Our youngest born, I could as well be brought
To knee his throne, and, squire-like, pension beg
To keep base life afoot. Return with her!

191. S.D.] *Johnson; not in Q, F.*   192. will you] *F;* wilt thou *Q.*   197. Sir]
not in Q2–3.   207. o'th'] of the *Q.*   208. owl] howl *Collier.*   210.
hot-blooded] hot bloud in *Q.*   212. beg] bag *Q1.*   213. afoot] *Q;* a foote
F.

194. *finds*] deems (Fr. *trouver*), detects.

195. *dotage*] Heilman, *op. cit.*, p. 141, says that this 'is Goneril's favourite word for age: it is her way of denying that age has dignity or deserts, and that it has a place in Nature; she conceives of it only as a state which compels submission to her and her sister's desires'.

195–6. *O . . . hold*] Cf. *Ant.*, IV. xiv. 39.

197. *disorders*] misconduct.

198. *advancement*] promotion, honour.

207. *wage*] combat, contend.

208. *owl*] Collier, following the Collier MS., read *howl.* This is not an improvement, in spite of the lines quoted by Collier in support of it, *All's W.*, III. ii. 119–21.

209. *Necessity's . . . pinch*] Cf. Florio's words, Appendix, p. 237.

210. *hot-blooded*] passionate. Cf. I. ii. 23.

212. *knee his throne*] Schmidt ex-

Persuade me rather to be slave and sumpter
To this detested groom.   [*Pointing at Oswald.*
Gon.   At your choice, Sir.   215
Lear. I prithee, daughter, do not make me mad:
I will not trouble thee, my child; farewell.
We'll no more meet, no more see one another;
But yet thou art my flesh, my blood, my daughter;
Or rather a disease that's in my flesh,   220
Which I must needs call mine: thou art a boil,
A plague-sore, or embossed carbuncle,
In my corrupted blood. But I'll not chide thee;
Let shame come when it will, I do not call it;
I do not bid the thunder-bearer shoot,   225
Nor tell tales of thee to high-judging Jove.
Mend when thou canst; be better at thy leisure;
I can be patient; I can stay with Regan,
I and my hundred knights.
Reg.   Not altogether so;
I look'd not for you yet, nor am provided   230
For your fit welcome. Give ear, Sir, to my sister;
For those that mingle reason with your passion
Must be content to think you old, and so—

215. S.D.] *Johnson, subst.; not in Q, F.*   216. I] *F;* Now I *Q.*   220. that's in]
F; that lies within *Q.*   222. or] *F;* an *Q.*   225. thunder-bearer] *F;*
thunder bearer *Q.*   226. high-judging] *F;* high iudging *Q.*   229. so] *F;* so
sir *Q.*   230. look'd] *F;* looke *Q.*   231. Sir] *not in Q 2–3.*   233. you old]
F; you are old *Q.*   so—] *Rowe;* so, *Q, F.*

plains 'to travel thither on the knees'.
Cf. *Cor.*, v. i. 5, and *Leir*, 2294: 'Ide
creepe along, to meet him on my
knee.' But the phrase is more likely to
mean 'kneel before his throne'.

214. *sumpter*] packhorse, or possibly
pack-horse driver. In Florio, *op. cit.*,
II. 143, the word has the former meaning. Cotgrave defines *Sommier* 'a
Sumpter horse, and generally any
toyling and load-carrying drudge or
groom'.

221. *boil*] Cotgrave (s.v. *Bosse*) gives
it as a synonym of 'plague-sore'.

222. *embossed*] swollen, tumid, knob-
bed like the boss of a shield. Palsgrave
has 'Botch, a sore; *bosse de pestilence*';

and Cotgrave, '*Embosser*, to swell, or
arise in bunches, hulches, knobs; to
grow knottie, or knurrie'. C. Leech
compares Elyot's *The Governour*, II. iv:
'And the goutes, carbuncles . . . and
other lyke sores and sickenesses, which
do procede of bloode corrupted'.

225. *thunder-bearer*] Jupiter.

226. *high-judging*] that is supreme
judge; or 'judging in heaven'
(Schmidt). There is the same ambiguity in 'high heaven' (*Meas.*, II. ii.
121).

232. *mingle . . . passion*] Dilute your
passionate words with a little common
sense, examine them in the cold light
of reason.

But she knows what she does.

Lear.   Is this well spoken?

Reg. I dare avouch it, sir: what! fifty followers?   235
   Is it not well? What should you need of more?
   Yea, or so many, sith that both charge and danger
   Speak 'gainst so great a number? How, in one house,
   Should many people, under two commands,
   Hold amity? 'Tis hard; almost impossible.   240

Gon. Why might not you, my Lord, receive attendance
   From those that she calls servants, or from mine?

Reg. Why not, my Lord? If then they chanc'd to slack ye
   We could control them. If you will come to me,
   For now I spy a danger, I entreat you   245
   To bring but five-and-twenty; to no more
   Will I give place or notice.

Lear. I gave you all—

Reg.   And in good time you gave it.

Lear. Made you my guardians, my depositaries,
   But kept a reservation to be follow'd   250
   With such a number. What! must I come to you
   With five-and-twenty? Regan, said you so?

Reg. And speak't again, my Lord; no more with me.

Lear. Those wicked creatures yet do look well-favour'd
   When others are more wicked; not being the worst   255
   Stands in some rank of praise. [*To Goneril.*] I'll go
      with thee:
   Thy fifty yet doth double five-and-twenty,
   And thou art twice her love.

Gon.   Hear me, my Lord.
   What need you five-and-twenty, ten, or five,

---

234. spoken] *F;* spoken now *Q.*   238. Speak] *F;* Speakes *Q.*   one] *F;*
a *Q.*   243. chanc'd] *F;* chanc'st *Q.*   ye] *F;* you *Q.*   250. kept] keep
F3–4.   254. look] *F;* seem *Q.*   well-favour'd] *hyphened Q2; unhyphened Q1,
F1–2.*   256. S.D.] *Hanmer; not in Q, F.*

243. *slack ye*] come short of their
duty towards you. Cf. *Oth.,* IV. iii.
88.

248. *I . . . all*] Cf. *Leir,* 2144:
'Ah, cruell *Ragan,* did I giue thee
all?'

249. *guardians . . . depositaries*] stew-

ardesses and trustees. Cf. Appendix,
p. 236.

250. *reservation*] a saving clause. Cf.
I. i. 132.

254-6. *Those . . . praise*] Steevens
compares *Cym.,* V. v. 215-17.

254. *well-favour'd*] good-looking.

To follow in a house where twice so many   260
Have a command to tend you?
Reg.   What need one?
Lear. O! reason not the need; our basest beggars
Are in the poorest thing superfluous:
Allow not nature more than nature needs,
Man's life is cheap as beast's. Thou art a lady;   265
If only to go warm were gorgeous,
Why, nature needs not what thou gorgeous wear'st,
Which scarcely keeps thee warm. But, for true need,—
You Heavens, give me that patience, patience I need!—
You see me here, you Gods, a poor old man,   270
As full of grief as age; wretched in both!
If it be you that stirs these daughters' hearts
Against their father, fool me not so much
To bear it tamely; touch me with noble anger,
And let not women's weapons, water-drops,   275
Stain my man's cheeks! No, you unnatural hags,
I will have such revenges on you both
That all the world shall—I will do such things,
What they are, yet I know not, but they shall be

261. need] *F;* needes *Q.*   262. need] *F;* deed *Q.*   265. life is] *F;* life as *Q1;*
life's as *Q2-3.*   267. wear'st] *F;* wearest *Q.*   270. man] *F;* fellow *Q.*
271. grief] gteefe *Q2.*   273. so] *F;* to *Q1-3;* too *Q2.*   274. tamely] *F;*
lamely *Q.*   275. And] *F;* O *Q.*   278. shall—] *Q2, F;* shall, *Q.*   279.
are, yet] *Q2;* are yet, *F;* are yet *Q1.*

260. *follow*] be your attendants.

262. *reason not*] do not argue about.
Heilman, *op. cit.*, p. 169, commenting
on this speech, observes that 'Lear not
only defines the effect upon humanity
of the use of mere need as a measuring
stick for perquisites, but he shrewdly
demonstrates that his daughters do not
themselves observe the canon of need.'

263. *Are . . . superfluous*] have, however little they possess, something
above what is necessary for bare existence. Cf. iv. i. 66 and iii. iv. 35.

264.] The first nature is 'human
nature', the second 'animal nature'
(G. K. Hunter).

266-8. *If . . . warm*] If it were gorgeous merely to be warm, you would

not need the fashionably scanty attire
you are now wearing.

268. *But . . . need*] Lear is about to
explain the difference between true
need and the perverted needs of
fashionable women, when he breaks
off to pray for his own chief need at the
moment—patience or fortitude.

273. *fool*] Empson, *op. cit.*, p. 134,
remarks that 'the heavens themselves,
in this break-up of the human order,
are becoming fools like everyone else,
only malicious ones.' But the passage
probably means 'do not make me such
a fool as'.

278-80. *I will . . . earth*] Ritson cites
Golding's *Ovid's Metamorphoses*, vi.
784-5: 'The thing that I doe purpose

The terrors of the earth. You think I'll weep;   280
No, I'll not weep:
I have full cause of weeping, [*Storm heard at a distance.*]
    but this heart
Shall break into a hundred thousand flaws
Or ere I'll weep. O Fool! I shall go mad.
        [*Exeunt Lear, Gloucester, Gentleman, and Fool.*

Corn. Let us withdraw, 'twill be a storm.   285
Reg. This house is little: the old man and's people
    Cannot be well bestow'd.
Gon. 'Tis his own blame; hath put himself from rest,
    And must needs taste his folly.
Reg. For his particular, I'll receive him gladly,   290
    But not one follower.
Gon.   So am I purpos'd.
    Where is my Lord of Gloucester?
Corn. Follow'd the old man forth. He is return'd.

Re-enter GLOUCESTER.

Glou. The King is in high rage.
Corn.   Whither is he going?
Glou. He calls to horse; but will I know not whither.   295
Corn. 'Tis best to give him way; he leads himself.

---

282. S.D.] *Capell; Storm and Tempest F; not in Q.*   283. into a hundred thousand] *F;* in a *roo.* thousand *Q1;* in a thousand *Q2.*   flaws] flowes *Q.*   284. Or ere] Ere *Q2.*   S.D.] *Ringler; Exeunt Lear, Leister . . . Q; Exeunt F; Exeunt Lear, Gloucester, Kent, and Fool Q2.*   286. and's] *F2–4;* an'ds *F;* and his *Q.*   291. *Gon.*] *F; Duke Q.*   purpos'd] *F;* puspos'd *Q1.*   293. *Corn.*] *F; Reg. Q.*   S.D.] *Dyce; after 292 Q, F.*   294–5. rage . . . whither] *F;* rage, and wil I know not whether *Q.*   296. *Corn.*] *F; Reg. Q.*   best] *F;* good *Q.*

---

on is great, what ere it is; / I know not what it may be yet.'

282. S.D.] The Heavens answer.

283. *flaws*] fragments. Bailey, *Eng. Dict.*, 1721, thus defines the word. The word was also used by Shakespeare to mean 'crack' (*LLL.*, v. ii. 415), and also 'gust of passion' (*Mac.*, III. iv. 63). There may be a quibble on two or three of these meanings here.

284. *Or ere*] before; both words separately also mean 'before'.

287. *bestow'd*] lodged.

288. '*Tis . . . hath*] F takes over the defective punctuation of Q (Duthie). Both omit the semicolon.

hath] 'he' is understood.

rest] repose of mind.

290. *For his particular*] as far as he personally is concerned.

296. *give him way*] give him his own way, let him go.

he . . . himself] He insists on having his own way (Kittredge).

Gon. My Lord, entreat him by no means to stay.
Glou. Alack! the night comes on, and the bleak winds
          Do sorely ruffle; for many miles about
          There's scarce a bush.
Reg.   O! Sir, to wilful men,   300
          The injuries that they themselves procure
          Must be their schoolmasters. Shut up your doors;
          He is attended with a desperate train,
          And what they may incense him to, being apt
          To have his ear abus'd, wisdom bids fear.   305
Corn. Shut up your doors, my Lord; 'tis a wild night:
          My Regan counsels well: come out o'th'storm.   [*Exeunt.*

298. bleak] *Q*; high *F*.   299. ruffle] *F*; russell *Q*; rustle *Capell*.   300.
There's] There is *Q3*.   scarce] *F*; not *Q*.   304. to] too *Q2–3, F1*.   306.
wild] wil'd *F1–2*.   307. Regan] Reg *Q1*.   o'th'] *F3–4*; oth' *F1–2*; at'h *Q1*;
ath *Q2–3*.

298. *bleak*] The F reading may be an
echo of *high* (l. 294).

299. *ruffle*] to bluster, to be noisy and
turbulent. The word is used by Harsnett. Cf. Appendix, p. 239.

303. *with*] by.

desperate train] It is not clear where
Lear's knights are supposed to go, or
if he brought them with him. Cf. II. iv.
61. Perhaps Regan is making a ficti-
tious excuse for her conduct.

304. *incense*] provoke, instigate.

305. *To . . . abus'd*] Cf. I. iii. 21.

wisdom] As Heilman points out (*op.
cit.*, p. 233) Regan means by wisdom,
looking out for oneself. 'Here a veri-
table exaggeration of cool sanity is
transmuted into moral madness.'

306. *Shut . . . doors*] Gloucester, in
spite of his feelings (cf. III. vii. 57 ff.),
obeys.

ACT III

SCENE I.—[*A Heath.*]

A storm, with thunder and lightning. Enter KENT
and a Gentleman, meeting.

Kent. Who's there, besides foul weather?
Gent. One minded like the weather, most unquietly.
Kent. I know you. Where's the King?
Gent. Contending with the fretful elements;
Bids the wind blow the earth into the sea,   5
Or swell the curled waters 'bove the main,
That things might change or cease; tears his white hair,
Which the impetuous blasts, with eyeless rage,
Catch in their fury, and make nothing of;
Strives in his little world of man to out-storm   10

ACT III

Scene 1

S.D. *A Heath*] Rowe; not in Q, F.   *A storm . . .*] Rowe, subst.; *Storm still* F;
not in Q.   *meeting*] *Capell; severally* F; *at several doors* Q.   1. Who's there] F;
What's here Q; Who's here *Malone.*   besides] F; beside Q.   4. elements]
F; element Q.   6. main] moon *Jennens.*   7–15. tears . . . take all] Q; *not
in* F.   10. out-storm] *conj. Steevens;* out-scorne Q.

4. *elements*] Cf. III. ii. 15–16.
6. *curled*] Cf. *2H4*, III. i. 23.
main] land. Cf. Hakluyt, Everyman
ed., v. 207: 'Our men repaired to
their boates, and passed from the
maine to a small Iland.' Shakespeare
usually uses the word as a synonym for
sea. Cf. *Sonn.*, lxiv. 7; lxxx. 8.

7. *things*] everything, the order of the
world. Cf. v. iii. 16 and *Mac.*, III. ii. 16.

8. *eyeless*] blind, sightless. Cf. *Mac.*,
I. vii. 23, where in my edition I followed the general consensus of opinion
in assuming that 'sightless' meant 'in-
visible'. Perhaps it too means 'blind'.

9. *make nothing of*] show no respect
for (Kittredge); the opposite of 'to
make much of'. Heath interprets:
'disperse to nothing as fast as he tears
it off'.

10. *little . . . man*] microcosm, the
little world, the earth (as distinguished
from the macrocosm, the great world,
the universe), a name often given to
man. Cf. Jonson, *Masque of Hymen*, 46;
Tourneur, *The Atheist's Tragedy*, III.
iii. 47.

out-storm] Steevens, in making this
conjecture, quoted *The Lover's Complaint*, 7: 'Storming her world with

The to-and-fro-conflicting wind and rain.
This night, wherein the cub-drawn bear would couch,
The lion and the belly-pinched wolf
Keep their fur dry, unbonneted he runs,
And bids what will take all.
Kent.   But who is with him?   15
Gent. None but the Fool, who labours to out-jest
His heart-strook injuries.
Kent.   Sir, I do know you;
And dare, upon the warrant of my note,
Commend a dear thing to you. There is division,
Although as yet the face of it is cover'd   20
With mutual cunning, 'twixt Albany and Cornwall;
Who have—as who have not, that their great stars
Thron'd and set high?—servants, who seem no less,
Which are to France the spies and speculations
Intelligent of our state. What hath been seen,   25
Either in snuffs and packings of the Dukes,

11. to-and-fro-conflicting] *hyphened Capell.*   13. belly-pinched] *hyphened Pope.*
17. heart-strook] *F;* heart strooke *Q.*   18. note] *F;* Arte *Q.*   19. Commend]
Commended *Q3.*   20. is] *F;* be *Q.*   22-9. Who have . . . furnishings] *F;*
not in Q.   23. Thron'd] *F;* Throne *Theobald.*

sorrow's wind and rain'. This line contains the same reference to the microcosm, and the Q compositor elsewhere confused c/t and m/n (cf. collations IV. ii. 12, II. i. 123).

11. *to-and-fro-conflicting*] swaying about in mad, angry conflict. Cf. IV. vii. 32 and *Tim.*, IV. iii. 230.

12. *cub-drawn*] sucked by her cubs, and so ravenous and ferocious. Cf. *AYL.*, IV. iii. 115, 127. Kittredge compares *Arden of Feversham*, II. ii. 118-20: 'Such mercy as the staruen Lyones, / When she is dry suckt of her eager young, / Showes to the prey that next encounters her'.

12. *couch*] lie in its lair.

14. *unbonneted*] Cf. *Oth.*, I. ii. 23.

15. *take all*] the cry of the gambler, staking all on a last throw. Cf. *Ant.*, IV. ii. 8.

16-17. *labours . . . injuries*] to drive out, exorcise them by jesting; or perhaps, to outdo the greatness of his

master's wrongs by the wild extravagance of his jests.

17. *heart-strook*] Cf. II. iv. 157.

18. *upon . . . note*] on the strength of my observation, knowledge of you.

19. *Commend*] entrust.

dear] important.

20. *is*] Q has *be*: but the indicative may be used for subjunctive since there is no reference to futurity, and since no element of doubt is involved (Duthie).

23. *who . . . less*] who do not seem less than servants, i.e. spies.

24. *speculations*] spies; the abstract used for the concrete, as in II. iv. 146.

25. *Intelligent*] giving information. Cf. III. v. 10 and III. vii. 11.

26. *snuffs*] resentments, quarrels, huffs. The word was often used in quibbles, since it could also mean a burning candlewick. Cf. *MND.*, v. i. 254; *LLL.*, v. ii. 22; *1H4*, I. iii. 41.

packings] plots, intrigues. Cf. *Shr.*,

Or the hard rein which both of them have borne
Against the old kind King; or something deeper,
Whereof perchance these are but furnishings—
But, true it is, from France there comes a power   30
Into this scatter'd kingdom; who already,
Wise in our negligence, have secret feet
In some of our best ports, and are at point
To show their open banner. Now to you:
If on my credit you dare build so far   35
To make your speed to Dover, you shall find
Some that will thank you, making just report
Of how unnatural and bemadding sorrow
The King hath cause to plain.
I am a gentleman of blood and breeding,   40

27. have] *F2–4;* hath *F1.*   30–42. But . . . office to you] *Q; not in F.*   31.
scatter'd] *Q;* shatter'd *Hanmer.*   32. feet] *Q1;* fee *Q2;* see *Q3;* sea *Pope;*
seat *conj. Upton;* foot *Capell.*

v. i. 121, and *Cym.*, III. v. 80. See also
Leir, 1932: 'There is good packing
"twixt your King and you".' The
word is connected with the vb *pack,* to
plot, scheme, intrigue; and *pack* in this
sense may be derived either from sb.
pack (in sense of *gang*) or *pack* (of cards).
'To pack cards with' is to make a
cheating arrangement with. Cf. *Ant.,*
IV. xiv. 19, where there may be a
quibble on the two senses.

27. *the . . . borne*] how inflexibly
firm, how stiff-necked they have been;
or perhaps it means 'the cruel way they
have proceeded'.

29. *furnishings*] trimmings, pretexts.
Schmidt remarks: 'Whether these in-
complete sentences are due to the poet,
or to the style in which the scene has
been transmitted to use, cannot be
decided.' As 22–9 are lacking in Q, and
30–42 in F (the compositor may have
thought the marginal addition of 22–9
was meant to be substituted for 30–42,
beside which it was written), it is quite
possible that a line or two has been
omitted from both texts at this point,
in which Kent's sentence was completed. Or Shakespeare may have
intended him to break off in the

middle of his explanation. Any explanation of France's invasion that
detracted from its disinterestedness
would have been dramatically wrong.
On the other hand, France could not
have heard by this time of ill-usage of
Lear sufficient to justify an invasion.
Shakespeare's manipulation of time
for dramatic ends compelled him to be
ambiguous and vague on the subject of
the French invasion. If, however, we
follow Steevens and most later editors
in putting a semicolon after *state* (25),
the *what* in that line might be taken to
mean 'namely, to note and report
what'. In which case the sense would
be completed at *furnishings.*

30. *power*] army.

31. *scatter'd*] divided, unsettled, dis-
united (Johnson).

32. *have . . . feet*] have gained a secret
foothold. Cf. III. vii. 45.

33. *at point*] ready. Cf. I. iv. 323.

35. *my credit*] your trust in me.

36. *To*] as to.

37. *making*] for making.
just] accurate.

38. *bemadding*] maddening. Cf.
Cym., II. ii. 37, 'madding'.

39. *plain*] complain of.

And from some knowledge and assurance offer
This office to you.
Gent. I will talk further with you.
Kent.   No, do not.
For confirmation that I am much more
Than my out-wall, open this purse, and take   45
What it contains. If you shall see Cordelia,—
As fear not but you shall—show her this ring,
And she will tell you who that fellow is
That yet you do not know. Fie on this storm!
I will go seek the King.   50
Gent. Give me your hand. Have you no more to say?
Kent. Few words, but, to effect, more than all yet;
That, when we have found the King, in which your
    pain
That way, I'll this, he that first lights on him
Holla the other.   [*Exeunt severally.* 55

SCENE II.—[*Another part of the Heath.*] *Storm still.*

Enter LEAR *and Fool.*

Lear. Blow, winds, and crack your cheeks! rage! blow!
You cataracts and hurricanoes, spout

43. further] *F;* farther *Q 1–2.*   44. I am] *F;* I *Q.*   47. fear] doubt *Q 2–3.*
48. that] *F;* your *Q.*   53. in . . . pain] *F; not in Q.*   54. That . . . this] *F;*
Ile this way, you that *Q.*   55. S.D.] *Theobald; Exeunt Q, F.*

Scene II
S.D. *Another . . . Heath*] *Capell.*   *Storm still*] *F; not in Q 1.*   1. winds] *F;*
wind *Q.*   2. cataracts] caterickes *Q.*   hurricanoes] Hyrricano's *F 1;*
Hircanios *Q 1–2;* Hercantos *Q 3.*

41. *assurance*] trustworthy information.

42. *office*] service, duty (i.e. the journey to Dover).

45. *out-wall*] exterior. Cf. *Tw.N.,* I. ii. 48, and *Sonn.,* cxlvi. 4.

48. *fellow*] companion.

52. *to effect*] in importance.

53–4. *in which . . . this*] in which task, you go that way, while I go this.

Scene II
1–5. *Blow . . . thunderbolts*] For Harsnett parallels see Appendix, p. 239.

2. *cataracts*] the flood-gates of the heavens, the earliest meaning of the word (cf. Gen., vii. 11); or possibly 'waterspouts'. Eden, *West India,* 1555 (ed. Arber, p. 386), mentions 'that in certeyne places of the sea, they sawe certeyne stremes of water which they

Till you have drench'd our steeples, drown'd the cocks!
You sulph'rous and thought-executing fires,
Vaunt-couriers of oak-cleaving thunderbolts,   5
Singe my white head! And thou, all-shaking thunder,
Strike flat the thick rotundity o'th'world!
Crack Nature's moulds, all germens spill at once
That makes ingrateful man!

Fool. O Nuncle, court holy-water in a dry house is better   10
than this rain-water out o'door. Good Nuncle, in,

---

3. our] *F;* The *Q.*   drown'd] *Q; drown F.   4. thought-executing] *F;
unhyphened Q.   5. of] *F;* to *Q.   6. Singe] sing *Q2–3.   all-shaking]
unhyphened Q.   7. Strike] *F;* Smite *Q.   o'th'] *F;* of the *Q.   8. moulds]
F; Mold Q.   9. makes] *F;* make *Q.   10. holy-water] *F; unhyphened Q.*
11. this rain-water] *F;* the Rain-water *F3–4; unhyphened Q.   o'] *F;* a *Q.*

---

caule spoutes faulynge owt of the ayer into the sea. . . . Sum phantasie that these shoulde be the catractes of heaven whiche were all opened at Noe's flood.'

hurricanoes] This form of the word is rare. Cf. *Troil.*, v. ii. 272: 'The dreadful spout, / Which shipmen do the hurricano call'. The word has been found in this sense in only one other passage, Drayton, *Mooncalfe*, 1627, 494: 'As that which men the hurricano call'. Drayton may have been echoing Shakespeare.

3. *drown'd*] submerged.

cocks] weathercocks.

4–5. *You . . . thunderbolts*] Pringle Barret, *M.L.N.*, 1928, pp. 316–17, compares *Tp.*, I. ii. 201–3: 'Jove's lightnings, the precursors / O' th' dreadful thunderclaps, more momentary / And sight-outrunning were not.'

4. *thought-executing*] Barret points out that Johnson's explanation, 'doing execution with rapidity equal to thought', is supported by the parallel passage in *The Tempest.* Moberly, however, explains 'executing the thought of him who casts you'.

5. *Vaunt-couriers*] forerunners, harbingers, heralds. Originally the word meant the foremost scouts in an army.

Cf. 'precursors' in the passage quoted from *The Tempest.*

oak-cleaving thunderbolts] a favourite image of Shakespeare's. Cf., e.g., *Tp.*, v. i. 44–6; *Meas.*, II. ii. 115–16; *Cor.*, v. iii. 153.

7. *rotundity*] Delius thinks that from the context 'the roundness of gestation' as well as the sphere of the globe is here suggested.

8. *moulds*] the moulds used by Nature in forming men.

germens] the germs or seeds of matter. Cf. *Mac.*, IV. i. 59, and *Wint.*, IV. iv. 488–9. Lear wishes to prevent the birth of any more people, so that the ungrateful race of man will die out.

spill] destroy.

9. *ingrateful*] ungrateful.

10. *court holy-water*] flattery. Malone cites Cotgrave, *op. cit.*, *Eau beniste de Cour.* 'Court holy water; . . . faire words, flattering speeches, glosing, soothing, palpable cogging'. The phrase is used by Florio (see Appendix, p. 237), and Harsnett makes frequent mention of holy-water. Eliot, *Ortho-Epia Gallica*, explains: 'I shall be sprinckled with the Court holy-water, that is to say, I shall haue a deluge of ceremonies, but as many apes tailes as dinners and breakefasts.'

ask thy daughters blessing; here's a night pities
neither wise men nor Fools.

Lear. Rumble thy bellyful! Spit, fire! spout, rain!
　　Nor rain, wind, thunder, fire, are my daughters:　　15
　　I tax you not, you elements, with unkindness;
　　I never gave you kingdom, call'd you children,
　　You owe me no subscription: then let fall
　　Your horrible pleasure; here I stand, your slave,
　　A poor, infirm, weak, and despis'd old man.　　20
　　But yet I call you servile ministers,
　　That will with two pernicious daughters join
　　Your high-engender'd battles 'gainst a head
　　So old and white as this. O, ho! 'tis foul.

Fool. He that has a house to put's head in has a good　　25
　　head-piece.
　　　　　　　The cod-piece that will house
　　　　　　　　Before the head has any,
　　　　　　　The head and he shall louse;
　　　　　　　　So beggars marry many.　　30

---

12. ask] *F;* and ask *Q.*　　13. wise men] wisemen *F;* wise man *Q.*　　Fools]
F; foole *Q.*　　14. bellyful] *Malone;* belly full *Q, F.*　　16. tax] *F;* taske *Q.*
18. then] *F;* Why then *Q.*　　22. will . . . join] *F;* haue . . . ioin'd *Q.*　　23.
high-engender'd] *F; unhyphened Q.*　　battles] *F;* battel *Q.*　　24. O, ho!] *F;*
O *Q.*　　25. put's] *F;* put his *Q.*

---

12. *ask . . . blessing*] ask a blessing
from your daughters. Cf. v. iii. 10 with
its two objects.

14. *thy bellyfull*] to thy heart's content. The storm here, as in the opening
line of the scene, is personified.

15. *fire*] dissyllabic.

16. *tax*] to bring a charge of something against. Cf. I. iv. 342 and *Meas.,*
v. i. 312. Moberly compares *AYL.,* II.
vii. 174.

18. *subscription*] allegiance, submission, obedience. Cf. I. ii. 24 (Q) and
III. vii. 63.

21. *ministers*] agents.

23. *high-engender'd*] engendered in
the heavens. Kittredge thinks there is
also a suggestion of the meaning
'sublime'.

battles] battalions.

25. *put's*] put his.

26. *head-piece*] a pun: (*a*) a helmet,
a covering for the head, (*b*) a head, i.e.
brain.

27. *cod-piece*] part of male attire,
worn by men in front of the close-
fitting hose; it is here used for the
phallus.

27–30. *The . . . many*] The man who
satisfied his sexual appetites before he
has a house to live in will end up by
marrying a wife, and share her lice.
Danby, *op. cit.,* p. 111, suggests that
l. 30 refers to the beggar's long train of
doxies, and he compares the rake's
progress described by Edgar, III. iv.
83 ff., of the proud gallant who becomes a naked Bedlamite. But Poor
Tom was perhaps a servingman, not a
courtier.

> The man that makes his toe
> What he his heart should make,
> Shall of a corn cry woe,
> And turn his sleep to wake.

For there was never yet fair woman but she made   35
mouths in a glass.

Enter KENT.

Lear. No, I will be the pattern of all patience;
I will say nothing.
Kent. Who's there?
Fool. Marry, here's grace and a cod-piece, that's a wise   40
man and a Fool.
Kent. Alas! Sir, are you here? things that love night
Love not such nights as these; the wrathful skies
Gallow the very wanderers of the dark,
And make them keep their caves. Since I was man   45
Such sheets of fire, such bursts of horrid thunder,
Such groans of roaring wind and rain, I never

---

31. The] That *F3-4*.   33. of] *F;* haue *Q.*   35. but] hut *Q uncorr.*   36.
S.D.] *F; after 37 Q.*   37. pattern] patience *F3-4*.   40-1. wise man] *Pope;*
wiseman *Q, F.*   42. are] *F;* sit *Q.*   44. wanderers] *F;* wanderer *Q.*
45. make] *F;* makes *Q.*   47. never] *F;* ne're *Q.*

31-4. *The . . . wake*] The man who
cherishes a mean part of his body to
the exclusion of what is really worth
cherishing, shall suffer lasting harm,
and from the very part he so foolishly
cherished. The Fool is glancing at
Lear's folly in casting out Cordelia and
enriching her evil sisters. Kittredge
quotes Greene, *Euphues his Censure,*
1587 (ed. Grosart, VI. 191): 'Finding
it folly to sett that at his heart which
other set at their heele.'

35-6. *For . . . glass*] Probably an
irrelevant piece of nonsense, 'such as
was often used to distract attention
from too keen a piece of satire' (Kittredge, following Furness). The Fool is
referring to the habit women have of
practising pretty faces in a mirror; and
may be glancing obliquely at the
vanity and hypocrisy of Goneril and
Regan.

37. *I . . . patience*] Cf. *Leir,* 755-6:
'But he, the myrrour of mild patience, /
Puts vp all wrongs, and neuer giues
reply.'

40. *grace*] the King's grace, i.e. the
King; or an honourable man.

cod-piece] Douce remarks that the
Fool 'was usually provided with this
unseemly part of dress in a more
remarkable manner than other persons'.

40-1. *a wise . . . Fool*] 'He leaves it to
Kent to decide which is which' (Kittredge). After the Fool's allusion to the
King as a codpiece in l. 27, the audience, too, will share the ambiguity.

44. *Gallow*] terrify. It is now used
only in S.W. Midland dialect, and by
whale-fishers.

wanderers . . . dark] wild beasts.

45. *And . . . caves*] Cf. III. i. 12.

46. *bursts*] peals.

Remember to have heard; man's nature cannot carry
Th'affliction nor the fear.
Lear.   Let the great Gods,
That keep this dreadful pudder o'er our heads,   50
Find out their enemies now. Tremble, thou wretch,
That hast within thee undivulged crimes,
Unwhipp'd of Justice; hide thee, thou bloody hand,
Thou perjur'd, and thou simular of virtue
That art incestuous; caitiff, to pieces shake,   55
That under covert and convenient seeming
Has practis'd on man's life; close pent-up guilts
Rive your concealing continents, and cry
These dreadful summoners grace. I am a man
More sinn'd against than sinning.
Kent.   Alack! bare-headed!
Gracious my Lord, hard by here is a hovel;   61
Some friendship will it lend you 'gainst the tempest;
Repose you there while I to this hard house,—

49. fear] *F;* force *Q.*   50. pudder] *F;* Powther *Q1;* Thundring *Q2-3.*
54. simular] *F;* simular man *Q1-2;* simulier man *Q3.*   55. to] *F;* in *Q.*
57. Has] *F;* hast *Q.*   58. concealing continents] *F;* concealed centers *Q.*
60. than] *F4;* then *F1-3;* their *Q.*   63. while] *F;* whilst *Q.*

48. *carry*] bear, endure.

49–60. *Let . . . sinning*] Baldwin, *op. cit.*, II. 532, compares Juvenal, *Satires,* XIII. 223–6.

50. *pudder*] hubbub, turmoil. Lamb preferred this reading to that of Q. Steevens quotes Beaumont and Fletcher, *The Scornful Lady,* II. ii (ed. Glover, I. 251): 'Some fellows would have cryed now, and have curst thee, / and faln out with their meat, and kept a pudder.' Mr F. Kermode calls my attention to the *pothering pole* used in Herefordshire for knocking down cider apples. He suggests that Lear may be alluding to the shower of missiles from above when the pothering pole is plied. This, however, is improbable.

51. *Find . . . now*] 'by the terror which such offenders must show' (Kittredge).

53. *of*] by.

54. *perjur'd*] perjured one, perjurer.
simular] simulator, counterfeiter.

This is more common as adj. (hence the Q reading) but *N.E.D.* quotes Tindale: 'Christ . . . calleth them ypocrites, that is to saye Simulars.'

55. *caitiff*] wretch.
to . . . shake] Cf. *All's W.,* IV. iii. 192.

56. *seeming*] hypocrisy. Cf. *Meas.,* II. iv. 150.

57. *practis'd on*] plotted against. Cf. *H5,* II. ii. 99.
guilts] crimes.

58. *Rive . . . continents*] burst the covering that hides you. Cf. *Ant.,* IV. xiv. 40.

58–9. *cry . . . grace*] cry for mercy from the dread ministers of vengeance; a summoner was an officer who haled offenders before the ecclesiastical courts.

59–60. *I . . . sinning*] I, as opposed to the hypocritical sinners described in this speech.

62. *lend*] afford.

63. *hard*] cruel.

More harder than the stones whereof 'tis rais'd,
Which even but now, demanding after you,   65
Denied me to come in,—return and force
Their scanted courtesy.

Lear.   My wits begin to turn.
Come on, my boy. How dost, my boy? Art cold?
I am cold myself. Where is this straw, my fellow?
The art of our necessities is strange,   70
And can make vile things precious. Come, your hovel.
Poor Fool and knave, I have one part in my heart
That's sorry yet for thee.

Fool.   *He that has and a little tiny wit,*
                    With hey, ho, the wind and the rain,   75
               Must make content with his fortunes fit,
                    Though the rain it raineth every day.

Lear. True, boy. Come, bring us to this hovel.

                                   [*Exeunt Lear and Kent.*
Fool. This is a brave night to cool a courtezan.
      I'll speak a prophecy ere I go: 80

---

64. harder than] *F;* hard then is *Q.*   stones] *F;* stone *Q.*   65. you] *F;*
me *Q.*   67. wits begin] *F;* wit begins *Q.*   71. And] *F;* that *Q.*   vile]
Pope; vilde *Q, F.*   your] *F;* you *Q.*   72. in] *F;* of *Q.*   73. That's sorry]
F; That sorrowes *Q.*   74. *has and*] *F;* has *Q.*   75. hey, ho] height-ho *F2–4.*
77. *Though*] *F;* for *Q.*   78. boy] *F;* my good boy *Q.*   S.D.] *Capell; Exit F;
not in Q.*   79–96. This . . . time] *F; not in Q.*

65. *Which*] the owners of which; or
the people in it. Cf. II. ii. 1.
    demanding after] asking for.
    66. *Denied . . . in*] refused me admit-
tance. Cf. *Wint.*, v. ii. 139.
    70. *The . . . strange*] Necessity has a
strange power of transforming, like
that of the Alchemists who changed
lead into gold. Florio, *op. cit.*, VI. 299,
says: 'Nature hath like a kinde mother
observed this, that such actions as shee
for our necessities hath enjoyned unto
us, should also be voluptuous un to us.'
(Cited G. C. Taylor. See Appendix,
p. 235.)
    74. He . . . wit] An adaptation of
Feste's song, *Tw.N.*, v. i. 398, and
probably sung by the same actor. The
Fool may be referring to Lear, or to
himself.

78. *True*] Lear admits that he must
make his happiness fit his fortunes.
    bring] conduct.
    79. *brave*] fine, suitable. This line
and the rest of the scene are omitted by
Q, and some have thought it to be an
interpolation.
    80. *a prophecy*] The verses that follow
are a parody of some pseudo-Chaucer-
ian verses to be found in Puttenham,
Arte of English Poesie (ed. Arber, p. 232).
Thynne's edition of Chaucer prints
them as follows: 'When faithe fayleth
in preestes sawes / And lordes hestes
are holden for lawes / And robbery
is holden purchace / And lechery is
holden solace / Than shal the londe of
albyon / Be brought to great confu-
syon.' Warburton pointed out that
81–4 refer to the actual state of affairs,

When priests are more in word than matter;
When brewers mar their malt with water;
When nobles are their tailors' tutors;
No heretics burn'd, but wenches' suitors;
When every case in law is right;   85
No squire in debt, nor no poor knight;
When slanders do not live in tongues;
Nor cut-purses come not to throngs;
When usurers tell their gold i'th'field;
And bawds and whores do churches build;   90
Then shall the realm of Albion
Come to great confusion:
Then comes the time, who lives to see't,
That going shall be us'd with feet.
This prophecy Merlin shall make; for I live before   95
his time.   [*Exit.*

SCENE III.—[*A Room in Gloucester's Castle.*]

Enter GLOUCESTER *and* EDMUND, *with lights.*

Glou. Alack, alack! Edmund, I like not this unnatural
dealing. When I desir'd their leave that I might pity
him, they took from me the use of mine own house;

Scene III

S.D. *A . . . Castle*] Rowe, subst.; not in Q, F.   *Enter . . . Edmund*] F; *Enter
Gloster and the Bastard Q.*   *with lights*] Q; not in F.   3. *took*] tooke
me *Q1*.

while 85–90 are Utopian. He suggested, perhaps rightly, that 91–2
should be inserted after 84.
    83. *tutors*] teaching them their job.
Kittredge cites *Shr.*, IV. iii. 86 ff.
    84. *burn'd*] there is a punning refer-
ence to the pox.
    89. *tell*] count.
    90. *do . . . build*] as a sign of repen-
tance.
    94. *going . . . feet*] feet shall be used
for walking.
    95. *Merlin*] Shakespeare probably
derived his knowledge of Merlin's pro-

phecies from Holinshed. Bethell,
*Shakespeare and the Popular Dramatic
Tradition,* 1947, p. 86, points out that
the Fool's concluding remark makes
him step out of the remote period as a
contemporary.

Scene III

    1–2. *unnatural dealing*] Sidney uses
the phrase 'vnnaturall dealings' in
the story Shakespeare used for his
under-plot. Cf. Introduction, p.
xxxiv.
    2. *pity*] take pity on, relieve.

charg'd me, on pain of perpetual displeasure, neither
to speak of him, entreat for him, or any way sustain   5
him.

Edm. Most savage and unnatural!

Glou. Go to; say you nothing. There is division between
the Dukes, and a worse matter than that. I have
receiv'd a letter this night; 'tis dangerous to be   10
spoken; I have lock'd the letter in my closet. These
injuries the King now bears will be revenged home;
there is part of a power already footed; we must
incline to the King. I will look him and privily re-
lieve him; go you and maintain talk with the Duke,   15
that my charity be not of him perceiv'd. If he ask for
me, I am ill and gone to bed. If I die for it, as no less
is threatened me, the King, my old master, must be
reliev'd. There is strange things toward, Edmund;
pray you, be careful.   [*Exit.*   20

Edm. This courtesy, forbid thee, shall the Duke
Instantly know; and of that letter too:
This seems a fair deserving, and must draw me
That which my father loses; no less than all:
The younger rises when the old doth fall.   [*Exit.*   25

4. perpetual] *F;* their *Q;* their perpetual *Jennens.*   5. or] *F;* nor *Q.*   8.
There is] *F;* There's a *Q.*   between] *F;* betwixt *Q.*   13. there is] *F;*
ther's *Q.*   footed] *F;* landed *Q.*   14. look] *F;* seeke *Q.*   17. If] *F;*
though *Q.*   for it] *F;* for't *Q.*   19. strange things] *F;* some strange thing *Q.*
23. draw me] draw to me *Q2–3.*   25. The] *F;* then *Q.*   doth] *F;* doe *Q.*

5. *sustain*] care for.

9. *worse*] i.e. the French invasion.

12. *home*] to the full.

13. *footed*] landed. Cf. III. i. 32 and
note.

14. *incline to*] take the side of. Cf.
Wint., I. ii. 304.
  look] seek for. Cf. *AYL.*, II. v. 34.

16. *of*] by.

17. *If . . . it*] Gloucester, who had

earlier offered reasons of policy (11–
14), now displays some moral stamina
for the first time.

19. *is*] A singular verb is often followed by a plural subject. There is no
need to adopt the Q reading.
  toward] impending.

21. *forbid*] forbidden.

23. *fair deserving*] an action which
will deserve to be rewarded.

SCENE IV.—[*The Heath. Before a Hovel.*]

Enter LEAR, KENT, *and Fool.*

Kent. Here is the place, my Lord; good my Lord, enter:
   The tyranny of the open night's too rough
   For nature to endure.   [*Storm still.*
Lear.   Let me alone.
Kent. Good my Lord, enter here.
Lear.   Wilt break my heart?
Kent. I had rather break mine own. Good my Lord, enter.   5
Lear. Thou think'st 'tis much that this contentious storm
   Invades us to the skin: so 'tis to thee;
   But where the greater malady is fix'd,
   The lesser is scarce felt. Thou'ldst shun a bear;
   But if thy flight lay toward the roaring sea,   10
   Thou'ldst meet the bear i'th'mouth. When the mind's
      free
   The body's delicate; this tempest in my mind
   Doth from my senses take all feeling else
   Save what beats there—filial ingratitude!
   Is it not as this mouth should tear this hand   15

Scene IV

S.D. *The Heath . . . Hovel*] *Rowe, subst.; not in Q, F.*   3. S.D.] *F; not in Q.*
4. here] *F; not in Q.*   6. contentious] *F;* crulentious *Q uncorr., Q2–3;* tempestious *Q corr.*   7. skin: so] *Rowe;* skinso: *F1;* skin so: *F2;* skin, so: *F3–4;* skin,
so *Q.*   9. Thou'ldst] *F;* thou wouldst *Q2–3.*   10. thy] they *F1.*   lay]
light *F4.*   roaring] *F;* raging *Q uncorr., Q2–3.*   11. i'th'] *F;* it'h *Q.*   12.
this] *Q corr.;* the *Q uncorr., Q2, F; not in Q3.*   14. beats] *Q corr., F;* beares *Q
uncorr., Q2–3.*   there—] *Singer;* their *Q;* there, *F1–2;* there. *F3–4, Rowe;*
there: *Delius, Schmidt.*   15. this hand] his hand *F3–4.*

2. *open night*] night in the open.
   4. *Wilt . . . heart?*] Steevens suggests
that Lear is addressing his own heart;
but Lear's next speech explains the
meaning. He thinks that by remaining
outside in the storm, he will have his
thoughts distracted from the ingratitude which will otherwise break his
heart.
   8–9. *But . . . felt*] Cf. *Cym.*, IV. ii. 243.
   11–14. *When . . . ingratitude*] Cf.
Appendix, p. 238.

   11. *free*] at ease. Cf. *Oth.*, III. iii. 340;
Middleton and Rowley, *A Fair
Quarrel*, I. i. 399: 'Then 'tis no prison
when the mind is free.'
   12. *delicate*] sensitive, averse to
pain.
   14. *beats*] a quibble: (*a*) throbs,
thinks laboriously, cf. *Tp.*, I. ii. 176;
(*b*) rages, as of a tempest.
   there—filial ingratitude] as Delius
pointed out, 'filial ingratitude' is in
apposition to 'what beats there'.

For lifting food to't? But I will punish home:
No, I will weep no more. In such a night
To shut me out? Pour on; I will endure.
In such a night as this? O Regan, Goneril!
Your old kind father, whose frank heart gave all,—   20
O! that way madness lies; let me shun that;
No more of that.

Kent.   Good my Lord, enter here.

Lear. Prithee, go in thyself; seek thine own ease:
This tempest will not give me leave to ponder
On things would hurt me more. But I'll go in.   25
[*To the Fool.*] In, boy; go first. You houseless poverty,—
Nay, get thee in. I'll pray, and then I'll sleep.

                                        [*Fool goes in.*

Poor naked wretches, whereso'er you are,
That bide the pelting of this pitiless storm,
How shall your houseless heads and unfed sides,   30
Your loop'd and window'd raggedness, defend you
From seasons such as these? O! I have ta'en
Too little care of this. Take physic, Pomp;
Expose thyself to feel what wretches feel,
That thou mayst shake the superflux to them,   35
And show the Heavens more just.

---

16. to't] to it *Q2–3*.   home] *F;* sure *Q.*   17–18. In . . . endure] *F; not in Q.*   20. gave] *F;* gaue you *Q.*   22. here] *F; not in Q.*   23. thine own] *F;* thy one *Q1;* thy owne *Q2.*   26. S.D.] *Johnson; not in Q.*   26–7. In, boy . . . sleep] *F; not in Q.*   26. poverty,—] *Rowe;* pouertie. *F.*   27. S.D.] *Johnson; Exit F (after 26); not in Q.*   29. storm] *F;* night *Q.*

16. *home*] Cf. III. iii. 12.

26. *houseless poverty*] the abstract for the concrete; the phrase is expanded in 28 ff.

27. *pray*] the prayer is not to the gods, but to the poor.

29. *bide*] endure. Cf. *Tw.N.*, II. iv. 97.

30–1. *How . . . raggedness*] D. G. James, *The Life of Reason*, 1949, p. 147, comments: 'If the reader will read the . . . lines carefully, and will bear in mind that "house" is two words and not one, having in its second and little known meaning the sense of "textile covering"; if also he will consider the

phrases "unfed sides" and "loop'd and window'd raggedness", he will see what a fusion of ideas is here; the body as the house of the soul and the house as protection for the body are ideas fused in the way I have spoken of.'

31. *loop'd and window'd*] full of holes and openings. The original meaning of window appears to have been *wind-eye*, i.e. eye, or hole, to admit the wind.

33–6. *Take . . . just*] Cf. Gloucester's words, IV. i. 65–70.

35. *superflux*] superfluity. Cf. Appendix, p. 239.

36. *And . . . just*] Cf. *Leir*, 1909, 'The heauens are iust'; and v. iii. 169.

Edg. [*Within.*] Fathom and half, fathom and half!
    Poor Tom!   [*The Fool runs out from the hovel.*
Fool. Come not in here, Nuncle; here's a spirit.
    Help me! help me!   40
Kent. Give me thy hand. Who's there?
Fool. A spirit, a spirit: he says his name's poor Tom.
Kent. What art thou that dost grumble there i'th'straw?
    Come forth.

Enter EDGAR *disguised as a madman.*

Edg. Away! the foul fiend follows me! Through the sharp   45
    hawthorn blow the cold winds. Humh! go to thy bed
    and warm thee.
Lear. Didst thou give all to thy daughters?
    And art thou come to this?
Edg. Who gives any thing to poor Tom? whom the foul   50

37–8. Fathom . . . Tom] *F; not in Q.*   37. S.D.] *Theobald; not in F.*   38
S.D.] *Theobald (after 40); Enter Edgar and Foole (after 36) F.*   42. A spirit, a
spirit] *F;* A spirit *Q.*   name's] name is *Q2–3.*   43. i'th'] *F;* in the *Q.*
44. S.D.] *Capell; not in Q, F.*   46. blow] *F;* blowes *Q.*   cold winds] *New
Camb.;* windes *F;* cold wind *Q.*   Humh!] *F;* Humph *Rowe; not in Q.*   bed]
F; cold bed *Q.*   48. Didst . . . daughters?] *F;* Hast thou giuen all to thy two
daughters? *Q;* Didst . . . two daughters? *Singer.*

---

37. *Fathom . . . half*] suggested by the
floods of rain. Edgar pretends to be a
mariner shipwrecked or spoiled by
pirates, as described in Harman's
Caveat (New Camb.).

46. *Humh!*] E. A. Armstrong, *op.
cit.*, p. 45, points out that 'Shakespeare
uses the word in twenty contexts and
in twelve of these there is death or
sleep imagery.' Cf. I. ii. 52–3.

46–7. *go . . . thee*] Cf. *Shr.*, Induction,
i. 10, where nearly the same words are
used: 'Go by Jeronimy; go to thy cold
bed, and warm thee.' In this parallel
passage, as Theobald points out, there
are allusions to Kyd's *Spanish Tragedy*
(ed. Boas, III. xii. 31; II. v. 1). See also
note on III. iv. 97 *post*. The Q reading,
accepted by most editors, was probably a corruption caused by the fami-
liarity of the *Shrew* passage, or 'an
interpolation by the actor to get an

effective antithesis' (Duthie). Staunton
says the phrase 'go to thy cold bed'
means only 'go cold to bed'.

48. *Didst . . . daughters?*] Empson, *op.
cit.*, p. 137, comments: 'Madness has
come. No doubt the appearance of the
wild Edgar . . . is the accident that
made him unable to shun it any
longer.'

50. *gives*] Edgar takes his cue from
Lear's *give* (48).

50–4. *whom . . . pew*] Theobald
pointed out that the substance of these
lines is to be found in Harsnett's
Declaration. Cf. Appendix, p. 242.
Steevens quoted Marlowe, *Doctor
Faustus*, ed. Tucker Brooke, 632–4:
'then swordes and kniues, / Poyson,
gunnes, halters, and invenomd steele /
Are layde before me to dispatch my
selfe.' Kittredge cites Greene and
Lodge, *A Looking Glass for London*, 1594

fiend hath led through fire and through flame,
through ford and whirlpool, o'er bog and quagmire;
that hath laid knives under his pillow, and halters in
his pew; set ratsbane by his porridge; made him
proud of heart, to ride on a bay trotting-horse over   55
four-inch'd bridges, to course his own shadow for a
traitor. Bless thy five wits! Tom's a-cold. O! do de,
do de, do de. Bless thee from whirlwinds, star-
blasting, and taking! Do poor Tom some charity,
whom the foul fiend vexes. There could I have him   60
now, and there, and there again, and there.   [Storm still.
Lear. What! has his daughters brought him to this pass?

51. through fire] *Q; though Fire Fi.*   through flame] *F; not in Q.*   52.
ford] foord *Q; Sword F; Swamp Collier MS.*   whirlpool] *F; whirlipoole Q 1–2.*
53. hath] *F; has Q.*   54. porridge] *F; pottage Q.*   55. trotting-horse]
hyphened Steevens.   56. four-inch'd] *hyphened Capell.*   57, 58. Bless] *Q;
Blisse F.*   57–8. O . . . de.] *F; not in Q.*   58–9. star-blasting] *F; starre-*
blusting *Q.*   61. and there, and] *F, Q2; and there and and Q1.*   there
again] here again *F4.*   and there.] *F; not in Q.*   S.D.] *F; not in Q.*   62.
What! has] *Duthie; Ha's F1; Has F2–3; Have F4; What, Q; What! have Theobald.*

(ed. Collins, I. 204), S.D. 'The Euill
Angel tempteth him, offering the
knife and rope.'

54. *pew*] 'gallery in a house or outside a chamber window' (Kittredge).

porridge] broth. The modern meaning of the word was not used in Shakespeare's day.

55. *trotting-horse*] a horse trained to
trot and amble in a stately and
measured fashion.

56. *four-inch'd bridges*] Cf. Jonson,
The Magnetic Lady, V. viii (ed. Herford
and Simpson, VI. 589): 'a poore
Squire . . . / That talk'd in's sleepe;
would walke to Saint Iohn's wood, /
And Waltham Forrest, scape by all the
ponds, / And pits i'the way; run over
two-inch bridges; / With his eyes fast,
and i'the dead of night!'

course] chase.

57. *Bless*] Duthie cites *N.E.D.* '*bliss*
vb . . . trans. To give joy or gladness to
. . . to gladden, make happy.' The
word became blended with *bless* in the
16th–17th centuries, but was derived
from O.E. *blissian*. But see III. vi. 56,
where the more usual word is em-

ployed, and III. iv. 58 where *bless* is
more appropriate.

five wits] Malone points out that in
Hawes, *The Pastime of Pleasure*, XXIV. 2,
the five wits are enumerated as common wit, imagination, fantasy, estimation, and memory. Cf. Sir John
Davies, *Nosce Teipsum* (ed. Grosart,
1876, pp. 70 ff.) for a similar list. The
five wits were sometimes confused with
the five senses, but Shakespeare distinguishes between them, as Malone
points out. Cf. *Sonn.*, cxli. 9–10: 'But
my five wits nor my five senses can /
Dissuade one foolish heart from serving
thee.'

Tom's a-cold] Cf. Orlando Gibbons's
'The London Cry': 'Poor naked Bedlam, Tom's a cold . . . God Almighty
bless thy wits' (F. P. Wilson).

57–8. *do . . . de.*] He is presumably
shivering. Cotgrave defines *Friller*,
'To shiuer, chatter, or didder for
cold.'

58–9. *star-blasting*] Cf. Harsnett,
Appendix, p. 241.

59. *taking*] infection, evil influences.
Cf. II. iv. 161.

Couldst thou save nothing? Would'st thou give 'em
    all?

Fool. Nay, he reserv'd a blanket, else we had been all
    sham'd.   65

Lear. Now all the plagues that in the pendulous air
    Hang fated o'er men's faults light on thy daughters!

Kent. He hath no daughters, Sir.

Lear. Death, traitor! nothing could have subdu'd nature
    To such a lowness but his unkind daughters.   70
    Is it the fashion that discarded fathers
    Should have thus little mercy on their flesh?
    Judicious punishment! 'twas this flesh begot
    Those pelican daughters.

---

63. Would'st] *F;* didst *Q.*   'em] *F;* them *Q.*   67. light] *F;* fall *Q.*

66–7. *Now . . . faults*] Boswell cites
Tim., v. iii. 108–9; Schmidt compares
The Birth of Merlin, IV. i. 220 (*Shakes.
Apoc.*): 'Knowest thou what pendulous
mischief roofs thy head?' But there is
a closer parallel with Harsnett, *op. cit.,*
p. 159. Cf. Appendix, p. 242.

67. *fated*] invested with the power of
fatal determination (Johnson). Cf.
All's W., I. i. 232, 'the fated sky'.

69. *subdu'd nature*] reduced his
natural powers.

72. *little . . . flesh*] referring either
to Edgar's wretchedness, or, more
likely, to the pins and thorns in his
flesh.

74. *pelican*] Cf. *Leir,* 512–13: 'I am as
kind as the Pellican / That kils it selfe,
to saue her young ones liues.' Wright
quotes *Batman vppon Bartholome,* ed.
1582, fol. 186: 'The Pellican loueth
too much her children. For when the
children bee haught, and begin to
waxe hoare, they smite the father and
the mother in the face, wherfore the
mother smiteth them againe and
slaieth them. And the thirde daye the
mother smiteth her selfe in her side
that the bloud runneth out, and shed-
deth that hot bloud vppon the bodies
of her children. And by virtue of the
bloud the birdes that were before dead,
quicken againe.' Green, *Shakespeare*

and the Emblem Writers, p. 395, cites
Whitney, *Choice of Emblems,* p. 87: 'The
Pellican, for to reuiue her younge, /
Doth pierce her breast, and geue them
of her blood.' He also cites Reusner, II.
73, where the pelican is compared to a
king: 'For people and for sanctioned
law heart's life a king will pour; / So
from this blood of mine do I life to my
young restore.' In some references to
the pelican, it is said that the mother
bird does not revive her young ones
with her blood, but feeds them with it.
Cf. *Edward III,* III. v. 110–13 (*Shakes.
Apoc.,* p. 90): 'A Pelican, my Lord, /
Wounding her bosome with her
crooked beak, / That so her nest of
young ones may be fed / With drops of
blood that issue from her hart'. Lear
seems to go further, and imply that the
young pelicans strike at the breasts of
the old ones, to drain their life out.
Green, *op. cit.,* p. 426, on l. 76, quotes
Augustine, *Confessions,* I. xii: 'De
peccante me ipso juste retribuebas
mihi. Jussisti enim, et sic est, ut poena
sua sibi sit omnis inordinatus animus.'
(By my own sin Thou didst justly
punish me. For it is even as Thou hast
appointed, that every inordinate
affection should bring its own punishment.) With this may also be compared v. iii. 169–70.

Edg. Pillicock sat on Pillicock hill: 75
    Alow, alow, loo, loo!
Fool. This cold night will turn us all to fools and madmen.
Edg. Take heed o'th'foul fiend. Obey thy parents; keep
    thy word justly; swear not; commit not with man's
    sworn spouse; set not thy sweet heart on proud array.   80
    Tom's a-cold.
Lear. What hast thou been?
Edg. A servingman, proud in heart and mind; that curl'd
    my hair, wore gloves in my cap, serv'd the lust of my
    mistress' heart, and did the act of darkness with her;   85

75. on] one *Q3.*   Pillicock] *F;* pelicocks *Q1–2;* pelicacks *Q3.*   76. Alow,
alow] *F;* Halloo, halloo *Theobald;* a lo *Q.*   78. o'th'] *F;* at' h *Q1;* of the *Q2–3.*
79. word justly] *Pope;* words Iustice *F1;* words iustly *Q;* word, Justice *F2–4.*
80. set not] set on *F3–4.*   sweet heart] *Q;* Sweet-heart *F.*

75. *Pillicock . . . hill*] Collier cites
Ritson, *Gammer Gurton's Garland:*
'Pillycock, Pillycock sat on a hill; /
If he's not gone, he sits there still.'
This may belong to a later date than
Edgar's rhyme, which was doubtless
suggested by *pelican.* Pillicock was a
term of endearment, meaning 'darling'
(Florio), 'prettie knaue' (Cotgrave).
But it is also used as a synonym for
phallus. Cf. Rabelais (Tudor Trans-
lations), 1. 56; Florio, *World of Words,*
thus translates *Puga.*
    76. *Alow . . . loo!*] Variously ex-
plained. 'A wild "halloo" as if he were
calling a hawk'.—Cf. *Ham.,* 1. v. 116
(Kittredge); 'A cry to excite dogs'
(Craig).—Cf. *Troil.,* v. vii. 10; 'the
noise of the Bedlam's horn' (Perrett).
Perhaps it is intended as the refrain of
the song.
    78–80. *Obey . . . array*] Edgar recites
a kind of catechism.
    79. *word justly*] Most editors adopt
Pope's improvement of the Q reading
but Schmidt, Harrison, and Duthie
follow F. Duthie interprets: 'Keep the
justice of thy words.' Schmidt, similarly: 'Be as just in deeds as in words.'
(Cf. catechism: 'To be true and iuste
in al my dealynge'.) Perhaps in this
passage, depending for its effect on
echoes from the scriptures and the

prayer-book, the simpler reading is to
be preferred.
    commit] i.e. adultery, as in the
7th Commandment, and *Oth.,* IV. ii.
72.
    80. *proud array*] Noble, *op. cit.,* com-
pares 1 Tim., ii. 9: 'Likewise also the
women, that they aray themselues in
comely apparell . . . not in braided
heare, either golde, or pearles, or
costly aray'.
    83. *servingman*] Knight supposes this
to be a *cavaliere servente,* a lover (cf.
Gent., II. iv. 106). Schmidt supposes it
to be used in the ordinary sense of servant. Craig quotes Cocles, *Physio-
gnomie,* Sig. A, III. 9: 'A courtier or
servingman'. Shakespeare may have
intended either, as Edgar's account
would fit either a fashionable lover or
a servant who turned his good looks to
account. Davenport, *N.Q.* (1953),
p. 21, suggests that a vague memory
was stirring in Shakespeare's mind of
Donne's fourth Elegy, which mentions
servingman, oaths, whistling silks, un-
creaking shoes, betrayal, harlot, and
hell.
    83–4. *curl'd my hair*] Malone cites a
Harsnett passage. See Appendix,
p. 240.
    84. *wore . . . cap*] favours from his
mistress. Cf. *Troil.,* IV. iv. 73.

swore as many oaths as I spake words, and broke
them in the sweet face of Heaven; one that slept in
the contriving of lust, and wak'd to do it. Wine lov'd
I deeply, dice dearly, and in woman out-paramour'd
the Turk: false of heart, light of ear, bloody of hand;   90
hog in sloth, fox in stealth, wolf in greediness, dog in
madness, lion in prey. Let not the creaking of shoes
nor the rustling of silks betray thy poor heart to
woman: keep thy foot out of brothels, thy hand out
of plackets, thy pen from lenders' books, and defy   95
the foul fiend. Still through the hawthorn blows
the cold wind; says suum, mun, hey no nonny.

89. deeply] *Q;* deerely *F.*   90. of hand] hand *F2;* handed *F3–4.*   93.
rustling] *F;* rus1ngs *Q1;* ruslings *Q2–3.*   silks] sickles *Q3.*   94. woman]
F; women *Q.*   brothels] *F;* brothell *Q.*   95. plackets] *F;* placket *Q.*
books] *F;* booke *Q.*   96. the hawthorn] thy Hawthorn *F3–4.*   97.
says suum, mun] *F; not in Q.*   hey no nonny] *Eccles;* ha, no, nonny *Steevens;*
hay no on ny *Q;* nonny *F.*

88. *contriving*] plotting, presumably
in his sleep.

89–90. *Wine . . . woman*] Cf. Florio,
Second Fruites, p. 105: 'Shun wine, dice,
and letchery, / Else will you come to
beggery.'

89. *out-paramour'd*] had more mistresses than.

90. *the Turk*] the Grand Turk, the
Sultan.

light of ear] credulous of evil, ready
to listen and receive malicious reports
(Johnson). Kittredge cites *The Schole-
House of Women,* 43–9 (ed. Hazlitt,
Early Popular Poetry, IV. 107): 'So light
of eare they be and sowre, / That of the
better they neuer record, / The worse
reherce they word by word.'

91–2. *hog . . . prey*] The Seven Deadly
Sins were often figured under the
names of animals. Malone cites a
Harsnett passage. Cf. p. 240. Florio,
Second Fruites, p. 165, has a similar list:
'lyon for surguedry, goate for let-
cherie, dragon for crueltie'.

92. *prey*] preying.

creaking] Creaking shoes were fashionable. Kittredge cites Rowley, *A
Shoo-maker a Gentleman,* II. i, in which a
shoemaker tells Leodice that he has

made her a 'tunable heele' . . . 'A
creake Madam, for a Musicall creake
nere a Boy in Feversham yet went
beyond me.'

94–5. *keep . . . books*] Florio, *Second
Fruites,* pp. 99–105, has a number of
similar injunctions.

95. *plackets*] a placket was an opening in a petticoat, jocosely derived by
Middleton (*Any Thing for a Quiet Life,*
II. ii) from '*placet: a placendo,* a thing or
place to please'. It was also used as a
synonym for wench.

lenders] moneylenders.

97. *suum*] imitating the noise of the
wind.

hey no nonny] presumably the refrain
of a song. Cf. *Ado,* II. iii. 71. Whiter in
an unpublished note points out that in
Fletcher, *The Humorous Lieutenant,* IV.
iv (ed. Glover and Waller, II. 347), the
phrase is used, as here, in proximity to
placket: 'Was that brave Heart made
to pant for a placket? . . . / That noble
Mind to melt away and moulder / For
a hey nonny nonny!' See also *The Wit
of a Woman,* 1604, C. 1ᵛ: 'These
dauncers sometimes do teach them
trickes above trenchmore, yea and
sometimes such lavoltas, that they

Dolphin my boy, boy; sessa! let him trot by.   [*Storm still.*
Lear. Thou wert better in a grave than to answer with
    thy uncover'd body this extremity of the skies. Is   100
    man no more than this? Consider him well. Thou

98. boy, boy] *F;* boy, my boy *Q.*
Q2; ceas *Q3.*   S.D.] *F; not in Q.*
thy *Q.*   101. than] *F;* but *Q.*

sessa!] *Malone;* sesey *F;* caese *Q1;* cease
99. Thou] *F;* Why thou *Q.*   a] *F;*

mount so high, that you may see their
hey nonny, nony no.' Drayton, *Shepherd's Garland,* 1593 (ed. Hebbel, I. 55),
speaks of 'These noninos of filthie
ribauldry'. J. M. Nosworthy suggests,
privately, that the Q reading may be
the best a reporter or compositor could
do with 'Hayronomy' or 'heyronomy'
(i.e. Jeronimy, Hieronimo). This and
III. iv. 46-7 echo a passage from *The
Taming of the Shrew,* in which Shakespeare gibes at *The Spanish Tragedy:* but
in neither place does he use the name
Hieronimo, unless Nosworthy's conj.
is sound.

98. *Dolphin*] Steevens gives a stanza
from an old ballad written on some
battle fought in France, in which
Dolphin is the Dauphin. This was
probably a fabrication; but as Jonson,
Bartholomew Fair, v. iv (ed. Herford
and Simpson, VI. 127), uses the phrase
'hee shall be *Dauphin* my boy' it is clear
that Edgar was quoting from some
song or ballad, unless Jonson was
echoing Edgar. J. Crow has called my
attention to the Newcastle Play of
Noah (*The Non-Cycle Mystery Plays,* ed.
O. Waterhouse, 1909, p. 25) which
contains the following lines: 'I pray to
Dolphin, prince of dead, / Scald you all
in his lead.' According to Holthausen,
Dolphin means 'Dauphin' in this context, and he is identified with the devil
because of the English hatred of the
French. Edgar has just spoken of the
fiend.

sessa!] Cf. *Shr.,* Induction, 6; 'let
the world slide, sessa'. Cf. also III.
vi. 70 and IV. vi. 200 *post.* It is probably
a mere interjection, perhaps an incitement to speed. Johnson thought it was
the Fr. word *cessez,* pronounced *cessey,*
and meaning 'be quiet, have done'.

From the context and III. vi. 72, it
would seem to mean rather 'Off you
go!'

99. *Thou...better*] it would be better
for you to be.

answer] encounter, bear the brunt.
Cf. *Cor.,* I. iv. 52.

100. *extremity*] extreme severity. Cf.
Wint., v. ii. 129.

100-1. *Is ... well*] Noble, *op. cit.,*
compares Heb., ii. 6: 'What is man,
that thou shouldest bee mindful of
him? or the sonne of man, that thou
wouldest consider him?'

101-7. *Thou ... lendings*] G. C.
Taylor cites the following passages
from Florio's Montaigne: 'Miserable
man; whom if you consider well what
is he?' 'Truely, when I consider man
all naked... I finde we have had much
more reason to hide and cover our
nakedness than any creature else. We
may be excused for borrowing those
which nature had therein favored
more than us . . . and under their
spoiles of wooll, of haire, of feathers,
and of silke, to shroud us.' 'And that
our wisedome should learne of beasts,
the most profitable documents, belonging to the chiefest and most
necessary parts of our life. . . Wherewith (with reason) men have done, as
perfumers doe with oyle, they have
adulterated her with so many argu-
mentations, and sofisticated her.' To
these passages may be added: 'man is
the onely forsaken and out-cast creature, naked on the bare earth . . .
having nothing to cover and arme
himselfe withall but the spoile of
others; whereas Nature hath clad and
mantled all other creatures, some with
huskes... with wooll,... with hides...
and with silke . . .: whereas man only

ow'st the worm no silk, the beast no hide, the sheep
no wool, the cat no perfume. Ha! here's three on's
are sophisticated; thou art the thing itself; un-
accommodated man is no more but such a poor,		105
bare, forked animal as thou art. Off, off, you lend-
ings! Come; unbutton here.			[*Tearing off his clothes.*

Fool. Prithee, Nuncle, be contented; 'tis a naughty night
to swim in. Now a little fire in a wild field were like
an old lecher's heart; a small spark, all the rest on's		110
body cold. Look! here comes a walking fire.

Enter GLOUCESTER, *with a torch.*

Edg. This is the foul Flibbertigibbet: he begins at cur-
few, and walks till the first cock; he gives the web
and the pin, squinies the eye, and makes the hare-

103. Ha] *F; not in Q.*		on's] ones *Q2–3.*		106–7. lendings] *Q corr., F;*
leadings *Q uncorr., Q2–3.*		107. Come . . . here] *F;* come on bee true *Q uncorr.,*
Q2–3; come on *Q corr.*		S.D.] *Rowe; not in Q, F.*		108. contented] *F;*
content *Q.*		'tis] *F;* this is *Q.*		109. wild] wide *Jennens (conj. Capell).*
110. on's] *F;* in *Q.*		111. S.D.] *F (after 107)*; Enter Gloster *Q.*		112. foul]
F; foule fiend *Q.*		Flibbertigibbet] *F;* Sriberdegibit *Q uncorr.;* fliberdegibek
Q corr.; Sirberdegibit *Q2–3.*		113. till the] *Q;* at *F.*		gives] gins *Q uncorr.,*
Q2–3.		114. and the pin, squinies] *Duthie (conj. Greg)*; and the pin, squints *F;*
the pin-queues *Q uncorr.;* & the pin, squemes *Q corr.;* the pin-queuer *Q2;* the
pinquever *Q3;* and the pin, squinies conj. *Anon ap. Cambridge.*		114–15.
hare-lip] *F;* harte lip *Q uncorr., Q2–3;* hare lip *Q corr.*

(Oh silly wretched man) can neither
goe, nor speake, nor shift, nor feed himselfe, unlesse it be to whine and weepe
onely, except hee be taught' (*op. cit.,*
III. 250, 268; VI. 189–90; III. 215–16.)

102. *beast*] ox, or similar animal.

103. *cat*] the civet cat.

104. *sophisticated*] adulterated. See
note to 101–7 above. Shakespeare
does not use the word again.

104–5. *unaccommodated*] without the
trappings of civilization. Cf. *2H4*, III.
ii. 72–7; *Oth.,* I. iii. 239; *Meas.,* III. i.
14. It is never used by Shakespeare in
the modern sense.

106. *forked*] two-legged. Falstaff,
2H4, III. ii. 334, calls Shallow 'a forked
raddish with a head fantastically
carved upon it'.

106–7. *lendings*] borrowed articles.

107. *unbutton here*] Lear wishes to

identify himself with the poor naked
wretches, unaccommodated men.

108. *naughty*] wicked.

109. *fire*] presumably he sees Gloucester's torch. Perhaps the sequence of
thought would be improved if this
sentence and the next were transposed.

wild] Jennens's emendation is unnecessary. *Wild* suggested the lecher's
body, unfruitful, out of condition. It is
just possible that Shakespeare wrote
vilde = vile.

110. *old lecher's*] The Fool does not
know that he is speaking of Gloucester, though the audience, from the
previous scene, expects his arrival.

112. *Flibbertigibbet*] The name is
taken from Harsnett. Cf. Appendix,
p. 240.

113. *first cock*] midnight.

113–14. *the web and the pin*] cataract:

lip; mildews the white wheat, and hurts the poor   115
creature of earth.

> *Swithold footed thrice the old;*
> *He met the night-mare, and her nine-fold;*
> *Bid her alight,*
> *And her troth plight,*   120
> *And aroint thee, witch, aroint thee!*

Kent. How fares your Grace?
Lear. What's he?
Kent. Who's there? What is't you seek?
Glou. What are you there? Your names?   125
Edg. Poor Tom; that eats the swimming frog, the toad,
   the todpole, the wall-newt, and the water; that in
   the fury of his heart, when the foul fiend rages, eats

---

116. earth] the earth *F3–4.*   117. *Swithold*] *F;* swithald *Q;* St Withold *Theobald.*   old] wold *Theobald (conj. Bishop).*   118. *He . . . night-mare*] *Q corr., F;* a nellthu night more *Q uncorr.;* anelthu night Moore *Q2;* anelthunight Moor *Q3.*   *nine-fold*] nine foles *conj. Tyrwhitt;* nine foals *conj. Farmer.*   119. *alight*] a-light *F;* O light *Q.*   120. *troth plight*] *Q;* troth-plight *F.*   121. *aroint . . . aroint*] (aroynt) *F;* arint *Q.*   witch] *Q corr., F;* with *Q uncorr., Q2–3.*   127. todpole] Tod-pole *F;* tode pold *Q uncorr., Q2–3;* tod pole *Q corr.;* tadpole *Johnson.*   wall-newt] *Q corr., F;* wall-wort *Q uncorr., Q2–3.*   128. fury] fruite *Q2–3.*

cf. *Wint.,* I. ii. 291. Cotgrave explains *taye* as 'a pin or web in the eye'. Holland, *Pliny,* 1601, p. 229, speaks of 'eyes dim and overcast either with the pin and web, or cataract'.

114. *squinies*] Greg, *Variants,* pp. 165–7, argues that the F 'squints' may be a sophistication. The word *squiny* is used IV. vi. 135; and it is to be found in Armin, *Nest of Ninnies,* 1608 (ed. 1880, p. 48). In the same book (p. 45) he uses *squened,* and in *The Italian Taylor* (ed. 1880, p. 175) *squeaning.* Armin probably played the part of the Fool on the first production of *King Lear.*

115. *white*] nearly ripe. Cf. John, IV. 35: 'the fields . . . white already to harvest'.

117–21. Swithold . . . aroint thee] Kittredge explains these lines as a charm. 'To recite how St Withold encountered the demon and her nine fold (her nine offspring) and subdued

her, served as a charm against her power.' He quotes from Thomas Blundevill, *The Foure Chiefest Offices belonging to Horsemanshippe,* 1571, xxiii, a charm, from 'an olde Englyshe writer', containing the lines: 'He walked day so did he night, / Untill he hir founde, / He hir beate, and he hir bounde, / Till truely hir trouth she him plyght, / That she woulde not come within the night.'

117. old] wold.

118. night-mare] an incubus, a demon from O.E. *mare.* It has no connection with the word meaning a female horse.

her nine-fold] Kittredge explains 'her nine offspring'; Capell explains 'her nine imps or familiars'.

121. aroint] be gone. Cf. *Mac.,* I. iii. 6.

127. *todpole*] tadpole.
wall-newt] wall-lizard.
water] i.e. water-newt.

cow-dung for sallets; swallows the old rat and the
ditch-dog; drinks the green mantle of the standing　130
pool; who is whipp'd from tithing to tithing, and
stock-punish'd, and imprison'd; who hath had
three suits to his back, six shirts to his body,

> Horse to ride, and weapons to wear,
> But mice and rats and such small deer,　　135
> Have been Tom's food for seven long year.

Beware my follower. Peace, Smulkin! peace, thou
fiend!

Glou. What! hath your Grace no better company?

Edg. The Prince of Darkness is a gentleman; Modo he's　140
called, and Mahu.

---

132. stock-punish'd] *Q;* stockt, punish'd *F.* ──── had] *Q; not in F.* 136.
Have]F; Hath *Q.* 137. Smulkin] *F;* snulbug *Q;* Smolkin *Theobald (Harsnett).*
141. Mahu] *F;* ma hu─*Q.*

129. *for sallets*] as a substitute for
salads. Hamlet uses the word for
'something tasty' (II. ii. 462), and this
subsidiary meaning adds point to
Edgar's remark.

130. *ditch-dog*] dead dog thrown into
a ditch.

green mantle] scum. Cf. *Mer.V.,* I. i.
89. Craig suggests it means duck-
weed, and it may mean water covered
with weed.

131. *whipp'd . . . tithing*] a tithing was
a district containing ten families.
Vagabonds, under the statute of 1597,
were liable to be whipped and sent
from parish to parish, until they
reached their own, if that could be
determined.

132. *stock-punish'd*] punished by being put in the stocks. The F reading is
awkward as it puts a general word,
punished, sandwiched between two
particular punishments, *stocked* and
imprisoned.

133. *three suits*] Cf. II. ii. 14, and
note.

135-6. But . . . year] Capell notes
that this couplet is a version of one in
the popular romance, *Bevis of Hampton,*
ed. Kölbing, p. 74: 'Ratons and

myce and soche smale dere, / That
was hys mete that seven yere.'

135. deer] game.

137. *follower*] familiar, fiend.

Smulkin] Cf. Harsnett, Appendix,
p. 242.

140-1. *The . . . Mahu*] Cf. Harsnett.
Appendix, p. 240. Blunden, *Shakespeare's Significances* (Bradby, *Shakespeare Criticism,* 1919-35, p. 331),
suggests that Modo recalled a passage
in Horace, *Epistles,* II. i: 'Ille per
extentum funem mihi posse videtur /
Ire poeta, meum qui pectus inaniter
angit, / Irritat, mulcet, falsis terroribus
implet, / Ut magus; et modo me
Thebis, modo ponit Athenis.' Blunden
argues that this passage led to the
mention of 'learned Theban' and
'good Athenian' (154, 177) and to the
later echo from one of Horace's Odes
(III. vi. 82). Baldwin, *op. cit.,* II. 520,
quotes Drant's translation (1567) of
Horace's lines: 'That poet on a
stretched rope may walke and neuer
fall, / That can stere vp my passions,
or quicke my sprytes at all. / Stere me,
chere me, or with false feares of bugges
fill vp my brest, / At *Athens* now, and
now at *Thebes,* by charminge make me

Glou. Our flesh and blood, my lord, is grown so vile,
     That it doth hate what gets it.
Edg. Poor Tom's a-cold.
Glou. Go in with me. My duty cannot suffer   145
     T'obey in all your daughters' hard commands:
     Though their injunction be to bar my doors,
     And let this tyrannous night take hold upon you,
     Yet I have ventured to come seek you out
     And bring you where both fire and food is ready.   150
Lear. First let me talk with this philosopher.
     What is the cause of thunder?

---

142. blood ... vile] *F;* bloud is growne so vild my Lord *Q.*   143. gets it] it gets
F3–4.   144, 170. a-cold] *hyphened Rowe.*   146. T'obey] *F;* to obey *Q.*
147. Though] Though all *F3–4.*   150. fire and food] *F;* food and fire *Q.*

---

rest.' Baldwin goes on to show that
Cooper, *Thesaurus,* defines *magus* as
'Dictio Persica, qua apud eos sapiens
significatur, eos enim Persae magos
vocant, quos Graeci philosophos,
Latini sapientes ... Cic. *A wise man: a
great learned philosopher.*' Cf. 'philosopher ... learned Theban' (151, 154)
'Persian' (III. vi. 79). This theory may
be supported by the fact that the chain
of ideas could have been suggested by
Harsnett, who quotes, and translates,
a passage from Horace's next epistle:
'Dreames and Magicall affrights, /
Wonders, witches, walking sprights, /
What Thessalian Hags can doe, / All
this seemes a iest to you.' The two
passages are linked by their mention
of terrors and magic.

142–3. *Our ... gets it*] Gloucester,
reminded perhaps by some tone or
inflection in his son's voice (Cowden
Clarke) links Edgar's supposed villainy with that of Goneril and Regan.

142. *Our ... blood*] humanity, our
children.

143. *gets*] begets.

151. *philosopher*] The word could
mean a natural scientist.

152. *What ... thunder?*] This question was much discussed. G. S.
Gordon, *Shakespearian Comedy,* 1944,
pp. 126–8, points out that Lear mis-

takes Edgar for a professional wise
man, acquainted with the secrets of
Nature, such as were formerly kept by
all kings. In the Middle Ages 'one of
the most popular forms of instructive
reading was the dialogue and catechism.' One such dialogue was called
The Book of Sidrach, or *The Sapience of
Nature.* Gordon asserts that a 16th-
century translation contains such
questions as 'What is the cause of
eclipses? Why are the planets seven?
Why has the snail a house?' Cf. I. v.
27, 34 where the Fool, reversing the
usual procedure, puts the 'reasons of
nature' to his master. *Boccus and
Sydrac,* the only version I have seen,
contains the question (No. 122)
'whereof cometh the thounder?' But
though it mentions seven planets
(No. 143) and 'whereof snayles come'
(No. 224) it does not seem to discuss
the Fool's other questions. Ovid,
Metamorphoses (tr. Golding, xv. 74 ff.)
tells how Pythagoras taught 'The first
foundation of the world: the cause of
every thing: / What nature was: and
what was God: whence snow and
lyghtning spring: / And whether *Jove*
or else the wynds in breaking clowdes
doo thunder: / What shakes the earth:
what law the starres doo keepe theyr
courses under'.

Kent. Good my Lord, take his offer; go into th'house.

Lear. I'll talk a word with this same learned Theban.
     What is your study?   155

Edg. How to prevent the fiend, and to kill vermin.

Lear. Let me ask you one word in private.

Kent. Importune him once more to go, my Lord;
     His wits begin t'unsettle.

Glou.   Canst thou blame him?

                                             [*Storm still.*

     His daughters seek his death. Ah! that good Kent;   160
     He said it would be thus, poor banish'd man!
     Thou say'st the king grows mad; I'll tell thee, friend,
     I am almost mad myself. I had a son,
     Now outlaw'd from my blood; he sought my life,
     But lately, very late; I lov'd him, friend,   165
     No father his son dearer; true to tell thee,
     The grief hath craz'd my wits. What a night's this!
     I do beseech your Grace,—

Lear.   O! cry you mercy, Sir:
     Noble philosopher, your company.

Edg. Tom's a-cold.   170

Glou. In, fellow, there, into th'hovel: keep thee warm.

Lear. Come, let's in all.

Kent.   This way, my Lord.

Lear.   With him;

153. Good my] *F; my* good *Q.*   th'house] *F;* the house *Q.*   154. talk]
take *F3–4.*   same] *F;* most *Q.*   157. me] us *F3–4.*   158. once more] *F;
not in Q.*   159. t'] *F;* to *Q.*   S.D.] *F; not in Q.*   160. Ah] *F;* O *Q.*
164. he] a *Q1.*   166. true] truth *Q2–3.*   167. hath] has *Q2–3.*   168.
Grace,—] *Capell;* Grace. *Q,F.*   168–9. mercy, Sir: Noble] *F;* mercy noble *Q.*
171. into th'] *F;* in't *Q1.*

154. *learned Theban*] Jonson, *Pan's Anniversary* (ed. Herford and Simpson, VII. 532), uses the words: 'Then comes my learned *Theban*, the Tinker, I told you of.' This may be an echo of this scene; but it looks as though both Jonson and Shakespeare were using an expression, the meaning of which has been lost.

155. *study*] department of research.

156. *prevent*] use preventative measures against, avoid.

kill vermin] Blunden, *op. cit.,* p. 332, compares III. vi. 22.

164. *outlaw'd . . . blood*] condemned to outlawry, through corruption of blood. Those subject to attainder (stain or corruption of blood) formerly suffered such loss. Cf. *1H6,* III. i. 159. Gloucester may merely mean, however, that Edgar has been disowned.

167. *The . . . wits*] Cf. III. iv. 77.

168. *cry you mercy*] I beg your pardon.

    I will keep still with my philosopher.

Kent. Good my Lord, soothe him; let him take the fellow.

Glou. Take him you on.   175

Kent. Sirrah, come on; go along with us.

Lear. Come, good Athenian.

Glou. No words, no words: hush.

Edg.   *Child Rowland to the dark tower came,*

           His word was still: *Fie, foh, and fum,*   180

           I smell the blood of a British man.   [*Exeunt.*

SCENE V.—[*A Room in Gloucester's Castle.*]

Enter CORNWALL *and* EDMUND.

Corn. I will have my revenge ere I depart his house.

Edm. How, my lord, I may be censured, that nature thus
gives way to loyalty, something fears me to think of.

1 79. *tower came*] *F;* towne come *Q.*

Scene v

S.D. *A . . . Castle*] *Capell; not in Q, F.*   1. my] *not in F3–4.*   his] *F;* the *Q;*
this *Hanmer.*

    174. *soothe*] humour. Cf. *Err.,* iv. iv.
82. The word is used by Harsnett, *op.
cit.,* p. 185.

    179. Child . . . came] Probably a
line from a lost ballad. The fragments
quoted in Jamieson, *Illustrations of
Northern Antiquities,* 1814, p. 402, and
Child, *English and Scottish Ballads,*
1864, I. 245, are 'manifestly of modern
composition' (Kittredge).

    Child] a candidate for knighthood.

    Rowland] Roland, Charlemagne's
nephew, and the hero of *The Song of
Roland* and other poems.

    180. *His . . . still*] Edgar's remark,
meaning 'His watchword or motto
was always' (Kittredge).

    180–1. Fie . . . man] the Giant's
speech from the story of *Jack the Giant-
Killer.* It is given, by an intentional
incongruity, to the heroic Child Rowland. Cf. Nashe, *Have with You to
Saffron-Walden,* 1596 (ed. McKerrow,
III. 37): 'O, tis a precious apotheg-

maticall Pedant, who will finde matter
inough to dilate a whole daye of the
first inuention of *Fy, fa, fum,* I smell the
bloud of an Englishman.' Nashe's
words could serve as a warning to
commentators. E. Yardley, *N.Q.,*
30 May 1896, attempts to associate
Rowland and the Giant. Helen was
carried off by a sea-monster and
immured in an enchanted castle. Her
brother, Childe Rowland, traversed
the seas in quest of her. She concealed
him during the temporary absence of
the monster. But the monster, when he
returned, smelt the blood of a Christian
man.

Scene v

    2. *How . . . censured*] what people will
think of me.

    nature] my natural feelings as a
son.

    3. *something . . . of*] rather frightens
me. Cf. *3H6,* v. ii. 2.

Corn. I now perceive it was not altogether your brother's
evil disposition made him seek his death; but a pro- 5
voking merit, set a-work by a reproveable badness in
himself.

Edm. How malicious is my fortune, that I must repent to
be just! This is the letter he spoke of, which approves
him an intelligent party to the advantages of France. 10
O Heavens! that this treason were not, or not I the
detector!

Corn. Go with me to the Duchess.

Edm. If the matter of this paper be certain, you have
mighty business in hand. 15

Corn. True or false, it hath made thee Earl of Gloucester.
Seek out where thy father is, that he may be ready for
our apprehension.

Edm. [*Aside.*] If I find him comforting the King, it will
stuff his suspicion more fully. [*Aloud.*] I will persever 20
in my course of loyalty, though the conflict be sore
between that and my blood.

Corn. I will lay trust upon thee; and thou shalt find a
dearer father in my love. [*Exeunt.*

---

9. letter] *Q;* Letter which *F.*   11. this] *F;* his *Q.*   were not] *F;* were *Q.*
19. S.D.] *Theobald; not in Q, F.*   20. S.D.] *Duthie; not in Q, F.*   24. dearer]
Q; deere *F.*   S.D.] *F; Exit Q.*

5–7. *a provoking . . . himself*] 'a provoking merit' has been taken to mean
'a virtue apt to be provoked', 'a consciousness of his own worth which
urged him on' and 'an anticipative
merit, a meritorious forestalling of
crime by its punishment'. Similarly
'badness in himself' has been taken to
mean Edgar's wickedness, and also
Gloucester's. The passage should probably be interpreted: 'Edgar's repre-
hensible wickedness was provoked to
mete out to Gloucester the death that
he deserved'. Although Gloucester
deserved to die, only an evil son would
attempt to murder his father.

9. *just*] righteous, i.e. that he has
revealed his father's treason.

9–10. *approves him*] proves him to
be.

10. *intelligent party*] intelligencer,
spy, providing information. Some take
it to mean 'well informed of'.

to the advantages] for the assistance.

18. *apprehension*] arrest.

19. *comforting*] used in the legal
sense of 'supporting, helping'. Lord
Campbell says: 'The indictment
against an accessory after the fact, for
treason, charges that the accessory
"comforted" the principal traitor
after knowledge of the treason.'

20. *persever*] continue. The accent is
on the second syllable.

22. *blood*] natural feelings of a son.

SCENE VI.—[*A Chamber in a Farmhouse adjoining the Castle.*]

Enter GLOUCESTER *and* KENT.

Glou. Here is better than the open air; take it thankfully.
I will piece out the comfort with what addition I
can: I will not be long from you.

Kent. All the power of his wits have given way to his
impatience. The Gods reward your kindness!   5
[*Exit Gloucester.*

Enter LEAR, EDGAR, *and Fool.*

Edg. Frateretto calls me, and tells me Nero is an angler in
the Lake of Darkness. Pray, innocent, and beware
the foul fiend.

Scene VI

S.D. *A . . . Castle*] Malone; *A Chamber, Rowe; A Chamber, in a Farmhouse. Theobald;
A Room in some of the out-buildings of the Castle. Capell.   Enter . . . Kent*] F; *Enter
Gloster and Lear, Kent, Foole, and Tom* Q.   4. have] Q, F; has *Pope;* hath
Capell.   to his] F; to Q.   5. reward] F; deserue Q; preserve *conj.
Capell.   Exit Gloucester*] Capell; *Exit (after 3)* F; *not in* Q.   Enter . . . Fool*] F;
at beginning of scene Q.   7. and] F; *not in* Q.

S.D.] Perrett, comparing III. iv. 153,
suggests that Theobald's placing of
this scene in a farmhouse is wrong.
Perhaps Capell's suggestion, 'A Room
in some of the outbuildings of the
Castle' is better.
  2. *piece*] eke. Cf. *Wiv.*, III. ii. 34.
  4. *have*] attracted into the plural by
the intervening *wits* (Kittredge).
  6. *Frateretto*] another name from
Harsnett. See Appendix, p. 240.
  6–7. *Nero . . . Darkness*] Upton
pointed out that according to Rabelais
(II. 30) Nero played on the hurdy-
gurdy in hell; it was Trajan who
angled (for frogs). But F. E. Budd,
R.E.S. (1935), pp. 421–9, shows that
Shakespeare's knowledge of Nero's
angling was taken from Chaucer, *The
Monk's Tale*, ll. 485–6; and that the
mention of Nero was suggested by
Harsnett's *Declaration*. Immediately
after the first mention of Frateretto, a

Fiddler comes in to provide 'musicke
in hell'. In the same context, Harsnett
mentions the '*stygian* lake' and 'a
Caesars humor'; and there are later
references to the bottomless pit. See
Appendix, p. 240. Edith Sitwell,
A Notebook on William Shakespeare, pp.
48–9, suggests 'the lake of darkness'
means 'the bottomless depth of human
nature' and she compares *Meas.*, III.
i. 93: 'His filth within being cast, he
would appeare / A pond as deepe as
hell.' She also suggests that Shakespeare had read Pausanias, *Description
of Greece*, II. 37, where he describes an
attempt by Nero to sound the depth of
the Alcyonian Lake, through which
Dionysus went to Hell to fetch up
Semele. It is unlikely that Shakespeare
read Pausanias in the original, but it is
possible that he read of Nero's experiment elsewhere. John Berryman,
T.L.S., 30 March 1946, points out that

Fool. Prithee, Nuncle, tell me whether a madman be a
　　　gentleman or a yeoman?　　　　　　　　　　　　　10
Lear. A King, a King!
Fool. No; he's a yeoman that has a gentleman to his son;
　　　for he's a mad yeoman that sees his son a gentleman
　　　before him.
Lear. To have a thousand with red burning spits　　15
　　　Come hizzing in upon 'em—
Edg. The foul fiend bites my back.
Fool. He's mad that trusts in the tameness of a wolf, a
　　　horse's health, a boy's love, or a whore's oath.
Lear. It shall be done; I will arraign them straight.　　20
　　　[*To Edgar.*] Come, sit thou here, most learned justicer;

9. be] may be *Q2–3.*　　12–15. *Fool.* No . . . him. *Lear.*] *F; not in Q.*　　13. mad]
not in F3–4.　　16. hizzing] *F;* hiszing *Q1;* hissing *Q2–3.*　　'em—] *Theobald;*
'em. *F;* them. *Q.*　　17–55. *Edg.* The foul .ʾ. 'scape] *Q; not in F.*　　18. trusts]
trust *Q3.*　　19. health] *Q;* heels *Singer (conj. Warburton).*　　21. S.D.] *Capell;*
not in Q; To the Fool Hanmer.　　justicer] *Theobald;* Iustice *Q.*

Nero was guilty of matricide, and that
Edgar, who speaks this line, is accused
of parricide. Higgins, in the 1587
edition of *The Mirror for Magistrates*
(*Cordila*, l. 370) mentions the 'darke-
some *Stygian lake*'.

12–14. *No . . . before him*] Shakespeare is thought to have secured a
coat of arms for his father. Schmidt
suggests that there is a pun on *mad* and
made. Davenport, *N.Q.* (1953), p. 21,
compares Joseph Hall's lines on a
yeoman: 'Old driueling *Lolio* drudges
all he can, / To make his eldest sonne a
Gentleman . . .' Lolio's son is ungrateful: 'Could neuer man worke thee a
worser shame / Then once to minge
thy fathers odious name . . . / His
father dead, tush, no it was not hee, /
He findes recordes of his great
pedigree' (*Virgid.*, 1598, IV. ii).

15–16. *To . . . upon 'em*] See Harsnett,
Appendix, p. 241.

16. *hizzing*] This form of *hissing*
'suggests the whizzing sound of the
redhot weapons as they are to be
brandished by a thousand assailants'
(Kittredge).

19. *horse's health*] perhaps his seller's
account of his condition. But see *Shr.*,
I. ii. 81 and III. ii. 50–6. Warburton
read 'a horse's heels'. Cf. Ray,
Proverbs, ed. 1879, p. 546: 'Trust not a
horse's heels, nor a dog's tooth.'

20. *arraign*] Lear suddenly abandons
his intention of using armed force, and
decides to bring his daughters to trial
instead. R. Peacock, *The Poet in the
Theatre*, 1946, p. 128, comments on the
trial: 'Lear, scarcely rescued from the
fury of nature, his ideas scattered by
suffering, conducts a trial of his
daughters. It is an illumination that
produces from the sub-conscious the
effects of order. At the moment of
greatest breakdown we are given a
judgement that represents amidst
chaos the memory of civilization.
Moral assumptions are at the centre
of tragedy.'

21. *justicer*] P. A. McElwaine, *N.Q.*,
23 Sept. 1911, suggests that this is a
corruption of 'Justiciar', a high officer
in the time of William I, who took the
king's place when he was abroad.
Cotgrave uses it as a synonym for

[*To the Fool.*] Thou, sapient sir, sit here. Now, you
    she foxes!

Edg. Look where he stands and glares! Want'st thou eyes
    at trial, madam?

         Come o'er the bourn, Bessy, to me,—   25

Fool. [Sings.]   *Her boat hath a leak,*
             And she must not speak;
        Why she dares not come over to thee!

Edg. The foul fiend haunts poor Tom in the voice of a
    nightingale. Hoppedance cries in Tom's belly for   30
    two white herring. Croak not, black angel; I have no
    food for thee.

Kent. How do you, sir? Stand you not so amaz'd:
    Will you lie down and rest upon the cushions?

Lear. I'll see their trial first. Bring in their evidence.   35

---

22. S.D.] *Capell; not in Q; To Edgar Hanmer.*   Now] *Q2–3;* no *Q1.*   23.
he] *Q;* she *Theobald.*   Want'st] *Q2;* wanst *Q1.*   Want'st . . . eyes] *Q;*
Wantonizeth thou *conj. Staunton;* Wanton'st thou eyes *Jennens (conj. Seward).*
24. trial] *Q2–3;* tral *Q1.*   25. *bourn*] *Camb.;* boorne *Capell;* broome *Q.*
26. S.D.] *Craig (conj. Camb.).*   27. *speak;*] *conj. Schmidt;* speake, *Q.*   34.
cushions] cushings *Q1.*   35. in their] *Q;* in the *Pope.*

'Justice'. The word is actually an
emendation of Theobald's. Cf. III. vi.
55 and IV. ii. 79; also *Cym.,* v. v. 214.

23. *Look . . . glares*] a fiend; or Lear.

23–4. *Want'st . . . madam?*] Do you
want to have spectators at your trial,
madam? Look where he, a fiend,
stands, and glares. K.D. (*N.Q.,* 2 Dec.
1905) conjectures 'worse than eyes at
trol-madam'. Cf. *Wint.,* IV. iii. 92.
Steevens explained: 'Do you want to
attract admiration, even while you
stand at the bar of justice?' Eccles gave
the speech to Lear, changing *he* to *she.*

23. *eyes*] Bell, unnecessarily, thought
this represented the crier's proclamation at the opening of court, *Oyez.*

25. *Come . . . me*] from a song in
which a lover calls upon his sweet-
heart to come to him across a stream.
Wager, *The Longer thou Livest the More
Fool thou Art,* quotes from the same
song: 'Com ouer the Boorne besse /
My little pretie Besse, / Com ouer the
Boorne besse to me.' (Cf. *Harleian
Miscellany,* ed. Park, x. 260.)

bourn] burn, brook. Capell's emendation.

26–8. Her . . . thee] The Fool
improvises.

29. *The . . . voice*] Edgar pretends
that the Fool's singing is that of a fiend
disguised as a nightingale.

30. *Hoppedance*] Harsnett's form is
'Hoberdidance'.

cries] His stomach is rumbling because it is empty. Cf. III. ii. 14.

31. *white herring*] either pickled herring (Steevens); or fresh, unsmoked
herring (Kittredge). Nashe, *Lenten
Stuffe,* 1599 (ed. McKerrow, III. 204)
speaks of 'herrings, which were as
white as whales bone when hee hung
them vp, nowe lookt as red as a
lobster'; and, *op. cit.,* p. 223: a white
pickled herring? why it is meate for a
Prince!'

Croak] rumble. Cf. Harsnett, Appendix, p. 242.

33. *amaz'd*] dumbfounded.

35. *their evidence*] those who are to
testify against them.

[*To Edgar.*] Thou robed man of justice, take thy
    place;
[*To the Fool.*] And thou, his yoke-fellow of equity,
Bench by his side. [*To Kent.*] You are o'th'commission,
Sit you too.

Edg. Let us deal justly.   40

      Sleepest or wakest thou, jolly shepherd?
         Thy sheep be in the corn;
      And for one blast of thy minikin mouth,
         Thy sheep shall take no harm.

Purr, the cat is grey.   45

Lear. Arraign her first; 'tis Goneril. I here take my oath
before this honourable assembly, she kick'd the poor
King her father.

Fool. Come hither, mistress. Is your name Goneril?

Lear. She cannot deny it.   50

Fool. Cry you mercy, I took you for a joint-stool.

---

36. S.D.] *Capell; not in Q.*   robed] robbed *Q.*   37. S.D.] *Capell; not in Q.*
38. S.D.] *Capell; not in Q.*   o'th'] *Q2, subst.;* ot'h *Q1.*   40–1. justly.
Sleepest] *Theobald;* iustly sleepest *Q1;* iustly, sleepest *Q2.*   45. Purr, the] Pur
the *Q;* Purr! the *most dd.*   47. she] *not in Q1.*   51. joint-stool] ioyne stoole *Q1.*

---

36. *robed*] Edgar's blanket appears as judicial robes here, and later (79) as the Persian attire of a Magus.

37. *yoke-fellow*] partner. Cf. *H5*, IV. vi. 9. Harsnett uses several words hyphened with *fellow*.

38. *Bench*] Take your seat on the bench.

o'th'commission] commissioned as a justice. P. A. McElwaine points out that 'we speak of "commission of the peace", but we also speak of "commission of Assize".'

41–4. Sleepest . . . harm] Probably a fragment, or an adaptation of an old song. Steevens quotes from *Interlude of the Nature of the Four Elements*, 1510: 'Slepyst thou, wakyst thou geffery coke.' Whiter, in an unpublished note, compares an obscure passage in *Gent.*, I. i. 77–80.

43. for one blast] Kittredge explains: 'for the time it takes to play one strain on your shepherd's pipe'. As H.

Myers points out (*The TLS,* 18 January 1980) sheep have to be introduced gradually to corn or grass each season; otherwise 'they swell up and can easily die'. Cf. Hardy's *Far from the Madding Crowd*, Chapter 21.

minikin] delicate, dainty, neat, *concinnus.* It was also a musical term, as in the apocryphal Marlowe poem, ed. Cunningham, 1870, p. 271 : 'I cannot lisp, nor to some fiddle sing, / Nor run upon a high stretched minikin.' Here it means the thin string of gut used for the treble string of the lute or viol, and hence shrill (*N.E.D.*).

45. *Purr*] The name was probably suggested by the name of one of Harsnett's demons (see Appendix, p. 240); but Edgar is referring to a demon or familiar in the shape of a grey cat, and this may be its noise, rather than its name.

51. *Cry . . . stool*] This proverbial expression is found in J. Withal, *Short*

Lear. And here's another, whose warp'd looks proclaim
What store her heart is made on. Stop her there!
Arms, arms, sword, fire! Corruption in the place!
False justicer, why hast thou let her 'scape?   55
Edg. Bless thy five wits!
Kent. O pity! Sir, where is the patience now
That you so oft have boasted to retain?
Edg. [*Aside.*] My tears begin to take his part so much,
They mar my counterfeiting.   60
Lear. The little dogs and all,
Tray, Blanch, and Sweetheart, see, they bark at me.
Edg. Tom will throw his head at them. Avaunt, you curs!
            Be thy mouth or black or white,
            Tooth that poisons if it bite;   65
            Mastiff, greyhound, mongrel grim,
            Hound or spaniel, brach or lym;

---

53. store] stuff *conj. Jennens;* stone *Collier (conj. Theobald).*   made on] *Capell;*
made an *Q;* made of *Theobald.*   58. retain] remain *F3–4.*   59. S.D.]
Rowe; not in Q, F.   60. They] *F;* Theile *Q1;* They'l *Q2–3.*   66–7.
mongrel grim, Hound] *Rowe, subst.;* Mongrill, Grim, Hound *F;* mungril,
grim-hound *Q.*   67. lym] *Hanmer;* him *Q;* Hym *F.*

Dictionary, 1554: 'Antehac te cornua habere putabam, I cry you mercy, I took you for a joyn'd stool.' It was a facetious apology for overlooking a person, 'a ridiculous instance of making an offence worse, by a foolish and improbable apology' (Nares). Steevens cites Lyly, *Mother Bombie,* IV. ii: 'I crie you mercy, I tooke you for a joynt stoole.'

joint-stool] joyned stool; a low stool with three or four legs fitted into it, made by a joiner, as distinguished from a carpenter who works more on the rough.

It has been suggested (*N.Q.,* 23 July 1904, p. 66) that the Fool may mean: 'I took you for one of the bench, not a prisoner.' Cf. *Narcissus,* 1603, 'Some of them are heires, all of good abilitye; I beseech your lordshipp with the rest of the ioyned stooles, I would say the bench, take my foolish iudgement, and lett them fine for it.'

52. *warp'd*] perverse, unnatural, distorted by evil passions.

53. *store*] material, stock (Craig). Perhaps 'of evil passions' is understood. But as the word could mean treasure, there may be an unintentional echo of Matt., vi. 21. Perhaps it should be emended to *stuff* (Jennens) or to *stone* (Theobald): the latter may be supported by III. vi. 76 and v. iii. 256; and *r* for *n* is a common misreading. Cf. collations of IV. ii. 21.

60. *mar . . . counterfeiting*] See Appendix, p. 239.

66. *grim*] Ridley suggests that the comma before this word means that it conceals a kind of dog, and is not an adj. But the comma may merely indicate that the adj. applies to all three kinds of dog.

67. *brach*] Cf. I. iv. 110.

lym] lymmer, a species of bloodhound, so called from the liam, or leather thong, by which he was led.

Or bobtail tike or trundle-tail;
Tom will make him weep and wail:
For, with throwing thus my head,   70
Dogs leap'd the hatch, and all are fled.
Do de, de, de. Sessa! Come, march to wakes and
fairs and market-towns. Poor Tom, thy horn is dry.
Lear. Then let them anatomize Regan, see what breeds
about her heart. Is there any cause in nature that   75
make these hard hearts? [*To Edgar.*] You, sir, I
entertain for one of my hundred; only I do not like
the fashion of your garments: you will say they are
Persian; but let them be chang'd.

68. Or] *F; not in Q.*   tike] tight *F1–3.*   trundle-tail] *Q;* Troudle taile *F.*
69. him] *F;* them *Q.*   71. leap'd] leapt *F;* leape *Q.*   72. Do . . . de.] *F;*
loudla doodla *Q.*   Sessa!] *Malone;* sese: *F; not in Q.*   76. make] *F;* makes
Q.   these hard hearts?] *Rowe;* these hard-hearts. *F;* this hardnes *Q.*
S.D.] *Capell; not in Q, F.*   77. for] *F;* you for *Q.*   78. garments] garment
Q2–3.   you will] *F;* youle *Q.*   79. Persian] *F;* Persian attire *Q.*

68. *trundle-tail*] or trindle-tail, a dog
with a long drooping tail, which he
seems to trundle along after him
(Kittredge).

70. *For . . . head*] After this line in
Edwin Booth's Prompt Book there is a
S.D.: 'Throws straw crown to left.'
There is no warrant for this. It may
mean that Edgar jerks his head at the
imaginary dogs. In Gielgud's 1950
production, Edgar made as though to
lift his head from his shoulders. Two
other suggestions occur to me: (i)
Edgar throws his horn at them. As
'head' means the antlers of a deer it
could be stretched to mean the ox's
horn of Poor Tom. (ii) Edgar might
put his horn on his head, and pretend
he is an ox attacking the dogs with it.

71. *hatch*] the lower half of a divided
door. 'To leap the hatch' means to
make a hurried exit.

72. *Do . . . de.*] Cf. III. iv. 57–8.
Sessa] Cf. III. iv. 98.

72–3. *Come . . . market-towns*]
Steevens suggests this is a line from a
song in which a vagabond calls upon
a companion to accompany him on his
rounds.

73. *thy . . . dry*] Aubrey, *Natural
History of Wiltshire,* ed. 1847, p. 93,
mentions that 'Bedlam beggars wore
about their necks a great horne of an
ox in a string or bawdrie, which, when
they came to an house for almes they
did wind, and they did put the drink
given them into this horne whereto they did put a stopple.' This was
the formula used in begging for a
drink; but Edgar also means that he is
unable to play his part any longer
(Steevens).

74–5. *what . . . heart*] as though
her heart had become as hard as
horn.

76. *make*] subjunctive (Schmidt).
Cf. Abbott *367.

77. *entertain*] engage, take into service. Cf. *Cæs.,* v. v. 60.

hundred] i.e. the hundred knights.
But one of Harsnett's devils was a
Centurion and 'had a hundred vnder
his charge'. Cf. Appendix, p. 240.

79. *Persian*] Horace, *Odes,* i. 38. Cf.
note on III. iv. 140–1. A Persian em-
bassy visited England early in James
I's reign.

chang'd] Carter, *Shakespeare and Holy*

Kent. Now, good my Lord, lie here and rest awhile.   80
Lear. Make no noise, make no noise; draw the curtains:
    so, so. We'll go to supper i'th'morning.
Fool. And I'll go to bed at noon.

Re-enter GLOUCESTER.

Glou. Come hither, friend: where is the King my master?
Kent. Here, Sir; but trouble him not, his wits are gone.   85
Glou. Good friend, I prithee, take him in thy arms;
    I have o'erheard a plot of death upon him.
    There is a litter ready; lay him in't,
    And drive toward Dover, friend, where thou shalt
      meet
    Both welcome and protection. Take up thy master: 90
    If thou should'st dally half an hour, his life,
    With thine, and all that offer to defend him,
    Stand in assured loss. Take up, take up;
    And follow me, that will to some provision
    Give thee quick conduct.
Kent.   Oppressed nature sleeps.   95
    This rest might yet have balm'd thy broken sinews

80. and rest] *Q; not in F.*   82. so, so] *F;* so, so, so *Q.*   morning.] *F;*
morning, so, so, so. *Q.*   83. And . . . noon] *F; not in Q.*   S.D.] *Q; after 79 F.*
88. in't] in it *Q 2–3.*   89. toward] *F;* towards *Q.*   93. take up] *F;* to keepe
Q uncorr., Q 2–3; the King *Q corr.*   95–9. Oppressed . . . behind] *Q; not in F.*
95. Oppressed] Opprest *Theobald.*   96. sinews] *Q;* senses *Theobald.*

Scripture, points out that Shakespeare may have been influenced by Dan., vi. 8: 'that it be not changed, according to the lawe of the Medes and Persians which altereth not'.

81. *curtains*] Lear imagines he is in his own bed.

82. *supper . . . morning*] since we have none to-night. Gloucester was to provide food, but Lear needs rest above all.

83. *And . . . noon*] Blunden, *op. cit.,* p. 336, suggests that there are seven meanings to this sentence, including 'a pun on the people's name for the scarlet pimpernel. The weak-bodied Fool with his coxcombe looks like that flower. It is the last time that the Fool speaks during the play. He presages his untimely death with a secondary meaning in the word "bed" of "grave". He takes off his coxcombe for the last time to please the audience.' Hilda M. Hulme cites from John Heywood a wife's complaint of her husband's infidelity: 'It seemeth ye wolde make me go to bed at noone.' She suggests that the Fool's last words are a comment on Lear's withdrawal 'into the world of hallucination'.

87. *upon*] against.

96. *broken sinews*] racked nerves. Schmidt cites, *V.A.,* 903: 'A second fear through all her sinews spread.'

Which, if convenience will not allow,
Stand in hard cure. [*To the Fool.*] Come, help to
    bear thy master;
Thou must not stay behind.

Glou.   Come, come, away.
                    [*Exeunt Kent, Gloucester, and the Fool,*
                                    bearing off the King.

Edg. When we our betters see bearing our woes,   100
We scarcely think our miseries our foes.
Who alone suffers, suffers most i'th'mind,
Leaving free things and happy shows behind;
But then the mind much sufferance doth o'erskip,
When grief hath mates, and bearing fellowship.   105
How light and portable my pain seems now,
When that which makes me bend makes the king
    bow;
He childed as I father'd! Tom, away!
Mark the high noises, and thyself bewray
When false opinion, whose wrong thoughts defile
    thee,   110
In thy just proof repeals and reconciles thee.

98. S.D.] *Theobald; not in Q.*   99. S.D.] *Capell; Exeunt F; Exit Q.*   100–13.]
Q; not in F.   102. suffers, suffers] suffers *Q2–3.*   110. thoughts defile]
thought defiles *Theobald.*

Delius compares *Tw.N.*, II. v. 83: 'We
break the sinews of our plot.' Sir John
Davies, *Nosce Teipsum* (ed. Grosart, I.
70) has, in a section on Feeling:
'Lastly, the feeling power which is
life's root, / Through every living
power itself doth shed / By sinews,
which extend from head to foot, / And
like a net, all o'er the body spread.'
Theobald's emendation, *senses*, is
therefore unnecessary.

98. *Stand . . . cure*] can hardly be
cured. Cf. 93 *ante*, and *Oth.*, II. i. 51.

.100–13. *When . . . lurk*] Wright
thought this soliloquy was spurious.
But its style is not unlike other passages, *Cor.*, II. iii. 120–31; *Oth.*, I. iii.
210–20; *Mac.*, v. iv. 16–21. It was
necessary to bring out the parallelism
between the two plots.

103. *free*] care-free.

105. *bearing*] endurance, suffering.

106. *portable*] endurable.

108. *He . . . father'd*] He had cruel
children, as I have a cruel father.

109. *Mark . . . noises*] observe the
signs of discord among the great;
'attend to the great events that are
approaching' (Johnson).

thyself bewray] reveal thyself, throw
off thy disguise.

111. *just proof*] proof of thy integrity.

repeals] repeals the sentence of outlawry, and recalls thee to thy proper
position.

reconciles thee] i.e. to thy father.
Plural and singular words were often
rhymed by Shakespeare, and there is
no need to read 'thought defiles' in the
previous line.

What will hap more to-night, safe 'scape the King!
Lurk, lurk.   [*Exit.*

SCENE VII.—[*A Room in Gloucester's Castle.*]

Enter CORNWALL, REGAN, GONERIL, EDMUND,
               and Servants.

Corn. [*To Goneril.*] Post speedily to my Lord your husband; show him this letter: the army of France is
   landed. Seek out the traitor Gloucester.
                            [*Exeunt some of the Servants.*
Reg. Hang him instantly.
Gon. Pluck out his eyes.   5
Corn. Leave him to my displeasure. Edmund, keep you
   our sister company: the revenges we are bound to
   take upon your traitorous father are not fit for your
   beholding. Advise the Duke, where you are going, to
   a most festinate preparation: we are bound to the   10
   like. Our posts shall be swift and intelligent betwixt
   us. Farewell, dear sister; farewell, my Lord of Gloucester.

               Enter OSWALD.

How now! where's the King?
Osw. My Lord of Gloucester hath convey'd him hence: 15
   Some five or six and thirty of his knights,

113. S.D.] *Theobald; not in Q.*

               Scene VII
S.D. *A . . . Castle*] *Rowe, subst.; not in Q, F.*   *Regan*] *not in F3–4.*   2. him]
Q; hin F1 uncorr.   3. traitor] *F; vilaine Q.*   S.D.] *Capell; not in Q, F.*
7. revenges] *F; reuenge Q.*   10. festinate] *F2; festiuate F1; festuant Q.*
11. posts] *F; post Q.*   intelligent] *F; intelligence Q.*   13. S.D.] *Collier;
Enter Steward F, at 14 Q.*

   112. *What*] whatever, whatsoever.   10. *festinate*] hasty, urgent. Cf.
Cf. Abbott, *254.   *LLL.*, III. i. 6.
                                                   preparation] i.e. for war.
               Scene VII   10–11. *we . . , like*] We intend to do
   2. *letter*] Cf. III. iii. 10 ff. and III. v.   the same.
9.   11. *posts*] speedy messengers on
   7. *bound*] ready, prepared to, pur-   horseback.
posing to; or possibly, obliged.   *intelligent*] giving information.

Hot questrists after him, met him at gate;
Who, with some other of the Lord's dependants,
Are gone with him toward Dover, where they boast
To have well-armed friends.
Corn.   Get horses for your mistress.
Gon. Farewell, sweet Lord, and sister.   21
Corn. Edmund, farewell. [*Exeunt Goneril, Edmund, and Oswald.*
                    Go seek the traitor Gloucester,
Pinion him like a thief, bring him before us.
                              [*Exeunt other Servants.*
Though well we may not pass upon his life
Without the form of justice, yet our power   25
Shall do a court'sy to our wrath, which men
May blame but not control. Who's there? The traitor?

Re-enter Servants, with GLOUCESTER *prisoner.*

Reg. Ingrateful fox! 'tis he.
Corn. Bind fast his corky arms.
Glou. What means your Graces? Good my friends, consider
    You are my guests: do me no foul play, friends.   31
Corn. Bind him, I say.   [*Servants bind him.*
Reg.   Hard, hard. O filthy traitor!
Glou. Unmerciful lady as you are, I'm none.
Corn. To this chair bind him. Villain, thou shalt find—
                              [*Regan plucks his beard.*
Glou. By the kind Gods, 'tis most ignobly done   35
    To pluck me by the beard.
Reg. So white, and such a traitor!

17. questrists] *F;* questrits *Q.*   19. toward] *F;* towards *Q.*   22. S.D.] *Dyce;*
Exit Gon. and Bast. (*after 21*) *Q; Exit* (*after 21*) *F.*   23. S.D.] *Capell; not in Q, F.*
24. well] *F; not in Q.*   27. S.D.] *Capell; Enter Gloster brought in by two or three Q;*
Enter Gloucester, and Servants (*after* comptroll) *F.*   30. means] *Q, F;* mean *F4.*
32. S.D.] *Rowe; not in Q, F.*   33. I'm none] *F;* I am true *Q.*   34. find—] *Q;*
finde. *F.*   S.D.] *Johnson; not in Q, F.*

17. *questrists*] seekers. Probably a
Shakespearian coinage.
    24. *pass . . . life*] pass the death sen-
tence on him. Cf. *Meas.*, II. i. 23.
    26. *do a court'sy*] yield, give way. Cf.
H5, v. ii. 293. Other explanations:
'indulge, gratify' (Johnson); 'bend to
our wrath as a courtesy is made by
bending the body' (Steevens); to
oblige (Schmidt).
    29. *corky*] sapless, dry and withered.
Cf. Harsnett, Appendix, p. 239.
    32. *filthy*] odious. Cf. *Oth.*, v. ii. 149.
    33. *Unmerciful*] merciless.

Glou.   Naughty lady,
These hairs, which thou dost ravish from my chin,
Will quicken, and accuse thee: I am your host:
With robbers' hands my hospitable favours   40
You should not ruffle thus. What will you do?
Corn. Come, sir, what letters had you late from France?
Reg. Be simple-answer'd, for we know the truth.
Corn. And what confederacy have you with the traitors
Late footed in the kingdom?
Reg.   To whose hands   45
You have sent the lunatic King: speak.
Glou. I have a letter guessingly set down,
Which came from one that's of a neutral heart,
And not from one oppos'd.
Corn.   Cunning.
Reg.   And false.
Corn. Where hast thou sent the King?
Glou.   To Dover.   50
Reg. Wherefore to Dover? Wast thou not charg'd at peril—
Corn. Wherefore to Dover? Let him answer that.
Glou. I am tied to th'stake, and I must stand the course.
Reg. Wherefore to Dover?
Glou.   Because I would not see
Thy cruel nails pluck out his poor old eyes;   55
Nor thy fierce sister in his anointed flesh

43. simple-answer'd] *Hanmer;* simple answer'd *F;* simple answerer *Q.*   45.
Late] Lately *Q2-3.*   46. You have sent] *Q1, F;* have you sent *Q2-3.*   51.
peril—] *Q;* perill. *F.*   52. answer] *F;* first answer *Q.*   54. Dover] *F;*
Douer sir *Q.*   54-9. Because . . . fires] *arranged Cuningham; lines end* nails /
sister / fangs / head / up / fires *Q, F.*   56. anointed] *Q corr., F;* aurynted *Q
uncorr., Q2-3.*

37. *Naughty*] wicked.

39. *quicken*] assume life.

40. *hospitable favours*] features of your host.

41. *ruffle*] treat with such violence. Cf. II. iv. 299.

42. *late*] lately.

43. *Be simple-answer'd*] give a straight answer.

44. *confederacy*] conspiracy.

45. *footed*] landed. Cf. III. iii. 13.

47. *guessingly set down*] written with-

out certain knowledge. Cf. III. iii. 10.

51. *at peril*] on peril of death.

53. *to th'stake*] like a baited bear. Cf. *Mac.,* v. vii. 2.

course] a relay of dogs set on a baited bear.

54-9. *Because . . . fires*] This arrangement is rhythmically superior to that of Q, F, and it is better to have *flesh* separated from *rash* by the line-ending.

56. *anointed flesh*] the flesh of the anointed king.

Rash boarish fangs. The sea, with such a storm
As his bare head in hell-black night endur'd,
Would have buoy'd up, and quench'd the stelled fires;
Yet, poor old heart, he holp the heavens to rain.   60
If wolves had at thy gate howl'd that dearn time,
Thou should'st have said 'Good porter, turn the key.'
All cruels else subscribe: but I shall see

---

57. Rash] *Q; stick F.*   58. As his bare] *F;* of his lou'd *Q uncorr., Q2–3;* on his lowd *Q corr.*   hell-black night] *Pope;* Hell-blacke-night *F;* hell blacke night *Q.* 59. buoy'd] *F;* layd *Q uncorr., Q2–3;* bod *Q corr.;* boil'd *Warburton.*   stelled] *F, Q corr.;* steeled *Q uncorr., Q2–3.*   60. holp] *F;* holpt *Q.*   rain] *F;* rage *Q.* 61. howl'd] *F;* heard *Q.*   dearn] *Q;* sterne *F.*   63. subscribe] *F;* subscrib'd *Q.*

---

57. *Rash*] strike obliquely with the tusk, as a boar does. Cf. Spenser, *Faerie Queene,* IV. ii. 17. Nares quotes Warner, *Albion's England,* 1586, VII. 36: 'Ha! cur, avant, the boar so rashe thy hide.' The F reading 'stick' is probably an actor's substitution, or a sophistication; but it may possibly be a substitution on Shakespeare's part to avoid the thrice repeated 'sh'.

58. *hell-black*] Capell suggested that Shakespeare derived this epithet from Hakluyt, VIII. 304 (Everyman ed.): 'to guide the ship in the hell-darke night, when we could not see any shore.' On p. 302 Hakluyt uses the word 'unmerciful'. Cf. 33 *ante.*

59. *buoy'd up*] risen up, as a cork buoy when sunk in water; or, as Schmidt suggests, used transitively: 'The sea would have lifted up the fixed fires and extinguished them.' There is something to be said for Warburton's emendation *boil'd* which suggests the fury of the waves more obviously than the F reading; but it should nevertheless be rejected, as *buoy'd* is so unusual a word that it is unlikely to be a guess.

stelled fires] Theobald explains 'starry fires', as if from the Latin, *stella.* But Nares, Schmidt, and Onions take it to mean 'fixed lights'. Cf. *Lucr.,* 1444: 'To find a face where all distress is stell'd'; and *Sonn.,* xxiv: 'Mine eye hath play'd the painter, and hath stell'd / Thy beauty's form in table of

my heart.' The word, from M.E. *stellen,* O.E. *stellan,* means *fixed* in all three passages. But there is no reason why Shakespeare should not have had the secondary meaning of *starry* in mind: indeed, it is impossible to believe he did not. 'Fixed stars' are stars, as opposed to 'wandering stars' (planets).

60. *holp*] helped.

61. *dearn*] dreary, dread, dire. Cf. *Per.,* III. Chorus, 15. The F word is comparatively weak, and doubtless a sophistication.

62–4. *Thou . . . children*] This passage has been much discussed. The problems involved are (i) Should the inverted commas be closed after *key,* or after *subscribe*? (ii) Does *cruels* mean 'cruel acts' or 'cruel creatures'? (iii) Are we to accept F *subscribe,* or Q *subscrib'd*?

It will be convenient to discuss them in the reverse order. As the F reading makes good sense, certainly as good as that of Q, we should accept it. *Subscribe* can be taken as a 3rd plural present indicative, or as an imperative. It can mean 'yield', 'surrender', 'submit', 'assent', 'make acknowledgement of'. It is more natural to take *cruels* to mean 'cruel creatures', like the wolves mentioned in the context. Cf. *Sonn.,* cxlix. But Verity and Perrett take it to mean 'cruel acts'. As Duthie points out, Shakespeare uses 'vulgars' (common

The winged vengeance overtake such children.
Corn. See't shalt thou never. Fellows, hold the chair.   65
    Upon these eyes of thine I'll set my foot.
Glou. He that will think to live till he be old,
    Give me some help! O cruel! O you Gods!
Reg. One side will mock another; th'other too.
Corn. If you see vengeance,—
First Serv.   Hold your hand, my Lord.   70
    I have serv'd you ever since I was a child,
    But better service have I never done you
    Than now to bid you hold.
Reg.   How now, you dog!
First Serv. If you did wear a beard upon your chin
    I'd shake it on this quarrel.

66. these] *F;* those *Q.*   68. you] *F;* ye *Q.*   69. th'other] *F;* tother *Q.*
70. vengeance,—] *Q;* vengeance. *F.*   71. you] *not in Q1.*

people, *Wint.*, II. i. 94), 'potents' (powerful people, *John*, II. i. 358), and 'resolutes' (resolute people, *Ham.*, I. i. 98). If we end the quotation after *subscribe*, we may paraphrase: 'Good porter, unlock the door and let the wolves in. All other cruel creatures yield to compassion on occasion, on such a night as this; and so will I too.' Schmidt compares *Troil.*, IV. v. 105–6: 'Hector in his blaze of wrath subscribes / To tender objects' (i.e. gives up his anger at the sight of objects of compassion). The objection to this arrangement is that Regan would be unlikely to admit her cruelty to the porter, though Duthie claims that it is quite consonant with the mood of the speech that Gloucester should attribute to Regan a cynical avowal of such self-knowledge. If, on the other hand, we take 'All cruels else subscribe' to be outside the quotation, we can interpret in two ways: (*a*) 'All other cruel creatures yield to feelings of compassion under strong provocation; you alone do not' (Duthie). (*b*) 'Leave on one side all other cruel creatures.' In the light of the *Troilus and Cressida* quotation (*a*) seems preferable.
    Perrett is the most persuasive of those who take *cruels* to mean 'cruel deeds'. He paraphrases: 'Never mind about your other cruel deeds, . . . subscribe them, let us leave them out of consideration—but for that impious act of shutting out your father in such a storm . . . I shall see the winged vengeance overtake you and Goneril, such children.' But I think Duthie's interpretation, given above, is the better.
    If we read 'subscrib'd', it may be taken as a 3rd plural past indicative ('All other cruel creatures yielded to feelings of compassion'—Duthie.) In any case, the general meaning of the passage is clear. Gloucester is telling Regan that she has been more cruel to her father then she would have been to wolves, and because of this unnaturalness displayed by her and by her sister, he will see the swift vengeance of heaven overtake them.

64. *winged vengeance*] divine vengeance, like a bird of prey. But he may be thinking of winged spirits, or of lightning. Cf. IV. ii. 46–7; II. iv. 162–3; and Ps., cxliv. 6: 'Send forth the lyghtnyng, and scater them, shute out thyne arowes, and consume them.'

Reg.　　　　　　　　　　　　What do you mean?　　　75
Corn. My villain!　　　　　　　　　[*They draw and fight.*
First Serv. Nay then, come on, and take the chance of anger.
Reg. Give me thy sword. A peasant stand up thus!
　　　　　　　　　　[*Takes a sword and runs at him behind.*
First Serv. O! I am slain. My Lord, you have one eye left
　　To see some mischief on him. Oh!　　　[*Dies.*　80
Corn. Lest it see more, prevent it. Out, vile jelly!
　　Where is thy lustre now?
Glou. All dark and comfortless. Where's my son Edmund?
　　Edmund, enkindle all the sparks of nature
　　To quit this horrid act.
Reg.　　　　　　　　Out, treacherous villain!　　　85
　　Thou call'st on him that hates thee; it was he
　　That made the overture of thy treasons to us,
　　Who is too good to pity thee.
Glou. O my follies! Then Edgar was abus'd.
　　Kind Gods, forgive me that, and prosper him!　　　90
Reg. Go thrust him out at gates, and let him smell
　　His way to Dover.　　　　　[*Exit one with Gloucester.*
　　　　　　　　How is't, my Lord. How look you?
Corn. I have receiv'd a hurt. Follow me, Lady.
　　Turn out that eyeless villain; throw this slave
　　Upon the dunghill. Regan, I bleed apace:　　　95
　　Untimely comes this hurt. Give me your arm.
　　　　　　　　　[*Exit Cornwall, led by Regan.*
Second Serv. I'll never care what wickedness I do
　　If this man come to good.

75. *Reg.*] *See note below.*　　　76. S.D.] *Q; not in F.*　　　77. Nay] *F;* Why *Q.*
78. S.D.] *Q; Killes him. F.*　　　79. *First Serv.*] *Capell; Servant Q, F.*　　you have]
F; yet haue you *Q;* yet you have *Steevens.*　　80. him] them *Dyce.*　　S.D.]
Q2; not in Q1, F.　　84. enkindle] *F;* vnbridle *Q.*　　85. treacherous] *F; not in*
Q.　　92. S.D.] *F; not in Q.*　　96. S.D.] *Theobald; Exit Q; Exeunt F.*
97–105.] *Q; not in F.*　　97. *Second Serv.*] *Capell; Servant Q.*

75. *What . . . mean*] ascribed
to Regan by Kittredge, after a suggestion by Craig. Furness thought
the words should be given to Cornwall.

76. *villain*] perhaps punning on the
old meaning, 'serf'.

77. *take . . . anger*] run the risk of
fighting while angry.

87. *made the overture*] made the discovery, disclosed.

89. *abus'd*] wronged, deceived.

92. *How look you?*] How do you
seem to me? How are you feeling?

Third Serv.   If she live long,
    And in the end meet the old course of death,
    Women will all turn monsters.   100
Second Serv. Let's follow the old Earl, and get the Bedlam
    To lead him where he would: his roguish madness
    Allows itself to any thing.
Third Serv. Go thou; I'll fetch some flax and whites of eggs
    To apply to his bleeding face. Now, heaven help him!
                        [Exeunt severally.

98. *Third Serv.*] *Capell; 2 Servant Q.*   101. *Second Serv.*] *Capell; 1 Serv. Q.*
102. roguish] *Q uncorr., Q2–3; not in Q corr.*   104. *Third Serv.*] *Capell; 2 Ser. Q.*
105. S.D.] *Theobald; Exit Q.*

99. *old*] customary, natural.

100. *Women . . . monsters*] because they will not fear divine vengeance, whatever their crimes.

102–3. *his . . . thing*] Because he is a vagabond and a madman, he cannot be called to account.

104. *flax . . . eggs*] Bailly, *Two Treatises concerning Diseases of the Eye*, 1616, p. 53, recommends for a hurt eye: 'Apply thereupon a plaster of flax and the white of an egg.'

ACT IV

SCENE I.—[*The Heath.*]

Enter EDGAR.

Edg. Yet better thus, and known to be contemn'd,
Than, still contemn'd and flatter'd, to be worst.
The lowest and most dejected thing of Fortune
Stands still in esperance, lives not in fear:
The lamentable change is from the best;   5
The worst returns to laughter. Welcome, then,

ACT IV

Scene 1

S.D. *The Heath*] *Capell; An open Country Rowe; not in Q, F.*   1. and known]
unknown *Collier (conj. Johnson).*   2. flatter'd ... worst] ... worst: *F;* flattered
to be worst, *Q;* flatter'd. To be worst *Pope;* flatter'd to be worse *conj. Tyrwhitt.*
3. dejected] deject *F3–4.*   4. esperance] *F;* experience *Q.*   6–9. Welcome
... blasts] *F; not in Q.*

1–2. *Yet ... worst*] Perrett is one of the few critics who defends the F punctuation. He paraphrases: 'Better thus, openly despised, than to be in fact worst, when flattered and yet nevertheless despised.' He suggests that a dash should be inserted before 'worst' to bring out this meaning, but I cannot see any point in doing this. I would rather explain: ''Tis better to be thus contemned and known to yourself to be contemned' (Johnson, who adds that 'when a man divests himself of his real character he feels no pain from contempt, because he supposes it incurred only by a voluntary disguise which he can throw off at pleasure') 'than to be worst, that is to be equally contemned, but to be unconscious of people's scorn because it is masked by flattery.' Pope's emended punctuation makes the passage easier,

though Perrett objects to making 'to be worst' subject of the next sentence. This is not an insuperable objection, because Shakespeare often changes the construction in the middle of a sentence, and 'thing' is the real subject of 'stands'. Cf. *Leir,* 2077–8: 'Why, say the worst, the worst can be but death, / And death is better than for to despaire.'

3. *most ... Fortune*] a thing most dejected of Fortune. Shakespeare often transposes the adjective in this way.

dejected] abased, cast down.

thing] The word is used contemptuously.

of] at the hands of.

4. *Stands ... esperance*] is always in a condition of hope. Cf. *Troil.*, v. ii. 121.

lives ... fear] Steevens quotes Milton, *Paradise Regain'd*, III. 206.

6. *returns to laughter*] must inevitably

Thou unsubstantial air that I embrace:
The wretch that thou hast blown unto the worst
Owes nothing to thy blasts. But who comes here?

Enter GLOUCESTER, *led by an old Man.*

My father, poorly led? World, world, O world!   10
But that thy strange mutations make us hate thee,
Life would not yield to age.

9. But who comes] *F;* Who's *Q.*   S.D.] *after* age (*12*) *Q; Enter Gloucester
and an Oldman F (after* blasts, *9*).   10. poorly led?] *Q2, F;* poorlie, leed
Q uncorr.; parti, eyd *Q corr.;* poorly 'rayd *conj. Muir.*   11. hate] hold *conj.*
A. Walker.

change for the better. Cf. *Mac.,* IV. ii. 24; Kittredge cites Wilkins, *The Miseries of Inforst Marriage,* 1607: 'When things are at the worst, tis hopt theyle mend.'

9. *Owes*] When a man's debts are paid, he fears no creditors (Kittredge).

10. *poorly led*] Greg, *Variants,* p. 169, calls this one of the worst cruxes of the play. The F reading makes sense, and it agrees substantially with that of the Q, uncorrected; but the corrector of Q evidently thought that the copy had a different reading, even though he failed to decipher it. As, according to Greg, the F reading is exceedingly feeble, and as this sheet of Q from which F was printed was uncorrected, it is possible that 'parti, eyd' conceals what Shakespeare actually wrote, which may have been corrupted by an actor, misheard by a scribe, misread by the corrector of Q, and perverted by the compositor. Such a chain of accidents would make Shakespeare's words irrecoverable. But the Paphlagonian King and his kind son are first described as 'an aged man, and a young, scarcely come to the age of a man both poorly arrayed'. Shakespeare may therefore have written 'poorly 'rayd'. This aphetic form of 'arrayed' makes reasonably good sense, and might, by the accidents mentioned above, have been variously

corrupted into 'leed' and 'eyd'. When I proposed this emendation in *T.L.S.,* 3 June 1949, Miss Janet Leeper suggested to me that if the MS. had had 'arayed' with the initial *a* deleted by a vertical stroke, this might have been read as the 'l' of 'leed'. Mr J. C. Maxwell mentions that 'poorly rayd' occurs in Tottel's *Songes and Sonettes* (ed. Arber, p. 108). On the other hand, Mr Wilson Knight points out that Edgar would notice that his father was being led before he noticed his clothes, and R. Flatter (*T.L.S.,* 22 July 1949) points out that *-ly* represents *like* (cf. Abbott, *447), and that *poorely led* means 'led like a poor man', i.e. like a beggar. Under the circumstances, therefore, I have retained the F reading, though one would be happier about it if one knew why the Q corrector had made the change he did.

10–12. *World . . . age*] We are only reconciled to growing old, and to the consequent approach of death, by the changes and chances of this mortal life which make us hate it. Montaigne has a similar thought (tr. Florio, 1. 105): 'Consider we by the ordinary mutations, and daily declinations which we suffer, how Nature deprives us of the sight of our losse and empairing: what hath an aged man left him of his youths vigour, and of his fore-past life?'

Old Man.   O my good Lord!
   I have been your tenant, and your father's tenant,
   These fourscore years.
Glou. Away, get thee away; good friend, be gone: 15
   Thy comforts can do me no good at all;
   Thee they may hurt.
Old Man.   You cannot see your way.
Glou. I have no way, and therefore want no eyes;
   I stumbled when I saw. Full oft 'tis seen,
   Our means secure us, and our mere defects   20
   Prove our commodities. Oh! dear son Edgar,
   The food of thy abused father's wrath;
   Might I but live to see thee in my touch,
   I'd say I had eyes again.
Old Man.   How now! Who's there?
Edg. [*Aside.*] O Gods! Who is't can say 'I am at the
     worst'?   25
   I am worse than e'er I was.
Old Man.   'Tis poor mad Tom.
Edg. [*Aside.*] And worse I may be yet; the worst is not
   So long as we can say 'This is the worst.'
Old Man. Fellow, where goest?
Glou.   Is it a beggar-man?
Old Man. Madman and beggar too.   30

---

14. These . . . years] *F;* this forescore— *Q.*   17. You] *F;* Alack sir, you *Q.*
20. Our . . . us] Our mean secures us *Pope;* Our needs secure us *Singer.*
21. Oh] *F;* ah *Q.*   25, 27, 37, 51, 53. S.D.] *Johnson; not in Q, F.*   25. the]
not in F2.   28. So] *F;* As *Q.*

13. *tenant*] Perrett points out that this word can mean vassal.

16. *comforts*] attempts to assist me. Cf. III. v. 19 note.

19. *I . . . saw*] Heilman, *op. cit.*, pp. 41–64, has a commentary on these words which express one of the central paradoxes of the play.

20. *Our . . . us*] our resources, our prosperity, make us careless. Cf. *Oth.*, I. iii. 10; and Jonson, *Poems,* ed. Herford and Simpson, VIII. 113: 'Man may securely sinne, but safely neuer.' Others take the words to mean: 'Our mean or moderate condition makes us secure.'

20–1. *our . . . commodities*] Our disadvantages prove advantages.

22. *The . . . wrath*] that on which his anger fed, the object of his anger.

abused] deceived, deluded.

25–6. *O . . . was*] Edgar is referring to his opening words in this scene.

27–8. *the worst . . . worst*] So long as we can comfort ourselves with such reflections as IV. i. 1–9 we are not without hope, and therefore not actually at the worst.

Glou. He has some reason, else he could not beg.
　　I'th'last night's storm I such a fellow saw,
　　Which made me think a man a worm. My son
　　Came then into my mind; and yet my mind
　　Was then scarce friends with him. I have heard
　　　　more since: 35
　　As flies to wanton boys, are we to th'Gods;
　　They kill us for their sport.
Edg. [*Aside.*]　　　　　　　　How should this be?
　　Bad is the trade that must play fool to sorrow,
　　Ang'ring itself and others. [*Aloud.*] Bless thee, master!
Glou. Is that the naked fellow?
Old Man.　　　　　　　　　Ay, my Lord.   40
Glou. Then, prithee, get thee away. If, for my sake,
　　Thou wilt o'ertake us, hence a mile or twain,
　　I'th'way toward Dover, do it for ancient love;
　　And bring some covering for this naked soul,
　　Which I'll entreat to lead me.

31. He] A *Q1*.　　32. I'th'] *F;* In the *Q.*　　36. flies] *F;* flies are *Q.*　　to
wanton] *F1–2;* to th' wanton *Q, F3–4.*　　37. kill] *F;* bitt *Q1;* bit *Q2–3;* hit
conj. Delius.　　this] their *F2.*　　38. play fool to] *F;* play the foole to *Q,*
F3–4; play to foole *F2.*　　41. Then, prithee] *Q; not in F.*　　away] *F;* gon *Q.*
42. hence] *F;* here *Q.*　　43. toward] to *Q2–3;* towards *Capell.*　　45. Which]
F; Who *Q.*

31. *He . . . reason*] He is not entirely
without intelligence.
　33. *worm*] Cf. Job, xxv. 6: 'How
much more man, a worme, euen the
sonne of man, which is but a worme?'
(Geneva).
　36–7. *As . . . sport*] William A. Armstrong, *T.L.S.*, 14 Oct. 1949, suggests
that Shakespeare transmuted Sidney,
Arcadia, ed. Feuillerat, III. x, pp. 406–
7: 'for els to thinke that those powers
(if there be any such) above, are moved
either by the eloquence of our prayers,
or in a chafe by the folly of our actions;
carries as much reason as if flies should
thinke, that men take great care which
of them hums sweetest, and which of
them flies nimblest.' Cf. Introduction,
p. xxxvii and Florio, *op. cit.*, VI. 29: 'The
gods perdie doe reckon and racket us
men as their tennis-balles.' Montaigne
was translating from Plautus. Emp-

son, *op. cit.*, p. 196, remarks that
'Gloucester does not say it in pass-
ing but as a summing-up of what
Lear has repeatedly implied.' But
as Chambers points out, *King Lear*,
1940, p. 30, 'the gods *are* giving Gloucester his wish, and, if he can but
be saved from despair, he will live
to know it. Shakespeare's irony
runs deep.'
　37. *How . . . be?*] This may mean,
'How did he come to forgive me?' or
'How did he lose his eyes?' Moberly,
however, thinks that Edgar is ques-
tioning the truth of his father's last
pessimistic remark.
　38. *Bad . . . trade*] Craig explains 'He
treads an evil path', *trade* being a
variant of *tread*. Cf. *R2*, III. iii. 156. But
it is more likely to mean business, occupation. Edgar has to act as a Fool to
his sorrowing father.

Old Man.   Alack, sir! he is mad.   45
Glou. 'Tis the times' plague, when madmen lead the blind.
    Do as I bid thee, or rather do thy pleasure;
    Above the rest, be gone.
Old Man. I'll bring him the best 'parel that I have,
    Come on't what will.   [*Exit.*
Glou.   Sirrah, naked fellow,—   50
Edg. Poor Tom's a-cold. [*Aside.*] I cannot daub it further.
Glou. Come hither, fellow.
Edg. [*Aside.*] And yet I must. Bless thy sweet eyes, they
    bleed.
Glou. Know'st thou the way to Dover?
Edg. Both stile and gate, horse-way and foot-path. Poor   55
    Tom hath been scar'd out of his good wits: bless thee,
    good man's son, from the foul fiend! Five fiends have
    been in poor Tom at once; as Obidicut, of lust;
    Hoberdidance, prince of dumbness; Mahu, of steal-
    ing; Modo, of murder; Flibbertigibbet, of mopping   60

49. 'parel] *Rowe;* Parrell *Q, F.*   50. S.D.] *F; not in Q.*   51. a-cold] *Rowe;*
a cold *Q, F.*   daub] *F;* dance *Q.*   further] *F;* farther *Q.*   53. And . . .
must] *F; not in Q.*   56. scar'd] *F3–4;* scard *Q;* scarr'd *F1–2;* scarred
Schmidt.   56–7. thee . . . son] *F;* the good man *Q.*   57–62. Five . . . master]
Q; not in F.   58. as . . . lust] *Hudson (conj. S. Walker);* of lust, as Obidicut *Q.*
59. Hoberdidance] Hobbididence *Q.*   60. Flibbertigibbet] *Pope;* Stiberde-
gebit *Q.*   60–1. mopping and mowing] *Theobald;* Mobing, & Mohing *Q;*
moping and Mowing *Pope;* mobbing and mowing *Jennens.*

46. *'Tis . . . blind*] Gloucester uses his
own situation as a symbol: when the
rulers are mad, and the people blind.
    48. *the rest*] all.
    49. *'parel*] apparel. Cf. Marlowe,
The Jew of Malta, IV. iv (1830–1):
'Here's goodly 'parrell, is there
not?'
    51. *daub it further*] dissemble any
more. Cf. *R3*, III. v. 29. The figure is
taken from plastering mortar. Cf. II.
ii. 63.
    55. *horse-way*] bridle-path. Cf. T.
Heywood, *A Maydenhead Well Lost*
(*Works*, ed. Pearson, 1874, IV. 121):
'I have one for the horse-way, another
for the foot-way, and a third for the
turning-stile.'
    57. *Five fiends*] Percy notes a Hars-
nett parallel. Cf. Appendix, p. 240.

58. *as . . . lust*] I have adopted Hudson's arrangement of these words,
following S. Walker (*Crit. Exam.*, II.
249).
    Obidicut] a corruption of Harsnett's
Hoberdicut. See Appendix, p. 241,
for this and the other devils mentioned
here.
    60–1. *mopping and mowing*] Malone
cited a Harsnett parallel. See Appendix, p. 242. Cf. *Tp.*, IV. i. 47 and II. ii.
9 ff. The second of these passages also
contains an echo from Harsnett. The
phrase means 'grimacing and making
faces', *mow* being derived from Fr.
moue. Huloet, *Dictionary*, 1572, defines
'mow' or 'to make a mow': 'It seemeth
a word derived of the thing, for we
cannot pronounce the word mowe but
we almost make a mowe.'

and mowing; who since possesses chambermaids and
waiting-women. So, bless thee, master!

Glou. Here, take this purse, thou whom the heav'ns' plagues
Have humbled to all strokes: that I am wretched
Makes thee the happier: Heavens, deal so still!   65
Let the superfluous and lust-dieted man,
That slaves your ordinance, that will not see
Because he does not feel, feel your power quickly;
So distribution should undo excess,
And each man have enough. Dost thou know Dover? 70

Edg. Ay, master.

Glou. There is a cliff, whose high and bending head
Looks fearfully in the confined deep;

---

66. lust-dieted] lust-dieting *Capell.*   67. slaves] *F;* stands *Q.*   68. does] doth
Q2–3.   69. undo] *F;* vnder *Q.*   73. fearfully] *F;* firmely *Q.*   in] on *Rowe.*

61–2. *who . . . waiting-women*] Theobald pointed out the allusion to Sara and Friswood Williams and Anne Smith, three chambermaids in the family of Edmund Peckham who were supposed to be possessed, and whose examination is reported by Harsnett.

64. *Have . . . strokes*] have brought so low as to accept humbly the bitterest strokes of Fortune.

65–70. *Heavens . . . enough*] Cf. III. iv. 33 ff.

66. *superfluous*] pampered, having too much. Cf. II. iv. 263.

lust-dieted] whose desires are fed to the full, feeding gluttonously. But Gloucester may be thinking specifically of his own adultery.

67. *That . . . ordinance*] 'who, instead of paying the deference and submission due to your ordinance, treats it as his slave, by making it subservient to his views of pleasure and interest, and trampling on and spurning it whenever it ceases to be of service to him in either of these respects' (Heath). Steevens gives examples of 'slaves' for 'enslaves' from Massinger, *A New Way to Pay Old Debts,* IV. iii etc. Wright gives others. J. Sledd, however, *M.L.N.*, 1940, p. 595, ingeniously suggests that *slaves* is used in the sense of

tears away or rends from O.E.—*slæfan.* He does not give any Elizabethan parallels. Shakespeare uses *sliver* in the next scene, IV. ii. 34, and it is just possible that he was quibbling here. Warburton suggested *braves.* Moberly refers to the parable of Dives and Lazarus, but the duty of almsgiving is not exclusively Christian.

68. *feel*] Craig takes this to mean 'suffer pain'; but it may mean rather 'feel sympathy'. The man is blind and without wisdom because he does not put himself in the place of his poor neighbours.

72. *cliff*] Gloucester wants to leap off Dover Cliff partly because the exigencies of the plot demand that he should meet Lear who has gone to Dover. But cf. Introduction, p. xlv.

bending] beetling.

73. *fearfully*] so as to inspire terror in one who looks over the edge (Kittredge). But the cliff is personified.

in] into. Malone suggests that Shakespeare thought of the sea as a mirror.

confined] restrained, by the cliffs. Cf. *John,* II. i. 23–4. Capell suggests that Shakespeare was thinking of the narrow Straits of Dover confined on both sides by the land.

Bring me but to the very brim of it,
And I'll repair the misery thou dost bear   75
With something rich about me; from that place
I shall no leading need.
Edg.   Give me thy arm:
Poor Tom shall lead thee.   [*Exeunt.*

SCENE II.—[*Before the Duke of Albany's Palace.*]

Enter GONERIL *and* EDMUND.

Gon. Welcome, my Lord; I marvel our mild husband
Not met us on the way.

Enter OSWALD.

Now, where's your master?
Osw. Madam, within; but never man so chang'd.
I told him of the army that was landed;
He smil'd at it: I told him you were coming;   5
His answer was 'The worse': of Gloucester's treachery,
And of the loyal service of his son,
When I inform'd him, then he call'd me sot,
And told me I had turn'd the wrong side out:
What most he should dislike seems pleasant to him;   10
What like, offensive.
Gon. [*To Edmund.*]   Then shall you go no further.
It is the cowish terror of his spirit

77. I shall] Shall I *Q2-3.*   leading] lending *F2, 4, Rowe.*   78. S.D.] *F;*
not in *Q.*

Scene II

S.D. Before . . . Palace] Capell, subst.; not in *Q, F.*   S.D.] *Theobald; Enter Goneril
and Bastard Q; Enter Goneril, Bastard, and Steward F.*   2. S.D.] *Theobald, subst.;
not in F; Enter Steward (after master) Q.*   10. most . . . dislike] *F; hee should
most desire Q.*   11. S.D.] *Hanmer; not in Q, F.*   12. cowish] *Q, F;* currish
conj. Wright.   terror] *F;* curre *Q uncorr., Q2-3;* terrer *Q corr.*

Scene II

1. *Welcome*] i.e. to my palace.
2. *on the way*] i.e. from Gloucester's
castle.
8. *sot*] fool.
9. *turn'd . . . out*] put a wrong com-

plexion on the matter, since Gloucester was not a traitor, nor Edmund
loyal. Cf. *Ado*, III. i. 68.
12. *cowish*] cowardly. *N.E.D.* cites
Rem, *Lawless Love, Vision of Rawe
Devise*, 1579: 'Amid the crewe of

That dares not undertake; he'll not feel wrongs
Which tie him to an answer. Our wishes on the way
May prove effects. Back, Edmund, to my brother;   15
Hasten his musters and conduct his powers:
I must change arms at home, and give the distaff
Into my husband's hands. This trusty servant
Shall pass between us; ere long you are like to hear,
If you dare venture in your own behalf,   20
A mistress's command. Wear this; spare speech;
                                        [*Giving a favour.*
Decline your head: this kiss, if it durst speak,
Would stretch thy spirits up into the air.

---

15. Edmund] Edgar *Q1*.   17. arms] *Q;* names F.   21. command] *Q corr.*,
F; coward *Q uncorr.*, *Q2–3*.   S.D.] *Johnson; Gives him a ring Hanmer; Puts on
a chaine Collier MS.; not in Q,F.*

---

cowish carped knights'. Cotgrave
defines *Couard*, 'a coward, a dastard, a
cow'. Wright conjectures *currish*. Cf.
Mer.V., IV. i. 292. The word is used by
Armin, *op. cit.*, p. 52, and it is also to be
found in Harsnett, *Declaration*, p. 98.
This seems to me very possible. The
uncorrected Q reading is 'cowish
curre'. If the copy had read 'cowish
terrer', with a marginal correction
'curr', the compositor might easily
have substituted 'curr' for 'terrer'
instead of for 'cow'. The corrector,
seeing that something was wrong,
might have restored 'terrer' without
realizing the intentions of the writer.
The initial mistake of 'cowish' might
be due to a mishearing. The F was
printed from a Q of which this sheet
was uncorrected, but though the correction of *cowish* might have been
overlooked in preparing the copy for
F, it is safer to retain *cowish* than to
emend it.

13. *undertake*] show enterprise or
courage, or assume responsibility.

13–14. *he'll . . . answer*] He will
ignore insults which, if he noticed, he
would be obliged to resent.

13. *feel*] notice, appear to notice.

14. *answer*] retaliation. Cf. *Cym.*,
v. iii. 79.

Our . . . way] our hopes, as we jour-
neyed here, that we should be able to
consummate our love, or get rid of my
husband.

15. *May . . . effects*] may be fulfilled.

17. *change*] exchange.

arms] the insignia of our sexes, the
sword and the distaff. Cf. *Cym.*, v. iii.
32–4. Budd, *R.E.S.*, 1935, p. 427, compares these lines from *The Monk's Prologue* in Chaucer's *Canterbury Tales*:
'Whan she comth hoom, she rampeth
in my face, / And cryeth, "false
coward, wreek thy wyf! / By *corpus*
bones! I wol have thy knyf, / And thou
shalt have my distaf and go spinne!" /
Fro day to night right thus she wol
biginne;— / "Allas!" she seith, "that
ever I was shape / To wedde a milksop
or a coward ape, / That wol be overlad
with every wight!"'

19. *like*] likely.

21. *A . . . command*] Goneril is quibbling on the word 'mistress'. She is
presumably going to ask Edmund to
murder Albany.

22. *Decline . . . head*] either for her to
kiss him, or to put a chain round his
neck.

23. *Would . . . air*] Heilman, *op. cit.*,
p. 314, suggests that this and the following lines contain 'several kinds of

Conceive, and fare thee well.

Edm. Yours in the ranks of death.

Gon.   My most dear Gloucester!

[*Exit Edmund.*

Oh! the difference of man and man.   26
To thee a woman's services are due:
A fool usurps my bed.

Osw.   Madam, here comes my Lord.

[*Exit.*

Enter ALBANY.

Gon. I have been worth the whistle.

Alb.   O Goneril!

You are not worth the dust which the rude wind   30
Blows in your face. I fear your disposition:
That nature, which contemns it origin,
Cannot be border'd certain in itself;
She that herself will sliver and disbranch
From her material sap, perforce must wither   35

---

24. fare thee] *F;* far you *Q1;* farye *Q2–3.*   25. S.D.] *Rowe; Exit (after* death)
F; not in Q.   26. Oh... man] *F; not in Q.*   difference] *F;* strange difference
Pope.   27. a] *not in Q uncorr., Q2–3.*   28. A . . . bed] *Q corr.;* My foote
vsurps my body *Q uncorr.;* My foote vsurps my head *Q2–3;* My Foole vsurpes my
body *F;* My fool . . . bed *Malone.*   28. *Exit*] *Q; not in F.*   29. whistle] *F,*
Q uncorr., Q2–3; whistling *Q corr.*   30. rude] *not in Q2–3.*   31–50. I . . . deep]
Q; not in F.   32. it] *Q uncorr., Q2;* ith *Q corr.;* its *Q3.*   35. material] *Q;*
maternal *Theobald.*

sexual innuendo'. Goneril puns on
spirits and *conceive,* and Edmund puns
on *death,* as Lear does, IV. vi. 195.

28. *A . . . bed*] Greg, *Variants,*
p. 171, argues that it is more likely that
the compositor of the Q should have
misread 'bed' as 'body', than that the
reader should have miscorrected
'body' to 'bed'. On these grounds he
concludes that what the copy actually
read was 'My foole vsurps my bed.'
Duthie, however, thinks that the F
reading is the more forceful, and that
the Q corrector may have altered
'body' by mistake, taking the 'o' for an
'e' and the 'y' for a tail to the 'd'.

29. *worth . . . whistle*] The usual form
of the proverb, 'It is a poore dog that is
not worth the whistling,' led to the

Q corruption. Bransom, *The Tragedy
of King Lear,* p. 140, remarks: 'Once,
when he was in love with her, he
would have come on the road to meet
her.'

31. *fear*] have fears concerning.

32. *it*] its.

33. *Cannot . . . itself*] cannot be kept
within fixed bounds, cannot be trusted
not to break the pale. Cf. IV. vi. 268.

34. *sliver*] tear off. Cf. *Mac.,* IV. i. 28.
disbranch] sever, cut off.

35. *material*] forming the substance
of a thing, nourishing, essential,
necessary.

perforce . . . wither] Cf. *Oth.,* v. ii. 15.
Perrett compares *Leir,* 1242–3: 'If so
the stocke be dryed with disdayne, /
Withered and sere the branch must

And come to deadly use.

Gon. No more; the text is foolish.

Alb. Wisdom and goodness to the vile seem vile;
Filths savour but themselves. What have you done?
Tigers, not daughters, what have you perform'd?   40
A father, and a gracious aged man,
Whose reverence even the head-lugg'd bear would lick,
Most barbarous, most degenerate! have you madded.
Could my good brother suffer you to do it?
A man, a prince, by him so benefited!   45
If that the heavens do not their visible spirits
Send quickly down to tame these vilde offences,
It will come,
Humanity must perforce prey on itself,
Like monsters of the deep.

42. even] *Q1; not in Q2–3.*   45. benefited] *Q corr.;* beneflicted *Q uncorr., Q2–3.*
47–8. Send . . . come] *so Malone;* one line in *Q.*   47. these] *Jennens (conj. Heath);*
the *Q uncorr., Q2–3;* this *Q corr.*   vilde] *Q2–3;* vild *Q1;* wild *Collier;* vile *Pope.*
49. Humanity] *Q corr.;* Humanly *Q uncorr., Q2–3.*

needes remaine.' Cf. also *R3*, II. ii. 41.

36. *come . . . use*] be used as a faggot
for the burning. See Heb., vi. 8.

37. *text*] on which you have been
preaching. Craig takes it to mean
'quotation'.

39. *Filths . . . themselves*] To the filthy
all things taste filthy. Kittredge cites:
Pravis omnia prava. Cf. also Tit., i. 15.

42. *head-lugg'd*] tugged by the head.
Wright quotes a Harsnett parallel. See
Appendix, p. 241. Cf. also *1H4*, I. ii. 83.

43. *madded*] driven mad.

46. *visible*] in visible form (Kittredge). Cf. *Leir*, 1651–2: 'How canst
thou suffer such outragius acts / To be
committed without iust reuenge?'

47. *tame . . . vilde*] The old spelling of
'vile' here preserved suggests there
may be a quibble intended on *vilde* and
wild, the opposite of tame.

offences] offenders; the abstract for
the concrete.

48. *It . . . come*] This effective short
line allows room for a dramatic pause
before the climax of Albany's speech.

49–50. *Humanity . . . deep*] Cf. the
Shakespearian addition to *Sir Thomas*

More (86–7): 'men like ravenous
fishes / Would feed on one another,'
and *Troil.*, I. iii. 123–4: 'Must make
perforce an universal prey, / And last
eat up himself'. There are many
parallels in contemporary and preceding literature. F. P. Wilson, *Shakespeare Survey 3*, p. 20, refers to *Everyman*,
Prologue; *Pride of Life*, 361–2; and
Ponet, *Short Treatise on Politic Power*,
1556, p. 10: Ponet argues that if there
were no acceptance of authority, 'the
rich would oppress the poor, and the
poor seek the destruction of the rich,
to have that he had: the mighty would
destroy the weak, and as *Theodoretus*
sayeth, the great fish eat up the small,
and the weak seek revenge on the
mighty; and so one seeking the others
destruction all at length should be
undone and come to destruction.' The
idea goes back even beyond Theodoretus. See Hesiod, *Works and Days*,
in a passage thus translated by George
Chapman, I. 434–7: 'Fish, fowl, and
savage beasts, (whose law is power) /
Jove lets each other mutually devour, /
Because they lack the equity he gives /

Gon.   Milk-liver'd man!   50
That bear'st a cheek for blows, a head for wrongs;
Who hast not in thy brows an eye discerning
Thine honour from thy suffering; that not know'st
Fools do those villains pity who are punish'd
Ere they have done their mischief. Where's thy drum;
France spreads his banners in our noiseless land,   56
With plumed helm thy state begins to threat,

51. bear'st] *F;* bearest *Q.*   for wrongs] of wrongs *F3–4.*   52. eye discerning]
Rowe; eye-discerning *F;* eye deseruing *Q.*   53–9. that . . . so] *Q; not in F.*
54. those] *Q1;* these *Q2–3.*   56. noiseless] *Q corr.;* noystles *Q uncorr.*
57. thy . . . threat] *Jennens;* thy slayer begin threats *Q uncorr.;* thy state begins
thereat *Q corr.;* thy slaier begins threats *Q2;* thy slayer begins his threats
Theobald; the slayer begins threats *Hanmer;* this Lear begins threats *conj. Leo;*
his state begins thereat *Duthie (conj. Greg).*

To govern men, as far best for their lives.' The following references may be added: Bestiary in Arundel MS. 292, ed. R. Morris, 1872, 505–16; Whitney, *Emblems,* p. 52: 'The mightie fishe deuowres the little frie'; Christopher Dawson, *The Making of Europe,* 1939, p. 267 (citing an example from A.D. 909); and the well-known drawing by Pieter Bruegel. But it should be noted that whereas most of these writers compare the rich to big fish and the poor to little fish, Shakespeare suggests that the violation of order would lead to actual cannibalism. The more commonplace comparison is to be found in a doubtful scene in *Pericles,* II. i. 29–34.

50. *Milk-liver'd*] white-livered, cowardly.

51. *a cheek for blows*] Noble compares Matt., v. 39.

52–3. *an . . . suffering*] an eye to distinguish between what can be honourably borne and what should be resented.

54–5. *Fools . . . mischief*] Apparently she refers to Lear, as the news of Gloucester's punishment has not yet arrived and she would not expect her husband to have heard of it. The implication is that Lear is a villain because he is in league with France. The French invasion is the *wrong*

Albany is suffering meekly; and Goneril returns to the subject after referring to Lear's punishment. Malone, however, thinks that Goneril is referring not to Lear, but to the King of France; and Furness and Kittredge believe that she means that only fools will pity Albany if he is defeated or dethroned without striking a blow. This last interpretation seems to me highly unlikely, since Goneril harps on Albany's feebleness and foolishness, not on his villainy; and she regards the repelling of the invader not as mischief but as a patriotic duty. I think *villains* can scarcely apply to the King of France, since he has not been punished, though it might conceivably mean that he is about to be defeated.

56. *noiseless*] because the drum has not sounded.

57. *thy . . . threat*] This is Jennens's reading. It makes sense, though Shakespeare is unlikely to have written it. Greg, *Variants,* p. 174, points out that there would certainly appear to have been no 'to' in the copy. The letters 'reat' are common to both uncorrected and corrected copies of Q; but Greg adds 'what reading may be concealed in the last four letters I am at a loss to imagine'. Duthie conjectures 'road' (i.e. inroad) but this is not very happy. Both Greg and Duthie suggest 'his' for

Whil'st thou, a moral fool, sits still, and cries
   'Alack! why does he so?'
Alb.   See thyself, devil!
Proper deformity shows not in the fiend   60
   So horrid as in woman.
Gon.   O vain fool!
Alb. Thou changed and self-cover'd thing, for shame,
Be-monster not thy feature. Were't my fitness
To let these hands obey my blood,
They are apt enough to dislocate and tear   65
Thy flesh and bones; howe'er thou art a fiend,
A woman's shape doth shield thee.
Gon. Marry, your manhood—mew!

---

58. Whil'st] *Q corr.*; Whil's *Q uncorr., Q2–3*; while *Capell.*   sits] *Q*; sit'st *Theo-bald.*   cries] *Q*; cry'st *Theobald.*   60. deformity] deformiry *Q2–3*.   shows] seemes *Q uncorr., F.*   62–9. Thou . . . news] *Q*; *not in F.*   62. self-cover'd] *Q*; self-converted *Theobald*; false-cover'd *Singer*; self-discover'd *conj. Cartwright*; self-colour'd *Moberly*; sex-cover'd *Hudson (conj. Crosby).*   64. hands] hands of mine *conj. Stevens.*   65. dislocate] *Q3*; dislecate *Q1–2.*   68. —mew!] *Cambridge (conj. Daniel)*; mew— *Q corr.*; now— *Q uncorr., Q2–3.*

'thy', because, in the absence of 'And', the line requires a new subject; but we cannot assume this, and 'state' would be awkwardly applied to the French army. Possibly a line has dropped out. But 'threat' could easily be misread or mis-written as 'thereat' and the word 'to' may have been omitted by the scribe responsible for the copy.

58. *moral*] moralizing.

60–1. *Proper . . . woman*] Deformity, appropriate to the fiend, seems more horrible in a woman, because of its inappropriateness. Delius explains 'deformity which conceals itself under a pleasing, fair outside'. Cf. 'proper-false', *Tw.N.*, ii. ii. 30. Albany may be referring to moral deformity, or to Goneril's face distorted by evil passions. Cf. *Leir*, 2582, 'Thou fiend in likenesse of a humane creature'.

62. *changed*] transformed.

self-cover'd] Various explanations: (i) having the real self concealed by a woman's shape; (ii) having assumed the appearance of a fiend, so concealing your woman's self; (iii) hidden

from thyself (Kinnear, who compares *Ant.*, ii. ii. 90–1, and *Luc.*, 633 ff.); (iv) dressed in one's native semblance, Goneril having betrayed her wickedness by changing countenance (Schmidt). There are also numerous conjectural emendations (cf. collations above), none of which need detain us. I incline to the second of these explanations. Goneril has bemonstered her appearance by allowing the fiendish passions of her self to show on her countenance.

63. *feature*] appearance, not merely her face. Cf. *Leir*, 2581: 'Nay, peace thou monster, shame vnto thy sexe.'

Were't . . . fitness] if it were proper for me.

64. *hands*] Steevens's conjecture is attractive, but Abbott *508 argues that a foot may be omitted from a line when there is any marked pause arising from emotion.

blood] instinct, passion.

65. *apt*] ready.

66. *howe'er*] but although.

68. *mew!*] The word is often used as

Enter a Messenger.

Alb. What news?

Mess. O! my good Lord, the Duke of Cornwall's dead;   70
   Slain by his servant, going to put out
   The other eye of Gloucester.

Alb.   Gloucester's eyes!

Mess. A servant that he bred, thrill'd with remorse,
   Oppos'd against the act, bending his sword
   To his great master; who, thereat enrag'd,   75
   Flew on him, and amongst them fell'd him dead;
   But not without that harmful stroke, which since
   Hath pluck'd him after.

Alb.   This shows you are above,
   You justicers, that these our nether crimes
   So speedily can venge! But, O poor Gloucester!   80
   Lost he his other eye?

Mess.   Both, both, my Lord.
   This letter, Madam, craves a speedy answer;
   'Tis from your sister.   [*Presents a letter.*

Gon. [*Aside.*]   One way I like this well;
   But being widow, and my Gloucester with her,
   May all the building in my fancy pluck   85
   Upon my hateful life: another way,

68. S.D.] F (*after 61*); *Enter a Gentleman* (*after 69*) Q *1*; (*after 68*) Q *2–3*.   69. news?] newes. Q *1*.   72. eyes!] eyes? Q *;* eyes. F.   73. thrill'd] F *;* thrald. Q. 75. thereat enrag'd] Q *;* threat-enrag'd F.   79. You justicers] Q *corr.*; your Iustices Q *uncorr.*, Q *2–3*; You Iustices F.   83. *Presents a letter*] Collier MS., *subst.*; *not in* Q, F.   Aside] *Johnson*; *not in* Q, F.   85. in] F *;* on Q *;* of Capell.

an interjection; and here Goneril, by imitating a cat's noise, suggests that Albany is effeminate. Craig adopted this reading, following a conjecture by Daniel. Kittredge, Duthie, and others retain the Q reading. Kittredge explains: 'Your valour seems to be feeble. . . Shut it up in the mews awhile, as we confine an ailing falcon that requires diet and medicine.' Ridley, who also retains the Q reading 'your manhood mew', interprets: 'If all that is troubling you is the difference in sex, put off your manhood

("mew" = moult, shed) and I shall be happy to meet you on equal terms.'

73. *thrill'd*] excited, moved, pierced. *remorse*] compassion.

74. *bending*] directing.

75. *To*] against.

76. *fell'd*] they felled.

79. *justicers*] judges. Cf. IV. ii. 46.

nether crimes] crimes committed here below.

85. *building . . . fancy*] castles in the air. Cf. *Cor.*, II. i. 216.

86. *hateful*] her life will be hateful to

The news is not so tart. [*Aloud.*] I'll read, and answer.

                                       [*Exit.*

Alb. Where was his son when they did take his eyes?

Mess. Come with my Lady hither.

Alb.   He is not here.

Mess. No, my good Lord; I met him back again.   90

Alb. Knows he the wickedness?

Mess. Ay, my good Lord; 'twas he inform'd against him,
    And quit the house on purpose that their punishment
    Might have the freer course.

Alb.   Gloucester, I live
    To thank thee for the love thou show'dst the king,   95
    And to revenge thine eyes. Come hither, friend:
    Tell me what more thou know'st.   [*Exeunt.*

SCENE III.—[*The French Camp near Dover.*]

Enter KENT *and a Gentleman.*

Kent. Why the King of France is so suddenly gone back
    know you no reason?

Gent. Something he left imperfect in the state, which
    since his coming forth is thought of; which imports

87. tart] *F;* tooke *Q.*   *Aloud*] not in *Q, F.*   *Exit*] *Q; not in F.*   95.
show'dst] *F;* shewdest *Q.*   96. thine] *F;* thy *Q.*   97. know'st] *F;*
knowest *Q.*   S.D.] *F; Exit Q.*

Scene III

S.D. *The . . . Dover*] Steevens; *Dover Theobald; not in Q, F.*   1–55. Why . . . with
me] *Q; not in F.*   2. no] *Q1;* the *Q2–3.*

her, because her plans for the future
have been ruined.

    90. *back*] on his way back.

Scene III

    3–4. *Something . . . of*] Greg, *M.L.R.,*
1940, p. 445, comments: 'The public
explanation was, no doubt, on these
lines, but (unless Shakespeare is being
more perfunctory than we have any
right to assume) we can hardly be
intended to take it at its face value.

The real reason . . . was that Cordelia
succeeded in persuading her husband to abandon his purpose of wrest-
ing a portion of the kingdom for himself and retire to his own land, thus
leaving her free to use his army in
defence of her father, should the
occasion arise.' Shakespeare had to
be wary in writing of a foreign invasion.

    4. *imports*] portends. Cf. *R3,* III. vii.
68.

to the kingdom so much fear and danger that his　5
　personal return was most requir'd and necessary.
Kent. Who hath he left behind him general?
Gent. The Marshal of France, Monsieur La Far.
Kent. Did your letters pierce the queen to any demon-
　stration of grief?　　　　　　　　　　　　　　　10
Gent. Ay, sir; she took them, read them in my presence;
　And now and then an ample tear trill'd down
　Her delicate cheek; it seem'd she was a queen
　Over her passion; who, most rebel-like,
　Sought to be king o'er her.
Kent.　　　　　　　　　　O! then it mov'd her.　15
Gent. Not to a rage; patience and sorrow strove
　Who should express her goodliest. You have seen
　Sunshine and rain at once; her smiles and tears
　Were like, a better way; those happy smilets
　That play'd on her ripe lip seem'd not to know　20

10. grief?] *Q2;* griefe. *Q1.*　　11. sir] *Theobald;* say *Q.*　　14. Over] ore
Q2–3.　　16. a rage] rage *Q3.*　　strove] *Pope;* streme *Q.*　　19. like,]
Duthie; like; *Hudson;* like *Q;* lik't *conj. Daniel.*　　better way] wetter May
Theobald (Warburton); better day *Steevens (conj. Theobald);* better May *Malone
(conj. Tollet).*　　20. seem'd] *Pope;* seeme *Q.*

9. *pierce*] Cf. *thrill'd*, IV. ii. 73.
12. *trill'd*] trickled.
13. *delicate*] lovely. Cf. *Oth.*, II. iii. 20.
14. *passion*] emotion.
rebel-like] Perrett fancifully suggests that Shakespeare was influenced by the rebellion of Cordelia's nephews described in several of his sources.
16. *patience*] self-control.
17. *express . . . goodliest*] give her the most beautiful expression (Kittredge).
17–24. *You . . . it*] J. F. Danby compares Sidney, *Arcadia* (ed. Feuillerat), p. 376: 'her teares came dropping downe like raine in Sunshine, and she not taking heede to wipe the teares, they ranne downe upon her cheekes, and lips, as upon Cherries which the dropping tree bedeweth.' On the next page Cecropia tells Philoclea to 'Take a glasse, and see whether these tears become your eies: although, I must confesse, those eies are able to make tears comely.' Here we have the same

balancing of opposites, the same image of sunshine and rain at once, the same reference to the weeper's unconsciousness of her tears, and the same suggestion that she makes tears seem comely. There may even be an echo of the cherries in the epithet 'ripe', commonplace though it is. Steevens quoted part of the Sidney passage and also Henry Wotton, *A Courtlie Controversie of Cupid's Cautels*, 1578, p. 289: 'who hath viewed in the spring time, raine and sunne-shine in one moment, might beholde the troubled countenance of the gentlewoman, after she had read and over-read the letters.'
19. *a better way*] but after a better fashion. Daniel's emendation would give the same meaning; but it is not necessary, and the numerous other conjectures are to be deplored.
smilets] little smiles.
20. *seem'd*] Pope's emendation is probably right, though Shakespeare

What guests were in her eyes; which parted thence,
As pearls from diamonds dropp'd. In brief,
Sorrow would be a rarity most belov'd,
If all could so become it.

Kent.   Made she no verbal question?

Gent. Faith, once or twice she heav'd the name of 'father'   25
Pantingly forth, as if it press'd her heart;
Cried 'Sisters! sisters! Shame of ladies! sisters!
Kent! father! sisters! What? i'th'storm! i'th'night?
Let pity not believe it!' There she shook
The holy water from her heavenly eyes,   30
And clamour moisten'd, then away she started
To deal with grief alone.

Kent.   It is the stars,

22. dropp'd.] dropt; *Q2;* dropt *Q1.*   24. question?] *Q2;* question. *Q1.*
29. pity] it *Capell.*   not] ne'er *Pope.*   believe it] *Pope;* be beleeft *Q.*
There] *Q;* Then *Pope.*   31. And] That *New Camb.*   clamour moisten'd]
Capell; clamour moystened her *Q;* clamour-moisten'd *conj. S. Walker.*

elsewhere drops into the historic present.

21. *which*] i.e. the guests.

22. *pearls . . . dropp'd*] Shakespeare often calls tears 'pearls', and once refers to eyes as diamonds. Cf. *Wiv.,* III. iii. 58. The implication here is that Cordelia's eyes were shining with tears, as well as naturally beautiful.

24. *If . . . it*] if it could be as becoming to others as to her.

Made . . . question?] Did she *say* nothing, apart from what you gathered from her tears?

question] speech.

25. *heav'd*] uttered with difficulty.

29–31. *There . . . moisten'd*] The general meaning of this passage is that Cordelia's emotion was calmed by a flood of tears: that seems to be the one point on which almost all critics are agreed. (Walker and Furness take 'her . . . moisten'd' to mean 'her heavenly and wet-with-wailing eyes'.) The Q reading is clumsy, as the 'her' is hyper-metrical, would involve the assumption that 'clamour' means tears, and not outcry, and was probably copied by mistake from the previous line. We

can discard 'clamour-motion'd', 'clamour soften'd', 'clammer'd moisture' and 'dolour master'd' (R. G. Brown, *T.L.S.,* 23 Dec. 1944). We are left with the question of whether to hyphen *clamour moisten'd* or not. With the hyphen we can take it to mean 'having her emotion calmed by a flood of tears, as the storm is assuaged by a shower of rain' (Craig) or 'with her cheeks wet with her outburst of sorrow' (White). If the hyphen is omitted the phrase can mean 'exclamations moistened with tears' (Heath, who takes the phrase as an ablative absolute); or 'moistened clamour', i.e. she drowned her exclamations with tears (Capell). The last explanation is probably the most satisfactory. I would only add that the sprinkling of the holy water seems to consecrate the clamour. Kittredge suggests that the Gentleman is using the elegant and artificial language expected of courtiers.

29. *There*] Pope's emendation, 'then', is open to the objection that it weakens the force of the same word two lines later. 'There' means 'at that point'.

The stars above us, govern our conditions;
Else one self mate and make could not beget
Such different issues. You spoke not with her since?   35
Gent. No.
Kent. Was this before the king return'd?
Gent.   No, since.
Kent. Well, sir, the poor distressed Lear's i'th'town;
Who sometime, in his better tune, remembers
What we are come about, and by no means   40
Will yield to see his daughter.
Gent.   Why, good sir?
Kent. A sovereign shame so elbows him: his own unkindness,
That stripp'd her from his benediction, turn'd her
To foreign casualties, gave her dear rights
To his dog-hearted daughters, these things sting   45
His mind so venomously that burning shame
Detains him from Cordelia.
Gent.   Alack! poor gentleman.
Kent. Of Albany's and Cornwall's powers you heard not?
Gent. 'Tis so, they are afoot.
Kent. Well, sir, I'll bring you to our master Lear,   50
  And leave you to attend him. Some dear cause
Will in concealment wrap me up awhile;
When I am known aright, you shall not grieve
Lending me this acquaintance. I pray you,
Go along with me.   [*Exeunt.*   55

34. make] *Q1;* mate *Q2–3.*   48. not?] *Q2;* not. *Q1.*   55. S.D.] *Pope;*
Exit *Q.*

33. *conditions*] characters.
34. *one self*] one and the same.
  make] partner. Cf. Lyly, *Mother Bombie*, III. iv. 15; and *Sonn.*, ix. 4.
39. *sometime*] sometimes.
  better tune] lucid intervals. Cf. IV. vii. 16 and *Ham.*, III. i. 166.
42. *sovereign*] over-mastering.
  elbows him] stands at his elbow and reminds him of the past (Wright); forcibly thrusts him back. . . His compunction for his cruelty towards his child mastering his eagerness to approach her (Craig). The second of these interpretations is preferable: it

fits in with the iterative image of the play.
43. *turn'd*] turned out.
44. *casualties*] chances. Cf. *Per.*, v. i. 94.
45. *dog-hearted*] fierce, pitiless. Cf. *Cor.*, I. i. 28; *Oth.*, v. ii. 361.
48. *powers*] armies.
49. *afoot*] on the march.
51. *dear cause*] important reason. We are not told what.
53. *aright*] i.e. as Kent.
54. *Lending . . . acquaintance*] for having been acquainted with me.

SCENE IV.—[*The Same.*]

Enter, with drum and colours, CORDELIA, *Doctor,*
and Soldiers.

Cor. Alack! 'tis he: why, he was met even now
      As mad as the vex'd sea; singing aloud;
      Crown'd with rank fumiter and furrow-weeds,
      With hardocks, hemlock, nettles, cuckoo-flowers,
      Darnel, and all the idle weeds that grow   5
      In our sustaining corn. A century send forth;

Scene IV

S.D. *The Same*] *A Camp Rowe; the Same. A Tent. Capell; not in Q, F.   Enter . . .*
Soldiers] *Enter . . . Gentlemen, and Souldiers F; Enter Cordelia, Doctor, and others Q.*
2. mad as] made *F3–4.*   vex'd] vent *Q.*   3. fumiter] *Theobald;* femiter *Q;*
Fenitar *F.*   4. hardocks] *F3–4;* hor-docks *Q;* Hardokes *F1–2;* burdocks
Hanmer; Harlocks *Steevens (conj. Farmer);* Hoar-docks *Collier (conj. Steevens).*
6. sustaining] sustayning, *Q.*   century] *Q, F3–4;* Centery *F1–2;* sent'ry
Johnson.   send] *F;* is sent *Q1–2;* is set *Q3.*

2. *vex'd*] Cf. *Tp.*, I. ii. 229.
3. *rank*] luxuriant.
fumiter] fumitory. Farren, *Essays on
Mania,* 1833, p. 73, says that its leaves
are of a bitter taste, and the juice was
formerly employed in cases of hypo-
chondrism and black jaundice. Blunden, *op. cit.,* p. 335, cites Clare,
Shepherd's Calendar: 'fumitory too—a
name / That Superstition holds to
fame'.
furrow-weeds] weeds that spring up
in the furrow, in ploughed land.
4. *hardocks*] the hoar or white dock
(Craig); burdock (*N.E.D.*, Onions);
corn blue-bottle (Skeat); knapweed
(Wright); harlocks (Farmer). Drayton, *Shepherd's Garland,* VIII. 156, mentions the Harlocke.
hemlock] used as a poison and as a
narcotic.
nettles] 'that throngs about graves'
(Blunden).
cuckoo-flowers] These have been
identified with a dozen different
plants, including *Lychnis flos-cuculi,*
Ragged Robin (Beisly); Ladies'
Smocks, *Cardamine pratensis* (Wright);
and the Bedlam Cowslip. The last

would be an apt flower for the mad
Lear; but the *Cardamine pratensis* was
used by the Greeks and Romans for
almost all affections of the head, and
according to Farren was used as late as
the last century as a remedy for convulsions, epilepsy, and other diseases
of the brain.
5. *Darnel*] tares, any hurtful weed,
Lolium temulentum, i.e. wild rye grass.
Lyte, *Herbal,* 1578, says Darnell 'is a
vitious graine that combereth or
anoyeth corne, especially Wheat'.
Blunden calls it 'sickly and usurping'.
It has narcotic powers.
idle] unprofitable, worthless, opposed to 'sustaining' corn, which is the
staff of life.
6. *century*] a hundred soldiers.
Perrett curiously takes it as a reference
to Lear's hundred knights, now restored to him. The word is also an
obsolete variant of 'sentry'; but one
sentry would not be much use as a
search party. Craig, who reads
'sentry', argues that century is an
anachronism since Lear lived before
the Roman occupation. But cf.
'cohorts', I. ii. 145.

Search every acre in the high-grown field,
And bring him to our eye.　　　　　[*Exit an Officer.*
　　　　　　　　　What can man's wisdom
In the restoring his bereaved sense?
He that helps him take all my outward worth.　　　10
Doct. There is means, Madam;
　　Our foster-nurse of nature is repose,
　　The which he lacks; that to provoke in him,
　　Are many simples operative, whose power
　　Will close the eye of anguish.
Cor.　　　　　　　　All bless'd secrets,　　　15
　　All you unpublish'd virtues of the earth,
　　Spring with my tears! be aidant and remediate
　　In the good man's distress! Seek, seek for him,
　　Lest his ungovern'd rage dissolve the life
　　That wants the means to lead it.

Enter a Messenger.

Mess.　　　　　　　　News, Madam;　　　20
　　The British powers are marching hitherward.
Cor. 'Tis known before; our preparation stands
　　In expectation of them. O dear father!
　　It is thy business that I go about;
　　Therefore great France　　　　　　25

7. high-grown] *F;* hie growne *Q.*　　8. S.D.] *Malone; not in Q, F.*　　wisdom]
wisdome do *Q2–3.*　　10. helps] can help *Q.*　　11. *Doct.*] *Q; Gent. F.*　　is]
are *Rowe.*　　17. remediate] remediant *Johnson.*　　18. good man's] Good-
mans *F1–2.*　　distress] *Q;* desires *F1–3;* desire *F4.*

8. *What . . . wisdom*] what does man's
science know?
　　9. *In . . . restoring*] to restore.
bereaved] robbed, impaired.
　　10. *helps*] cures.
worth] possessions.
　　11. *There . . . means*] Kellogg, *Shakespeare's Delineation of Insanity,* N.Y.,
1866, p. 26, suggests that Shakespeare
was wiser than the doctors of his day in
his prescription.
　　13. *provoke*] induce.
　　14. *simples*] medicinal herbs.
　　15. *anguish*] generally used by
Shakespeare of physical pain.

16. *virtues*] efficacious medicinal
plants (Kittredge).
　　17. *aidant . . . remediate*] helpfully
remedial. 'Remediate' may be a coinage, perhaps to avoid the jingle that
would be caused by 'remediant'.
　　19. *rage*] frenzy.
　　20. *the means*] i.e. his reason.
　　22. *preparation*] our troops, ready for
battle.
　　23–4. *father! . . . about*] Bethell,
*Shakespeare and the Popular Dramatic
Tradition,* 1946, p. 60, compares Luke,
ii. 49: 'Knew yee not that I must goe
about my father's businesse?'

My mourning and importun'd tears hath pitied.
No blown ambition doth our arms incite,
But love, dear love, and our ag'd father's right.
Soon may I hear and see him!   [*Exeunt.*

SCENE V.—[*A Room in Gloucester's Castle.*]

Enter REGAN *and* OSWALD.

Reg. But are my brother's powers set forth?
Osw.   Ay, Madam.
Reg. Himself in person there?
Osw.   Madam, with much ado:
    Your sister is the better soldier.
Reg. Lord Edmund spake not with your Lord at home?
Osw. No, Madam.   5
Reg. What might import my sister's letter to him?
Osw. I know not, Lady.
Reg. Faith, he is posted hence on serious matter.
    It was great ignorance, Gloucester's eyes being out,

---

26. importun'd] *F;* important *Q;* importunate *Capell;* importune *Harrison.*
27. No] Now *F3–4.*   incite] *F;* insite *Q2;* in sight *Q1.*   28. ag'd] aged *Q2.*
right] Rite *F1–2.*   29. S.D.] *F; Exit Q.*

Scene v

S.D. *A . . . Castle*] *Capell; not in Q, F.*   *Oswald*] Steward *Q, F.*   2. there] *F;*
not in Q.   3. sister is] sister's *Q2–3.*   4. Lord] *F;* Lady *Q.*   6. letter]
letters *Q1.*

26. *importun'd*] importunate. Shake-speare uses the passive form with an active meaning in *1H4,* I. iii. 183 (where *disdain'd* means disdainful). In the present passage the epithet is transferred from the King of France to Cordelia's tears. The Q reading, 'important', also means importuned. It is possible, however, that the F reading is a misreading of *importune* (also meaning importunate): it would be a simple *e/d* error.

27. *blown*] puffed up, inflated with the pride of conquest. Cf. 1 Corinthians, xiii. 4–5: 'Loue suffereth long

. . . it is not puffed vp: . . . it seeketh not her owne things' (Geneva).

Scene v

2. *with much ado*] after much fuss and persuasion. Albany was not certain where his duty lay.

6. *What . . . him?*] Regan evidently returns to a topic discussed before the opening of the scene.

import] bear as its purport, express, signify.

8. *serious matter*] important business.

9. *ignorance*] folly.

To let him live; where he arrives he moves   10
All hearts against us. Edmund, I think, is gone,
In pity of his misery, to dispatch
His nighted life; moreover, to descry
The strength o'th'enemy.
Osw. I must needs after him, Madam, with my letter.   15
Reg. Our troops set forth to-morrow; stay with us,
The ways are dangerous.
Osw.   I may not, Madam;
My Lady charg'd my duty in this business.
Reg. Why should she write to Edmund? Might not you
Transport her purposes by word? Belike,   20
Some things—I know not what. I'll love thee much,
Let me unseal the letter.
Osw.   Madam, I had rather—
Reg. I know your Lady does not love her husband;
I am sure of that: and at her late being here
She gave strange œilliads and most speaking looks   25
To noble Edmund. I know you are of her bosom.
Osw. I, Madam!
Reg. I speak in understanding; y'are, I know't:
Therefore I do advise you, take this note:
My Lord is dead; Edmund and I have talk'd   30
And more convenient is he for my hand

---

11. Edmund] *F;* and now *Q.*   14. o'th'enemy] *F;* at'h army *Q1;* of the Army
Q2–3.   15. Madam] *F; not in Q.*   letter] *F;* letters *Q.*   16. troops set]
F; troope sets *Q.*   21. Some things] *F;* Some thing *Q1;* Something *Q2;*
Something.— *Pope.*   22. I had] *F;* I'de *Q.*   25. œilliads] *Dyce;* aliads *Q;*
Eliads *F1;* Iliads *F2–4;* œliads *Rowe.*   28. y'are] *F;* for *Q.*

12. *In . . . misery*] presumably
ironical.

13. *nighted*] darkened, because he is
blind.

18. *charg'd my duty*] earnestly enjoined me to carry out her instructions.

20. *Belike*] probably.

21. *Some things . . .*] Obviously she
suspects that Edmund and Goneril are
lovers.

25. *œilliads*] This is clearly the word
represented by the F spelling. Cf.
Wiv., I. iii. 68. Cotgrave defines the
word as 'an amorous look, affectionate

wink'; and Steevens quotes R.
Greene, *Disputation between a He and
a She Cony-Catcher,* 1592 (ed. G. B.
Harrison, p. 5), 'amorous glaunces,
smirking œyliades'.

speaking looks] Cf. Florio, *op. cit.,*
III. 211.

26. *of her bosom*] in her confidence.

29. *take this note*] take note of what I
say. Delius wrongly assumes that
Regan is referring to her letter.

30. *have talk'd*] have come to an
understanding.

31. *convenient*] fitting.

Than for your Lady's. You may gather more.
If you do find him, pray you give him this,
And when your mistress hears thus much from you,
I pray desire her call her wisdom to her: 35
So, fare you well.
If you do chance to hear of that blind traitor,
Preferment falls on him that cuts him off.

Osw. Would I could meet him, Madam: I should show
What party I do follow.

Reg.   Fare thee well.   [*Exeunt.*   40

SCENE VI.—[*The Country near Dover.*]

Enter GLOUCESTER *and* EDGAR *dressed like a peasant.*

Glou. When shall I come to th'top of that same hill?
Edg. You do climb up it now; look how we labour.
Glou. Methinks the ground is even.
Edg.   Horrible steep:
Hark! do you hear the sea?
Glou.   No, truly.
Edg. Why, then your other senses grow imperfect   5
By your eyes' anguish.
Glou.   So may it be, indeed.

36. fare you well] *F*; farewell *Q*.   39. him] *Q; not in F*.   should] would
Q1-2.   40. party] *F*; Lady *Q*.   S.D.] *F*; *Exit Q*.

Scene vi

S.D. *The . . . Dover*] *Theobald*; *Fields . . . Dover Capell*; *The Country Rowe.*
Enter . . . peasant] *Theobald*; *Enter Gloucester and Edgar F*; *Enter Gloster and*
Edmund Q.   1. I] *F*; we *Q*.   2. up it now] *F*; it vpnow *Q1*; it vp now
Q2-3.

32. *You . . . more*] You may deduce
more from my hints.

33. *this*] either a token or a letter.
Only one letter, Goneril's, is found on
Oswald after his death; but as L.
Campbell, *Tragic Drama*, 1904, p. 251,
suggests, Shakespeare may choose this
way of revealing Regan's passion, but
would not wish to weaken the scene of
Oswald's death by the complication of
two letters.

34. *thus much*] what I have told you.

Scene vi

5-6. *your . . . anguish*] Cf. Florio,
op. cit., iv. 70: 'Our senses are not
onely altered, but many times dulled,
by the passions of the mind.' But
anguish probably means the physical pain Gloucester is suffering,
rather than his grief at the loss of his
eyes.

Methinks thy voice is alter'd, and thou speak'st
In better phrase and matter than thou didst.

Edg. You're much deceiv'd; in nothing am I chang'd
But in my garments.

Glou.   Methinks you're better spoken.   10

Edg. Come on, sir; here's the place: stand still. How fearful
And dizzy 'tis to cast one's eyes so low!
The crows and choughs that wing the midway air
Show scarce so gross as beetles; half way down
Hangs one that gathers sampire, dreadful trade!   15
Methinks he seems no bigger than his head.
The fishermen that walk upon the beach
Appear like mice, and yond tall anchoring bark
Diminish'd to her cock, her cock a buoy
Almost too small for sight. The murmuring surge,   20
That on th'unnumber'd idle pebble chafes,
Cannot be heard so high. I'll look no more,
Lest my brain turn, and the deficient sight
Topple down headlong.

7. alter'd] *F;* altered *Q.*   speak'st] *F;* speakest *Q.*   8. In] *F;* With *Q.*
9. You're] *Rowe;* Y'are *Q2-3, F;* Y'ar *Q1;* You are *Steevens.*   deceiv'd] *F;*
deceaued *Q.*   10. you're] *Rowe;* y'are *Q2-3, F;* y'ar *Q1;* you are *Capell.*
15. sampire] *Q1-2, F;* samphier *Q3;* samphire *Rowe.*   17. walk] *Q;*
walk'd *F.*   beach] beake *Q2-3.*   18. yond] yon *Q1-2.*   19. a buoy]
F; a boui *Q1;* aboue *Q2-3.*   21. pebble chafes] *F;* peeble chaffes *Q1;*
peebles chafe *Q2-3;* pebbles chafes *Pope.*   22. so] *F;* its so *Q1;* it is so
Q2-3.

10. *you're . . . spoken*] You speak with
better accent, propriety, and grace.
Shakespeare marks the change by
making him speak in verse.

11-24. *How . . . headlong*] Cf. Florio,
op. cit., IV. 67-8, where Montaigne
discusses the effect of dizzy heights.

13. *choughs*] jackdaws (*Corvus mone-
dula*); or, less likely, Cornish choughs
(*Pyrrhocorax*) which are sometimes to
be met with on Beachy Head, and
may well then have been common on
Dover Cliff (Craig).

15. *sampire*] samphire, *herbe de Saint
Pierre,* an aromatic plant used for
pickles. Drayton, *Poly-Olbion,* XVIII.
763-4, as Malone points out, associates the plant with Dover: 'Rob

Dovers neighbouring Cleeves of Sam-
pyre, to excite / His dull and sickly
taste, and stirre up appetite'. Evelyn,
Accetaria, calls a recipe for pickling it
'the Dover receipt'.

19. *cock*] cock-boat, a small ship's
boat.

21. *unnumber'd*] innumerable, num-
berless. Cf. Drayton, *op. cit.,* I. 72:
'th'unnumbered fowl'.

idle] barren (Warburton); moved
by a kind of continual and frivolous
agitation to no purpose or effect
(Eccles).

pebble] often used as a plural, as
pearl is used for *pearls.*

23-4. *and . . . headlong*] and I, my
sight failing me, fall headlong (Kitt-

Glou.   Set me where you stand.

Edg. Give me your hand; you are now within a foot   25
Of th'extreme verge: for all beneath the moon
Would I not leap upright.

Glou.   Let go my hand.
Here, friend, 's another purse; in it a jewel
Well worth a poor man's taking: fairies and Gods
Prosper it with thee! Go thou further off;   30
Bid me farewell, and let me hear thee going.

Edg. Now fare ye well, good sir.

Glou.   With all my heart.

Edg. [*Aside.*] Why I do trifle thus with his despair
Is done to cure it.

Glou. [*Kneeling.*]   O you mighty Gods!
This world I do renounce, and in your sights   35
Shake patiently my great affliction off;
If I could bear it longer, and not fall
To quarrel with your great opposeless wills,
My snuff and loathed part of nature should
Burn itself out. If Edgar live, O, bless him!   40
Now, fellow, fare thee well.

Edg.   Gone, sir: farewell.
          [*Gloucester throws himself forward and falls.*

---

26. th'extreme] the extreme *Q2–3*.   29. fairies] fairiegs *Q3*.   30. further]
F; farther *Q*.   32. ye] *F;* you *Q*.   33. I do] do I *F3–4, Rowe*.   34. Is]
tis *Q2–3, F3–4*.   S.D.] *He kneeles Q; not in F*.   39. snuff] *F;* snurff *Q1*.
40. him] *F; not in Q*.   41. Gone] Good *F2–4*.   S.D.] *He fals Q; not in F;
He leaps and falls along. Rowe*.

---

redge). His body, to which sight belongs, falls with the actual organs of
sight.

   23. *deficient*] Cf. *Oth.*, i. iii. 63.

   26. *extreme*] The accent is on the first
syllable.

   27. *leap upright*] because he is so close
to the edge that even if he jumped
straight up in the air he would be in
grave danger of toppling over the cliff.

   28. *another purse*] Cf. iv. i. 63.

   29. *fairies*] Kittredge suggests that
this refers to the superstition that hidden treasure is guarded by fairies, and
that they make it multiply miracu-

lously in the possession of the dis-
coverer. Cf. *Wint.*, iii. iii. 121 ff.

   33–4. *Why . . . cure it*] Abbott, *411,
points out that this sentence is a confusion of two constructions: 'Why I
trifle is to cure' and 'My trifling is done
to cure.' Such a confusion is, of course,
common in colloquial speech.

   37–8. *fall To quarrel*] begin to rebel
against, and so fall into a worse sin
than suicide.

   38. *opposeless*] irresistible.

   39. *snuff*] the smouldering wick of a
candle. His brief candle is nearly burnt
out. Cf. i. iv. 215 note.

And yet I know not how conceit may rob
The treasury of life when life itself
Yields to the theft; had he been where he thought
By this had thought been past. Alive or dead?　　　45
Ho, you sir! friend! Hear you, sir! speak!
Thus might he pass indeed; yet he revives.
What are you, sir?

Glou.　　　　　　　　Away, and let me die.

Edg. Hadst thou been aught but gossamer, feathers, air,
So many fathom down precipitating,　　　50
Thou'dst shiver'd like an egg; but thou dost breathe,
Hast heavy substance, bleed'st not, speak'st, art sound.
Ten masts at each make not the altitude
Which thou hast perpendicularly fell:
Thy life's a miracle. Speak yet again.　　　55

Glou. But have I fall'n or no?

Edg. From the dread summit of this chalky bourn.
Look up a-height: the shrill-gorg'd lark so far
Cannot be seen or heard: do but look up.

Glou. Alack! I have no eyes.　　　60
Is wretchedness depriv'd that benefit
To end itself by death? 'Twas yet some comfort,
When misery could beguile the tyrant's rage,
And frustrate his proud will.

Edg.　　　　　　　　Give me your arm:
Up: so; how is't? Feel you your legs? You stand.　　　65

42. may] my *Q1*.　　　45. had thought] thought had *Q2–3*.　　　46. friend]
F; not in Q.　　　49. gossamer] *Campbell*; goss'mer *Pope*; gosmore *Q*; Gozemore
F.　　　51. Thou'dst] *F*; Thou hadst *Q*.　　　52. speak'st] speakest *Q1*; speak
F3–4.　　　56. fall'n] falne *F*; fallen *Q*.　　　no?] no I *Q1*.　　　57. summit]
Rowe; Summet *F2–4*; Somnet *F1*; sommons *Q1*; summons *Q2–3*.　　　58. a-
height] *hyphened Warburton*.　　　shrill-gorg'd] *F*; shrill gorg'd *Q*; shrill-gor'd
F2–3; shrill gor'd *F4, Rowe*.　　　63. tyrant's] tyrants *Q*; Tyranrs *F1*.　　　65. is't]
F; not in Q.

42. *conceit*] imagination, delusion.
44. *Yields*] consents.
47. *pass*] die.
50. *precipitating*] Cf. Appendix, p. 236.
53. *at each*] one on top of the other.
54. *fell*] fallen.
57. *bourn*] boundary of the sea, confining it. Cf. *Troil.*, II. iii. 260.
58. *a-height*] on high.
shrill-gorg'd] shrill-throated, shrill-voiced. Cf. *Ham.*, I. i. 149–51.
63–4. *When . . . will*] See Appendix, p. 237.
63. *beguile*] cheat.
65. *Feel you*] can you use; or, possibly, have you any feeling in.

Glou. Too well, too well.

Edg.   This is above all strangeness.
Upon the crown o'th'cliff what thing was that
Which parted from you?

Glou.   A poor unfortunate beggar.

Edg. As I stood here below methought his eyes
Were two full moons; he had a thousand noses,   70
Horns whelk'd and wav'd like the enridged sea:
It was some fiend; therefore, thou happy father,
Think that the clearest Gods, who make them honours
Of men's impossibilities, have preserved thee.

Glou. I do remember now; henceforth I'll bear   75
Affliction till it do cry out itself
'Enough, enough,' and die. That thing you speak of
I took it for a man; often 'twould say
'The Fiend, the Fiend': he led me to that place.

Edg. Bear free and patient thoughts. But who comes here?

67. o'th'] *F*; of the *Q*.   cliff what] *Q*; Cliffe. What *F*.   68. unfortunate]
unfortune *F2*.   beggar] *F*; bagger *Q1*.   69. methought] *Q2*; me thought
F; me thoughts *Q1*.   70. he] *F*; a *Q*.   71. whelk'd] *Hanmer*; welk't
Q1; welkt *Q2*; wealk'd *F1–2*; walk'd *F3–4*.   enridged] *Q*; enraged *F*.
73. make them] *F*; made their *Q*.   77. die. That] die that *Q1*.   78.
'twould] *F*; would it *Q1*; would be *Q2–3*.   80. Bear free] *F*; Bare free *Q1*;
Bare, free *Q2–3*.

69–74. *As . . . thee*] Kittredge compares *Ham.*, I. iv. 69–78.

71. *whelk'd*] twisted, convolved
(Malone). Cf. Golding, *Metamorphoses*, v. 416–17: '*Joves* ymage which
the Lybian folke by name of Hammon
serve, / Is made with crooked welked
hornes that in ward still do terve.'

enridged] furrowed. F reads 'enraged', but Shakespeare is not thinking
of a rough sea. Kittredge compares
Ven., 818–20, and *Lucr.*, 1436–42.

72. *father*] old man; Edgar uses the
term ambiguously, and does not reveal
his identity.

73. *clearest*] 'open and righteous'
(Theobald); 'the purest, the most free
from evil' (Johnson); 'clear-sighted'
(Capell); 'bright, pure, glorious'
(Schmidt); 'who perform miracles to
make themselves clear to those who do
not believe' (Stewart, *Textual Diffi-*

culties, 1914, p. 113); 'this word, which
expresses the pure and luminous
essence of the divinity, reflects the
clear, and profound nature of the man
who utters it' (Reyher, *Essai sur les
Idées . . . de Shakespeare*, p. 500). An
anglicization of *candidissimi dei* (G. K.
Hunter).

73–4. *who . . . impossibilities*] 'who
derive to themselves honour and
reverence from man, by doing things
which he reckons impossible' (Capell).
Furness compares Luke, xviii. 27:
'The things which are impossible with
men are possible with God.'

76–7. *till . . . die*] This may mean 'till
Affliction recognizes that I have been
afflicted enough and itself dies'; or
else 'till Affliction recognizes that I
have borne enough, and allows me to
die a natural death'.

80. *free*] free from sorrow, happy:

Enter LEAR, *fantastically dressed with wild flowers.*

The safer sense will ne'er accommodate   81
His master thus.
Lear. No, they cannot touch me for coining; I am the
king himself.
Edg. O thou side-piercing sight!   85
Lear. Nature's above art in that respect. There's your
press-money. That fellow handles his bow like a
crow-keeper: draw me a clothier's yard. Look, look!
a mouse. Peace, peace! this piece of toasted cheese
will do't. There's my gauntlet; I'll prove it on a   90

---

80. S.D.] *Capell; Enter Lear mad (after* thus, *82) Q; Enter Lear (after* thoughts) *F.*
81. ne'er] neare *Q1;* nere *Q2;* ne're *F.*   83. coining] *Q;* crying *F.*   85.
side-piercing] *F;* side piercing *Q.*   86. Nature's] *F;* Nature is *Q.*   89.
piece of] *F; not in Q.*   90. do't] *F;* do it *Q.*

---

a sorrowful man is enslaved to his grief.

81–2. *The . . . thus*] The sounder sense (i.e. a man in his right senses) would never get himself up in this fashion. Cf. *Meas.*, I. i. 72.

83. *coining*] Lear's mad speeches have an undertone of meaning, and although he leaps from one subject to another it is often possible to see that there is a subconscious connection between them. *Coining*, which was a royal prerogative, leads to the thought of *press-money*. This suggests watching recruits at target-practice and war. War suggests *peace*, which in turn suggests *piece*, and also a challenge and brown *bills*. *Bills* suggests *bird*, bird suggests an arrow in flight, and its target. See Introduction, p. xxxviii, for parallels with *Titus Andronicus*. It may be mentioned that *coining* often had a sexual significance. See *Meas.*, II. iv. 45; *Edward III*, II. i. 258; Tourneur, *The Revenger's Tragædie*, II. ii. 60.

85. *side-piercing*] heart-rending.

86. *Nature's . . . respect*] 'a born King can never take his natural rights' (Schmidt). The relative importance of art and nature was often discussed in Shakespeare's day. See, for example, Puttenham, *The Arte of English Poesie*, III. xxv (ed. Arber, pp. 308 ff.); *Wint.*, IV. iv. 87 ff.; and *All's W.*, II. i. 121.

87. *press-money*] money paid to recruits when they enlisted.

88. *crow-keeper*] a scarecrow with a bow awkwardly tucked under its arm (cf. *Rom.*, I. iv. 6); or, possibly, a boy employed to scare away rooks. Douce quotes from Ascham, *Toxophilus*, ed. Arber, p. 145: 'An other coureth downe, and layeth out his buttockes, as though he shoulde shoote at crowes.'

me] for me.

clothier's yard] The standard English arrow was a cloth-yard in length. Cf. *Chevy Chase*, 180: 'An arrow of a cloth yard long / Up to the head he drew.' Stewart, *Textual Difficulties*, p. 84, says that 'a bowman who could draw a clothier's yard was one who, when the butt of the shaft was at his nose, had the strength to force the bow out the full length of the arm.'

89. *mouse*] possibly as imaginary as the dogs in III. vi. 62.

90. *gauntlet*] a leather glove plaited with steel, the throwing down of which was a challenge.

     giant. Bring up the brown bills. O! well flown bird;
     i'th'clout, i'th'clout: hewgh! Give the word.
Edg. Sweet marjoram.
Lear. Pass.
Glou. I know that voice.   95
Lear. Ha! Goneril, with a white beard! They flattered
     me like a dog, and told me I had the white hairs in
     my beard ere the black ones were there. To say 'ay'
     and 'no' to every thing that I said! 'Ay' and 'no'
     too was no good divinity. When the rain came to   100
     wet me once and the wind to make me chatter,
     when the thunder would not peace at my bidding,
     there I found 'em, there I smelt 'em out. Go to, they
     are not men o'their words: they told me I was every
     thing; 'tis a lie, I am not ague-proof.   105
Glou. The trick of that voice I do well remember:

91–2. bird; i' . . . hewgh!] *F;* bird in the ayre, hagh *Q.*   96. Ha . . . beard!] *F;*
Ha Gonorill, ha Regan, *Q.*   97. the white] *F;* white *Q.*   99. every thing
that] *F;* euery thing *Q1;* all *Q2–3.*   100. too] toe *Q1.*   101. the wind]
wind *F2–4.*   103. 'em . . . 'em] *F;* them . . . them *Q.*   104. o'] *F;* of *Q.*
105. ague-proof] *F;* argue-proofe *Q.*

    91. *brown bills*] brown billmen. A
brown bill was a halberd painted to
keep off rust.
    well . . . bird] The falconer's cry
when the hawk was successful; but
Lear is probably referring to the flight
of the arrow.
    92. *clout*] the mark shot at. Cf. *LLL.,*
IV. i. 136.
    hewgh] an imitation of the noise
made by the arrow.
    word] watchword, password.
    93. *Sweet marjoram*] Blunden, *op. cit.,*
p. 333, says that according to Culpeper
this was a remedy for diseases of the
brain.
    96. *Goneril . . . beard*] This has been
interpreted in two ways: (i) Lear takes
Gloucester for Goneril in disguise;
(ii) Lear is addressing Goneril, and
asking how she could be so cruel to her
father with a white beard.
    97. *like a dog*] as a dog fawns on his
master.
    97–9. *the . . . there*] told me I had

the wisdom of age before I was old
enough to grow a beard. The idea was
prompted by the sight of Gloucester's
beard.
    98–9. *To . . . said*] to agree with me
always, whether I was right or wrong,
like the flatterer in one of Hall's
Satires, VI. 1, cited by Kittredge:
'Smiles on his master for a meale or
two; / And loues him in his maw,
loaths in his heart, / Yet soothes, and
yeas and nays on eyther part'. *Ay and
No* may have been suggested by
Gloucester's 'I know'.
    100. *no . . . divinity*] not good theo-
logy, because it went against the
biblical injunction, James, v. 12: 'But
let your yea, bee yea, and your nay,
nay, lest ye fall into condemnation.'
Though here and in Matt., v. 37, the
injunction is against swearing, and St
Paul in 2 Corinthians, i. 18, cited by
Moberly and others, is avowing his
consistency.
    106. *trick*] peculiarity, intonation.

Is't not the King?

Lear.   Ay, every inch a king:
When I do stare, see how the subject quakes.
I pardon that man's life. What was thy cause?
Adultery?   110
Thou shalt not die: die for adultery! No:
The wren goes to't, and the small gilded fly
Does lecher in my sight.
Let copulation thrive; for Gloucester's bastard son
Was kinder to his father than my daughters   115
Got 'tween the lawful sheets. To't, Luxury, pell-mell!
For I lack soldiers. Behold yond simp'ring dame,
Whose face between her forks presages snow;
That minces virtue, and does shake the head
To hear of pleasure's name;   120

107–17. Ay . . . soldiers] *lines end* King. / quakes. / cause? / Adultery? / Fly / thriue; / Father, / sheets. / Souldiers. *F; lines end* king: / quakes, / cause? / Adultery? / No; / fly / sight. / son / daughters / sheets. / soldiers. *Johnson; prose Q.*   107. every] euer *Q 1.*   111. die: die] *F;* die *Q.*   113. Does] *F;* doe *Q.*   107. every] euer *Q 1.*   117. lack] want *Q2.*   117–25. Behold . . . inherit] *arranged Johnson; prose Q, F.*   yond] *F1–2;* yon *Q, F3;* you *F4.*   118. presages] *F;* presageth *Q.*   119. does] *F;* do *Q.*   120. To] *F; not in Q.*

---

107. *King*] The word recalls Lear to the thought of sovereignty with which he began (Kittredge).

107–17. *Ay . . . soldiers*] prose in Q, mislined verse in F.

109. *cause*] charge, offence.

111. *die . . . adultery*] Noble compares Levit., xx. 10, and John, vii. 5.

112. *The . . . to't*] Florio, *op. cit.*, v. 116, translates Montaigne's quotation from Catullus: 'No pigeons hen, or paire, or what worse name / You list, makes with hir Snow-white cock such game. / With biting bill to catch when she is kist, / As many-minded women when they list.' Montaigne goes on to discuss the worship of Priapus.

115. *kinder*] Gloucester now knows of Edmund's 'kindness'.

116. *Luxury*] lust. Cf. *Ham.*, I. v. 83.
pell-mell] promiscuously.

117–31. *Behold . . . for thee*] Q and F both print this as prose. Johnson printed it as verse except for the last five lines. Tucker Brooke thinks the whole speech is good honest prose.

118. *Whose . . . snow*] who seems to be frigidly chaste.

forks] legs; but H. C. Hart suggests that it may mean instruments for keeping up women's hair. Stubbes, *Anatomy of Abuses*, ed. 1877–9, p. 67, mentions that women's hair 'is vnderpropped with forks, wyers, and I can not tel what'.

119. *minces virtue*] affects the coy timidity of virtue. Cotgrave translates '*faire la sadinette*', 'to mince it, niceifie it, . . . be very squeamish, backward, or coy'.

120. *pleasure's name*] the very name of pleasure. Florio, *op. cit.*, IV. 131, remarks: 'Wee have taught Ladies to blush, onely by hearing that named, which they nothing feare to doe.'

The fitchew nor the soiled horse goes to't
With a more riotous appetite.
Down from the waist they are Centaurs,
Though women all above:
But to the girdle do the Gods inherit,   125
Beneath is all the fiend's: there's hell, there's
    darkness,
There is the sulphurous pit—burning, scalding,
Stench, consumption; fie, fie, fie! pah, pah!
Give me an ounce of civet, good apothecary,
To sweeten my imagination.   130
There's money for thee.

Glou.   O! let me kiss that hand.

---

121. The] *F; to Q.*   123 .they are] tha're *Q 1.*   126–8. Beneath ... pah!]
arranged Muir; prose Q, F.   127. There is] *F;* there's *Q.*   sulphurous] *F;*
sulphury *Q.*   128. consumption] *F;* consumation *Q.*   129–31. Give ...
hand] *arranged Muir; lines end* apothecary, / thee. *Johnson.*   129. civet,] *Q;*
Ciuet: *F.*   130. To] *Q; not in F.*

---

121. *fitchew*] pole-cat; 'a cant term
for a prostitute' (Dyce).

soiled] wanton with rich feeding in
the springtime.

123. *Centaurs*] Heilman, *op. cit.*, p.
100, says: 'The Centaur is exactly the
right image here ... it exhibits man as
a rational animal.' Cf. his remark on
Regan and Goneril, p. 234: 'The paradox is that these free minds, un-
burdened by any conventional or traditional allegiances, become slaves to
the uncontrolled animal desire, mech-
anisms for the attainment of irrational
objectives.'

125. *But . . . inherit*] The Gods
possess only that part of the body
above the waist.

inherit] possess, hold sway.

126. *Beneath . . . fiend's*] Furness
quotes a passage by Ingleby about an
early Christian heretical sect called the
Paterniani 'whose opinion was that the
upper parts of a man's body were
made, indeed, by God, but the lower
parts, from the girdle, they held were
made by the devil'. The priests who
were exposed by Harsnett tried to
exorcise the devils from the lower parts

of the body. See Appendix, p. 240.

126–31. *there's . . . for thee*] Johnson
and Jennens printed this as verse,
though most editors treat it as prose.
The present arrangement is rather
different from Johnson's. The verse
form brings out the point of having
there is instead of *there's* (127) and the
three *fies* and the two *pahs* conveniently fill out a line.

130. *To . . . imagination*] Here I have
followed the Q reading; the F reading,
which may be explained by the accidental omission of *to* in the MS., is
perfectly possible, but seems rather
awkward in rhythm. Cf. Marston,
The Fawne, II. i (ed. Wood, p. 161):
'Sweeten your imaginations, with
thoughts of—ah why women are the
most giddie, uncertain motions under
heaven . . . onely meere chancefull
appetite swayes them.' This juxtaposition of satire on women with the
phrase quoted suggests that Marston
was imitating Shakespeare, but as *The
Fawne* may have been written some
time before its publication in 1606 the
influence may have been the other
way round.

Lear. Let me wipe it first; it smells of mortality.

Glou. O ruin'd piece of Nature! This great world
    Shall so wear out to naught. Dost thou know me?

Lear. I remember thine eyes well enough. Dost thou
        squiny at me?   135
    No, do thy worst, blind Cupid; I'll not love.
    Read thou this challenge; mark but the penning of it.

Glou. Were all thy letters suns, I could not see.

Edg. [*Aside.*] I would not take this from report; it is,
    And my heart breaks at it.   140

Lear. Read.

Glou. What! with the case of eyes?

Lear. O, ho! are you there with me? No eyes in your
    head, nor no money in your purse? Your eyes are in
    a heavy case, your purse in a light: yet you see how   145
    this world goes.

Glou. I see it feelingly.

Lear. What! art mad? A man may see how this world

132–4. Let . . . me?] *lines end* first, / Mortality. / world / naught. / Me? *F.*
132. Let me] *F;* Here *Q.*   134. Shall] *F;* should *Q.*   Dost thou] *F;* Do
you *Q.*   135–7. I . . . it.] *arranged Muir; prose Q, F.*   135. thine] *F;* thy *Q.*
squiny] squint *Q3.*   at] *F;* on *Q.*   137. this] *F;* that *Q.*   but] *F; not
in Q.*   of it] *F;* oft *Q1;* on't *Q2–3.*   138. thy] *F;* the *Q.*   see] *F;* see
one *Q, F2–3.*   139–40.] *arranged Theobald; lines end* report *and* it *F; prose Q.*
142. the] this *Rowe.*   144. nor no] nor *Q2–3.*   145. a heavy] heavy *F3–4.*
148. this] *F;* the *Q.*

133. *This great world*] the universe.
Cf. III. i. 10.

135. *squiny*] squint. Cf. III. iv. 114.

136–7. *No . . . penning of it*] This is
usually printed as, and may be, prose.

136. *blind Cupid*] the sign of a brothel.
Sidney's *Arcadia,* II. xiv, contains a
poem about blind Cupid, and Miso is
warned not to love.

137. *challenge*] Lear's mind jumps
back to his earlier speech, IV. vi. 90.
Kittredge suggests the enemy is blind
Cupid, but this is unlikely since he
gives the challenge to Gloucester to
read, and it is Gloucester he has taken
for Cupid.

139. *this*] the scene he is witnessing.

142. *case*] the sockets which had
once held the eyes. Cf. *Per.,* III. ii. 99;
Wint., v. ii. 14.

143. *are . . . me?*] Is that what you
mean? Cf. *AYL.,* v. ii. 32.

145. *heavy case*] sad plight, with a
pun on *case.*

your purse . . . light] a quibble on *light*
which means *empty* and *merry.* Cf.
Cym., v. iv. 167: 'purse and brain both
empty,—the brain the heavier for
being too light, the purse too light
being drawn of heaviness'. There
is a reference to the proverb:
'A heavy purse makes a light heart.'
Whiter, in an unpublished note,
compares Jonson, *The New Inn,* I. i.
16.

145–6. *how . . . goes*] Cf. Florio, *op.
cit.,* v. 85: 'Thus goes the world.'

147. *feelingly*] another quibble: (*a*)
by my sense of feeling; (*b*) keenly.
Lear takes him to mean (*a*).

goes with no eyes. Look with thine ears: see how
yond justice rails upon yond simple thief. Hark, in   150
thine ear: change places, and, handy-dandy, which
is the justice, which is the thief? Thou hast seen a
farmer's dog bark at a beggar?

Glou. Ay, Sir.

Lear. And the creature run from the cur? There thou
          might'st behold   155
The great image of Authority:
A dog's obey'd in office.
Thou rascal beadle, hold thy bloody hand!
Why dost thou lash that whore? Strip thine own back;
Thou hotly lusts to use her in that kind   160
For which thou whipp'st her. The usurer hangs
          the cozener.
Thorough tatter'd clothes small vices do appear;
Robes and furr'd gowns hide all. Plate sin with gold,

149. thine] thy *Q.*   150. yond . . . yond] *F;* yon . . . yon *Q.*   151. thine]
F; thy *Q.*   change . . . and] *F; not in Q.*   handy-dandy] handy, dandy
Q1; handy dandy *Q2–3.*   152. justice] *F;* theefe *Q.*   thief] *F;* Iustice
Q.   154. Ay] *not in F3–4.*   155–7.] *arranged Muir; prose Q, F.*   157.
dog's obey'd] *F;* dogge, so bade *Q1;* dogge, so bad *Q2–3.*   158–61. Thou
. . . cozener] *arranged Pope; prose Q, F.*   159. thine] *Q;* thy *F.*   160. Thou]
F; thy bloud *Q.*   162–9. Thorough . . . seem] *arranged Rowe; prose Q, F.*
162. Thorough] *F;* Through *Q.*   tatter'd clothes] *F;* tottered raggs *Q1;*
tattered ragges *Q2–3.*   small] *Q;* great *F.*   163. hide] *F;* hides *Q.*
163–8. Plate . . . lips] *F; not in Q.*   163. Plate sin] *Theobald;* Plate sins
Pope; Place sinnes *F.*

150. *simple*] of low estate, ordinary.

151. *handy-dandy*] i.e. take your
choice. It is a well-known children's
game. Florio mentions it, *op. cit.,* v.
259. But as G. K. Hunter points out,
Langland (B. IV. 75) uses it to mean
bribery. There are several passages in
Montaigne's essays on the guilt of
judges. One adulterous one condemns
an adulterer (*op. cit.,* VI. 85); 'one
same magistrate doth lay the penalty
of his change on such as cannot do
withal. . . A horrible image of justice'
(v. 21); and 'Justice . . . is used but for
a cloake and ornament' (III. 191).

155. *creature*] human being.

157. *A . . . office*] Montaigne mentions 'that there are Nations, who

receive and admit a Dogge to be their
King' (*op. cit.,* III. 210).

158. *beadle*] parish constable.

160. *kind*] manner.

161. *The . . . cozener*] a magistrate
who has been guilty of the crime of
usury passes sentence on one guilty
only of petty cheating.

cozener] cheat.

162. *small*] The reading of Q. The F
reading, 'great', would mean that all
vices are great when looked at through
tattered clothes; but it would be difficult to convey that meaning in a
theatre. It would be easier if *great* were
printed after *do.*

163. *Robes . . . all*] Lear is still thinking of judges. Cf. *Lucr.,* 93: 'Hiding

And the strong lance of justice hurtless breaks;
Arm it in rags, a pigmy's straw does pierce it.   165
None does offend, none, I say, none; I'll able 'em:
Take that of me, my friend, who have the power
To seal th'accuser's lips. Get thee glass eyes;
And, like a scurvy politician, seem
To see the things thou dost not. Now, now, now,
            now;   170
Pull off my boots; harder, harder; so.
Edg. [*Aside.*] O! matter and impertinency mix'd;
Reason in madness.
Lear. If thou wilt weep my fortunes, take my eyes;
I know thee well enough; thy name is Gloucester;   175
Thou must be patient; we came crying hither:
Thou know'st the first time that we smell the air
We wawl and cry. I will preach to thee: mark.

170–1. To . . . so] *arranged Capell; prose Q, F.*   170. Now . . . now;] *F;* no
now *Q.*   172. impertinency mix'd] impertinency, mixt *Q2–3.*   174–
204. If . . . to] *verse F; prose Q.*   174. fortunes] *F;* fortune *Q.*   178. wawl] *F;*
wayl *Q.*   mark] *F;* marke me *Q.*

base sin in pleats of majesty'. See also
the following passage from Barclay,
The Mirrour of good Maners, ed. 1885,
p. 34: 'What difference betwene a
great thiefe and a small, / Forsooth no
more but this to speake I dare be
bolde, / The great sitteth on benche in
costly furres of pall, / The small thiefe
at barre standeth trembling for colde, /
The great thieues are laded with great
chaynes of golde, / The small thiefe
with yron chayned from all refuge, /
The small thiefe is iudged, oft time the
great is Iudge.'

Plate] Theobald's emendation is
certainly correct—clothe in plate-
armour.

166. *None . . . offend*] Florio, *op. cit.*,
v. 245, has the following passage: 'I
say not, that none should accuse except
hee bee spotlesse in himselfe: For then
none might accuse.' But Montaigne
derived this injunction from the
Gospels.

able] vouch for, warrant, authorize.
167. *that*] piece of information;

or perhaps an imaginary pardon.
169. *scurvy*] vile.

politician] trickster, one who follows
Machiavelli's 'policy', not a politician
in the modern sense of the word.

172. *matter . . . impertinency*] sense and
nonsense. Florio uses the word impertinency.

176. *we . . . hither*] Noble compares
Wisdom, vii. 3, 5: 'And when I was
borne, I receiued the common aire,
and fell vpon the earth, which is of like
nature, crying and weeping at the first
as all other doe. . . For there is no king
that had any other beginning of birth.'
Cf. Montaigne (tr. Florio, I. 107): 'So
wept we, and so much did it cost us to
enter into this life.'

178. *We wawl . . . cry*] Anders compares Holland's *Pliny*, VII, Proem (ed.
1601, p. 152): 'man alone, poore
wretch, she (Nature) hath laid all
naked upon the bare earth, euen on
his birth-day, to cry and wraule presently from the very first houre that he
is borne into this world.'

Glou. Alack, alack the day!

Lear. When we are born, we cry that we are come   180
　　To this great stage of fools. This' a good block!
　　It were a delicate stratagem to shoe
　　A troop of horse with felt; I'll put't in proof,
　　And when I have stol'n upon these son-in-laws,
　　Then, kill, kill, kill, kill, kill, kill!   185

Enter a Gentleman, with Attendants.

Gent. O! here he is; lay hand upon him. Sir,
　　Your most dear daughter—
Lear. No rescue? What! a prisoner? I am even
　　The natural fool of Fortune. Use me well;

---

181. This'] *Singer (conj. S. Walker)*; This *Q, F*; 'Tis *Hudson (conj. Ritson)*; This's *Camb.*   182. shoe] *F*; shoot *Q.*   183. felt] *F*; fell *Q.*   I'll . . . proof] *F*; not in Q.   184. stol'n] *F*; stole *Q.*   son-in-laws] Son in Lawes *Q1, F1*; sons-in-law *Q2–3*; Sonnes in Lawes *F2–3*; Sons-in-Laws *F4.*   185. S.D.] *Rowe*; Enter a Gentleman *F*; Enter three Gentlemen *Q.*   186. hand] *F*; hands *Q.* him. Sir] *Johnson*; him, Sir *Q, F.*   Sir] Sirs *Q2–3.*   187. Your . . . daughter] *F*; your most deere *Q1*; not in *Q2–3.*

---

181. *stage of fools*] See Introduction, p. xxxvii.

This'] this is.

block] The word was probably suggested by *stage*, since the stage was often called a scaffold. It is usually assumed that Lear takes off his hat to preach, and that his remark means 'This is a good hat' or 'This hat is made in a good fashion'; but it is unlikely that Lear would be wearing a hat in this scene, and it would be awkward for him to take Edgar's or Gloucester's. It is possible that Lear mistakes a stone or a stump of a tree for a mounting-block, and then quibbles on the word. Empson, *T.L.S.*, 19 Dec. 1952, suggested that this means a boot-block. Muir, *T.L.S.*, 30 Jan. 1953, supported the suggestion by reference to the first scene of *Julius Cæsar* where the sequence of ideas (*cobbler, surgeon, shoes, blocks, shout, weep*) probably suggested the sequence here. Perhaps the scaffold suggested the executioner's block, and thence the boot-block, the

mounting-block, and the hat-block. The mounting-block would suggest horses, as the block of a hat would suggest felt.

182. *delicate*] neat.

183. *felt*] Malone quotes a passage from Lord Herbert of Cherbury's *Life of Henry VIII* (ed. 1872, p. 147) about a joust, in which the horses 'to prevent sliding and noise, were shod with felt or flocks'.

I'll . . . proof] I'll try the experiment.

184. *son-in-laws*] This is the reading of Q and F, and is a possible colloquial plural. It is unwise to blame the printer for every mistake of grammar in Shakespeare's plays.

185. *kill, kill*] a cry of soldiers, meaning 'No quarter!' Cf. *Ven.*, 652.

189. *natural . . . Fortune*] born to be the sport of fortune. Cf. *Rom.*, II. i. 141. Empson, *op. cit.*, p. 145, seems to suggest that there is a quibble on *natural*, which can mean *imbecile* as well as *born*.

You shall have ransom. Let me have surgeons;   190
I am cut to th'brains.
Gent.   You shall have any thing.
Lear. No seconds? all myself?
Why this would make a man a man of salt,
To use his eyes for garden water-pots,
Ay, and laying autumn's dust. I will die bravely,   195
Like a smug bridegroom. What! I will be jovial:
Come, come; I am a king, masters, know you that?
Gent. You are a royal one, and we obey you.
Lear. Then there's life in't. Come and you get it, you
shall get it by running. Sa, sa, sa, sa.   200
                    [*Exit running. Attendants follow.*
Gent. A sight most pitiful in the meanest wretch,
Past speaking of in a King! Thou hast one daughter,
Who redeems nature from the general curse
Which twain have brought her to.
Edg. Hail, gentle sir!
Gent.   Sir, speed you: what's your will?   205
Edg. Do you hear aught, sir, of a battle toward?
Gent. Most sure and vulgar; every one hears that,

190. ransom] a ransom *Q2–3.*   surgeons] *F;* a surgeon *Capell;* a chirurgeon
Q2–3; a churgion *Q1.*   191. th'] the *Q1.*   193. a man a man of] *F;* a man
of *Q.*   195. Ay ... dust] *Q; not in F;* Ay, and for laying autumn's dust *Craig.*
After this Q2 inserts: Gent. Good Sir.   196. smug] *F; not in Q.*   197. masters]
F; my maisters *Q.*   199. Come and] *F;* nay and *Q1;* nay if *Q2–3;* Nay, an
Capell.   200. by] *F;* with *Q.*   Sa ... sa.] *F; not in Q.*   S.D.] *Capell,
subst.; Exit King running Q; Exit F.*   202. one] *Q;* a *F.*   204. have] *F;*
hath *Q.*   206. sir] *F; not in Q.*   207–8. Most ... sound] *divided as in Q1;
Q2–3 divide at* heares, *and F at* vulgar.   207. one] ones *Q2–3.*   hears]
here's *Q1.*

191. *cut ... brains*] used literally and
figuratively; he is vexed to madness,
but requires a surgeon for an imaginary wound in the head.

193. *a man of salt*] of salt tears.

195. *bravely*] two meanings: (*a*)
courageously, (*b*) in smart clothes.

196. *Like ... bridegroom*] Cf. *Meas.*,
III. i. 83–5, and note on IV. ii. 23 *ante.*
smug] spick and span.

199. *there's ... in't*] the case is not yet
desperate (Johnson).
and] if.

200. *Sa ... sa*] 'An old hunting cry to
call a hound or to urge the dogs forward in chase of the hare' from Fr. *ça,
ça!* It was used as a rallying cry, or
as an interjection of challenge and
defiance (Kittredge).

203. *general*] universal.

204. *twain*] not Adam and Eve, as
Danby fancifully suggests (*op. cit.*,
p. 125), but Goneril and Regan.

205. *gentle*] noble.

207. *vulgar*] in every one's mouth;
common knowledge.

Which can distinguish sound.

Edg.   But, by your favour,
How near's the other army?

Gent. Near, and on speedy foot; the main descry   210
Stands on the hourly thought.

Edg.   I thank you, sir: that's all.

Gent. Though that the Queen on special cause is here,
Her army is mov'd on.

Edg.   I thank you sir.   [*Exit Gentleman.*

Glou. You ever-gentle Gods, take my breath from me:
Let not my worser spirit tempt me again   215
To die before you please!

Edg.   Well pray you, father.

Glou. Now, good sir, what are you?

Edg. A most poor man, made tame to Fortune's blows;
Who, by the art of known and feeling sorrows,
Am pregnant to good pity. Give me your hand,   220
I'll lead you to some biding.

Glou.   Hearty thanks:
The bounty and the benison of Heaven
To boot, and boot!

Enter OSWALD.

Osw.   A proclaim'd prize! Most happy!
That eyeless head of thine was first fram'd flesh
To raise my fortunes. Thou old unhappy traitor,   225

208. Which] *F;* That *Q.*   sound] *F;* sence *Q.*   210. speedy foot] *F;* speed
fort *Q1;* speed for't *Q2–3.*   descry] *F;* descries *Q.*   211. Stands] *F;*
Standst *Q1.*   thought] *F;* thoughts *Q.*   213. Her] *F;* Hir *Q1;* His *Q2–3.*
S.D.] *Johnson; Exit Q; Exit F, after* on.   214. ever-gentle] *hyphened Capell.*
218. tame to] *F;* lame by *Q.*   221–3. Hearty . . . boot!] *F; prose Q.*   222.
bounty . . . benison] bornet and the beniz *Q uncorr.*   223. To . . . boot!] *F;*
to boot, to boot *Q corr., Q2–3;* to saue thee *Q uncorr.*   S.D.] *Collier; Enter
Steward Q,F.*   224. first] *not in Q uncorr.*   225. old] *F;* most *Q.*

210. *speedy foot*] advancing rapidly.
210–11. *the . . . thought*] We expect to
descry the main body any hour now.
215. *worser spirit*] evil angel, evil side
of my nature.
218. *tame*] submissive.
219. *by . . . sorrows*] instructed by the
heart-felt sorrows I have experienced.
Cf. *Wint.,* IV. ii. 8.

220. *pregnant*] disposed, susceptible.
221. *biding*] abode.
222. *benison*] blessing.
223. *To boot, and boot*] to reward you,
in addition to my thanks. 'To boot'
means both 'in addition' and 'to
enrich with an additional gift'.
proclaim'd] The accent is on the first
syllable.

Briefly thyself remember: the sword is out
That must destroy thee.
Glou.   Now let thy friendly hand
Put strength enough to't.   [*Edgar interposes.*
Osw.   Wherefore, bold peasant
Dar'st thou support a publish'd traitor? Hence;
Lest that th'infection of his fortune take   230
Like hold on thee. Let go his arm.
Edg. Chill not let go, zir, without vurther 'casion.
Osw. Let go, slave, or thou di'st.
Edg. Good gentleman, go your gait, and let poor volk
pass. And 'chud ha' bin zwagger'd out of my life,   235
'twould not ha' bin zo long as 'tis by a vortnight.
Nay, come not near th'old man; keep out, che vor'
ye, or ise try whither your costard or my ballow be
the harder. Chill be plain with you.

228. S.D.] *Johnson, subst.; not in Q, F.*   229. Dar'st] durst *Q1.*   230. that
th'] *F;* the *Q.*   232. zir] *F;* sir *Q.*   vurther] *F; not in Q.*   'casion] *F;*
cagion *Q.*   234. and] *F; not in Q.*   volk] voke *Q1.*   235. ha'] *F;*
haue *Q.*   zwagger'd] zwagged *F2–4.*   236. ha']*F;* haue *Q.*   zo] so *Q1.*
as 'tis] *F; not in Q.*   vortnight] fortnight *Q uncorr.*   237. th'] the *Q.*
238. ise] ice *F;* ile *Q.*   whither] *F;* whether *Q.*   costard] coster *Q uncorr.;*
costerd *Q.*   ballow] *F;* battero *Q uncorr.;* bat *Q corr., Q2–3.*

226. *thyself remember*] Think of thy
sins (so as to make thy peace with
heaven).

out] of its scabbard.

227. *friendly*] because it gives him the
death he desires.

229. *publish'd*] proclaimed.

232–42. *Chill . . . foins*] conventional
stage dialect, 'approximating to that
of Somersetshire', but used for a
variety of other counties. It is identical
with the Devonshire dialect in *The
London Prodigal* (1605), performed by
Shakespeare's company. See Gill,
Logonomia Anglica, 1621, p. 23.

232. *Chill*] I will. Cf. *The London
Prodigal,* II. i. 40; Gill, *op. cit.,* p. 32.

234. *go your gait*] go your way.

volk] folk.

235. *And 'chud*] if I could. Cf. *The
London Prodigal,* III. iii. 7, where *chud* =
should.

237–8. *che vor' ye*] The usual explana-

tion is 'I warn you'; but the passage
quoted by Capell from *The Contention
between Liberality and Prodigality,* II. iii. 4
('by gisse sir tis high time che vore ye')
and one quoted by Craig from *The
London Prodigal,* v. i. 349 ('Well, che
vor ye, he is changed') make it clear
that the phrase means 'I warrant you'.
See also *The London Prodigal,* II. iv. 80,
III. iii. 43, and v. i. 355; and Gill, *op.
cit.,* p. 32.

238. *ise*] I shall.

costard] literally a kind of apple
(Drayton, *Poly-Olbion,* XVIII. 684) but
often used humorously for the head.

ballow] cudgel. Wright, *English
Dialect Dictionary,* 1896, shows that in
Nottingham a staff beaked with iron
was called 'a ballowe staff'. Tucker
Brooke, *Essays on Shakespeare,* 1948,
p. 106, calls this 'a possibly poetic, but
quite unknown weapon, a "ballow"
instead of a plain batoon'.

Osw. Out, dunghill!   240

Edg. Chill pick your teeth, zir. Come; no matter vor
     your foins.   [*They fight, and Edgar knocks him down.*

Osw. Slave, thou hast slain me. Villain, take my purse.
     If ever thou wilt thrive, bury my body;
     And give the letters which thou find'st about me   245
     To Edmund Earl of Gloucester; seek him out
     Upon the British party: O! untimely death.
     Death!   [*Dies.*

Edg. I know thee well: a serviceable villain;
     As duteous to the vices of thy mistress   250
     As badness would desire.

Glou.   What! is he dead?

Edg. Sit you down, father; rest you.
     Let's see these pockets: the letters that he speaks of
     May be my friends. He's dead; I am only sorry
     He had no other deathsman. Let us see: 255
     Leave, gentle wax; and, manners, blame us not:
     To know our enemies' minds, we rip their hearts;
     Their papers is more lawful.   [*Reads.*

     Let our reciprocal vows be remembered. You have many
     opportunities to cut him off; if your will want not, time   260
     and place will be fruitfully offer'd. There is nothing done
     if he return the conqueror; then am I the prisoner, and his
     bed my gaol; from the loathed warmth whereof deliver me,
     and supply the place for your labour.

               Your wife, so I would say—   265
                    Affectionate servant,
                         GONERIL.

241. Chill] Ile *Q1*.   zir] sir *Q1*.   vor] *F;* for *Q.*   242. S.D.] *Rowe; They
fight Q; not in F.*   247. British] *Q;* English *F.*   248. S.D.] *He dies Q; not
in F.*   253. these] *F;* his *Q.*   the] *F;* these *Q.*   254. sorry] sorrow *Q1.*
257. we] *F;* wee'd *Q.*   258. is] are *F2–4.*   S.D.] *A Letter Q; Reads the Letter
F; not in Q uncorr.*   259. our] *F;* your *Q.*   264. for] of *F3–4.*   266.
Affectionate] F; your affectionate *Q1;* and your affectionate *Q2–3.*   servant]
seruant and for you her owne for *Venter, Q1.*

240. *dunghill*] dunghill born, low
bred.
  242. *foins*] thrusts. Cf. *2H4*, II. i. 17.
  243. *Villain*] serf.
  247. *Upon*] among.
  255. *deathsman*] executioner.

256. *Leave*] by your leave.
259. reciprocal] See Appendix, p.
236.
  261. fruitfully] plentifully.
  266. servant] lover. The nonsense
that follows in Q1 may conceal sense,

O indistinguish'd space of woman's will!
A plot upon her virtuous husband's life,
And the exchange my brother! Here, in the sands,   270
Thee I'll rake up, the post unsanctified
Of murtherous lechers; and in the mature time
With this ungracious paper strike the sight
Of the death-practis'd Duke. For him 'tis well
That of thy death and business I can tell.   275
Glou. The King is mad: how stiff is my vile sense
That I stand up, and have ingenious feeling
Of my huge sorrows! Better I were distract:
So should my thoughts be sever'd from my griefs,
And woes by wrong imaginations lose   280
The knowledge of themselves.   [*Drum afar off.*
Edg.   Give me your hand:
Far off, methinks, I hear the beaten drum.
Come, father, I'll bestow you with a friend.   [*Exeunt.*

---

268. O] Of *F2-4*.   indistinguish'd] *Q1, F4*; indinguish'd *F1-3*; vndistinguist
Q2-3.   space] scope *conj. Theobald.*   will] *F*; wit *Q*.   270. the sands]
Q; rhe sands *F1*.   274. death-practis'd] *unhyphened Q*.   275. thy] his
Q2-3.   279. sever'd] *F*; fenced *Q*.   281. S.D.] *after* griefs (279) *F*; *A drum
a farre off Q*.   283. S.D.] *F*; *Exit Q*.

meaning perhaps 'and your own if you
dare venture for me'. Duthie suggests
the words were an actor's interpolation. Cf. IV. ii. 20.
  268. *O . . . will!*] O limitless range of
woman's lust!
  indistinguish'd] indefinable, beyond
the range of sight.
  270. *sands*] Perrett points out that
only Gloucester thinks they are on the
beach. Either Edgar is speaking for his
father's benefit, or Shakespeare forgot.
  271. *rake up*] cover up, as the embers
are covered with ashes so that the fire
will keep in.
  272. *mature*] accent on the first syllable. When time is ripe.
  273. *ungracious*] without grace,
wicked.
  274. *death-practis'd*] whose death is
plotted.

  276. *stiff*] obstinately unbending.
  vile sense] Empson, *op. cit.*, p. 146,
explains that Gloucester's sense is vile
because it seems disloyal to outlast
Lear's, but that *vile sense* is commonly
used for the senses of a source of pleasure, so that he might be regretting his
past sensualities which have coarsened
his sensibility. This is too ingenious. Gloucester calls his senses vile
because they still allow him to be
fully conscious of his sorrows, and
do not give him the relief of insanity.
  277. *ingenious*] conscious.
  278. *distract*] mad.
  280. *wrong imaginations*] illusions.
  283. *bestow*] lodge.
  friend] We are not told how the
fugitive Edgar has got in touch with a
friend.

SCENE VII.—[*A Tent in the French Camp.*]

Enter CORDELIA, KENT, *Doctor, and Gentleman.*

Cor. O thou good Kent! how shall I live and work
To match thy goodness? My life will be too short,
And every measure fail me.
Kent. To be acknowledg'd, Madam, is o'er-paid.
All my reports go with the modest truth,   5
No more nor clipp'd, but so.
Cor.   Be better suited:
These weeds are memories of those worser hours:
I prithee, put them off.
Kent.   Pardon, dear Madam;
Yet to be known shortens my made intent:
My boon I make it that you know me not   10
Till time and I think meet.
Cor. Then be't so, my good Lord. [*To the Doctor.*] How
does the King?
Doct. Madam, sleeps still.
Cor. O you kind Gods,
Cure this great breach in his abused nature!   15
Th'untuned and jarring senses, O! wind up
Of this child-changed father.
Doct.   So please your Majesty

Scene VII

S.D. *A . . . Camp*] Capell, *subst.; not in* Q, F.   *Enter . . . Gentleman*] Craig; Enter
Cordelia, Kent, and Gentleman F; Enter Cordelia, Kent and Doctor Q; Lear on a bed
asleep Steevens (Capell).   8. Pardon] *F;* Pardon me Q.   12. good] *not in*
Q2–3.   S.D.] *Theobald, subst.; not in* Q, F.   13. *Doct.*] Q; Gent. F.   16.
and] *not in* Q3.   jarring] *F;* hurrying Q.   17. *Doct.*] Q; Gent. F.

3. *measure fail me*] because Kent's
goodness is immeasurable. Cf. *Leir*,
2655–6: 'Yet all I can, I, were it ne're
so much / Were not sufficient, thy true
loue is such.'
5. *reports*] i.e. about Lear, and his
own service as Caius.
6. *clipp'd*] inaccurate through omission.
so] as I have described them.
suited] clothed.

7. *memories*] reminders.
9. *shortens . . . intent*] interferes with
the plan I have made.
16. *wind up*] tune, by tightening the
strings.
17. *child-changed*] 'changed to a
child' (Steevens); changed in mind by
the cruelty of his children (Malone).
Cf. *R3*, III. vii. 184, 'care-crazed'.
Cleanth Brooks thinks that the ambiguity is deliberate.

That we may wake the King? he hath slept long.
Cor. Be govern'd by your knowledge, and proceed
    I'th'sway of your own will. Is he array'd?   20

Enter LEAR *in a chair carried by Servants.*

Gent. Ay, Madam, in the heaviness of sleep
    We put fresh garments on him.
Doct. Be by, good Madam, when we do awake him;
    I doubt not of his temperance.
Cor.   Very well.   [*Music.*
Doct. Please you, draw near. Louder the music there!   25
Cor. O my dear father! Restoration hang
    Thy medicine on my lips, and let this kiss
    Repair those violent harms that my two sisters
    Have in thy reverence made!
Kent.   Kind and dear Princess!
Cor. Had you not been their father, these white flakes   30
    Did challenge pity of them. Was this a face
    To be oppos'd against the warring winds?
    To stand against the deep dread-bolted thunder?
    In the most terrible and nimble stroke
    Of quick, cross lightning? to watch—poor *perdu!*—   35
    With this thin helm? Mine enemy's dog,

18. That] *not in Q2–3.*   20. S.D.] *F; not in Q.*   21. *Gent.*] *F; Doct. Q.*
of] *F; of his Q.*   23. *Doct.*] *Capell; Gent. Q1, F; Kent Q2–3.*   Be . . .
Madam] *F;* Good madam be by *Q.*   24. not] *not in F1–2.*   24–5. Very . . .
there] *Q; not in F.*   24. S.D.] *Grant White, subst.; not in Q, F.*   29. Kind] *F;*
Klnd *Q1.*   31. Did challenge] *F;* Had challenged *Q.*   a face] face *F3–4.*
32. oppos'd] *F;* exposd *Q.*   warring] *Q;* iarring *F.*   33–6. To . . . helm?]
Q; not in F.   33. dread-bolted] *hyphened Theobald.*   35. *perdu]* Per du *Q;*
perdu! *Warburton.*   36. enemy's] *F;* iniurious *Q;* injurer's *Capell.*

24. *temperance*] sanity, normality.
25. *music*] Kittredge compares *Tp.*,
v. i. 58–9.
30. *white flakes*] snowy locks.
31. *challenge*] claim.
32. *warring*] The F reading, 'jarring',
was a mistake, the epithet being borrowed from l. 16 *ante.*
33. *deep*] bass.
    dread-bolted] furnished with the
dread thunder-bolt.
35. *perdu*] a sentry in a perilous position (*sentinelle perdue*). Cf. Tourneur,

The Atheist's Tragedy, II. vi. 4 (ed.
Nicoll, p. 210): 'I would you would
relieue me, for I am / So heauie that I
shall ha' much adoe / To stand out my
perdu.' Moberly suggests the word
means 'lost one'; and I think Shakespeare had the derivative meaning in
his mind.
36. *enemy's*] The Q reading 'iniurious' may be a misreading of *iniurers*,
and Capell's reading may be correct.
But, as Duthie points out, *iniurious* may
be a misreading of *enemies.*

Though he had bit me, should have stood that night
Against my fire. And wast thou fain, poor father,
To hovel thee with swine and rogues forlorn,
In short and musty straw? Alack, alack!   40
'Tis wonder that thy life and wits at once
Had not concluded all. He wakes; speak to him.
Doct. Madam, do you; 'tis fittest.
Cor. How does my royal Lord? How fares your Majesty?
Lear. You do me wrong to take me out o'th'grave;   45
    Thou art a soul in bliss; but I am bound
    Upon a wheel of fire, that mine own tears
    Do scald like molten lead.
Cor.   Sir, do you know me?
Lear. You are a spirit, I know; where did you die?
Cor. Still, still, far wide.   50
Doct. He's scarce awake; let him alone awhile.
Lear. Where have I been? Where am I? Fair daylight?
    I am mightily abus'd. I should e'en die with pity
    To see another thus. I know not what to say.
    I will not swear these are my hands: let's see;   55

41. thy] my *F3–4*.   43. *Doct.*] *Q; Gen. F.*   45. o'th'] *F;* ath *Q*.   48.
scald] *Q;* scal'd *F1*.   do . . . me?] *F;* know me *Q1;* know ye me? *Q2–3.*
49. You are] *F;* Yar *Q1;* Y'are *Q2–3.*   where] *Q1, F1–2;* when *Q2–3, F3–4.*
51. *Doct.*] *Q; Gent. F.*   53. e'en] even *F3–4.*

38. *Against*] before, opposite to.

39. *rogues*] vagabonds.

40. *short*] cut short for litter; scanty, insufficient; broken up into short lengths by constant use as bedding (Kittredge).

42. *all*] together.

47. *wheel of fire*] Lear thinks he is in hell. Cf. Appendix, p. 241. H. W. Crundell has pointed out to me that the torment of the wheel of fire, although not scriptural, is traditional in the medieval legends and visions of Hell and Purgatory. They all draw upon the New Testament Apocrypha. In *The Apocalypse of Peter*, the *Sibylline Oracles*, and *The Acts of Thomas*, the wheel of fire is the punishment inflicted upon the damned. Cf. M. R. James, *Apoc. N.T.*, pp. 390, 517, 525.

Owst, *Literature and Pulpit in Medieval England*, 1933, cites *The Pricke of Conscience*, 6576, 7124, which mentions scalding tears and molten lead. Holinshed discusses the authenticity of the stories of St Patrick's Purgatory, so we can assume that they were known to Shakespeare's contemporaries, though he probably derived his information from some intermediate source.

that] so that.

50. *wide*] astray, wandering. Cf. *Ado*, IV. i. 63.

53. *abus'd*] deluded. He thinks Cordelia must be an hallucination.

53–4. *I should . . . thus*] This is not to be taken as indulgence in self-pity, but as an objective statement to guide the audience in their emotional reactions.

I feel this pin prick. Would I were assur'd
Of my condition!

Cor.   O! look upon me, Sir,
And hold your hand in benediction o'er me.
No, Sir, you must not kneel.

Lear.   Pray, do not mock me:
I am a very foolish fond old man,   60
Fourscore and upward, not an hour more or less;
And, to deal plainly,
I fear I am not in my perfect mind.
Methinks I should know you and know this man;
Yet I am doubtful: for I am mainly ignorant   65
What place this is, and all the skill I have
Remembers not these garments; nor I know not
Where I did lodge last night. Do not laugh at me;
For, as I am a man, I think this lady
To be my child Cordelia.

Cor.   And so I am, I am.   70

Lear. Be your tears wet? Yes, faith. I pray, weep not:
If you have poison for me, I will drink it.
I know you do not love me; for your sisters
Have, as I do remember, done me wrong:
You have some cause, they have not.

Cor.   No cause, no cause.

Lear. Am I in France?

Kent.   In your own kingdom, Sir.   76

Lear. Do not abuse me.

Doct. Be comforted, good Madam; the great rage,
You see, is kill'd in him: and yet it is danger
To make him even o'er the time he has lost.   80

58. hand] *F*; hands *Q*.   59. No, Sir] *Q*; *not in F*.   me] *not in Q 1*.   61. not
. . . less] *F*; *not in Q*.   63. in . . . mind] perfect in my mind *Q 2–3*.   68. not]
no *Q 2–3*.   70. I am, I am] *F*; I am *Q*.   74. me] we *F 2*.   78. *Doct.*]
Q; *Gent. F.*   79. kill'd] *F*; cured *Q*; quell'd *conj. Collier.*   79–80. and . . .
lost] *Q*; *not in F*.

60. *fond*] in his dotage.

65. *mainly*] entirely.

69–70. *lady . . . child*] The contrast
between these two words indicates
Lear's return to sanity.

70. *I . . . am*] Ruskin, *Works*, ed.
1903, XIV. 17, remarks that 'all

Cordelia is poured forth in that
infinite "I am" of fulfilled love.'

77. *abuse*] deceive.

78. *rage*] frenzy, delirium.

80. *even o'er*] fill up the gap in; to
smooth over, render what had passed
unbroken in his recollection (Wright);

Desire him to go in; trouble him no more
Till further settling.

Cor. Will't please your Highness walk?

Lear.   You must bear with me.
Pray you now, forget and forgive: I am old and foolish.

       [Exeunt Lear, Cordelia, Doctor, and Attendants.

Gent. Holds it true, sir, that the Duke of Cornwall was so   85
    slain?

Kent. Most certain, sir.

Gent. Who is conductor of his people?

Kent. As 'tis said, the bastard son of Gloucester.

Gent. They say Edgar, his banish'd son, is with the Earl of   90
    Kent in Germany.

Kent. Report is changeable. 'Tis time to look about; the
    powers of the kingdom approach apace.

Gent. The arbitrement is like to be bloody. Fare you well,
    sir.   *[Exit.*   95

Kent. My point and period will be throughly wrought,
    Or well or ill, as this day's battle's fought.   *[Exit.*

---

83. Will't] *Rowe;* Wilt *Q, F.*   83–4. Will't . . . foolish] *as Capell; prose Q;
three lines, ending* me; / forgiue, / foolish. *F.*   84. you now] now *Q.*   S.D.]
Exeunt. Manet Kent, and Gent. Q; Exeunt F.   85–97.] *Q; not in F.*   85–
95. Holds . . . well, sir] *prose Q; verse Capell, lines ending* sir, / sir. / said, / Edgar, /
Kent, / changeable, / kingdom, / arbitrement, / sir. *Capell omits* that *(85), and* As
(89) and reads And the . . . most bloody *(94).*   92–5. Report . . . well, sir.]
prose Theobald; three lines, ending about, / apace, / sir. *Q.*   95. S.D.] *Theobald;
not in Q.*   97. S.D.] *Exit Q1; Exit Kent Theobald; not in Q2–3.*

Craig suggests the metaphor is taken
from the language of accountants, *to
even* means 'to make accounts even'.
Some take *even* to be an adj. and the
phrase might then mean 'precise
about', '*au fait* with'.

  82. *Till . . . settling*] till he is calmer.
Cf. *Wint.,* IV. iv. 482.

83. *walk*] withdraw.

85. *Holds it true*] is it still accepted.

88. *conductor*] leader, general.

94. *arbitrement*] decisive encounter.

96. *My . . . period*] my life's end and
object; the full-stop at the end of my
life's sentence.

ACT V

SCENE I.—[*The British Camp near Dover.*]

Enter, with drum and colours, EDMUND, REGAN, *Officers,*
Soldiers, and Others.

Edm. Know of the Duke if his last purpose hold,
Or whether since he is advis'd by aught
To change the course; he's full of alteration
And self-reproving; bring his constant pleasure.

> [*To an Officer, who goes out.*

Reg. Our sister's man is certainly miscarried.   5
Edm. 'Tis to be doubted, Madam.
Reg.   Now, sweet Lord,
You know the goodness I intend upon you:
Tell me, but truly, but then speak the truth,
Do you not love my sister?
Edm.   In honour'd love.
Reg. But have you never found my brother's way   10
To the forfended place?

ACT V
Scene 1

S.D. *Act V Scene* 1] *Act* IV *Scene* viii. *conj. Spedding.*   *The . . . Dover*] *Capell, subst.;*
not in Q, F; *A Camp Rowe.*   *Enter . . . Others*] *Enter . . . Regan, Gentlemen, and*
Souldiers F; *Enter Edmund, Regan, and their powers* Q.   3. *he's*] he is Q2–3.
alteration] abdication Q *uncorr.*   4. S.D.] *Capell, subst.; not in* Q, F.   8. *but*
truly] truly Q2–3.   9. In] F; I, Q1; I Q2–3.

1. *his last purpose*] i.e. to fight.
2. *advis'd*] induced.
3. *alteration*] vacillation.
4. *self-reproving*] self-reproach, con-
scientious scruples.
   constant pleasure] fixed decision. Cf.
I. i. 42.
   5. *man*] Oswald.
   miscarried] come to harm.

6. *doubted*] feared.
7. *intend . . . you*] mean to confer upon
you.
8. *but then*] even if the truth is un-
palatable to me.
9. *honour'd*] honourable.
11. *forfended*] forbidden. *Oth.*, v. ii.
32. Goneril's bed is forbidden by the
commandment against adultery.

Edm.   That thought abuses you.
Reg. I am doubtful that you have been conjunct
     And bosom'd with her, as far as we call hers.
Edm. No, by mine honour, Madam.
Reg. I never shall endure her: dear my Lord,   15
     Be not familiar with her.
Edm.   Fear me not.
     She and the Duke her husband!

     Enter, with drum and colours, ALBANY, GONERIL,
                    and Soldiers.

Gon. [*Aside.*] I had rather lose the battle than that sister
     Should loosen him and me.
Alb. Our very loving sister, well be-met.   20
     Sir, this I hear; the King is come to his daughter,
     With others whom the rigour of our state
     Forc'd to cry out. Where I could not be honest,
     I never yet was valiant: for this business,
     It touches us, as France invades our land,   25

11–13. *Edm.* That . . . hers] *Q; not in F.*   12–13. I am . . . hers] *as Q2–3;
prose Q1.*   15–16. I . . . her] *as F; prose Q1.*   16–17. Fear . . . husband!]
as Capell; one line Q, F.   16. me] *Q; not in F.*   17. S.D.] *F; Enter Albany
and Goneril with Troupes Q.*   18. S.D.] *Theobald; not in Q, F.*   18–19. I . . .
me] *arranged Theobald; prose Q1; two lines, divided after* battell *Q2–3; not in
F.*   19. loosen] cosin *Q3.*   21. Sir, this I hear] *Theobald;* Sir, this I heard
F; For this I heare *Q.*   23–8. Where . . . nobly] *Q; not in F.*   25. touches]
Q1; toucheth *Q2–3.*

12. *doubtful*] fearful.
conjunct] Cf. ii. ii. 115 (Q).
13. *bosom'd . . . her*] embraced her, breast to breast.
as . . . hers] in the fullest sense of the word, not merely in the sense of 'admitted to her confidence'.
15–17. *I . . . husband*] It is possible that 'I never shall endure her' should be given to Edmund (W. W. Lloyd, *N.Q.*, 11 June 1892) to complete line 14, that the rest of Regan's speech should be printed as a single line, and that Edmund's next speech should likewise be printed as one line. Otherwise we must take 'I never shall endure her' to mean 'I could never endure her to loosen you and me.'

Cf. Goneril's words, ll. 18–19, *post.*
16. *Fear me not*] Don't distrust me, don't worry about me on that account. F omits the pronoun, probably by accident.
18–19. *lose . . . loosen*] The Q spelling 'loose' brings out the quibble.
20. *be-met*] met.
22. *rigour of our state*] harshness of our rule.
23–8. *Where . . . nobly*] These lines are omitted in F, perhaps because they related to the French invasion; but it seems probable that the Q text is corrupt.
23. *Where*] in a case where.
24. *for*] as for.
25. *touches*] concerns.

Not bolds the King, with others, whom, I fear,
Most just and heavy causes make oppose.
Edm. Sir, you speak nobly.
Reg.   Why is this reason'd?
Gon. Combine together 'gainst the enemy;
For these domestic and particular broils   30
Are not the question here.
Alb.   Let's then determine
With th'ancient of war on our proceeding.
Edm. I shall attend you presently at your tent.
Reg. Sister, you'll go with us?
Gon. No.   35
Reg. 'Tis most convenient; pray go with us.
Gon. [*Aside.*] O, ho! I know the riddle. I will go.

As they are going out enter EDGAR, *disguised.*

26. Not bolds the] *Q; Not the old conj. Mason;* Not holds the *Pope.*   30. and...
broils] *F;* dore particulars *Q1;* doore particulars *Q2-3;* dear particulars *Ridley.*
31. the] *F;* to *Q.*   31-2. Let's ... proceeding] *arranged Q2-3; prose Q1;*
first line ends warre *F.*   32. proceeding] *F;* proceedings *Q.*   33. *Edm.* I ...
tent] *Q; not in F.*   36. pray] *F;* pray you *Q.*   37. *Aside*] *Capell; the whole*
line aside, Hanmer.   As ... disguised] *Theobald; Enter Edgar Q1; Exit. Enter*
Edgar Q2-3; Exeunt both the Armies; Enter Edgar F.

26-7. *Not ... oppose*] not because he
emboldens by supporting the King
and others who have been induced to
take up arms against us by genuine
grievances. This is presumably the
meaning, but the passage may be
corrupt. The repetition 'with others
whom' from l. 22 is suspicious, and
l. 27 seems to be a restatement of 'the
rigour ... out'. It is possible that a line
or two has dropped out before l. 26,
and that Albany said originally: 'We
intend to repel the invader, but not to
treat the King and his supporters as
enemies.'
26. *bolds*] emboldens, encourages,
supports. Cf. Wyatt, *Poems*, ed. Muir,
p. 43: 'And therwithall bolded I seke
the way how / To vtter the smert that
I suffre within.'
27. *heavy causes*] weighty reasons.
28. *reason'd*] mentioned. 'Why do
you want to waste time thus in arguing
with yourself about the justice of our
cause?' (Kittredge).

30. *and ... broils*] and private
quarrels. But this may well be a F
sophistication. Steevens interprets the
Q reading 'particulars at our very
doors'; but Malone, rightly I believe,
suspects that 'dore' is a misprint
for 'dear' (spelt 'dere' presumably),
the phrase meaning 'intimate details' rather than 'important quarrels', which is Malone's interpretation.
32. *th'ancient of war*] experienced
officers, 'brass-hats'.
33. *presently*] at once.
36. *convenient*] befitting.
37. *O ... go*] This may mean 'You
want to keep me under your eye so as
to observe my relations with Edmund';
or, 'You don't want me to attend the
council of war, where I shall be close
to Edmund.' If Regan was herself
going to attend the council, we must
assume that she did not wish to leave
Goneril behind with Edmund even for
a moment.

Edg. If e'er your grace had speech with man so poor,
　　Hear me one word.
Alb.　　　　　　　　I'll overtake you.
　　　　　　　[*Exeunt Edmund, Regan, Goneril, Officers,*
　　　　　　　　　　　　Soldiers, and Attendants.
　　　　　　　　　　　Speak.
Edg. Before you fight the battle, ope this letter.　　　　40
　　If you have victory, let the trumpet sound
　　For him that brought it: wretched though I seem,
　　I can produce a champion that will prove
　　What is avouched there. If you miscarry,
　　Your business of the world hath so an end,　　　　45
　　And machination ceases. Fortune love you!
Alb. Stay till I have read the letter.
Edg.　　　　　　　　　　I was forbid it.
　　When time shall serve, let but the herald cry,
　　And I'll appear again.
Alb.　　　　　　Why, fare thee well:
　　I will o'erlook thy paper.　　　　　[*Exit Edgar.* 50

Re-enter EDMUND.

Edm. The enemy's in view; draw up your powers.
　　Here is the guess of their true strength and forces
　　By diligent discovery; but your haste
　　Is now urged on you.
Alb.　　　　　　We will greet the time.　　[*Exit.*
Edm. To both these sisters have I sworn my love;　　55
　　Each jealous of the other, as the stung
　　Are of the adder. Which of them shall I take?

---

38. had] did *Q3.*　　man] one *Q2–3.*　　39. S.D.] *Theobald; see note to 37
above.*　　42. wretched] wretch *F2–4.*　　though] thoughts *Q3.*　　46. And
... ceases] *F; not in Q.*　　love] *Q;* loues *F.*　　49–50. Why . . . paper]
arranged as conj. S. Walker; one line Q, F.　　50. o'erlook] look ore *Q2–3.*　　thy]
F; the *Q.*　　S.D.] *Dyce; Exit after* again (*49*) *Q, F.*　　52. Here] *F;* hard
Q.　　guess] quesse *Q1.*　　54. S.D.] *not in Q2–3.*　　55. sisters] sister *Q1.*
56. stung] sting *Q.*

---

44. *avouched*] maintained.
miscarry] lose the battle, and perish.
46. *machination*] Cf. I. ii. 109–10.
50. *o'erlook*] peruse.
51. *powers*] troops.

53. *By ... discovery*] obtained by careful reconnoitring.
54. *greet the time*] meet the emer-
gency.
56. *jealous*] suspicious.

Both? one? or neither? Neither can be enjoy'd
If both remain alive: to take the widow
Exasperates, makes mad her sister Goneril;   60
And hardly shall I carry out my side,
Her husband being alive. Now then, we'll use
His countenance for the battle; which being done,
Let her who would be rid of him devise
His speedy taking off. As for the mercy   65
Which he intends to Lear and to Cordelia,
The battle done, and they within our power,
Shall never see his pardon; for my state
Stands on me to defend, not to debate.   [*Exit.*

SCENE II.—[*A Field between the two Camps.*]

Alarum within. Enter, with drum and colours, LEAR,
CORDELIA, *and their Forces; and exeunt.*

Enter EDGAR *and* GLOUCESTER.

Edg. Here, father, take the shadow of this tree

64. who] *F; that Q.*   65. the] *F; his Q.*   66. intends] *F;* entends *Q1*
extends *Q2–3.*

Scene II

S.D. *A . . . Camps*] Capell, subst.; not in Q, F.   *Alarum . . . exeunt*] F, subst.
Alarum. Enter the powers of France over the stage, Cordelia with her father in her hand Q.
1. tree] *F;* bush *Q.*

61. *carry . . . side*] make my game,
succeed in my ambitions. This is the
usual explanation, the image being
taken from a game of cards. But another explanation is possible, i.e. 'ful-
fil my side of the bargain with Goneril
—satisfy her lust in return for advancement'.
    63. *countenance*] authority, credit.
    65. *taking off*] killing. Cf. *Mac.*, I.
vii. 20.
    68. *Shall*] they shall.
    68–9. *for . . . debate*] I must take
active steps to maintain my position,
not merely think about it. Edmund
hopes that Goneril will kill Albany,
and kill, or be killed by, Regan, leaving

him free to marry the survivor. The
survival of Lear and Cordelia would
prejudice his chances of becoming
king of the united kingdom.
    69. *Stands on me*] concerns me much.
Cf. *Err.*, IV. i. 68, and *Ham.*, v. ii. 63.

Scene II

Spedding, *New Shakespeare Society
Transactions*, 1877–9, p. 11, argues that
as the battle is inadequately described,
Shakespeare must have intended the
fourth act to end after l. 4 of this scene.
This would make Act IV extremely
long, and the shortness of this scene
may be rather explained as an example of dramatic economy, since the

For your good host; pray that the right may thrive.
If ever I return to you again,
I'll bring you comfort.

Glou.   Grace go with you, sir!

[*Exit Edgar.*

Alarum; afterwards a retreat. Re-enter EDGAR.

Edg. Away, old man! give me thy hand: away!   5
King Lear hath lost, he and his daughter ta'en.
Give me thy hand; come on.

Glou. No further, sir; a man may rot even here.

Edg. What! in ill thoughts again? Men must endure
Their going hence, even as their coming hither: 10
Ripeness is all. Come on.

Glou.   And that's true too. [*Exeunt.*

---

4. go] be *F3–4.*   *Exit Edgar*] *Pope; Exit F, (after* comfort) *Q.   Re-enter Edgar*] *Enter Edgar F; not in Q1.*   8. further] *F;* farther *Q.*   9. What . . . endure] *one line Q; two in F.*   11. *Glou.* And . . . too] *not in Q.*   *Exeunt*] *F; Exit Q2–3; not in Q1.*

battle itself is not important. We are only interested in the result of the battle. In *Macbeth* and *Antony and Cleopatra* the battles are important since the heroes of both plays are soldiers.

2. *good host*] shelterer, entertainer.

3–4. *If . . . comfort*] dramatic irony. Cf. l. 5.

11. *Ripeness is all*] The one important thing with regard to death is that we should be ready for it. Steevens compares *Ham.*, v. ii. 234. The aphorism reads like a condensation of Montaigne's essay, 'That to philosophie is to learne how to die'. He discusses life's 'ordinary mutations' which reconcile us to death (*op. cit.*, I. 105; cf. IV. i. 11); he compares death with birth: 'So wept we, and so much did it cost us to enter into this life; and so did we spoile us of our ancient vaile in entring into it' (*op. cit.*, I. 107–8; cf. v. ii. 9–10); and he concludes that the actual length of our lives is unimportant: 'It consists not in number of

yeeres, but in your will, that you have lived long enough' (*op. cit.*, p. 112). In Elyot, *The Gouernour*, I. xxii (Everyman ed., p. 98), there is a discussion of Maturity: 'Maturitic is a mean betweene two extremities, wherein nothynge lacketh or exceedeth, and is in such a state that it may neyther encrease nor minysshe without losinge the denomination of Maturitie . . . *Maturum* in latyn maye be enterpretid ripe or redy, as fruite when it is ripe, it is at the very poynte to be gathered and eaten. . . Therefore that word maturitie, is translated to the actis of man, that whan they be done with suche moderation, that nothing in the doing may be sene superfluous or indigent, we may saye, that they be maturely doone: reseruyng the wordes rype and redy to frute and other things separate from affaires, as we haue nowe in usage.' Cf. Edgar's phrase 'mature time' (IV. vi. 272), and *Meas.*, v. i. 116, 'ripened time'.

SCENE III.—[*The British Camp near Dover.*]

Enter, in conquest, with drum and colours, EDMUND, LEAR
and CORDELIA, *prisoners; Officers, Soldiers, etc.*

Edm. Some officers take them away: good guard,
  Until their greater pleasures first be known
  That are to censure them.

Cor.   We are not the first
  Who, with best meaning, have incurr'd the worst.
  For thee, oppressed King, I am cast down;   5
  Myself could else out-frown false Fortune's frown.
  Shall we not see these daughters and these sisters?

Lear. No, no, no, no! Come, let's away to prison;
  We two alone will sing like birds i'th'cage:
  When thou dost ask me blessing, I'll kneel down,   10
  And ask of thee forgiveness: so we'll live,
  And pray, and sing, and tell old tales, and laugh
  At gilded butterflies, and hear poor rogues
  Talk of court news; and we'll talk with them too,
  Who loses and who wins; who's in, who's out;   15

Scene III

S.D. *The . . . Dover*] Malone; *not in Q, F.*   *Enter . . . Soldiers, etc.*] Capell, subst.;
Enter . . . Souldiers, Captaine F; Enter Edmund with Lear and Cordelia prisoners Q.
2. first] *F;* best *Q.*   5. I am] *F, Q3;* am I *Q1-2.*   8. No . . . no!] *F;* no,
no *Q.*   12. and sing] *Q1, F; not in Q2-3.*   13. hear poor rogues] heere
(poore Rogues) *F1;* hear—poor rogues!— *Schmidt.*   14. talk] talkd *F2.*
15. who's . . . who's] *F;* whose . . . whose *Q.*

2. *greater pleasures*] wishes of the
people of greater authority.

3. *censure*] judge, pass judgment on.
Cf. *Meas.*, I. iv. 72.

6. *Myself . . . frown*] Cf. Seneca,
Œdipus, I. i (tr. Nevile): '*Joc.* It is no
poinct of courage stout to yeelde to
fortunes frown. / *Œed.* Nay. Feare
could never cause mee stoupe nor
Fortune cast mee down.'

9. *cage*] a quibble, since the word
also means prison. Cf. *2H6*, IV. ii. 56.
Maxwell compares Spenser, *F.Q.*,
VI. vi. 4, 9.

10. *I'll . . . down*] Shakespeare
was probably thinking of the scene
in the source-play. See Appendix, p.
219.

12. *old tales*] improbable fictions of
bygone times. Cf. *Wint.*, v. ii. 66, and
AYL., I. ii. 128.

13. *gilded butterflies*] Craig suggests
that this means 'gay courtiers' as in
Marston's *Antonio and Mellida*, IV. i. 49:
'Troopes of pide butterflies, that
flutter still / In greatnesse summer,
that confirme a prince'. But it is more
likely that Lear is referring to actual
butterflies, the other meaning merely
suggesting the 'court news' in the
following line.

poor rogues] wretched creatures, presumably their fellow-prisoners or
jailers. In the F this phrase is in
parenthesis and must refer to Lear and
Cordelia.

And take upon's the mystery of things,
As if we were Gods' spies: and we'll wear out,
In a wall'd prison, packs and sects of great ones
That ebb and flow by th'moon.

Edm.   Take them away.

Lear. Upon such sacrifices, my Cordelia,   20
The Gods themselves throw incense. Have I caught
  thee?
He that parts us shall bring a brand from heaven,
And fire us hence like foxes. Wipe thine eyes;
The good years shall devour them, flesh and fell,

19. th'moon] *F;* the moon *Q2–3.*   23. eyes] eye *F2–4.*   24. good years] *F;*
good *Q;* goodjers *Theobald;* goujeres *Hanmer.*   them] em *Q.*   flesh] *F;*
fleach *Q.*

16. *take upon*] profess to understand
and explain.

the . . . things] the mysterious course
of worldly events, the mystery of
human life and destiny. Cf. the use of
res in Latin poetry; e.g. Virgil,
Georgics, ii. 490; Ovid, *Metamorphoses,*
xv. 68. G. C. Taylor compares Florio,
op. cit., iii. 368: 'These people . . . who
know nothing themselves, and yet will
take upon them to governe the world
and know all: . . . What cause doth
calme the Sea, what cleares the
yeare, . . . / What makes the Moones
darke Orbe to wax or wane, / What
friendly fewd of things both will and
can'.

17. *Gods'*] There is no apostrophe in
F or Q, and I follow Perrett in assuming that Shakespeare intended the
plural since he was writing of a pagan
world.

spies] This may mean 'angels commissioned to survey and report the
lives of men' (Johnson). Warburton,
less plausibly, explains: 'spies placed
on God Almighty to watch his
motions'.

18. *packs and sects*] cliques and
parties.

20. *such sacrifices*] as their renuncia-
tion of the world (Bradley); as those
Cordelia has made for Lear's sake
(Kittredge). I think Bradley is right;

but there seems also to be an underlying suggestion of human sacrifice,
which looks forward to the murder of
Cordelia. In an old note-book I have
found the suggestion, perhaps based
on T. Carter's *Shakespeare and Holy
Scriptures,* p. 442, that underlying
Lear's speech there are echoes of
several Old Testament stories—of
Jephthah's daughter, who was sacrificed, and of the destruction of Sodom
by a brand from heaven, of Samson
and the foxes, of Pharoah's dream of
the good and bad years.

21. *incense*] R. W. Chambers compares Wisdom, iii. 6.

Have . . . thee?] Cf. *Wiv.,* iii. iii. 45.
Falstaff is quoting from the second
song in Sidney's *Astrophel and Stella.*

22. *He . . . heaven*] We can never be
parted again by human agency.

23. *fire . . . foxes*] as foxes were driven
from their holes by fire and smoke.
Cf. the Harsnett parallel, Appendix,
p. 241.

24. *good years*] Cf. *Ado,* i. iii. 1; *2H4,*
ii. iv. 64, 191. See also Golding, *op.
cit.,* iii. 319: 'And what a goodyeare
have I won by scolding erst (she sed).'
The word *goodyear* 'came to be used in
imprecatory phrases, as denoting
some undefined malefic power or
agency' (*N.E.D.*). It may be derived
from the Dutch phrase 'wat goet iaer

Ere they shall make us weep: we'll see 'em starv'd
    first.   25
  Come.   [*Exeunt Lear and Cordelia, guarded.*
Edm. Come hither, captain; hark.
  Take thou this note;   [*Giving a paper.*
    Go follow them to prison.
One step I have advanc'd thee; if thou dost
As this instructs thee, thou dost make thy way   30
To noble fortunes; know thou this, that men
Are as the time is; to be tender-minded
Does not become a sword; thy great employment
Will not bear question; either say thou'lt do't,
Or thrive by other means.
Offi.   I'll do't, my Lord.   35
Edm. About it; and write happy when th'hast done.
  Mark,—I say, instantly, and carry it so
  As I have set it down.

25. 'em] *Q3, F3–4;* e'm *F1–2;* vm *Q1;* em *Q2.*   starv'd] *F;* starue *Q.*
26. Come] *not in Q2–3.*   S.D.] *Theobald; Exit F, Q2–3; not in Q1.*   28.
S.D.] *Malone.*   29. One] And *Q uncorr.*   32. tender-minded] *hyphened*
Rowe.   33. thy] my *Theobald.*   36. th'hast] *F;* thou hast *Q.*

is dat.' Florio translates 'Il mal anno
che dio ti dia' as 'With a good yeare to
thee!' According to Morwenstow
(*N.Q.*, v. 607, 1852) the Goujere is the
old Cornish name of the Fiend, and
this meaning was confirmed later
(*N.Q.*, 11 March 1876). Croft fantastically interprets as *gougers*, those
who gouge out people's eyes. (There is
no evidence that Lear had heard of
Cornwall's brutality to Gloucester,
though he knew Gloucester had lost
his eyes.) Nor is there any substance in
Hanmer's emendation, *goujeres* (i.e.
the pox), a word he ingeniously but
inadmissibly derived from the Fr.
gouje (defined by Cotgrave as 'a Souldiers Pug or Punke; a Whore that
followes the Camp'). In Pharaoh's
dream (Genesis, xli) the thin ears that
devoured the seven good ears symbolized seven years of famine; and the
words 'devour' (24) and 'starv'd' (25)
suggest that the story of Joseph was,
vaguely, at the back of Shakespeare's

mind. Lear may mean that Goneril
and Regan will be destroyed not by
misfortunes but by their evil prosperity, and till the day of their ruin he
and Cordelia will not deign to weep.
When Lear does weep next Goneril
and Regan are both dead.

flesh and fell] flesh and skin, i.e.
altogether.

33. *sword*] one who wields a sword,
a soldier.

34. *Will . . . question*] will not admit
discussion; either because it must be
done promptly, or because it is too
delicate a matter to be expressed in
words. Ragan (*King Leir*, 1309–10)
when bribing a man to murder Leir,
says: 'It is a thing of right strange consequence, / And well I cannot vtter it
in words.'

36. *write happy*] style yourself
happy.

37. *carry it so*] manage the affair in
such a way that it will appear that
Cordelia slew herself.

Offi. I cannot draw a cart nor eat dried oats;
    If it be man's work I'll do't.   [*Exit.* 40

    Flourish. Enter ALBANY, GONERIL, REGAN, *Officers,*
                and Soldiers.

Alb. Sir, you have show'd to-day your valiant strain,
    And Fortune led you well; you have the captives
    Who were the opposites of this day's strife;
    I do require them of you, so to use them
    As we shall find their merits and our safety   45
    May equally determine.
Edm.   Sir, I thought it fit
    To send the old and miserable King
    To some retention and appointed guard;
    Whose age had charms in it, whose title more,
    To pluck the common bosom on his side,   50
    And turn our impress'd lances in our eyes
    Which do command them. With him I sent the
        Queen;
    My reason all the same; and they are ready
    To-morrow, or at further space, t'appear
    Where you shall hold your session. At this time   55
    We sweat and bleed; the friend hath lost his friend,
    And the best quarrels, in the heat, are curs'd

39–40. I . . . do't] *Q; not in F.*   40. *Exit*] *Steevens; Exit Captaine F; not in
Q.*   *Flourish . . . Officers, and Soldiers*] *Flourish . . . another Captain, Soldiers F;
Enter Duke, the two Ladies, and others Q.*   41. show'd] *Q1, F;* shewne *Q2–3.*
43. Who] *F;* That *Q.*   44. I] *F;* We *Q.*   require them] *F;* require
then *Q.*   47. send] saue *Q uncorr.*   48. and . . . guard] *Q corr., Q2–3;
not in Q uncorr., F.*   49. had] *F;* has *Q.*   50. common] coren *Q uncorr.*
bosom] blossomes *Q2–3.*   on] *F;* of *Q.*   54. at] at a *Q2–3.*   t'appear]
F; to appeare *Q.*   55–60. At . . . place] *Q; not in F.*   56. We] *Q corr.,
Q2–3;* mee *Q uncorr.*

39. *I . . . oats*] I'm not a horse. I don't
want to be driven by necessity after
the war to become an agricultural
labourer.

41. *strain*] lineage, or, more probably
here, disposition.

43. *opposites*] opponents, enemies.

45. *merits*] deserts.

48. *retention*] confinement.

49. *Whose*] i.e. the King's.

50. *To . . . side*] win the hearts of the
common people.

51. *impress'd lances*] conscripted
lances, i.e. soldiers.

57. *quarrels*] causes.

in the heat] before passion has
cooled. Edmund is implying that
Lear and Cordelia would not get
a fair trial under the circumstances.

By those that feel their sharpness;
The question of Cordelia and her father
Requires a fitter place.
Alb.   Sir, by your patience,   60
I hold you but a subject of this war,
Not as a brother.
Reg.   That's as we list to grace him;
Methinks our pleasure might have been demanded,
Ere you had spoke so far. He led our powers,
Bore the commission of my place and person;   65
The which immediacy may well stand up,
And call itself your brother.
Gon.   Not so hot;
In his own grace he doth exalt himself
More than in your addition.
Reg.   In my rights,
By me invested, he compeers the best.   70
Alb. That were the most, if he should husband you.
Reg. Jesters do oft prove prophets.
Gon.   Holla, holla!
That eye that told you so look'd but a-squint.
Reg. Lady, I am not well; else I should answer
From a full-flowing stomach. General,   75
Take thou my soldiers, prisoners, patrimony;
Dispose of them, of me; the walls are thine;

58. sharpness] *Q corr., Q2–3;* sharpes *Q uncorr.*   63. might] *F;* should *Q.*
66. immediacy] *F;* imediate *Q.*   69. addition] *F;* aduancement *Q.*   rights]
F; right *Q.*   71. *Alb.] F; Gon. Q.*   73. a-squint] *hyphened Rowe.*   75. full-
flowing] *hyphened Theobald.*   77. Dispose . . . thine] *F; not in Q.*   the . . .
thine] *F;* they are all thine *Hanmer (conj. Theobald).*   are] *F2–4;* is *F1.*

58. *sharpness*] Greg argues that
sharpes may be the correct reading.
    62. *list*] wish.
    64. *spoke so far*] said so much.
    66. *immediacy*] Johnson says this
means 'supremacy in opposition to
subordination'; but it means more
probably 'being my immediate representative'.
    69. *your addition*] the titles and
offices you have bestowed upon him.
    70. *compeers*] equals.

72. *Jesters . . . prophets*] There's many
a true word spoken in jest.
    73. *That . . . a-squint*] Steevens com-
pares the proverb: 'Love being jealous,
makes a good eye look a-squint.'
    75. *From a full-flowing stomach*] with a
flood of angry words. 'Stomach' often
means 'anger'. Cf. *Tim.,* III. i. 234.
    77. *the walls . . . thine*] Theobald pro-
posed 'they all are thine.' Kinnear
suggested 'the whole is thine.' Wright
thinks it may refer to Regan's castle

Witness the world, that I create thee here
My lord and master.
Gon.   Mean you to enjoy him?
Alb. The let-alone lies not in your good will.   80
Edm. Nor in thine, Lord.
Alb.   Half-blooded fellow, yes.
Reg. [*To Edmund.*] Let the drum strike, and prove my
          title thine.
Alb. Stay yet; hear reason. Edmund, I arrest thee
On capital treason; and, in thy attaint,
This gilded serpent.   [*Pointing to Goneril.*
                        For your claim, fair sister,   85
I bar it in the interest of my wife;
'Tis she is sub-contracted to this lord,
And I, her husband, contradict your banes.
If you will marry, make your loves to me,
My lady is bespoke.
Gon.   An interlude!   90
Alb. Thou art arm'd, Gloucester; let the trumpet sound:
If none appear to prove upon thy person
Thy heinous, manifest, and many treasons,
There is my pledge;   [*Throws down a glove.*
                        I'll make it on thy heart,

---

79. him] *F;* him then *Q.*   80. let-alone] *hyphened Capell.*   82. *Reg.*] *F; Bast.*
Q.   S.D.] *Malone; not in Q, F.*   thine] *F;* good *Q.*   84. thy] *F;* thine *Q.*
attaint] *Q;* arrest *F.*   85. S.D.] *Johnson; not in Q, F.*   sister] *Q;* Sisters *F.*
86. bar] *Rowe;* bare *Q, F.*   87. this] her *Q2–3.*   88. your] *F;* the *Q.*
banes] *Q, F;* bans *Malone.*   89. loves] *F;* loue *Q.*   90–1. *Gon.* An interlude!
Alb.] *F; not in Q.*   91. let ... sound] *F; not in Q.*   92. person] *F;* head *Q.*
94. S.D.] *Malone, subst.; not in Q, F.*   make] *F;* proue *Q.*

(cf. 244 *post*). Steevens cites *Cym.*, II. i. 68: 'the walls of thy dear honour' and Schmidt thinks it refers to Regan's person, which surrenders itself like a vanquished fortress. This is obviously correct, and, as Kittredge points out, a woman's heart was often compared to a fortress, long before Shakespeare's time.

80. *The let-alone*] the power of saying 'Thou shalt not'.

81. *Half-blooded fellow*] bastard.

82. *strike*] strike up.

84. *attaint*] impeachment. The F reading 'arrest' was copied by mistake from the previous line.

85. *gilded*] superficially beautiful.

88. *banes*] banns.

90. *interlude*] play. Cf. *Cym.*, V. v. 228.

94. *pledge*] gage.

make] show or allege that something is the case (*N.E.D.*). Duthie suggests the Q reading may be either a synonym-substitution or else a memorial corruption. Cf. 92 *ante*, and 139 *post*.

Ere I taste bread, thou art in nothing less   95
Than I have here proclaim'd thee.
Reg.   Sick! O, sick!
Gon. [*Aside.*] If not, I'll ne'er trust medicine.
Edm. There's my exchange: [*Throws down a glove.*
                    What in the world he is
That names me traitor, villain-like he lies.
Call by the trumpet: he that dares approach,   100
On him, on you, who not? I will maintain
My truth and honour firmly.
Alb.   A herald, ho!
Trust to thy single virtue; for thy soldiers,
All levied in my name, have in my name
Took their discharge.
Reg.   My sickness grows upon me.   105
Alb. She is not well; convey her to my tent.   [*Exit Regan, led.*

Enter a Herald.

Come hither, herald,—Let the trumpet sound,—
And read out this.
Offi. Sound, trumpet!   [*A trumpet sounds.*
Her. [*Reads.*] *If any man of quality or degree within the lists* 110
of the army will maintain upon Edmund, supposed Earl of
Gloucester, that he is a manifold traitor, let him appear by
the third sound of the trumpet. He is bold in his defence.
Sound!   [*First trumpet.*

97. S.D.] *Rowe; not in* Q, F.   medicine] *F;* poyson Q.   98. S.D.] *Malone,*
subst.; not in Q, F.   he is] *Q;* hes *F1.*   100. the] *F;* thy Q.   102.] *After*
this line Q *inserts: Bast.* A Herald ho, a Herald.   103. virtue] vertues *F3–4.*
105. My] *F;* This Q.   106. *Exit . . . led*] *Theobald; not in* Q, F.   *Enter*
a Herald] after firmly (*102*) *F; not in* Q.   107. trumpet] Trumper *F1.*   109.
Offi.] *Capell; Cap.* Q.   Sound, trumpet!] *Q; not in* F.   S.D.] *F; not in* Q.
110. S.D.] *F; not in* Q.   110. *within the lists*] *F;* in the hoast Q.   112. *he is*] *F;*
he's Q.   by] *F;* at Q.   114–16. Sound . . . Again!] *Jennens, Duthie; Bast.*
Sound? Againe? *Q; Her.* Againe. *Her.* Againe. *F.*

97. *medicine*] a euphemism for poison.
98. *exchange*] glove thrown down in exchange; the technical term.
101. *maintain*] justify.
103. *virtue*] valour, Lat. *virtus.*

112. manifold] Cf. *Tp.*, v. i. 295.
114–16. *Sound . . . Again!*] It is better to give to the Herald all these instructions to the trumpeter, rather than to give the first to Edmund (as in Q). If the Herald calls for the second and

Again!   [*Second trumpet.*   115
Again!   [*Third trumpet.*
                                [*Trumpet answers within.*

Enter EDGAR, *armed, with a trumpet before him.*

Alb. Ask him his purposes, why he appears
    Upon this call o'th'trumpet.
Her.   What are you?
    Your name? your quality? and why you answer
    This present summons?
Edg.   Know, my name is lost;   120
    By treason's tooth bare-gnawn, and canker-bit:
    Yet am I noble as the adversary
    I come to cope.
Alb.   Which is that adversary?
Edg. What's he that speaks for Edmund Earl of
      Gloucester?
Edm. Himself: what say'st thou to him?
Edg.   Draw thy sword,
    That, if my speech offend a noble heart,   126
    Thy arm may do thee justice; here is mine:
    Behold, it is the privilege of mine honours,
    My oath, and my profession: I protest,
    Maugre thy strength, place, youth, and eminence,   130

---

115. S.D.] *not in Q.*   116. Third . . . within] *F; not in Q .   Enter . . . him.*]
Enter Edgar at the third sound, a trumpet before him Q; Enter Edgar armed F.
119. your] *F; and Q.*   120. Know] *F; O know Q.*   lost;] *Theobald;*
lost *Q.*   121. tooth] *Theobald;* tooth: *F, Q2–3;* tooth. *Q1.*   122. Yet
. . . as] *F;* yet are I mou't where is *Q1;* where is *Q2–3.*   123. cope] *F;*
cope with all *Q.*   Which] What *Q2–3.*   127. Thy] *F;* thine *Q.*   128.
the . . . honours] *Pope;* the priuiledge of my tongue *Q;* my priuiledge, The
priuiledge of mine Honours *F.*   129. and my] and *Q2–3.*   130. place,
youth] *F;* youth, place *Q.*

third blasts, he should also call for the
first, as Jennens points out.
    116. S.D. with . . . him] preceded by
a trumpeter.
    121. *canker-bit*] eaten by the cater-
pillar, withered.
    123. *cope*] encounter.
    128. *Behold . . . honours*] It is the
privilege of my knighthood to draw

my sword, as this which you now behold, for the purpose of challenging a
traitor, and it is my privilege to have
such a challenge accepted.
    129. *My . . . profession*] of the oath I
swore when I was made a knight, and
of my knighthood itself.
    130. *Maugre*] in spite of. Cf. *Tw.N.,*
III. i. 163.

Despite thy victor sword and fire-new fortune,
Thy valour and thy heart, thou art a traitor,
False to thy gods, thy brother, and thy father,
Conspirant 'gainst this high illustrious prince,
And, from th'extremest upward of thy head　　　135
To the descent and dust below thy foot,
A most toad-spotted traitor. Say thou 'No,'
This sword, this arm, and my best spirits are bent
To prove upon thy heart, whereto I speak,
Thou liest.

Edm.　　　　　In wisdom I should ask thy name;　　　140
But since thy outside looks so fair and war-like,
And that thy tongue some say of breeding breathes,
What safe and nicely I might well delay
By rule of knighthood, I disdain and spurn;
Back do I toss these treasons to thy head,　　　145
With the hell-hated lie o'erwhelm thy heart,
Which, for they yet glance by and scarcely bruise,

---

131. Despite] Despise *F.*　　　victor sword] *Capell;* victor-Sword *F;* victor,
sword *Q.*　　　fire-new] *hyphened Rowe.*　　　fortune] *F;* fortun'd *Q.*　　　133. thy
gods] the gods *Q2–3.*　　　134. Conspirant] *F;* Conspicuate *Q.*　　　136. below
thy foot] *F;* beneath thy feet *Q.*　　　138. are] *F;* As *Q1;* Is *Q2–3.*　　　140.
should] *F;* sholud *Q1.*　　　142. tongue] *F;* being *Q.*　　　143. What . . . delay]
F; not in Q.　　　144. rule] *F;* right *Q.*　　　145. Back . . . head] *not in Q2–3.*
Back] Heere *Q1.*　　　these] *F;* those *Q1.*　　　146. hell-hated lie] *F;* hell
hatedly *Q.*　　　o'erwhelm] *F;* oreturnd *Q.*　　　147. scarcely] scarely *F1.*

131. *victor*] victorious.

fire-new] brand new, straight from
the forge or mint. Cf. *Tw.N.*, III. ii. 23.

132. *heart*] courage. Cf. *Cor.*, v. vi.
99.

134. *Conspirant*] conspirator, or con-
spiring. The word is used as a sub-
stantive by Harsnett, *op. cit.*, p. 19.

135. *upward*] top. Cf. *Tp.*, I. ii. 50
('backward') and *Cym.*, III. iv. 6 ('in-
ward') for a similar use of adjectives as
substantives.

136. *descent*] the lowest part, i.e. the
sole.

137. *toad-spotted*] stained with in-
famy, as a toad is spotted and veno-
mous. Cf. *R2*, III. ii. 134, and *AYL.*, II. i.
13. Cotgrave defines *tache* as 'spotted,
stained . . . disgraced'.

140. *In wisdom*] because he was not
bound to fight with a man of lower
rank. Cf. v. iii. 151–2 *post.*

142. *say*] smack, taste, proof.

143. *safe and nicely*] cautiously and
punctiliously, with the letter of the
law on my side.

delay] postpone; or 'refuse'
(Schmidt).

144. *I . . . spurn*] i.e. I scorn to insist
on my legal rights under the code of
knighthood. Edmund changes the
construction in the middle of the
sentence.

146. *hell-hated*] hated as much as
hell.

147. *Which*] these treasons.

for] since.

glance] glide.

This sword of mine shall give them instant way,
Where they shall rest for ever. Trumpets, speak.

           [*Alarums. They fight. Edmund falls.*

Alb. Save him! save him!

Gon.   This is practice, Gloucester: 150
By th'law of war thou wast not bound to answer
An unknown opposite; thou art not vanquish'd,
But cozen'd and beguil'd.

Alb.   Shut your mouth, dame,
Or with this paper shall I stople it. Hold, sir;
Thou worse than any name, read thine own evil: 155
No tearing, lady; I perceive you know it.

Gon. Say, if I do, the laws are mine, not thine:
Who can arraign me for't?

Alb.   Most monstrous! O!
Know'st thou this paper?

Gon.   Ask me not what I know. [*Exit.*

---

149. S.D.] *Capell; Alarums. Fights. F; no* †*in Q.*   150.] *See note below.*   practice] *F; meere practise Q.*   151. th'] *F; the Q.*   war] *F; arms Q.*   wast] *F; art Q.*   answer] *offer Q2–3.*   153. Shut] *F; Stop Q.*   154. stople] *Q1; stop Q2–3, F.*   Hold, sir] *F; not in Q.*   155. name] *F; thing Q.*   156. No] *F; Nay no Q.*   158. can] *F; shal Q.*   O] *F; not in Q.*   158–9. Most . . . Know'st] *F; Monster, know'st Q2–3.*   159. Gon.] *Q; Bast. F.*   S.D.] *Q; after* for't *(158) F.*

---

149. *Where . . . ever*] His success in the combat will prove that Edgar is the traitor, and the treasons will remain with the victim.

150. *Save him!*] 'Albany desires that Edmund's life might be spared at present, only to obtain his confession, and to convict him openly by his own letter' (Johnson). Some editors give the words to Goneril. In some productions the words are spoken of Edgar, when he is temporarily disarmed.

practice] treachery.

154. *stople*] This is the reading of Q1; the F *stop* may be a sophistication, and perhaps 'Hold, sir' was added to fill out the line.

Hold, sir] Capell thought this was addressed to Edgar, asking him not to kill Edmund. Dyce thought the words were spoken to Edmund, 'Hold' being

commonly used when anyone presented anything to another (cf. *Mac.*, II. i. 4). Kittredge takes it to mean 'Just a moment!' Albany must attend to Goneril before showing the paper to Edmund. The letter was never delivered; and we are not told whether Regan's letter was also found on Oswald's body. Edmund could have seen neither, though Albany would not know this for certain. See previous note.

155. *Thou*] probably Goneril. Kirschbaum thinks it is addressed to Edmund. Bransom, *op. cit.*, p. 161, argues that the pronoun would not have been used of Goneril by Albany. But cf. IV. ii. 62.

156. *No tearing*] based on an incident in the source-play. See Introduction, p. xxviii.

158–9. *Who . . . know*] F puts

Alb. Go after her: she's desperate; govern her.   160

                                     [Exit an Officer.

Edm. What you have charg'd me with, that have I done,
    And more, much more; the time will bring it out:
    'Tis past, and so am I. But what art thou
    That hast this fortune on me? If thou'rt noble,
    I do forgive thee.

Edg.   Let's exchange charity.   165
    I am no less in blood than thou art, Edmund;
    If more, the more th'hast wrong'd me.
    My name is Edgar, and thy father's son.
    The Gods are just, and of our pleasant vices
    Make instruments to plague us;   170
    The dark and vicious place where thee he got
    Cost him his eyes.

Edm.   Th'hast spoken right, 'tis true.
    The wheel is come full circle; I am here.

Alb. Methought thy very gait did prophesy

160. S.D.] *Capell; not in* Q, F.   164. thou'rt] *F;* thou bee'st *Q.*   167. th' hast] *F;* thou hast *Q.*   169. vices] *F;* vertues *Q.*   170. plague us] *F;* scourge vs *Q.*   171. thee he] he thee *Q2–3.*   172. Th' hast] *F;* Thou hast *Q.* right] *F;* truth *Q.*   'tis true] *F; not in* Q.   173. circle] *F;* circled *Q.*

Goneril's exit after 'for't' and ascribes 'Ask . . . know' to the Bastard. Kirschbaum supports F; but Goneril needs an hysterical, not a defiant, exit line; Albany would not turn to Edmund to ask his question about the letter, and then belatedly give instructions about his wife; and it is difficult to reconcile Edmund's confession (161) with his defiance two lines earlier. Knight and Kirschbaum argue that as Goneril has already admitted she knows the letter it is unnecessary for Albany to ask again 'Know'st thou this paper?' But Goneril has only implied that she knows the paper in the words 'Say, if I do'; Albany wants a direct admission.

   165. *Let's exchange charity*] Let me forgive you for your crimes against me, as you have forgiven me for killing you.

   169. *The . . . just*] The dramatic answer to Gloucester's cry, IV. i. 36. Bishop Wordsworth compares Wis-

dom, xi. 16: 'That wherewith a man sinneth, by the same also shall he be punished.' Noble also compares Wisdom, xii. 23: 'Wherefore thou hast tormented the wicked that haue liued a dissolute life by their owne imaginations.' 'Wherefore, whereas men haue lied dissolutely and vnrighteously, thou hast punished them sore with their owne abominations.' Empson compares III. iv. 73. Cf. also *Leir*, 1909: 'The heauens are iust, and hate impiety.'

   171. *The . . . place*] the adulterous bed, and so the act of adultery.

   got] begot.

   173. *The . . . circle*] Cf. Tourneur, *The Revenger's Tragedy*, II. i. 77: 'This wheele comes about.' Kittredge thinks that Edmund is referring to the fact that he is back at the bottom where he was before Fortune's wheel began to revolve.

   174. *gait*] Cf. *Troil.*, IV. v. 14.

A royal nobleness: I must embrace thee: 175
Let sorrow split my heart, if ever I
Did hate thee or thy father.
Edg.   Worthy prince, I know't.
Alb. Where have you hid yourself?
How have you known the miseries of your father?
Edg. By nursing them, my lord. List a brief tale;   180
And when 'tis told, O! that my heart would burst!
The bloody proclamation to escape
That follow'd me so near,—O! our lives' sweetness,
That we the pain of death would hourly die
Rather than die at once!—taught me to shift   185
Into a madman's rags, t'assume a semblance
That very dogs disdain'd: and in this habit
Met I my father with his bleeding rings,
Their precious stones new lost; became his guide,
Led him, begg'd for him, sav'd him from despair;   190
Never—O fault!—reveal'd myself unto him,
Until some half-hour past, when I was arm'd;
Not sure, though hoping, of this good success,
I ask'd his blessing, and from first to last
Told him my pilgrimage: but his flaw'd heart,   195
Alack, too weak the conflict to support!
'Twixt two extremes of passion, joy and grief,
Burst smilingly.
Edm.   This speech of yours hath mov'd me,
And shall perchance do good; but speak you on;
You look as you had something more to say.   200
Alb. If there be more, more woeful, hold it in;

176–7. ever I Did] *F*; I did euer *Q*.   177. know't] know it *Q2–3*.   183.
follow'd] followeth *Q3*.   184. we] *F*; with *Q*.   186. t'assume] *F*; To
assume *Q*.   189. Their] *F*; The *Q*.   191. fault] *F*; Father *Q*.   192.
arm'd] armed *Q2*.   195. my] *Q*; our *F*.   his] this *F4*.   201. more,
more] any more more *Q2*; any more *Q3*.

176. *split my heart*] Cf. *R3*, I. iii. 300,
and *Wint.*, I. ii. 349.
   177. *Worthy*] noble.
   184. *That . . . die*] Cf. *Cym.*, v. i. 26–7,
and I Corinthians, xv. 31.
   185. *shift*] change. Cf. *Cym.*, I. ii. I.
   188. *rings*] sockets, without the
jewels which were his eyes.

191. *fault*] mistake. Delius suggests
it here means 'misfortune'. Cf. *Per.*,
IV. ii. 79.
   193. *success*] result of an action,
either good or bad.
   195. *flaw'd*] cracked, damaged by
flaw. Cf. Lear's death and see Introduction, p. xxxv.

For I am almost ready to dissolve,
Hearing of this.
Edg.　　　　　　　This would have seem'd a period
To such as love not sorrow; but another,
To amplify too much, would make much more,　　　205
And top extremity.
Whilst I was big in clamour came there in a man,
Who, having seen me in my worst estate,
Shunn'd my abhorr'd society; but then, finding
Who 'twas that so endur'd, with his strong arms　　210
He fasten'd on my neck, and bellow'd out
As he'd burst heaven; threw him on my father;
Told the most piteous tale of Lear and him
That ever ear receiv'd; which in recounting
His grief grew puissant, and the strings of life　　215
Began to crack: twice then the trumpets sounded,
And there I left him tranc'd.
Alb.　　　　　　　　　But who was this?
Edg. Kent, sir, the banish'd Kent; who in disguise
Follow'd his enemy king, and did him service
Improper for a slave.　　　　　　　　　220

Enter a Gentleman, with a bloody knife.

Gent. Help, help! O, help!
Edg.　　　　　　　What kind of help?
Alb.　　　　　　　　　　Speak, man.

203. Hearing of this] *not in Q2–3.*　　203–20. This . . . slave] *Q; not in F.*
207. in] *Q; not in Theobald.*　　208. worst estate] worser state *Theobald.*
212. him] *Theobald;* me *Q.*　　213. Told the most] *Q1;* And told the *Q2–3.*
220. S.D.] *Camb.; Enter a Gentleman F; Enter one with a bloudie knife Q.*　　221. O,
help!] *F; not in Q.*　　*Edg.] F; Alb. Q.*

202. *dissolve*] melt in tears. Cf. *Ant.*,
v. ii. 302.
203. *period*] highest point, limit.
204. *but*] only.
another] i.e. sorrow. Some think it
means 'another man', others that it
means 'another period'.
205. *To . . . much*] if I were to describe
it in detail. Shakespeare is using the
terms of rhetoric. Cf. Baldwin, *op. cit.*,
II. 228.

206. *top extremity*] go beyond the
extreme limit.
207. *big*] loud.
208. *estate*] condition.
212. *As*] as if.
215. *puissant*] powerful.
the . . . life] heartstrings. Kent is
dying.
217. *tranc'd*] senseless.
219. *enemy*] hostile. Cf. *Cor.*, IV. iv.
24.

Edg. What means this bloody knife?
Gent.   'Tis hot, it smokes;
    It came even from the heart of—O! she's dead.
Alb. Who dead? speak, man.
Gent. Your lady, sir, your lady: and her sister   225
    By her is poison'd; she confesses it.
Edm. I was contracted to them both: all three
    Now marry in an instant.
Edg.   Here comes Kent.

Enter KENT.

Alb. Produce the bodies, be they alive or dead;
                                    [*Exit Gentleman.*
    This judgment of the heavens, that makes us tremble,
    Touches us not with pity.
                    [*To Kent.*] O! is this he?   231
    The time will not allow the compliment
    Which very manners urges.
Kent.   I am come
    To bid my King and master aye good night;
    Is he not here?
Alb.   Great thing of us forgot!   235

---

222. *Edg.*] *F; speech continued to Alb.* Q.   this] *F; that* Q.   'Tis] *F;*
Its Q.   223. It] *not in F2–4.*   O! she's dead.] *not in* Q.   224. Who
. . . man] *F; Who man, speake?* Q.   226. confesses] *F; hath confest* Q*1;*
has confest Q*2–3.*   228. Here . . . Kent] *F;* Here . . . Kent sir *(after* pity,
231) Q.   S.D.] *F; after* pity *(231)* Q*2–3.*   229. the] *F; their* Q.   alive]
live F*3–4.*   S.D.] *Camb.; not in* Q, F; Exit Gent *(after* pity) *Malone.*   230.
judgment] Iustice Q.   231. us] *not in* Q*2–3.*   is this] *F; tis* Q.   he]
she F*2–4.*   233. Which] *F; that* Q.   235. thing] things Q*2–3.*

---

222. *smokes*] steams.

228. S.D.] F marks Kent's entrance
here, Q three lines later. He comes
slowly down the stage while Albany is
speaking.

229. *dead*] According to F the bodies
are brought in here; it seems more
natural to leave a short time, as Q
does, for Albany's order to be obeyed.
Kirschbaum, who argues for the F
arrangement, says that it is significant
that Kent makes no comment on

the bodies; but he does later (238).

232. *compliment*] ceremony.

233. *manners*] singular. Cf. *Rom.*,
v. iii. 213.

235. *Great . . . forgot*] Kittredge
remarks that 'this amnesia on every-
body's part is necessary for the climax
that follows.' But, after all, there is no
reason why Albany should suspect that
Lear and Cordelia were in danger;
and he had had plenty to occupy his
mind during the wasted ten minutes.

Speak, Edmund, where's the King? and where's
　　Cordelia?
Seest thou this object, Kent?
　　　　　[*The bodies of Goneril and Regan are brought in.*
Kent.　Alack! why thus?
Edm.　　　　　　　　　Yet Edmund was belov'd:
The one the other poison'd for my sake,
And after slew herself.　　　　　　　　　　　240
Alb.　Even so. Cover their faces.
Edm.　I pant for life; some good I mean to do
Despite of mine own nature. Quickly send,
Be brief in it, to th'castle; for my writ
Is on the life of Lear and on Cordelia.　　　245
Nay, send in time.
Alb.　　　　　　　　Run, run! O, run!
Edg.　To who, my Lord? Who has the office? send
Thy token of reprieve.
Edm.　Well thought on: take my sword,
Give it the captain.
Edg.　　　　　　Haste thee, for thy life.　[*Exit Officer.*
Edm.　He hath commission from thy wife and me　251
To hang Cordelia in the prison, and
To lay the blame upon her own despair,
That she fordid herself.

237. S.D.] *Q; after 229, F, subst.*　　240. after] *not in Q3.*　　243. mine]
F; my Q.　　244. in it, to th'] *F;* int toth' *Q1;* into the *Q2–3.*　　castle]
Chastle *F2.*　　245. Is] tis *Q2–3.*　　247. who] whom *F2–4.*　　has] *F;*
hath *Q.*　　249–50. sword, Give] sword the Captaine, Giue *Q1.*　　250. *Edg.*]
F; Duke Q1; Alb. Q2–3.　　S.D.] *Exit a Captain Schmidt; Exit Messenger
Theobald; Exit Edgar Malone; Exeunt Edgar and others Capell; not in Q, F.*
254. That . . . herself] *not in Q2–3.*

237. *object*] sight. Kirschbaum,
defending the Folio through thick and
thin, takes this to refer to Edmund,
lying wounded. It is more natural for
it to refer to the bodies of Goneril and
Regan, especially when one takes
Edmund's next speech into consideration. He is really answering Kent's
question. The bodies are brought on
the stage so that Lear can be confronted with his three daughters, as in
the first scene of the play.

238. *Yet . . . belov'd*] Heilman, *op. cit.*,

p. 234, remarks that Edmund's sole
thought is of himself. But it is a brilliant
stroke to reveal here that Edmund's
career of crime was caused by his feeling that he was not loved.

240. *after*] afterwards.

250. *Haste . . . life*] This speech is
given to Albany in Q.

S.D.] Capell, Malone, and many
editors assume that Edgar goes out;
but if we give the line to Edgar, some-
one else has to run to the castle.

254. *fordid*] destroyed. Cordelia

Alb.   The Gods defend her!
    Bear him hence awhile.   [*Edmund is borne off.*   255

    Re-enter LEAR, *with* CORDELIA *dead in his arms; Officer.*

Lear. Howl, howl, howl! O! you are men of stones:
    Had I your tongues and eyes, I'd use them so
    That heaven's vault should crack. She's gone for ever.
    I know when one is dead, and when one lives;
    She's dead as earth. Lend me a looking-glass;   260
    If that her breath will mist or stain the stone,
    Why, then she lives.
Kent.   Is this the promis'd end?
Edg. Or image of that horror?
Alb.   Fall and cease.
Lear. This feather stirs; she lives! if it be so,
    It is a chance which does redeem all sorrows   265
    That ever I have felt.
Kent. [*Kneeling.*]   O my good master!
Lear. Prithee, away.
Edg.   'Tis noble Kent, your friend.
Lear. A plague upon you, murderers, traitors all!
    I might have sav'd her; now she's gone for ever!
    Cordelia, Cordelia! stay a little. Ha!   270

---

255. *Edmund . . . off*] *Theobald; not in Q, F.   Re-enter*] *Dyce; Enter Q, F.
dead*] *Rowe; not in Q, F.   Officer*] *not in Q, F; Edgar, Officer and Others Malone.*
256. Howl, howl, howl] *F; four times Q.*   you] your *F1-2.*   257. I'd]
F; I would Q.   258. She's] O, she is *Q2-3.*   261. or] and *Q2-3.*   262.
Why, then she] she then *Q2-3.*   265. which] that *Q2-3.*   266. S.D.]
Theobald; not in Q, F.   O] *F; A Q.*   268. you, murderers] *F; your
murderous Q1; you murdrous Q2-3; you murtherers F2-4.*   270. Ha!]
not in Q2-3.

committed suicide in most of Shakespeare's sources. See Introduction
p. xxxi, and Appendix, p. 222.
    254. *The . . . her*] They do not.
    256. *men of stones*] Cf. *R3*, III. vii. 25.
Pope thought Shakespeare wrote
'stone'. But Walker compares *Mer.V.*,
IV. i. 31: 'hearts of flints'; and *R3*, III.
vii. 224: 'I am not made of stones.'
Shakespeare may have been thinking
of the story of Deucalion as told by
Ovid in *Metamorphoses*, I.

    258. *heaven's vault*] Cf. *Tp.*, v. i. 43.
The term is used by Florio, *op. cit.*,
III. 373.
    261. *stone*] a mirror of polished stone
or crystal.
    262. *promis'd end*] the Last Judg-
ment, the end of the world. Cf. IV. vi.
133-4.
    263. *Fall . . . cease*] Let the heavens
fall, and everything come to an end.
Delius takes the words as substantives,
in opposition to 'that horror'.

What is't thou say'st? Her voice was ever soft,
Gentle and low, an excellent thing in woman.
I kill'd the slave that was a-hanging thee.

Offi. 'Tis true, my lords, he did.

Lear.   Did I not, fellow?
I have seen the day, with my good biting falchion   275
I would have made them skip: I am old now,
And these same crosses spoil me. Who are you?
Mine eyes are not o'th'best: I'll tell you straight.

Kent. If Fortune brag of two she lov'd and hated,
One of them we behold.   280

Lear. This is a dull sight. Are you not Kent?

Kent.   The same;
Your servant Kent. Where is your servant Caius?

Lear. He's a good fellow, I can tell you that;
He'll strike, and quickly too. He's dead and rotten.

Kent. No, my good Lord; I am the very man,—   285

Lear. I'll see that straight.

---

271. say'st] sayest *Q1;* stay *Q3.*   272. woman] *F;* women *Q.*   273. a-
hanging] *hyphened Dyce.*   274. *Offi.] Capell; Cap. Q; Gent. F.*   275. have]
ha *Q2-3.*   with my good] that with my *Q2-3.*   276 them] *Q;* him *F.*
278. not] none *Q2-3.*   279. brag] bragd *Q.*   and] *F;* or *Q.*   281. This
. . . sight] *not in Q.*   This is] *F;* this' *Schmidt (conj. S. Walker).*   you not] *F;*
not you *Q.*   283. He's a] He's *F2.*   you] *F; not in Q.*

---

275. *I . . . day*] J. M. Nosworthy,
R.E.S., 1951, pp. 259–61, compares
Porter, *The Two Angry Women of
Abington,* 2382: 'Ha, I have seen the
day I could have danced in my fight';
and the following Shakespearian pas-
sages: *Rom.,* I. v. 23; *Wiv.,* II. i. 235;
Oth., v. ii. 261.

falchion] a light sword, with the
point a little bent inwards.

277. *crosses*] troubles.

spoil me] i.e. as a swordsman.

279–80. *If . . . behold*] 'If Fortune
. . . should brag of two persons, one
of whom she had highly elevated, and
the other she had woefully depressed,
we now behold the latter' (Mason).
Some think Kent is referring to himself; others think he is referring to Lear
and himself. In *N.Q.,* 18 Oct. 1890,
p. 305, the passage is paraphrased:

'If Fortune, in the history of the world,
pre-eminently loved and then hated
two persons, here in the miserable
example of my king we have one of
them.' Jennens who emended *we* to
you (*ye* Furness) explains that Kent
is answering Lear's question (277).
We may here have an example of a
change of thought in the middle of a
sentence, Kent meaning: 'If Fortune
brag of two people, one of whom she
loved and one hated—but no, Lear,
who was thrown down from great
prosperity, can serve as an example
of both.'

281. *dull sight*] melancholy spectacle; but some critics think that
Lear is referring to his own failing
eyesight.

286. *I'll . . . straight*] I'll attend to
that in a moment.

Kent. That from your first of difference and decay,
    Have follow'd your sad steps,—
Lear.   You are welcome hither.
Kent. Nor no man else. All's cheerless, dark, and deadly:
    Your eldest daughters have fordone themselves,   290
    And desperately are dead.
Lear.   Ay, so I think.
Alb. He knows not what he says, and vain is it
    That we present us to him.
Edg.   Very bootless.

               Enter an Officer.

Offi. Edmund is dead, my Lord.
Alb.   That's but a trifle here.
    You lords and noble friends, know our intent;   295
    What comfort to this great decay may come
    Shall be appli'd: for us, we will resign,
    During the life of this old Majesty,
    To him our absolute power: *[To Edgar and Kent.]*
                     You, to your rights,
    With boot and such addition as your honours   300
    Have more than merited. All friends shall taste
    The wages of their virtue, and all foes
    The cup of their deservings. O! see, see!

---

287. first] *F;* life *Q.*   288. Have] Hane *F2.*   You are] *Q2, F2–4;* Your are *F1;* You'r *Q1.*   290. fordone] *F;* foredoome *Q1;* fore-doom'd *Q2–3.* 291. Ay . . . think] *F;* So think I too *Q1;* So I think too *Q2–3.*   292. says] *F;* sees *Q.*   is it] *F;* it is *Q.*   293. S.D.] *Capell; Enter Captaine Q; Enter Messenger (after* him) *F.*   294. Offi.] *Capell; Capt. Q; Mess. F.*   296. great] *F; not in Q.*   299. S.D.] *Malone; To Edg. Rowe; not in Q, F.*   300. honours] *F;* honor *Q1.*

---

287. *first*] beginning.
    difference and decay] change and decline of fortunes.

289. *Nor . . . else*] This may mean: 'No, neither I, nor any man, is welcome.' Or it may mean: 'And there was no one else followed you in the days of your misfortunes' (though the Fool was also there). But I think it probably refers back to 'I am the very man' (285) and that it means

simply 'I am really him, and no one else.'
    290. *fordone*] destroyed.
    291. *desperately*] from despair.
    296. *great decay*] the ruined piece of nature, Lear.
    297. *resign*] Lear, then, dies a king (R. W. Chambers).
    300. *With . . . addition*] with such additional titles and rights.
    honours] noble deeds.

Lear. And my poor fool is hang'd! No, no, no life!
Why should a dog, a horse, a rat, have life,   305
And thou no breath at all? Thou'lt come no more,
Never, never, never, never, never!
Pray you, undo this button: thank you, Sir.
Do you see this? Look on her, look, her lips,
Look there, look there!   [*Dies.*

Edg.   He faints! My Lord, my Lord!

Kent. Break, heart; I prithee, break!

Edg.   Look up, my Lord. 311

Kent. Vex not his ghost: O! let him pass; he hates him
That would upon the rack of this tough world
Stretch him out longer.

Edg.   He is gone, indeed.

304. No, no, no] *F*; no, no *Q*.   305. have] of *Q1*.   306. Thou'lt] *F*;
O thou wilt *Q*.   307. Never] *five times F; thrice Q*.   308. Pray you] pray
Q2–3.   Sir] *F*; sir, O, o, o, o(o) *Q*.   309–10. Do . . . there!] *F*; *not
in Q*.   look, her lips,] *Johnson;* Looke her lips *F1;* look on her lips, *F2–4*.
310. S.D.] *He dies F; not in Q*.   My Lord, my Lord!] my Lord. *F4*.   311.
Kent.] *F; Lear. Q*.   up] to *F2–4*.   312. hates him] hates him much *Q2–3*.
313. rack] *F4;* wracke *Q, F1–3*.   tough] rough *Q3, Pope, Capell*.   314. He]
F; O he *Q*.

304. *fool*] Cordelia, a term of endearment. Sir Joshua Reynolds thought Lear was referring to the Fool. Brandl, Quiller-Couch, and Edith Sitwell have argued that the two parts of Cordelia and the Fool were taken by the same actor; but Thaler, *T.L.S.*, 13 Feb. 1930, shows that the parts could not have been doubled. Perrett points out that 'when Cordelia is away her place as the representative of utter truthfulness is taken by the Fool. In this respect the two characters are one.' And Empson, *op. cit.*, p. 152, while pointing out that the assumption that Lear is referring to the Fool must be wrong because in the rest of the speech he is obviously talking about Cordelia, remarks, following Bradley, 'that his mind has wandered so far that he no longer distinguishes the two. . . Lear is now thrown back into something like the storm phase of his madness, the effect of immediate shock, and the Fool

seems to him part of it. The only affectionate dependent he had recently has been hanged, and the only one he had then was the Fool.'

308. *button*] Lear feels a sense of suffocation, and imagines it is caused by the tightness of his clothes. J. W. Harvey suggests that Lear is referring to one of Cordelia's buttons; but I think this is unlikely. See letter in *T.L.S.*, 14 Nov. 1952, and later replies.

309. *Look*] Lear dies of joy, believing Cordelia to be alive (Bradley).

311. *Break . . . break*] Bradley suggests that Kent may be speaking of his own heart. Q, impossibly, gives the words to Lear who is already beyond speech.

312. *ghost*] departing spirit.

313. *tough*] obdurate, rigid, referring perhaps to the rack as well as to the world. Cf. Appendix, p. 240.

314. *longer*] syllepsis: (*a*) for a longer time, (*b*) with his body extended further by the rack.

Kent. The wonder is he hath endur'd so long: 315
    He but usurp'd his life.
Alb. Bear them from hence. Our present business
    Is general woe. [*To Kent and Edgar.*] Friends of my
        soul, you twain
    Rule in this realm, and the gor'd state sustain.
Kent. I have a journey, sir, shortly to go;   320
    My master calls me, I must not say no.
Edg. The weight of this sad time we must obey;
    Speak what we feel, not what we ought to say.
    The oldest hath borne most: we that are young
    Shall never see so much, nor live so long.   325
                 [*Exeunt, with a dead march.*

318. Is] *F;* Is to *Q.*   S.D.] *Johnson; not in Q, F.*   319. realm] *F;* kingdome
Q.   gor'd] good *Q2–3.*   state] *not in Q3.*   321. calls me] *F;* cals,
and *Q.*   no.] *Q, F1;* no. *Dyes. F2–4.*   322. Edg.] *F; Duke. Q.*   324.
hath] *F;* haue *Q.*   borne] bornue *Q3.*   325. S.D.] *F; not in Q.*

319. *gor'd state*] See Appendix, p. 236.

320. *journey*] to another world.

322–5. *The . . . long*] These lines are given to Albany by Q; and critics have argued that the last speech should be given to the person of highest rank who survives. But Edgar has to reply to Albany's speech, and the words 'We that are young' come somewhat more naturally from his mouth than from that of Albany.

APPENDICES

1. *THE TRUE CHRONICLE HISTORY OF KING LEIR*

This play, of over 2,500 lines, is too long to print in full. But most of it has little connection with Shakespeare's play, and all the significant parallels are given in the introduction or the notes. The three scenes given here relate to the division of the kingdom and to the reconciliation of Leir and Cordella.

SCENE III

Enter LEIR *and* PERILLUS

Leir. Perillus, go seek my daughters,
    Will them immediately come and speak with me.
Per. I will, my gracious Lord.   [*Exit.*
Leir. Oh, what a combat feeles my panting heart,
    'Twixt childrens loue, and care of Common weale!
    How deare my daughters are vnto my soule,
    None knowes, but he, that knowes my thoghts and secret
        deeds.
    Ah, little do they know the deare regard,
    Wherein I hold their future state to come:
    When they securely sleepe on beds of downe,
    These aged eyes do watch for their behalfe:
    While they like wantons sport in youthfull toyes,

This throbbing heart is pearst with dire annoyes.
As doth the Sun exceed the smallest Starre;
So much the fathers loue exceeds the childs.
Yet my complaynts are causelesse: for the world
Affords not children more conformable:
And yet, me thinks, my mind presageth still
I know not what; and yet I feare some ill.

Enter PERILLUS, *with the three daughters.*

Well, here my daughters come: I haue found out
A present meanes to rid me of this doubt.
Gon. Our royall Lord and father, in all duty,
We come to know the tenour of your will,
Why you so hastily haue sent for vs?
Leir. Deare *Gonorill*, kind *Ragan*, sweet *Cordella*,
Ye florishing branches of a Kingly stocke,
Sprung from a tree that once did flourish greene,
Whose blossoms now are nipt with Winters frost,
And pale grym death doth wayt vpon my steps,
And summons me vnto his next Assizes.
Therefore, deare daughters, as ye tender the safety
Of him that was the cause of your first being,
Resolue a doubt which much molests my mind,
Which of you three to me would proue most kind;
Which loues me most, and which at my request
Will soonest yeeld vnto their fathers hest.
Gon. I hope my gracious father makes no doubt
Of any of his daughters loue to him:
Yet for my part, to shew my zeale to you,
Which cannot be in windy words rehearst,
I prize my loue to you at such a rate,
I thinke my life inferiour to my loue.
Should you inioyne me for to tye a milstone
About my neck and leape into the Sea,
At your commaund I willingly would doe it:
Yea, for to doe you good, I would ascend
The highest Turret in all Brittany,
And from the top leape headlong to the ground:
Nay, more, should you appoynt me for to marry
The meanest vassayle in the spacious world,
Without reply I would accomplish it:
In briefe, commaund what euer you desire,
And if I fayle, no fauour I require.

Leir. O, how thy words reuiue my dying soule!
Cor. O, how I doe abhorre this flattery!
Leir. But what sayth *Ragan* to her fathers will?
Rag. O, that my simple vtterance could suffice,
    To tell the true intention of my heart,
    Which burnes in zeale of duty to your grace,
    And neuer can be quench'd, but by desire
    To shew the same in outward forwardnesse.
    Oh, that there were some other mayd that durst
    But make a challenge of her loue with me;
    I de make her soone confesse she neuer loued
    Her father halfe so well as I doe you.
    I then, my deeds should proue in playner case,
    How much my zeale aboundeth to your grace:
    But for them all, let this one meane suffice,
    To ratify my loue before your eyes:
    I haue right noble Suters to my loue,
    No worse then Kings, and happely I loue one:
    Yet, would you haue me make my choyce anew,
    I de bridle fancy, and be rulde by you.
Leir. Did neuer *Philomel* sing so sweet a note.
Cord. Did neuer flatterer tell so false a tale.
Leir. Speak now, *Cordella*, make my ioyes at full,
    And drop downe Nectar from thy hony lips.
Cor. I cannot paynt my duty forth in words,
    I hope my deede shall make report for me:
    But looke what loue the child doth owe the father,
    The same to you I beare, my gracious Lord.
Gon. Here is an answere answerlesse indeed:
    Were you my daughter, I should scarcely brooke it.
Rag. Dost thou not blush, proud Peacock as thou art,
    To make our father such a slight reply?
Leir. Why how now, Minion, are you growne so proud?
    Doth our deare loue make you thus peremptory?
    What, is your loue become so small to vs,
    As that you scorne to tell vs what it is?
    Do you loue vs, as euery child doth loue
    Their father? True indeed, as some,
    Who by disobedience short their fathers dayes,
    And so would you; some are so father-sick,
    That they make meanes to rid them from the world
    And so would you: some are indifferent,
    Whether their aged parents liue or dye;

And so are you. But, didst thou know, proud gyrle,
What care I had to foster thee to this,
Ah, then thou wouldst say as thy sisters do:
Our life is lesse, then loue we owe to you.

Cord. Deare father, do not so mistake my words,
Nor my playne meaning be misconstrued;
My toung was neuer vsde to flattery.

Gon. You were not best say I flatter: if you do,
My deeds shall shew, I flatter not with you.
I loue my father better then thou canst.

Cor. The prayse were great, spoke from anothers mouth:
But it should seeme your neighbours dwell far off.

Rag. Nay, here is one, that will confirme as much
As she hath sayd, both for my selfe and her.
I say, thou dost not wish my fathers good.

Cord. Deare father—.

Leir. Peace, bastard Impe, no issue of King *Leir*,
I will not heare thee speake one tittle more.
Call not me father, if thou loue thy life,
Nor these thy sisters once presume to name:
Looke for no helpe henceforth from me nor mine;
Shift as thou wilt, and trust vnto thy selfe:
My Kingdome will I equally deuide
'Twixt thy two sisters to their royall dowre,
And will bestow them worthy their deserts:
This done, because thou shalt not haue the hope,
To haue a childs part in the time to come,
I presently will dispossesse my selfe,
And set vp these vpon my princely throne.

Gon. I euer thought that pride would haue a fall.

Rag. Plaine dealing, sister: your beauty is so sheene,
You need no dowry, to make you be a Queene.

              [*Exeunt* LEIR, GONORILL, RAGAN.

Cord. Now whither, poore forsaken shall I goe,
When mine own sisters tryumph in my woe?
But vnto him which doth protect the iust,
In him will poore *Cordella* put her trust.
These hands shall labour, for to get my spending;
And so ile liue vntill my dayes haue ending.

Per. Oh, how I grieue, to see my Lord thus fond,
To dote so much vpon vayne flattering words.
Ah, if he but with good aduice had weyghed,
The hidden tenure of her humble speech,

Reason to rage should not haue giuen place,
Nor poore *Cordella* suffer such disgrace.   [*Exit.*

SCENE VI

Enter GONORILL *and* RAGAN

Gon. Sister, when did you see *Cordella* last,
       That pretty piece, that thinks none good ynough
       To speake to her, because (sir-reuerence)
       She hath a little beauty extraordinary?
Rag. Since time my father warnd her from his presence,
       I neuer saw her, that I can remember.
       God giue her ioy of her surpassing beauty;
       I thinke, her dowry will be small ynough.
Gon. I haue incenst my father so against her,
       As he will neuer be reclaymed agayne.
Rag. I was not much behind to do the like.
Gon. Faith, sister, what moues you to beare her such good will?
Rag. In truth I thinke, the same that moueth you;
       Because she doth surpasse vs both in beauty.
Gon. Beshrew your fingers, how right you can gesse:
       I tell you true, it cuts me to the heart.
Rag. But we will keepe her low enough, I warrant,
       And clip her wings for mounting vp too hye.
Gon. Who euer hath her, shall haue a rich marriage of her.
Rag. She were right fit to make a Parsons wife:
       For they, men say, do loue faire women well,
       And many times doe marry them with nothing.
Gon. With nothing! marry God forbid: why, are there any
            such?
Rag. I meane, no money.
Gon. I cry you mercy, I mistooke you much:
       And she is far too stately for the Church;
       Sheele lay her husbands Benefice on her back,
       Euen in one gowne, if she may haue her will.
Rag. In faith, poore soule, I pitty her a little.
       Would she were lesse fayre, or more fortunate.
       Well, I thinke long vntill I see my *Morgan*,
       The gallant Prince of Cambria, here arriue.
Gon. And so do I, vntill the Cornwall King
       Present himselfe, to consummate my ioyes.
       Peace, here commeth my father.

Enter LEIR, PERILLUS *and others.*

Leir. Cease, good my Lords, and sue not to reuerse
          Our censure, which is now irreuocable.
          We haue dispatched letters of contract
          Vnto the Kings of Cambria and of Cornwall;
          Our hand and seale will iustify no lesse:
          Then do not so dishonour me, my Lords,
          As to make shipwrack of our kingly word.
          I am as kind as is the Pellican,
          That kils it selfe, to saue her young ones liues:
          And yet as ielous as the princely Eagle,
          That kils her young ones, if they do but dazell
          Vpon the radiant splendor of the Sunne.
          Within this two dayes I expect their comming.

Enter KINGS OF CORNWALL *and* CAMBRIA.

          But in good time, they are arriu'd already.
          This haste of yours, my Lords, doth testify
          The feruent loue you beare vnto my daughters:
          And think your selues as welcome to King *Leir,*
          As euer *Pryams* children were to him.
Corn. My gracious Lord, and father too, I hope,
          Pardon, for that I made no greater haste:
          But were my horse as swift as was my will,
          I long ere this had seene your Maiesty.
Cam. No other scuse of absence can I frame,
          Then what my brother hath inform'd your Grace:
          For our vndeserued welcome, we do vowe,
          Perpetually to rest at your commaund.
Corn. But you, sweet Loue, illustrious *Gonorill,*
          The Regent, and the Soueraigne of my soule,
          Is *Cornwall* welcome to your Excellency?
Gon. As welcome, as *Leander* was to *Hero,*
          Or braue *Aeneas* to the Carthage Queene:
          So and more welcome is your Grace to me.
Cam. O, may my fortune proue no worse than his,
          Since heauens do know, my fancy is as much.
          Deare *Ragan,* say, if welcome vnto thee,
          All welcomes else will little comfort me.
Rag. As gold is welcome to the couetous eye,
          As sleepe is welcome to the Traueller,
          As is fresh water to sea-beaten men,
          Or moystned showres vnto the parched ground,

Or any thing more welcomer then this,
So and more welcome louely *Morgan* is.
Leir. What resteth then, but that we consummate,
The celebration of these nuptiall Rites?
My Kingdome I do equally deuide.
Princes, draw lots, and take your chaunce as falles.

Then they draw lots.

These I resigne as freely vnto you,
As earst by true succession they were mine.
And here I do freely dispossesse my selfe,
And make you two my true adopted heyres:
My selfe will soiorne with my sonne of Cornwall,
And take me to my prayers and my beades.
I know, my daughter *Ragan* will be sorry,
Because I do not spend my dayes with her:
Would I were able to be with both at once;
They are the kindest Gyrles in Christendome.
Per. I haue bin silent all this while, my Lord,
To see if any worthyer then my selfe,
Would once haue spoke in poore *Cordellaes* cause:
But loue or feare tyes silence to their toungs.
Oh, heare me speake for her, my gracious Lord,
Whose deeds haue not deseru'd this ruthlesse doome,
As thus to disinherit her of all.
Leir. Vrge this no more, and if thou loue thy life:
I say, she is no daughter, that doth scorne
To tell her father how she loueth him.
Who euer speaketh hereof to mee agayne,
I will esteeme him for my mortall foe.
Come, let vs in, to celebrate with ioy,
The happy Nuptials of these louely payres.

Exeunt omnes, manet PERILLUS.

Per. Ah, who so blind, as they that will not see
The neere approch of their owne misery?
Poore Lady, I extremely pitty her:
And whilest I liue, eche drop of my heart blood,
Will I strayne forth, to do her any good.   [*Exit.*

SCENE XXIV

Enter the GALLIAN KING *and* QUEENE, *and* MUMFORD, *with a basket, disguised like Countrey folke.*

King. This tedious iourney all on foot, sweet Loue,
        Cannot be pleasing to your tender ioynts,
        Which ne're were vsed to these toylesome walks.
Cord. I neuer in my life tooke more delight
        In any iourney, then I do in this:
        It did me good, when as we hapt to light
        Amongst the merry crue of country folke,
        To see what industry and paynes they tooke,
        To win them commendations 'mongst their friends.
        Lord, how they labour to bestir themselues,
        And in their quirks to go beyond the Moone,
        And so take on them with such antike fits,
        That one would think they were beside their wits!
        Come away, *Roger*, with your basket.
Mum. Soft, Dame, here comes a couple of old youthes,
        I must needs make my selfe fat with iesting at them.
Cor. Nay, prithy do not, they do seeme to be
        Men much o'regone with griefe and misery.
        Let's stand aside, and harken what they say.

                              [*Enter* LEIR *and* PERILLUS *very faintly.*

Leir. Ah, my *Perillus*, now I see we both
        Shall end our dayes in this vnfruitfull soyle.
        Oh, I do faint for want of sustenance:
        And thou, I know, in little better case.
        No gentle tree affords one taste of fruit,
        To comfort vs, vntill we meet with men:
        No lucky path conducts our luckless steps
        Vnto a place where any comfort dwels.
        Sweet rest betyde vnto our happy soules;
        For here I see our bodies must haue end.
Per. Ah, my deare Lord, how doth my heart lament,
        To see you brought to this extremity!
        O, if you loue me, as you do professe,
        Or euer thought well of me in my life,   [*He strips vp his arme.*
        Feed on this flesh, whose veynes are not so dry,
        But there is vertue left to comfort you.
        O, feed on this, if this will do you good,
        Ile smile for ioy, to see you suck my bloud.

Leir. I am no Caniball, that I should delight
  To slake my hungry iawes with humane flesh:
  I am no deuill, or ten times worse then so,
  To suck the bloud of such a peerelesse friend.
  O, do not think that I respect my life
  So dearely, as I do thy loyall loue.
  Ah, Brittayne, I shall neuer see thee more,
  That hast vnkindly banished thy King:
  And yet thou dost not make me to complayne,
  But they which were more neere to me than thou.
Cor. What do I heare? this lamentable voyce,
  Me thinks, ere now I oftentimes haue heard.
Leir. Ah, *Gonorill*, was halfe my Kingdomes gift
  The cause that thou didst seeke to haue my life?
  Ah, cruell *Ragan*, did I giue thee all,
  And all could not suffice without my bloud?
  Ah, poore *Cordella*, did I giue thee nought,
  Nor neuer shall be able for to giue?
  O, let me warne all ages that insueth,
  How they trust flattery, and reiect the trueth.
  Well, vnkind Girles, I here forgiue you both,
  Yet the iust heauens will hardly do the like;
  And only craue forgiuenesse at the end
  Of good *Cordella*, and of thee, my friend;
  Of God, whose Maiesty I haue offended,
  By my transgression many thousand wayes:
  Of her, deare heart, whom I for no occasion
  Turn'd out of all, through flatterers perswasion:
  Of thee, kind friend, who but for me, I know,
  Hadst neuer come vnto this place of wo.
Cor. Alack, that euer I should liue to see
  My noble father in this misery.
King. Sweet Loue, reueale not what thou art as yet,
  Vntill we know the ground of all this ill.
Cor. O, but some meat, some meat: do you not see,
  How neere they are to death for want of food?
Per. Lord, which didst help thy seruants at their need,
  Or now or neuer send vs helpe with speed.
  Oh comfort, comfort! yonder is a banquet,
  And men and women, my Lord: be of good cheare;
  For I see comfort comming very neere.
  O my Lord, a banquet, and men and women!
Leir. O, let kind pity mollify their hearts,

That they may helpe vs in our great extreames.
Per. God saue you, friends; & if this blessed banquet
    Affordeth any food or sustenance,
    Euen for his sake that saued vs all from death,
    Vouchsafe to saue vs from the gripe of famine.
                          [She bringeth him to the table.
Cor. Here father, sit and eat, here sit and drink:
    And would it were far better for your sakes.

    PERILLUS *takes* LEIR *by the hand to the table.*

Per. Ile giue you thanks anon: my friend doth faynt,
    And needeth present comfort.   *[Leir drinks.*
Mum. I warrant, he ne're stayes to say grace:
    O, theres no sauce to a good stomake.
Per. The blessed God of heauen hath thought vpon vs.
Leir. The thanks be his, and these kind courteous folke,
    By whose humanity we are preserued.

    They eat hungerly, Leir drinkes.

Cor. And may that draught be vnto him, as was
    That which old *Eson* dranke, which did renue
    His withered age, and made him young againe.
    And may that meat be vnto him, as was
    That which *Elias* ate, in strength whereof
    He walked fourty dayes, and neuer faynted.
    Shall I conceale me longer from my father?
    Or shall I manifest my selfe to him?
King. Forbeare a while, vntill his strength returne,
    Lest being ouer ioyed with seeing thee,
    His poore weak sences should forsake their office,
    And so our cause of ioy be turnd to sorrow.
Per. What chere, my Lord? how do you feele your selfe?
Leir. Me thinks, I neuer ate such sauory meat:
    It is as pleasant as the blessed Manna,
    That raynd from heauen amongst the Israelities:
    It hath recall'd my spirits home agayne,
    And made me fresh, as earst I was before.
    But how shall we congratulate their kindnesse?
Per. Infayth, I know not how sufficiently;
    But the best meane that I can think on, is this:
    Ile offer them my dublet in requitall;
    For we haue nothing else to spare.
Leir. Nay, stay, *Perillus,* for they shall haue mine.

Per. Pardon, my Lord, I sweare they shall haue mine.
> *Perillus proffers his dublet: they will not take it.*

Leir. Ah, who would think such kindnes should remayne
Among such strange and vnacquainted men:
And that such hate should harbour in the brest
Of those, which haue occasion to be best?

Cor. Ah, good old father, tell to me thy griefe,
Ile sorrow with thee, if not adde reliefe.

Leir. Ah, good young daughter, I may call thee so;
For thou art like a daughter I did owe.

Cor. Do you not owe her still? what, is she dead?

Leir. No, God forbid: but all my interest's gone,
By shewing my selfe too much vnnaturall:
So haue I lost the title of a father,
And may be call'd a stranger to her rather.

Cor. Your title's good still; for tis alwayes knowne,
A man may do as him list with his owne.
But haue you but one daughter then in all?

Leir. Yes, I haue more by two, then would I had.

Cor. O, say not so, but rather see the end:
They that are bad, may haue the grace to mend:
But how haue they offended you so much?

Leir. If from the first I should relate the cause,
Twould make a heart of Adamant to weepe;
And thou, poore soule, kind-hearted as thou art,
Dost weepe already, ere I do begin.

Cor. For Gods loue tell it, and when you haue done,
Ile tell the reason why I weepe so soone.

Leir. Then know this first, I am a Brittayne borne,
And had three daughters by one louing wife;
And though I say it, of beauty they were sped;
Especially the youngest of the three,
For her perfections hardly matcht could be:
On these I doted with a ielous loue,
And thought to try which of them lou'd me best,
By asking them, which would do most for me?
The first and second flattred me with words,
And vow'd they lou'd me better then their liues:
The youngest sayd, she loued me as a child
Might do: her answere I esteem'd most vild,
And presently in an outragious mood,
I turned her from me to go sinke or swym:
And all I had, euen to the very clothes,

I gaue in dowry with the other two:
And she that best deseru'd the greatest share,
I gaue her nothing, but disgrace and care.
Now mark the sequell: When I had done thus,
I soiournd in my eldest daughters house,
Where for a time I was intreated well,
And liu'd in state sufficing my content:
But euery day her kindnesse did grow cold,
Which I with patience put vp well ynough,
And seemed not to see the things I saw:
But at the last she grew so far incenst
With moody fury, and with causelesse hate,
That in most vild and contumelious termes,
She bade me pack, and harbour somewhere else.
Then was I fayne for refuge to repayre
Vnto my other daughter for reliefe,
Who gaue me pleasing and most courteous words;
But in her actions shewed her selfe so sore,
As neuer any daughter did before:
She prayd me in a morning out betime,
To go to a thicket two miles from the Court,
Poynting that there she would come talke with me:
There she had set a shaghayrd murdring wretch,
To massacre my honest friend and me.
Then iudge your selfe, although my tale be briefe,
If euer man had greater cause of griefe.

King. Nor neuer like impiety was done,
Since the creation of the world begun.

Leir. And now I am constraind to seeke reliefe
Of her, to whom I haue bin so vnkind;
Whose censure, if it do award me death,
I must confesse she payes me but my due:
But if she shew a louing daughters part,
It comes of God and her, not my desert.

Cor. No doubt she will, I dare be sworne she will.

Leir. How know you that, not knowing what she is?

Cor. My selfe a father haue a great way hence,
Vsde me as ill as euer you did her;
Yet, that his reuerend age I once might see,
Ide creepe along, to meet him on my knee.

Leir. O, no mens children are vnkind but mine.

Cor. Condemne not all, because of others crime:
But looke, deare father, looke, behold and see

    Thy louing daughter speaketh vnto thee.   *[She kneeles.*

Leir. O, stand thou vp, it is my part to kneele,
    And aske forgiuenesse for my former faults.   *[he kneeles.*

Cor. O, if you wish I should inioy my breath,
    Deare father rise, or I receiue my death.   *[he riseth.*

Leir. Then I will rise, to satisfy your mind,
    But kneele againe, til pardon be resigned.   *[he kneeles.*

Cor. I pardon you: the word beseemes not me:
    But I do say so, for to ease your knee.
    You gaue me life, you were the cause that I
    Am what I am, who else had neuer bin.

Leir. But you gaue life to me and to my friend,
    Whose dayes had else, had an vntimely end.

Cor. You brought me vp, when as I was but young,
    And far vnable for to helpe my selfe.

Leir. I cast thee forth, when as thou wast but young,
    And far vnable for to helpe thy selfe.

Cor. God, world and nature say I do you wrong,
    That can indure to see you kneele so long.

King. Let me breake off this louing controuersy,
    Which doth reioyce my very soule to see.
    Good father, rise, she is your louing daughter,   *[He riseth.*
    And honours you with as respectiue duty,
    As if you were the Monarch of the world.

Cor. But I will neuer rise from off my knee,
    Vntill I haue your blessing, and your pardon
    Of all my faults committed any way,
    From my first birth vnto this present day.

Leir. The blessing, which the God of *Abraham* gaue
    Vnto the trybe of *Iuda*, light on thee,
    And multiply thy dayes, that thou mayst see
    Thy childrens children prosper after thee.
    Thy faults, which are iust none that I do know,
    God pardon on high, and I forgiue below.   *[she riseth.*

Cor. Now is my heart at quiet, and doth leape
    Within my brest, for ioy of this good hap:
    And now (deare father) welcome to our Court,
    And welcome (kind *Perillus*) vnto me,
    Myrrour of vertue and true honesty.

Leir. O, he hath bin the kindest friend to me,
    That euer man had in aduersity.

Per. My toung doth faile, to say what heart doth think,
    I am so rauisht with exceeding ioy.

King. All you haue spoke: now let me speak my mind,
  And in few words much matter here conclude: [*he kneeles.*
  If ere my heart do harbour any ioy,
  Or true content repose within my brest,
  Till I haue rooted out this viperous sect,
  And repossest my father of his Crowne,
  Let me be counted for the periurdst man,
  That euer spake word since the world began.   [*rise.*
Mum. Let me pray too, that neuer pray'd before;
                                              [*Mumford kneeles.*
  If ere I resalute the Brittish earth,
  (As (ere't be long) I do presume I shall)
  And do returne from thence without my wench,
  Let me be gelded for my recompence.   [*rise.*
King. Come, let's to armes for to redresse this wrong:
  Till I am there, me thinks, the time seemes long.   [*Exeunt.*

2. HOLINSHED

Leir the sonne of Baldud was admitted ruler ouer the Britaines in the yeare of the world 3105, at what time Joas reigned in Juda. This Leir was a prince of right noble demeanor, gouerning his land and subiects in great wealth. He made the towne of Caerleir now called Leicester, which standeth vpon the riuer of Sore. It is written that he had by his wife three daughters without other issue, whose names were Gonorilla, Regan, and Cordeilla, which daughters he greatly loued, but specially Cordeilla the yoongest farre aboue the two elder. When this Leir therefore was come to great yeres, & began to waxe vnweldie through age, he thought to vnderstand the affections of his daughters towards him, and preferre hir whome he best loued, to the succession ouer the kingdome. Whervpon he first asked Gonorilla the eldest, how well she loued him: who calling hir gods to record, protested that she loued him more than hir owne life, which by right reason should be most deere vnto hir. With which answer the father being well pleased, turned to the second, and demanded of hir how well she loued him: who answered (confirming hir saiengs with great othes) that she loued him more than toong could expresse, and farre aboue all other creatures of the world.

Then called he his yoongest daughter Cordeilla before him, and asked of hir what account she made of him, vnto whome she made this answer as followeth: 'Knowing the great loue and fatherlie zeale that you haue alwaies borne towards me (for the which I maie not answere you otherwise than I thinke, and as my conscience leadeth me) I protest vnto you, that I haue loued you euer, and will continuallie (while I liue) loue you as my naturall father. And if you would more vnderstand of the loue that I beare you, assertaine your selfe, that so much as you haue, so much you are worth, and so much I loue you, and no more.' The father being nothing content with this answer, married his two eldest daughters, the one vnto Henninus the duke of Cornewall, and the other vnto Maglanus the duke of Albania, betwixt whome he willed and ordeined that his land should be diuided after his death, and the one halfe thereof immediatlie should be assigned to them in hand: but for the third daughter Cordeilla he reserued nothing.

Neuertheless it fortuned that one of the princes of Gallia (which now is called France) whose name was Aganippus, hearing of the beautie, womanhood, and good conditions of the said Cordeilla, desired to haue hir in mariage, and sent ouer to hir father, requiring that he might haue hir to wife; to whome answer was made, that he might haue his daughter, but as for anie dower he could haue none, for all was promised and assured to hir other sisters alreadie. Aganippus notwithstanding this answer of deniall to receiue anie thing by way of dower with Cordeilla, tooke hir to wife, onlie moued thereto (I saie) for respect of hir person and amiable vertues. This Aganippus was one of the twelue kings that ruled Gallia in those daies, as in the British historie it is recorded. But to proceed.

After that Leir was fallen into age, the two dukes that had married his two eldest daughters, thinking it long yer the gouernment of the land did come to their hands, arose against him in armour, and reft from him the gouernance of the land, vpon conditions to be continued for terme of life: by the which he was put to his portion, that is, to liue after a rate assigned to him for the maintenance of his estate, which in processe of time was diminished as well by Maglanus as by Henninus. But the greatest griefe that Leir tooke, was to see the vnkindnesse of his daughters, which seemed to thinke that all was too much which their father had, the same being neuer so little: in so much that going from the one to the other, he was brought to that miserie, that scarslie they would allow him one seruant to wait vpon him.

In the end, such was the vnkindnesse, or (as I maie saie) the vnnaturalnesse which he found in his two daughters, notwithstanding their faire and pleasant words vttered in time past, that being constreined of necessitie, he fled the land, & sailed into Gallia, there to seeke some comfort of his yongest daughter Cordeilla, whom before time he hated. The ladie Cordeilla hearing that he was arrived in poore estate, she first sent to him priuilie a certeine summe of monie to apparell himselfe withall, and to reteine a certeine number of seruants that might attend vpon him in honorable wise, as apperteined to the estate which he had borne: and then so accompanied, she appointed him to come to the court, which he did, and was so ioifullie, honorablie, and louinglie receiued, both by his sonne in law Aganippus, and also by his daughter Cordeilla, that his hart was greatlie comforted: for he was no lesse honored, than if he had beene king of the whole countrie himselfe.

Now when he had informed his sonne in law and his daughter in what sort he had been vsed by his other daughters, Aganippus caused a mightie armie to be put in a readinesse, and likewise a great nauie of ships to be rigged, to passe ouer into Britaine with Leir his father in law, to see him againe restored to his kingdome. It was accorded, that Cordeilla should also go with him to take possession of the land, the which he promised to leaue vnto hir, as the rightfull inheritour after his decesse, notwithstanding any former grant made to hir sisters or to their husbands in anie maner of wise.

Herevpon, when this armie and nauie of ships were readie, Leir and his daughter Cordeilla with hir husband tooke the sea, and arriuing in Britaine, fought with their enimies, and discomfited them in battell, in the which Maglanus and Henninus were slaine; and then was Leir restored to his kingdome, which he ruled after this by the space of two yeeres, and then died, fortie yeeres after he first began to reigne. His bodie was buried at Leicester in a vaut vnder the chanell of the riuer of Sore beneath the towne.

Cordeilla the yoongest daughter of Leir was admitted Q. and supreme gouernesse of Britaine, in the yeere of the world 3155, before the bylding of Rome 54, Vzia was then reigning in Juda, and Jeroboam ouer Israell. This Cordeilla after hir father's deceasse ruled the land of Britaine right worthilie during the space of fiue yeeres, in which meane time hir husband died, and then about the end of those fiue yeeres, hir two nephewes Margan and Cunedag, sonnes to hir aforesaid sisters, disdaining to be vnder the gouernment of a woman, leuied warre against hir, and destroied a great part of the land, and finallie tooke hir prisoner, and laid hir fast in ward, wherewith she tooke suche griefe, being a woman of a manlie courage, and despairing to recouer libertie, there she slue hirselfe.

3. EDMUND SPENSER

The Faerie Queene, Book Two, Canto X.

27

Next him king *Leyr* in happie peace long raind,
  But had no issue male him to succeed,
  But three faire daughters, which were well vptraind,
  In all that seemed fit for kingly seed:
  Mongst whom his realme he equally decreed
  To haue diuided. Tho when feeble age
  Nigh to his vtmost date he saw proceed,
  He cald his daughters; and with speeches sage
Inquyrd, which of them most did loue her parentage.

28

The eldest *Gonorill* gan to protest,
  That she much more then her owne life him lou'd:
  And *Regan* greater loue to him profest,
  Then all the world, when euer it were proou'd;
  But *Cordeill* said she lou'd him, as behoou'd:
  Whose simple answere, wanting colours faire
  To paint it forth, him to displeasance moou'd,
  That in his crowne he counted her no haire,
But twixt the other twaine his kingdome whole did shaire.

29

So wedded th'one to *Maglan* king of Scots,
  And th'other to the king of *Cambria*,
  And twixt them shayrd his realme by equall lots:
  But without dowre the wise *Cordelia*
  Was sent to *Aganip* of *Celtica*.
  Their aged Syre, thus eased of his crowne,
  A priuate life led in *Albania*,
  With *Gonorill*, long had in great renowne,
That nought him grieu'd to bene from rule deposed downe.

30

But true it is, that when the oyle is spent,
  The light goes out, and weeke is throwne away;
  So when he had resigned his regiment,
  His daughter gan despise his drouping day,
  And wearie waxe of his continuall stay.

Tho to his daughter *Regan* he repayrd,
Who him at first well vsed euery way;
But when of his departure she despayrd,
Her bountie she abated, and his cheare empayrd.

31

The wretched man gan then auise too late,
     That loue is not, where most it is profest,
     Too truely tryde in his extreamest state;
     At last resolu'd likewise to proue the rest,
     He to *Cordelia* him selfe addrest,
     Who with entire affection him receau'd,
     As for her Syre and king she seemed best;
     And after all an army strong she leau'd,
To war on those, which him had of his realme bereau'd.

32

So to his crowne she him restor'd againe,
     In which he dyde, made ripe for death by eld,
     And after wild, it should to her remaine:
     Who peaceably the same long time did weld:
     And all mens harts in dew obedience held:
     Till that her sisters children, woxen strong
     Through proud ambition, against her rebeld,
     And ouercommen kept in prison long,
Till wearie of that wretched life, her selfe she hong.

4. JOHN HIGGINS

Cordila shewes how by despaire when she was in prison she slue herselfe.
the yeare before Christe. 800.

My grandsyre *Bladud* hight that found the Bathes by skill,   [36
A fethered king that practisde for to flye and soare:
Whereby he felt the fall God wot against his will,
And neuer went, roode, raignde nor spake, nor flew no more.
Who dead his sonne my father *Leire* therefore,
Was chosen kinge, by right apparent heyre,
Which after built the towne of *Leircestere*.

He had three daughters, first and eldest hight *Gonerell*:
Next after hir, my sister *Ragan* was begotc:

The thirde and last was, I the yongest namde *Cordell*,
And of vs all, our father *Leire* in age did dote.
So minding hir that loude him best to note,
Because he had no sonne t'enioye his lande:
He thought to giue, where fauoure most he fande.

What though I yongest were, yet men me iudgde more wise
Then either *Gonorell*, or *Ragan* had more age,
And fayrer farre: wherefore my sisters did despise
My grace, and giftes, and sought my praise t'swage:
But yet though vice gainst vertue die with rage,
It cannot keepe her vnderneth to drowne,
But still she flittes aboue, and reapes renowne.

Yet nathelesse, my father did me not mislike:
But age so simple is, and easye to subdue:
As childhode weake, thats voide of wit and reason quite:
They thincke thers nought, you flater fainde, but all is true:
Once olde and twice a childe, tis said with you,
Which I affirme by proofe, that was definde:
In age my father had a childish minde.   [63

He thought to wed vs vnto nobles three, or Peres:
And vnto them and theirs, deuide and part the lande:
For both my sisters first he sent as first their yeares
Requirde their mindes, and loue, and fauour t'understand.
(Quod he) all doubtes of duty to abande,
I must assaye and eke your friendships proue:
Now tell me eche how much you do me loue.

Which when they aunswered, they loude him wel and more
Then they themselues did loue, or any worldly wight:
He praised them and said he would againe therefore,
The louing kindnes they deserude in fine requite:
So found my sisters fauour in his sight,
By flatery fayre they won their fathers hart:
Which after turned, him and mee to smart.

But not content with this he minded me to proue,
For why he wonted was to loue me wonders well:
How much dost thou (quoth he) *Cordile* thy father loue?   [80
I will (said I) at once my loue declare and tell:
I loude you euer as my father well,

No otherwise, if more to know you craue:
We loue you chiefly for the goodes you haue.

Thus much I said, the more their flattery to detect,
But he me answerd thereunto again with Ire,
Because thou dost thy fathers aged yeares neglect,
That loude the more of late then thy desertes require,
Thou neuer shalt, to any part aspire
Of this my realme, emong thy sisters twayne,
But euer shalt vndotid ay remayne.

Then to the king of *Albany* for wife he gaue
My sister *Gonerell*, the eldest of vs all:
And eke my sister *Ragan* for *Hinnine* to haue,
Which then was Prince of *Camber* and *Cornwall*:
These after him should haue his kingdome all
Betwene them both, he gaue it franke and free:
But nought at all, he gaue of dowry mee.

At last it chaunst the king of *Fraunce* to here my fame,
My beutie braue, was blazed all abrode eche where:
And eke my vertues praisde me to my fathers blame
Did for my sisters flattery me less fauoure beare.
Which when this worthy king my wrongs did heare,
He sent ambassage likte me more then life,
T'intreate he might me haue to be his wife.

My father was content withall his harte, and sayde,
He gladly should obtaine his whole request at will
Concerning me, if nothing I herein denayde:
But yet he kept by their intisment hatred still,
(quoth he) your prince his pleasure to fulfill,
I graunt and giue my daughter as you craue:
But nought of me for dowry can she haue.

King *Aganippus* well agreed to take me so,
He deemde that vertue was of dowries all the best:
And I contentid was to *Fraunce* my father fro
For to depart, & hoapte t'enioye some greater rest.
I maried was, and then my ioyes encreaste,
I gate more fauoure in this prince his sight,
Then euer princesse of a princely wight.

But while that I these ioyes enioyd, at home in *Fraunce*
My father *Leire* in *Britayne* waxed aged olde,
My sisters yet them selues the more aloft t'aduance,
Thought well they might, be by his leaue, or sans so bolde:
To take the realme & rule it as they wold.
They rose as rebels voyde of reason quite,
And they depriude him of his crowne and right. [125

Then they agreed, it should be into partes equall
Deuided: and my father threscore knightes & squires
Should alwayes haue, attending on him still at cal.
But in six monthes so much increasid hateful Ires,
That *Gonerell* denyde all his desires,
So halfe his garde she and her husband refte:
And scarce alowde the other halfe they lefte.

Eke as in *Scotlande* thus he lay lamenting fates,
When as his daughter so, sought all his vtter spoyle:
The meaner vpstarte gentiles, thought themselues his mates
And betters eke, see here an aged prince his foyle.
Then was he faine for succoure his, to toyle.
With all his knightes, to *Cornewall* there to lye:
In greatest nede, his *Raganes* loue to trye.

And when he came to *Cornwall*, *Ragan* then with ioye,
Receiued him and eke hir husbande did the lyke:
There he abode a yeare and liude without a noy,
But then they tooke, all his retinue from him quite
Saue only ten, and shewde him dayly spite,
Which he bewailde complayning durst not striue,
Though in disdayne they laste alowde but fiue.

On this he deemde him selfe was far that tyme vnwyse,
When from his doughter *Gonerell* to *Ragan* hee:
Departed erste yet eache did him poore king despise, [150
Wherfore to *Scotlande* once againe with hir to bee
And bide he went: but beastly cruell shee,
Bereaude him of his seruantes all saue one,
Bad him content him selfe with that or none.

Eke at what time he askte of eache to haue his garde,
To garde his grace where so he walkte or wente:
They calde him doting foole and all his hestes debarde,

Demaunded if with life he could not be contente.
Then he to late his rigour did repente,
Gainst me and sayde, *Cordila* now adieu:
I finde the wordes thou toldste mee to to true.

And to be short, to *Fraunce* he came alone to mee,
And tolde me how my sisters him our father vsde:
Then I besought my king with teares vpon my knee,
That he would aide my father thus by them misusde
Who nought at all my humble heste refusde:
But sent to euery coste of Fraunce for ayde,
Wherwith my father home might be conueide.

The soldiers gathered from eche quarter of the land,
Came at the length to know the king his mind & will: [170
Who did commit them to my fathers aged hand,
And I likewise of loue and reuerent mere goodwill
Desirde my king, he would not take it ill,
If I departed for a space withall:
To take a parte, or ease my fathers thrall.

This had: I parted with my father from my fere,
We came to *Britayne* with our royall campe to fight:
And manly fought so long our enmies vanquisht were
By martiall feates, and force by subiectes sword and might.
The Britishe kinges were fayne to yelde our right,
And so my father well this realme did guide,
Three yeares in peace and after that he dide.   [182

(Cordila reigns as queen of Britain for five years, and then on
the death of her husband she is dethroned and imprisoned by
her nephews, Morgan and Conidagus.)

Was euer lady in such wofull wreckfull wo:
Depriude of princely powre, berefte of libertie,
Depriud in all these worldly pompes, hir pleasures fro,
And brought from welthe, to nede, distresse, and misery?
From palace proude, in prison poore to lye:
From kingdomes twayne, to dungion one no more:
From Ladies wayting, vnto vermine store.

From light to darke, from holsome ayre to lothsom smell:
From odewr swete, to sweate: from ease, to grieuous payne:

From sight of princely wights, to place where theues do dwell:
From deinty beddes of downe, to be of strawe full fayne:
From bowres of heauenly hewe, to dennes of dayne:
From greatest haps, that worldly wightes atchieue:
To more distresse then any wretche aliue.

(Despair appears to her in prison and offers her various means
of suicide, including the knife with which Dido slew herself.
Cordila prays for vengeance on her nephews, and stabs herself, or is stabbed by Despair.)

5. SIR PHILIP SIDNEY

Arcadia, II. 10

The pitifull state, and storie of the Paphlagonian *vnkinde King, and his
kind sonne, first related by the son, then by the blind father.*

It was in the kingdome of *Galacia*, the season being (as in the
depth of winter) very cold, and as then sodainely growne to so
extreame and foule a storme, that neuer any winter (I thinke)
brought foorth a fowler child: so that the Princes were euen compelled by the haile, that the pride of the winde blew into their faces,
to seeke some shrowding place within a certaine hollow rocke
offering it vnto them, they made it their shield against the tempests
furie. And so staying there, till the violence thereof was passed, they
heard the speach of a couple, who not perceiuing them (being
hidde within that rude canopy) helde a straunge and pitifull disputation which made them steppe out; yet in such sort, as they might
see vnseene. There they perceaued an aged man, and a young,
scarcely come to the age of a man, both poorely arayed, extreamely
weather-beaten; the olde man blinde, the young man leading him:
and yet through all those miseries, in both these seemed to appeare
a kind of noblenesse, not sutable to that affliction. But the first
words they heard, were these of the old man. Well *Leonatus* (said
he) since I cannot perswade thee to lead me to that which should
end my griefe, & thy trouble, let me now entreat thee to leaue me:
feare not, my miserie cannot be greater then it is, & nothing doth
become me but miserie; feare not the danger of my blind steps, I
cannot fall worse then I am. And doo not I pray thee, doo not
obstinately continue to infect thee with my wretchednes. But flie,

flie from this region, onely worthy of me. Deare father (answered
he) doo not take away from me the onely remnant of my happi-
nesse: while I haue power to doo you seruice, I am not wholly
miserable. Ah my sonne (said he, and with that he groned, as if
sorrow straue to breake his harte,) how euill fits it me to haue such
a sonne, and how much doth thy kindnesse vpbraide my wicked-
nesse? These doleful speeches, and some others to like purpose (well
shewing they had not bene borne to the fortune they were in,)
moued the Princes to goe out vnto them, and aske the younger what
they were? Sirs (answered he, with a good grace, and made the
more agreeable by a certaine noble kinde of pitiousness) I see well
you are straungers, that know not our miserie so well here knowne,
that no man dare know, but that we must be miserable. In deede
our state is such, as though nothing is so needfull vnto vs as pittie,
yet nothing is more daungerous vnto vs, then to make our selues so
knowne as may stirre pittie. But your presence promiseth, that
cruelty shall not ouer-runne hate. And if it did, in truth our state is
soncke below the degree of feare.

This old man (whom I leade) was lately rightfull Prince of this
countrie of *Paphlagonia*, by the hard-harted vngratefulnes of a
sonne of his, depriued, not onely of his kingdome (whereof no
forraine forces were euer able to spoyle him) but of his sight, the
riches which Nature graunts to the poorest creatures. Whereby, &
by other his vnnaturall dealings, he hath bin driuen to such griefe,
as euen now he would haue had me to haue led him to the toppe of
this rocke, thence to cast himselfe headlong to death: and so would
haue made me (who receiued my life of him) to be the worker of his
destruction. But noble Gentlemen (said he) if either of you haue a
father, and feele what duetifull affection is engraffed in a sonnes
hart, let me intreate you to conuey this afflicted Prince to some
place of rest & securitie. Amongst your worthie actes it shall be
none of the least, that a King, of such might and fame, and so
vniustly oppressed, is in any sort by you relieued.

But before they could make him answere, his father began to
speake, Ah my sonne (said he) how euill an Historian are you, that
leaue out the chiefe knotte of all the discourse? my wickednes, my
wickednes. And if thou doest it to spare my eares, (the onely sense
nowe left me proper for knowledge) assure thy selfe thou dost mistake me. And I take witnesse of that Sunne which you see (with that
he cast vp his blinde eyes, as if he would hunt for light,) and wish
my selfe in worse case then I do wish my selfe, which is as euill as
may be, if I speake vntruely; that nothing is so welcome to my
thoughts, as the publishing of my shame. Therefore know you

Gentlemen (to whom from my harte I wish that it may not proue ominous foretoken of misfortune to haue mette with such a miser as I am) that whatsouer my sonne (ô God, that trueth binds me to reproch him with the name of my sonne) hath said, is true. But besides those truthes this also is true, that hauing had in lawful mariage, of a mother fitte to beare royall children, this sonne (such one as partly you see, and better shall knowe by my shorte declaration) and so enioyed the expectations in the world of him, till he was growen to iustifie their expectations (so as I needed enuie no father for the chiefe comfort of mortalitie, to leaue an other onesselfe after me) I was caried by a bastarde sonne of mine (if at least I be bounde to beleeue the words of that base woman my concubine, his mother) first to mislike, then to hate, lastly to destroy, to doo my best to destroy, this sonne (I thinke you thinke) vndeseruing destruction. What waies he used to bring me to it, if I should tell you, I should tediously trouble you with as much poysonous hypocrisie, desperate fraude, smoothe malice, hidden ambition, & smiling enuie, as in any liuing person could be harbored. But I list it not, no remembrance, (no, of naughtines) delights me, but mine own; & me thinks the accusing his traines might in some manner excuse my fault, which certainly I loth to doo. But the conclusion is, that I, gaue order to some seruants of mine, whom I thought as apte for such charities as my selfe, to leade him out into a forrest, & there to kill him.

But those theeues (better natured to my sonne then my selfe) spared his life, letting him goe, to learne to liue poorely: which he did, giuing himselfe to be a priuate souldier, in a countrie here by. But as he was redy to be greatly aduanced for some noble peeces of seruice which he did, he hearde newes of me: who (dronke in my affection to that vnlawfull and vnnaturall sonne of mine) suffered my self so to be gouerned by him, that all fauours and punishments passed by him, all offices, and places of importance, distributed to his fauourites; so that ere I was aware, I had left my self nothing but the name of a King: which he shortly wearie of too, with many indignities (if any thing may be called an indignity, which was laid vpon me) threw me out of my seat, and put out my eies; and then (proud in his tyrannie) let me goe, nether imprisoning, nor killing me: but rather delighting to make me feele my miserie; miserie indeed, if euer there were any; full of wretchednes, fuller of disgrace, and fullest of guiltines. And as he came to the crowne by so vniust meanes, as vniustlie he kept it, by force of stranger souldiers in *Cittadels*, the nestes of tyranny, & murderers of libertie; disarming all his own countrimen, that no man durst shew himself a wel-willer of mine: to say the trueth (I think) few of them being so (considering my cruell follie to my good sonne, and foolish kindness to my vnkinde bastard:) but if there were any who fell to pitie of so great a fall, and had yet any sparkes of vnstained duety lefte in them towardes me, yet durst they not shewe it, scarcely with giuing me almes at their doores; which yet was the onelie sustenaunce of my distressed life, no bodie daring to shewe so much charitie, as to lende me a hande to guide my darke steppes: Till this sonne of mine (God knowes, woorthie of a more vertuous, and more fortunate father) forgetting my abhominable wrongs, not recking danger, & neglecting the present good way he was in doing himselfe good, came hether to doo this kind office you see him performe towards me, to my vnspeakable griefe; not onely because his kindness is a glasse even to my blind eyes, of my naughtines, but that above all griefes, it greeues me he should desperatly aduenture the losse of his soul-deseruing life for mine, that yet owe more to fortune for my deserts, as if he would cary mudde in a chest of christall. For well I know, he that now raigneth, how much soeuer (and with good reason) he despiseth me, of all men despised; yet he will not let slippe any advantage to make away him, whose iust title (ennobled by courage and goodnes) may one day shake the seate of a neuer secure tyrannie. And for this cause I craued of him to leade me to the toppe of this rocke, indeede I must confesse, with meaning to free him from so Serpentine a companion as I am. But he finding what I purposed onely therein since he was borne, shewed himselfe disobedient vnto me. And now Gentlemen, you haue the true storie, which I pray you publish to the world, that my mischieuous proceedinges may be the glorie of his filiall pietie, the onely reward now left for so great a merite. And if it may be, let me obtaine that of you, which my sonne denies me: for neuer was there more pity in sauing any, then in ending me; both because therein my agonies shall ende, and so shall you preserue this excellent young man, who els wilfully folowes his owne ruine.

The matter in it self lamentable, lamentably expressed by the old Prince (which needed not take to himselfe the gestures of pitie, since his face could not put of the markes thereof) greatly moued the two Princes to compassion, which could not stay in such harts as theirs without seeking remedie. But by and by the occasion was presented: for *Plexirtus* (so was the bastard called) came thether with fortie horse, onely of purpose to murder this brother; of whose comming he had soone aduertisement, and thought no eyes of sufficient credite in such a matter, but his owne; and therefore came him selfe to be actor, and spectator. And as soone as he came, not regarding the weake (as he thought) garde of but two men, commaunded some of his followers to set their handes to his, in the killing of *Leonatus*. But the young Prince (though not otherwise armed but with a sworde) how falsely soeuer he was dealt with by others, would not betray him selfe: but brauely drawing it out, made the death of the first that assaulted him, warne his fellowes to come more warily after him. But then *Pyrocles* and *Musidorus* were quickly become parties (so iust a defence deseruing as much as old friendship) and so did behaue them among that companie (more iniurious, then valiant) that many of them lost their liues for their wicked maister.

Yet perhaps had the number of them at last preuailed, if the King of *Pontus* (lately by them made so) had not come vnlooked for to their succour. Who (hauing had a dreame which had fixt his imagination vehemently vpon some great daunger, presently to follow those two Princes whom he most deerely loued) was come in all hast, following as well as he could their tracke with a hundreth horses in that countrie, which he thought (considering who then raigned) a fit place inough to make the stage of any Tragedie.

But then the match had ben so ill made for *Plexirtus*, that his ill-led life, & worse gotten honour should haue tumbled together to destruction; had there not come in *Tydeus & Telenor*, with fortie or fiftie in their suit, to the defence of *Plexirtus*. These two were brothers, of the noblest house of that country, brought vp from their infancie with *Plexirtus*: men of such prowesse, as not to know feare in themselues, and yet to teach it others that should deale with them: for they had often made their liues triumph ouer most terrible daungers; neuer dismayed and euer fortunate; and truely no more setled in their valure, then disposed to goodnesse and iustice, if either they had lighted on a better friend, or could haue learned to make friendship a child, and not the father of Vertue. But bringing vp (rather then choise) hauing first knit their minds vnto him, (indeed craftie inough, eyther to hide his faultes, or neuer to shew them, but when they might pay home) they willingly held out the course, rather to satisfie him, then al the world; and rather to be good friendes, then good men: so as though they did not like the euill he did, yet they liked him that did the euill; and though not councellors of the offence, yet protectors of the offender. Now they hauing heard of this sodaine going out, with so small a company, in a country full of euill-wishing minds toward him (though they knew not the cause) followed him; till they found him in such case as they were to venture their liues, or else he to loose his: which they did with such force of minde and bodie, that truly I may iustly say, *Pyrocles & Musidorus* had neuer till then found any, that could make them so well repeate their hardest lesson in the feates of armes. And briefly so they did, that if they ouercame not; yet were they not ouercome, but caried away that vngratefull maister of theirs to a place of securitie; howoseuer the Princes laboured to the contrary. But this matter being thus far begun, it became not the constancie of the Princes so to leaue it; but in all hast making forces both in *Pontus* and *Phrygia*, they had in fewe dayes, lefte him but only that one strong place where he was. For feare hauing bene the onely knot that had fastned his people vnto him, that once vntied by a greater force, they all scattered from him; like so many birdes, whose cage had bene broken.

In which season the blind King (hauing in the chief cittie of his Realme, set the crowne vpon his sonne *Leonatus* head) with many teares (both of ioy and sorrow) setting forth to the whole people, his owne fault & his sonnes vertue, after he had kist him, and forst his sonne to accept honour of him (as of his newe-become subiect) euen in a moment died, as it should seeme: his hart broken with vnkindnes & affliction, stretched so farre beyond his limits with this excesse of comfort, as it was able no longer to keep safe his roial spirits. But the new King (hauing no lesse louingly performed all duties to him dead, then aliue) pursued on the siege of his vnnatural brother, asmuch for the reuenge of his father, as for the establishing of his owne quiet. In which siege truly I cannot but acknowledge the prowesse of those two brothers, then whom the Princes neuer found in all their trauell two men of greater habilitie to performe, nor of habler skill for conduct.

But *Plexirtus* finding, that if nothing else, famin would at last bring him to destruction, thought better by humblenes to creepe, where by pride he could not march. For certainely so had nature formed him, & the exercise of craft conformed him to all turnings of sleights, that though no man had lesse goodnes in his soule then he, no man could better find the places whence arguments might grow of goodnesse to another: though no man felt lesse pitie, no man could tel better how to stir pitie: no man more impudent to deny, where proofes were not manifest; no man more ready to confesse with a repenting manner of aggravating his owne euil, where denial would but make the fault fowler. Now he tooke this way, that hauing gotten a pasport for one (that pretended he would put *Plexirtus* aliue into his hands) to speak with the King his brother, he him selfe (though much against the minds of the valiant brothers, who rather wished to die in braue defence) with a rope about his necke, barefooted, came to offer himselfe to the discretion of *Leonatus*. Where what submission he vsed, how cunningly in making greater the faulte he made the faultines the lesse, how artificially he could set out the torments of his owne conscience, with the burdensome comber he had found of his ambitious desires, how finely seeming to desire nothing but death, as ashamed to liue, he begd life, in the refusing it, I am not cunning inough to be able to expresse: but so fell out of it, that though at first sight *Leonatus* saw him with no other eie, then as the murderer of his father; & anger already began to paint reuenge in many colours, ere long he had not only gotten pitie, but pardon, and if not an excuse of the fault past, yet an opinion of future amendment: while the poore villaines (chiefe ministers of his wickedness, now betraied by the author thereof,) were deliuered to many cruell sorts of death; he so handling it, that it rather seemed, he had rather come into the defence of an vnremediable mischiefe already committed, then that they had done it at first by his consent.

6. FLORIO AND *KING LEAR*

There have been numerous books and articles dealing with the influence of Florio's translation of Montaigne on Shakespeare, including J. M. Robertson's *Montaigne and Shakespeare* (1897), Elizabeth Robins Hooker's article (*P.M.L.A.*, 1902), and A. H. Upham's *The French Influence in English Literature* (1911). The best treatment of the subject is that by George Coffin Taylor in *Shakespeare's Debt to Montaigne* (1925), and there is a later essay, dealing only with *King Lear*, by W. B. Drayton Henderson (*S.A.B.*, Oct. 1939, Jan. 1940).

According to Taylor, there are twenty-three Montaigne passages echoed in *King Lear*, and 116 words used by Shakespeare in that play, and not used by him before 1603, which are to be found in Florio's translation. I have not been able to trace all these words, but the following list, which includes words used in a different sense before 1603, will give an idea of the extent of Florio's influence on the vocabulary of the play.

This list should be received with caution. Taylor gives 125 words that Shakespeare used in *Hamlet*, and not before; yet it is probable that that play was on the stage a year or two before the publication of Florio's translation. He may, of course, have read it in MS. Then one has to reckon with the fact that every play of Shakespeare's contains a number of words he does not use elsewhere; and many of the words in the list he could have seen in other books, or heard in conversation. Yet as there is no doubt that he did read Florio's translation, it is reasonable to assume that he enlarged his vocabulary by a study of it, especially as some of these words seem to be Florio's coinages.

Affectionate
Allowance
Amplify
Assaulted
Auricular
Avouched

Bastardizing
Bellyfull
Brim

Catastrophe
Changed
Clap
Cock
Compeer
Contentious
Creaking
Curiosity

Depositaries
Debauched
Depraved
Deride
Derogate
Descent
Disaster
Discommend
Dislocate
Disnatured
Dissipation
Distribution
Divisions

Eminence
Enormous
Epicurism
Evasion

Exist
Exposed

Fitly
Flawed
Flay
Ford
Frustrate

Goatish
Gored
Gratitude

Handy-dandy
Hafted
Hereditary
Heretofore

Imperfect
Impertinency
Impetuous
Improper
Incestuous
Intelligent
Interessed

Jovial
Justicer
Justification

Lowness

Marble-hearted
Marjoram
Menaces
Milky
Monopoly
Mortar

Mongrel
Mutation

Numbed

Parricide
Pilferings
Plaited
Planetary
Ponder
Portable
Precipitating

Rake up
Rarity
Reciprocal
Ripeness
Roguish
Roughness
Rumble

Sectary
Sharpness
Smilingly
Soliciting
Sophisticated
Sprigs
Sterility
Sumpter
Syllable

Trilled

Unquietly

Visible

Waywardness
Windowed

Taylor also gives a list of phrases used by Florio and in *King Lear*. Some of these are too commonplace to be significant—'essay of virtue' (Temple ed. ii. 131), 'heaven's vault' (iii. 373), 'felled him dead' (i. 11) and 'furred gown' (iii. 22). Another, 'court holy water' (ii. 140), is to be found in John Eliot. More interesting are those parallels in which the words juxtaposed are significant only from their juxtaposition. 'Depository and guardian' (vi. 40) may be compared with 'my guardians, my depositaries'; 'Necessitie must first pinch you by the throat' (ii. 143) may have suggested 'Necessity's sharp pinch'; 'Frustrate the Tyrants cruelty' (ii. 65) may have suggested the lines—

> When misery could beguile the tyrant's rage,
> And frustrate his proud will;

'The breath of a Lawyer' (iii. 86) resembles 'the breath of an unfee'd lawyer'; and 'Mangled estate', closely followed by 'Gored' (iii. 5–6) may be compared with 'gor'd state'. A few longer passages are quoted in the notes. These include Edgar's alleged views on fathers (I. ii. 45 ff.), Lear's remarks on 'unaccommodated man' (III. iv. 104–5), and some passages on justice in IV. vi.

Several critics have argued that Shakespeare was also influenced by Montaigne's philosophy, and Henderson claims that Shakespeare, in writing *King Lear*, made particular use of the *Apology for Raymond Sebonde*. Montaigne mentions that once 'some articles of their religion be made doubtfull and questionable', people will 'immediately reject (as a tyrannicall yoke) all impressions they had in former times received by the authoritie of Lawes, or reverence of ancient custome'—as Edmund repudiates custom (iii. 185. Cf. I. ii. 3). Montaigne wishes to trample human pride under foot

> to make them feele the emptinesse, vacuitie, and no worth of man; and violently to pull out of their hands the silly weapons of their reason (iii. 201);

and in many passages he exposes the weakness of unaccommodated man,

> man alone without other help, armed but with his owne weapons, and unprovided of the grace and knowledge of God (iii. 203. Cf. pp. 215, 250, 268, 309).

He considers 'the power and domination' of the stars,

> not onely upon our lives, and condition of our fortune... but also over our dispositions and inclinations, our discourses and wils, which they rule (iii. 205. Cf. IV. iii. 33, I. ii. 115 ff.).

It is the stars that make

> sonnes kill fathers, fathers sonnes destroy,
> Brothers for mutuall wounds their armes do bear (iii. 207)

Montaigne mentions that 'there are Nations, who receive and admit a Dogge to be their King' (iii. 210. Cf. iv. vi. 157). He refers to the speaking looks of lovers (iii. 211), the habits of ants (iii. 217. Cf. ii. iv. 65) and to the fact that

> we must be besotted ere we can become wise, and dazled before we can be led (ii. 284).

> The weaknesse of our judgement helps us more than our strength to compasse the same, and our blindnesse more than our cleare-sighted eyes (iii. 298).

> Our wisedome is lesse wise, then our folly (iv. 19).

These three passages link up with the theme of 'reason in madness' discussed in the Introduction (p. lv). Montaigne mentions that the Stoics supposed the soul to be situated 'within and about the heart' (iii. 377. Cf. iii. vi. 74–5). He discusses the effect of dizzy heights in a passage which may have contributed something to the description of Dover Cliff, and he says that

> if but a tree, a shrub, or any out-butting crag of a Rock presented it selfe unto our eyes, upon those steepie and high Alpes, some-what to uphold the sight, and divide the same, it doth somewhat ease and assure us from feare (iv. 68).

Shortly afterwards, he declares that 'our senses are . . . many times dulled by the passions of the mind' (iv. 70)—an idea that occurs twice in the play (iii. iv. 11–14, iv. vi. 5–6).

There are also several parallels with other essays. Montaigne declares that

> one same magistrate doth lay the penalty of his change on such as cannot do withal . . . and the guide striketh the blinde man he leadeth. A horrible image of justice (v. 21. Cf. iv. vi. 156).

He mentions that we are all sinners:

> I say not, that none should accuse, except hee bee spotlesse in himselfe: For then none might accuse (v. 245).

A judge who condemns an adulterer will write a love-letter to his fellow-judge's wife—'Thus goes the world, and so goe men' (vi. 85. Cf. iv. vi. 145–6). He quotes Catullus to the effect that women are as lustful as pigeons (v. 116). He declares that ladies 'blush, onely

by hearing that named, which they nothing feare to doe' (iv. 131);
and that

> the same woman from whom you came lately . . . will soone after
> even in your presence, raile and scold more bitterly against the
> same fault in her neighbour, than ever Portia or Lucrece could
> (vi. 85. Cf. iv. vi. 112 ff.).

Some of these ideas, perhaps all of them, Shakespeare might
have derived from other sources or invented on his own; but it
seems to me that it would be unreasonable to deny that Montaigne
had a substantial influence on the thought of *King Lear*. On the
other hand, it is difficult to go all the way with Henderson, some
of whose views are rather fanciful.

7. SAMUEL HARSNETT AND *KING LEAR*

I have discussed elsewhere Shakespeare's use of *A Declaration of
Egregious Popishe Impostures* (*R.E.S.* 1951, pp. 11–21). Here it will
be sufficient to print the relevant extracts with line references to
the corresponding passages in the play.

Sig. A 3. These lighter superfluities, whom they disgorge amongst you . . . in the
fashion of great Potentates, vntill Gods reuengefull arme doth vncase
them to the view of the world, and then they suffer the mild stroke of
iustice with a glorious ostentation (iii. iv. 28 ff.).

p. 1. The names of the Actors in this holy Comedie were these, *Edmunds* . . .

p. 12. the harbinger . . . the steward, the vauntcourrier, . . . and the Pandar
(iii. ii. 5).

p. 18. so violent, boystrous, and bigge, as that he will ruffle, rage, and hurle
in the ayre . . . and blow downe steeples, trees, may-poles (iii. ii. 1).

p. 19. with all conspirants in any badde practice (v. iii. 134).
marred the play (iii. vi. 59–60).

p. 22. spoyle the play (iii. vi. 59–60).

p. 23. an old corkie woman (iii. vii. 29).

p. 24. *Marwood* . . . being pinched with penurie (ii. iv. 209)
and hunger, did lie but a night, or two, abroad in the fieldes, and beeing
a melancholicke person, was scared with lightning, and thunder, that
happened in the night, & loe, an euident signe that the man was possessed . . . this pittifull creature . . . (iii. iv. 50 ff.).

p. 25. Ma: *Maynie* had a spice of the *Hysterica passio*, as seems from his youth,
hee himselfe termes it the Moother (ii. iv. 54–6).

p. 38. to frame themselues iumpe and fit vnto the Priests humors, to mop,
mow, iest, raile, raue, (iv. i. 60–1)
roare, commend, & discommend, and as the priests would haue them,
vpon fitting occasions (ii. ii. 106).

p. 41. brimstone (iv. vi. 127).

p. 41. mortified patience (III. ii. 37; II. iii. 15).

p. 42. there were two needles thrust into her legge . . . and she wist it not (II. iii. 15–16).

p. 43. she attempted to runne from the house, and to wade through a brooke (III. iv. 52).

p. 45. our *stygian* Imposters goe farre beyond that *stygian* lake (III. vi. 7).

p. 46. Captaine *Maho*, *Saras* deuil, Captaine *Modu*, Maynies deuil . . . (III. iv. 140–1).

p. 47. and therefore like a melancholick *Priuado*, he affects *Marwood* to lie in the fields, and to gape at the Moone, and so of a *Cæsars* humor, he raignes in *Marwood* alone (III. vi. 6).

Trayfords deuill, was a Centurion . . . and had a hundred vnder his charge (III. vi. 77). *Smolkin* (III. iv. 137).

Hiaclito, a Prince, & Monarch of the world . . . he said that hee had no fellowes, but two men, and an vrchin boy. It was little beseeming his state (I wis) beeing so mighty a Monarch, to come into our coasts so skuruily attended, except hee came to see fashions in England (III. iv. 140–1; III. vi. 78).

p. 48. hell was cleere, and had not a deuill to cast at a mad dogge (III. vi. 63).

p. 49. fiddle . . . (III. vi. 6).

except he allow theyr Commision that tenders him his oath: . . . (III. vi. 38).

Frateretto, Fliberdigibbet, Hoberdidance . . . (III. vi. 6, III. iv. 112, III. vi. 30). And least you should conceiue, that the deuils had no musicke in hell, especially that they would goe a maying without theyr musicke, the Fidler comes in with his Taber, & Pipe, and a whole Morice after hime, with motly visards for theyr better grace (III. vi. 6).

p. 50. now the many, rascality, or black-guard of (II. iv. 34)

hell, were God knows how many in her: for all were there tag, and ragge, cut and long-tayle (III. vi. 66 ff.).

. . . *Puffe*, and *Purre*, the two fat deuils, . . . (III. vi. 45).

These were all in poore *Sara* at a chop . . . shee poore wench had all hell in her belly (IV. i. 57–8).

p. 52. a shelter against what wind or weather so euer (III. ii. 62).

. . . Sara Williams was furnished with all the devils in hell, at a clap (I. iv. 292).

p. 54. *Maynie* . . . comes mute vpon the stage, with his haire curled vp. *Loe heere . . . comes vp the spirit* (III. iv. 83–4)

of pride . . . auarice . . . Enuie . . . Sloth . . . the seauen deadly sinnes . . . (III. iv. 91; IV. i. 57 ff.).

p. 55. hee slinkes closely away, like a dogge at the sight of a whip . . . (III. vi. 63).

p. 58. couch them as a curre at the sound of his Maisters whippe . . . (I. iv. 109–10).

p. 59. his lodge in a homely place (III. ii. 61).

p. 61. the bottomlesse pit of hell . . . (III. vi. 7).

to play bo-peepe (I. iv. 173).

p. 62. a pad in the straw (III. iv. 43).

vnsauorie smels . . . in a peculiar part of the body, but onely in the wenches (IV. vi. 128).

p. 63. lodging the deuil . . . in the inferiour parts (IV. vi. 126).

p. 66. afflicted, and tormented . . . tough weatherbeaten spirit (V. iii. 313–15).

p. 68. scalded (IV. vi. 127).

p. 73. launces, swords, and kniues dash through me ... lightning from heauen deuoure mee, ... rent with a thousand nayles ... (II. iii. 16).

Prometheus with his Vulture ... *Ixion* with his wheele (II. iv. 132; IV. vii. 47).

How doost thou vexe, how dost thou wring me? (III. iv. 60).

p. 74. thou art neuer but plaguing me with torment and fire: ... so cunningly to act, & feigne the passions, and agonies of the deuil, that the whole companie of spectators shal by his false illusions be brought into such commiserations, and compassion, as they shall all weepe, crie, and exclaime, as loud as the counterfet deuil ... (III. vi. 59–60).

p. 76. your dogges being curres (III. vi. 63).

p. 77. pue-fellow (III. vi. 37).

p. 80. sparrow-blasting, or sprite-blasting (III. iv. 58–9).

p. 89. In a wel sorted cry of hounds, the dogs are not all of a qualitie, and sise: some be great, some of a midle, some of a low pitch: some good at a hot chase, some at a cold sent: some swift, and shalow, some slow and sure: some deepe and hollow-mounted, some very pleasant, and merrie at traile ... (III. vi. 64 ff.).

p. 93. and how would he winch, skip, and curuet, hauing so many fiery needles in his skin at once? (II. iii. 15).

p. 94. thicke smoake, & vapour of hell; the swords, darts, and speares of fire, pointed with grisly death ... the Furies, and tormentors of hell, with black vgly visages, grisly with smoake, with whips of blood, and fire in theyr hands, theyr armes gored with blood: and a huge bunch of a thousand snakes crawling down theyr haire ... (III. vi. 15–16).

p. 95. streamers of scorching smoke ... breathing out fire, and brimstone ... burning (IV. vi. 127).

p. 97. fire him out of his hold, as men smoke out a Foxe out of his burrow: ... (V. iii. 23)

certaine deuils in the likenes of dogges (III. vi. 61).

p. 100. neather-stockes (II. iv. 10).

p. 101. in the likenes of a Toade ... (III. vi. 31).

p. 106. as men leade Beares by the nose, or Iack an Apes (II. iv. 8)

in a string ... deuil-blasting ... (III. iv. 58–9).

p. 108. in steede of thunder, and lightning to bring *Iupiter* vpon the stage ... thundring, clapping, and flashing out ... hearing the huge thunder cracke of adiuration ... (III. ii. 49).

p. 109. Brimstone ... vgly blacknes, smoake, scorching, broyling, and heate ... (IV. vi. 127).

p. 113. hunger-bitten (V. iii. 121).

p. 114. foule-mouthed fiend (III. iv. 60).

p. 115. vice-bitten (V. iii. 121).

p. 116. Bedlam ... hunger-bitten ... whips, scourges, serpents, scorpions, brimstone, coales, flames ... bottomlesse burning pit ... (II. iii. 14; V. iii. 121; IV. vi. 127).

p. 119. The Prince of hel ... Hoberdicut ... (III. iv. 140).

the poore deuil chattered his teeth (IV. i. 58; IV. vi. 101).

p. 120. on the racke (V. iii. 313).

p. 128. To disguise, difforme, and monster-like to mishape the nature (IV. ii. 60).

p. 136. against hayle, thunder, lightning, (III. ii)

biting of mad dogges ... (III. vi. 65).

sparrow-blasting ... (III. iv. 58–9).

p. 136. and she haue a little help of the Mother, Epilepsie, or *Cramp*, to teach her role her eyes, wrie her mouth, gnash her teeth, startle with her body, hold her armes and hands stiffe, make antick faces, girne, mow, and mop like an Ape, tumble like a Hedgehogge (iv. i. 60–1).

p. 137. Owle-blasted (iii. iv. 58–9).

p. 139. a dog of two colours . . . a Spaniell (iii. vi. 64, 67).

p. 140. a whirlewind (iii. iv. 58). *Smolkin* . . . whom *Sara* espied . . . to goe out at *Trayfords* right eare in the forme of a *Mouse* (iii. iv. 137).

p. 141. his deuils went out in the forme of those creatures, that haue neerest resemblance vnto those sinnes: as for example: the spirit of *Pride* went out in the forme of a *Peacocke* (forsooth): the spirit of *Sloth* in the likeness of an *Asse;* the spirit of *Enuy* in the similitude of a *Dog;* the spirit of *Gluttony* in the forme of a *Woolfe* . . . *Luxury* (iii. iv. 91 ff.).

p. 146. pined (i. iv. 72).

p. 159. that all the sensible accidents should be made pendulous in the ayre, like Archimedes *doue* . . . (iii. iv. 66).

p. 166. a Sisternity of mimpes, mops, and idle holy women, that shal grace *Modu* the deuil, with their idle holy presence and be as ready to cry out, at the mowing of an apish wench . . . (i. iv. 166).

p. 168. Prince of darkness (iii. iv. 140).

p. 195. if they heard any croaking in her belly, (a thing whereunto many women are subiect, especially when they are fasting) then they would make a wonderful matter of that. One time shee remembreth, that shee hauing the said croaking in her belly, or making of herselfe some such noyse in her bed, they said it was the deuill that was about the bedde, that spake with the voyce of a Toade (iii. vi. 31–2).

p. 214. did thrust a pinne into her shoulder (ii. iii. 16).

p. 219. one *Alexander* . . . hauing brought with him . . . a new halter, and two blades of kniues, did leaue the same vpon the gallerie floare in her Maisters house (iii. iv. 50 ff.).

p. 225. Nightingale (iii. vi. 30).

p. 228. to drowne or kill themselues (iii. iv. 50 ff.).

It should be added that the following words and phrases are used in *King Lear* and also by Harsnett: carpe (A3), intelligences (6), pestilent, pernicious (8), auricular (9), fashioned (34), frame (38), asquint (96), currish (98), allay (121), gaster (135), propinquitie (143), at a clap (164), what a good year (165), fellow Iustice (223), counterfeit Demoniack (252). Waltham Forest is mentioned on p. 166 (cf. note on iii. iv. 56). See also K. Muir, *N.Q.* (1952), pp. 555–6.

8. ADDITIONAL NOTES (1985)

Text. See Kenneth Muir, 'The Texts of King Lear' in *Shakespeare: Contrasts and Controversies* (1985). A few emendations, out of the many proposed by P. W. K. Stone in *The Textual History of King Lear* (1980), are recorded below.

Date. Gary Taylor, *R.E.S.* (1982), pp. 396–413, argues that the storm scenes were influenced by *Eastward Ho!* The play was published in the summer of 1605, but Shakespeare probably saw a performance a few months earlier.

Sources. Inga-Stina Ekeblad (Ewbank), *N.Q.* (1957), pp. 193–4, pointed out that in the anonymous *Selimus* there is a blinding on stage and a minor character called Regan. E. Slater, *N.Q.* (1978), p. 147, lists a number of links between *King Lear* and *Timon of Athens*. See also note to I. ii. 1–22 below.

Recent Criticism. 'Image of that Horror' by Joseph Wittreich (1984) traces the influence of the Apocalypse on the play. In the epilogue to my anthology, *King Lear: Critical Essays* (1984), I have brought up to date the interpretation of the play given in the present edition.

Text and Commentary.

I. i. 82. *least*] T. W. Craik, *N.Q.* (1956), p. 11, mentions that S. Batman, *The Doome warning all men to the iudgement* (1581), p. 439, speaks of Cordilla as 'least of all her sisters'.

I. i. 301. *compliment*] Gordon N. Ross, *Explicator*, 36, 4 (1978), pp. 25–6 and William Nelson, *R.Q.* (1974), pp. 193–5, argue convincingly for the retention of *complement*. Lear and France had quarrelled.

I. ii. 1–22. *Thou . . . bastards*] Brian Vickers, *M.L.R.* (1968), pp. 305–14, quotes the following passage from Thomas Milles, *The Treasurie of Ancient and Moderne Times* (1613), 'That the Bastard is more worthy to be esteemed than he that is lawfully borne or legitimate':

> The great Priviledges, which I see are duely appertayning to Bastards, and illegitimate Children . . . makes mee undertake the boldnesse, to preferre them before other; and to shew by good reasons, that they are greatly superiour to such, whome we call legittimate and lawfull borne Children. First of all (Gentlemen) I entreate yee to consider, that Bastards generally, are begot in more heat and vigour of love, with more agreeable conformity of willes, and far sweeter Union of spirites, then the most part of our Legittimate Children. Consider withall, that their conception is performed by stolne opportunities, warie preventions, watchfull discretion, and an infinite number of more ingenious deceipts, and amorous actions, then eyther needeth, or is required, in a settled condition of marriage, free from that fierie feare, which is the sole spurre unto a longing appetite. Such Conceptions (many times) are acted without anie gayetie of heart, without anie savourie pleasing of both the souls, or that height of affection and delight, that makes an act well done, before it be halfe

doone. Which is the reason (as I thinke) why we see many sightly and formall Fathers, to have Children dul of spirite, lame of disposition, and deformed in body. Contrarywise, yee shall not find a Bastard (for the most part of them) but he is ingenious, of sprightly judgement, and commonly accompanied with beseeming corpulence of bodie, and some other faire fore-telling rules, of good adventure and Fortune. Beside, it seemeth as a certainty that Nature had some peculier respect of Bastardes, in squaring them forth such liberall allowances, as to erect and builde magnificent houses, in places of solemne and publick note, yea, in most celebrate and stupendious Citties, as having this care, that in following times, they should rise to great request and honour. (pp. 723–4)

Edmund makes the same points. Vickers suggests that Milles had access to a second volume of *The Defence of Contraries*. The first volume (1593), translated by Anthony Munday, via the French, from the *Paradossi* of Ortensio Landi (1543), had a list of paradoxes advertised to follow in the second volume, including this one on bastards. It is significant that the other six paradoxes in Milles's book are all in Munday's list.

I. ii. 35. *I . . . spectacles*] One of the advantages of blindness, according to another of Munday's paradoxes is that the blind 'have no need of spectacles' (Vickers, *op. cit.*).

I. ii. 145. *cohorts*] Stone, *op. cit.*, emends to *courts*.

I. iv. 8. S.D.] John C. Meagher, *N.Q.* (1965), pp. 97–8, suggests that the attendants, here and elsewhere, should ignore Lear's command.

II. ii. 34. *Vanity*] Meagher, in *Shakespeare 1971*, ed. Leech and Margeson (1972) shows that in emblematic pictures Lady Vanity was often depicted with a mirror; and he suggests therefore that Goneril should carry a mirror.

II. iv. 14–21. *No . . . do't*] S. Unkowitz, *Shakespeare's Revision of 'King Lear'* (1980), argues convincingly against the conflation of Q and F in this passage.

II. iv. 54–5. *mother . . . passio*] The Jordan passage should read: '*Praefocatio . . . Matricis* Etc. In'.

III. i. 18. note] Stone emends to *heart*.

III. iv. 75. *Pillicock . . . hill*] Thomas D'Urfey's text in *Songs Compleat Pleasant and Divertive*, IV (1719) underlines the bawdy significance.

III. iv. 115. *mildews*] Mario L. D'Avanzo, *S.Q.*, XXVIII (1977), pp. 83–9, suggests that 'the mildewing of wheat may also refer to ergot, a poisonous blight growing on grain', which induces 'insanity, gangrene, convulsions, and death'.

III. vi. 45. *Purr . . . grey*] Adrienne Lockhart, *S.Q.*, XXVI (1975), p. 470, refers to John Heywood, *A Dialogue* (1546): 'When all candels be out, all cats be grey, All things are then of one colour'.

III. vii. 50. *buoy'd*] Stone supports Warburton's reading.

IV. i. 20. *Our means . . . us*] William Elton, *Neoph.*, XLVII (1963), pp. 225–7, cites Richard Rogers's *Seven Treatises* (1603), in which 'means' involve 'outward occasions' and G. Bucanus, who in his *Institutions* (1606) asserts that God's providence is accused by them 'who being preposterously secure neglect all meanes'. Gloucester 'attributes the error of false complacency to those who rest securely with good works, or means.' Our mere defects, 'our deficiency of works, may prove ironically less disadvantageous or harmful.'

IV. ii. 39. *Filths savour*] C. Camden, *M.L.N.*, LXXII (1957), p. 251, cites Palingenius' *The Zodiake of Life* (tr. B. Googe, 1576), p. 234: 'Things filthy, filthy folkes doe loue, and villaines villanie.'

IV. iii. 49. *so*] Stone proposes the emendation *said*.

IV. vi. 81. *safer sense*] Hilda Hume, *N.Q.* (1957), pp. 237–8, argues that Edgar's words mean: 'Gloucester's newly recovered and precarious mental balance . . . will never be able to maintain itself against the shock and horror of encountering Lear as he now is.' *accommodate* = adapt itself to.

IV. vi. 180–1. *When . . . fools*] See also William Fulbecke, *A Booke of Christian Ethicks* (1587): 'a child as soone as he is borne, giueth out no signe, which is proper to man, but onely weeping: and hath he not good cause of weeping, when he commeth into the *Theater* wherein Maliciousnes playeth her prize.'

IV. vii. 47. *wheel of fire*] Starnes and Talbot, *Classical Myth and Legend in Renaissance Dictionaries* (1955), pp. 115–16, suggest that the legend of Ixion was much in Shakespeare's mind throughout Act IV. See also William R. Elton, *King Lear and the Gods* (1966), p. 237, and O. B. Hardison, 'Myth and History in *King Lear*', *S.Q.*, XXVI (1975), pp. 227–42, where it is argued that the myth 'supplied Shakespeare with the philosophical issues in terms of which the action of the play is developed'.

V. iii. 24. *good years*] William Elton, *M.L.R.*, LIX (1964), pp. 177–8, shows that 'in addition to its expletive meaning, "good years" probably also signified prosperity, riches, abundance, or good fortune. Lear's words imply that the prosperity of the evil sisters may be transient.' Elton cites James v. 3 against worldly prosperity. 'Your gold and silver is cankered and the rust of them shall be a witnesse agaynst you, and shall eate your flesh as it were fire.' William E. Brady, *S.Q.*, xxi (1970), pp. 495–7, comments: 'When the evil years are overcome by the good years, Goneril, Regan and Edmund come to a natural end, as a species under new conditions becomes extinct for lack of prey.'

v. iii. 304. *fool*] John C. Meagher, *S.Q.*, xxxvi (1984), p. 18, rightly points out that Thaler did not show that the parts of Cordelia and the Fool *could* not have been doubled. Nevertheless the generally accepted view that the Fool was played by Armin, and that, as far as we know, he never played a female part, makes the doubling unlikely. It would be interesting to see it tried.